THE
PIE
AT
NIGHT

Also by Stuart Maconie

Cider with Roadies
Pies and Prejudice
Adventures on the High Teas
Hope and Glory
The People's Songs

THE
PIE
AT
NIGHT

IN SEARCH OF THE NORTH AT PLAY

STUART
MACONIE

EBURY
PRESS

1 3 5 7 9 10 8 6 4 2

Ebury Press, an imprint of Ebury Publishing
20 Vauxhall Bridge Road
London SW1V 2SA

Ebury Press is part of the Penguin Random House group of companies
whose addresses can be found at global.penguinrandomhouse.com

Penguin
Random House
UK

First published by Ebury Press in 2015

www.eburypublishing.co.uk

A CIP catalogue record for this book is available from the British Library

ISBN 9780091933814 (hardback)
ISBN 9781785031878 (trade paperback)

Printed and bound in Great Britain by Clays Ltd, St Ives PLC

CONTENTS

PROLOGUE
CLOCKING OFF

The train now leaving Stalybridge station is for the north …

They call it Stalyvegas. A good place to start I think. A town that just wants to have fun.

But where to start with Stalybridge itself? With its long, dark, wild hills and its long, dark, wild history? It has plenty of that. Luddites, those mocked and misunderstood symbols of industrial muscle, once raged through its streets, smashing looms, burning mills, generally earning themselves centuries of undeserved bad press. Chartists made it a stronghold, collected signatures, stoked the people's ire; strikers and plug rioters stalked the town, anger spread like a bloodstain across Lancashire, Yorkshire, Derbyshire, Staffordshire. Friedrich Engels came and found a town in disarray and a people in despair, despite some really rather lovely countryside.

> Stalybridge lies in a narrow, crooked ravine … and both sides of this ravine are occupied by an irregular group of cottages, houses and mills. On entering, the very first cottages are narrow, smoke-begrimed, old and ruinous; and as the first houses, so the whole town. A few streets lie in the narrow valley bottom, most of them run criss-cross, pell-mell, up hill and down, and in nearly all the houses, by reason of this sloping situation, the ground-floor is half-buried in the earth; and what multitudes of courts, back lanes and remote nooks

arise out of this confused way of building may be seen from the hills, whence one has the town, here and there, in a bird's-eye view almost at one's feet. Add to this the shocking filth, and the repulsive effect of Stalybridge … may be readily imagined.

Understandably, the tourist board doesn't go big on the above in the promotional literature.

Or shall we begin with a chorus of 'It's a Long Way to Tipperary', written, it's said, in an hour for a bet one boozy night in 1912 in Stalybridge's Newmarket Tavern by local lad Jack Judge? Then there's another claim to fame, the fact that the last surviving tripe shop in Britain is still about its rubbery, vinegary business on Stalybridge's Main Street. It is still a place of local pilgrimage, if only selling around a quarter of the mind-boggling, jaw-dropping, some would say stomach-turning 100lbs-a-day of the stuff they would sell 20 years ago.

Or shall we begin with that nickname; 'Stalyvegas', the city of lights in the wilderness, first used jokingly when the council went overboard on traffic lights and then used more abstractly and affectionately of a crazy, fun town in the middle of nowhere. An isolated town cradled by soft hills, turning rural again, feral even, as industry's tide recedes and the tripe trade slackens to be replaced by other passions; cocktail bars and bookies, tanning salons, Wetherspoons and pound shops.

But no. Let us begin on platform one of Stalybridge station where the trains clank and whizz and rumble their way between Lancashire and Yorkshire, and where stands what just might be the best pub in the north of England.

You'll need a drink after your journey. The northern rail train will be cramped and fetid, because it always is, packed sardine tight with the workers of Liverpool and Manchester and Bolton heading home to the hills; smart office girls in charcoal suits with pink paperbacks, hipster web designers with iPods and waxed 'tashes, exhausted labourers in blue serge overalls flecked with plaster nodding off against the rainy window, through which the landscape is gradually greening.

You won't get a seat, rest assured, so as the decrepit seventies 'Sprinter' train sighs into Stalybridge you will fall gratefully out of the grimy concertina doors and onto platform 1, where the much more welcoming door of the Stalybridge Buffet Bar will be open, and the little lights will be twinkling and your stool or your table and your pint and the night await you.

The evening has begun.

A long, long time ago, an unimaginably long time actually – somewhere between half a million and two million years – our distant ancestor *Homo erectus* made the most important discovery of his or her short, action-packed life.

No one can be sure when or how it happened. A stray, fugitive spark from the sharpening of a flint axe head perhaps; or a lightning strike in a primeval forest bringing a crackle of sudden heat and light and a plume of smoke in the depths of a stormy Pleistocene night. But whatever it took, whatever happened, at some unknowable but undeniable point in the earth's history, human beings discovered fire and how to control it.

We'll never know when that was; certainly before 230,000 BC when we have evidence of hearths in Terra Amata, southern France. But whenever it occurred, this step, according to many modern anthropologists, marked the real beginnings of our culture. Firstly, of course, it meant a giant culinary leap for mankind. But it gets more interesting than that. Raw food is harder to digest and far less calorific than cooked; gorillas and other big primates have to spend eight hours a day eating to get enough calories to feed their small brains. When we invented cooking, we beefed up our brains far more speedily and easily than before, without having to spend the day sitting around gormlessly munching and masticating. Cooking made us smarter.

So we became cleverer. But what to do with this new brain power and the capacity to embrace abstract thought? Mastery of fire brought a new social dimension to our existence, too. The glow and warmth of the campfire extended the short, harsh day beyond sunset. It brought us together in light and safety when the daily business of survival was over. It gave us entertainment, art, nightlife; all that good stuff. When humans mastered fire, they invented leisure.

A couple of million years later – in AD 1983 to be precise – the singer Cyndi Lauper put it rather well: 'When the working day is done, oh girls, they want to have fun'. Boys too of course. For as long as we have worked, we have played. We have played in different ways, at different times, for different reasons, and with different levels of engagement. *Homo erectus* gave way to brainier, brighter *Homo sapiens* but we have always still wanted to have fun down the long centuries, however constrained our time, however limited our choices. How one set of people have spent and still spend their free time – the working people of northern industrial Britain – is the subject of this book.

As soon as you enter the Buffet Bar on platform 1 of Stalybridge station, you know immediately that that grim trip was worth it. This is a place that feels both a little too good to be true and inescapably, quintessentially northern. Cosy lighting in the bar parlour, antique and mysterious railway bric-a-brac and memorabilia to lose oneself in, conspiratorial corners for secret assignations, a walnut bar to perch at with your novel or the crossword, at the end of which, under glass, glisten home-made hot pork pies, Eccles cakes and Victoria sponges. There are several real ales with enticing names, reeking of industry and Norse myth, a row of bottles of Vimto, and a tureen full of steaming broth 'freshly made'. The kindly, elderly lady ahead of you at the bar is greeted by name and with her usual, a hot elderflower cordial, at which point you will think that this is defintely too good to be true, or that I am a fantasist, or both. But no.

The lady served, her cordial carried away in a china mug, the barman turns to you to speak but pauses, noticing that the young serving girl has left the kitchen radio on and Heart FM is leaking through into the bar. 'Let me turn this rubbish off sir ...' he begins, giving you a quick, appraising glance as he does so, at your book, your man bag, your smartphone '… and now can I say that, as you don't seem to be here for the steamy movies or the knitting circle, are you a card carrying member of CAMRA?'

You are none of these but you are intrigued, and the barman can tell. 'Let me explain. First, a drink? A pint of Boltmakers? Named after our head brewers' local, the Boltmakers Arms in Keighley. "I'll tell you now and I'll tell you briefly, I don't never want to go to Keighley",' he drawls in Salfordian, quoting the great John Cooper Clarke. 'Nice little pub. Oasis sponsored the pub football team for a while I believe. Now, let me tell you what's going on here tonight.'

Steamy movies is the humorous name given to the weekly showings of old black-and-white steam train footage in the back bar. He indicates a group of men of a certain age in caps and anoraks, some with pipes, which makes me think of David Hockney's sage observation that no pipe smoker would ever have road rage. One raises a cap in salute, increasing the sensation that I am in some kind of Lancashire *Twin Peaks*. 'The knitters are through there,' and he points to a clutch of women of varying ages taking needles and multicoloured yarns out of carpet bags and with a variety of drinks in front of them; spritzers, tea, halves of mild. Other regular attractions advertised on the pub's crowded wall include Laurel and Hardy Night, a poetry reading and several quizzes.

Next to them is a menu upon which my eye falls hungrily. 'Now then, sir,' the barman begins apologetically, 'if you've come for our infamous black peas' – this a northern delicacy, often enjoyed around Bonfire Night and delicious in a Dickensian sort of way – 'then I have to tell you that they haven't really been soaking for long enough yet. It wouldn't be right to serve them for you. I can offer you a delicious hot pork pie from Saddleworth and mushy peas though, and after that perhaps a home-made pudding.'

'Yes, that would be marvellous,' I answer weakly, the evening beginning to take on the quality of a dream. On the wall a sign reads that this is has been voted CAMRA's pub of the year. I'm just surprised it isn't every year.

In a daze of pleasure, I find a corner table. I have come here to start a new book and to re-read the end of an old one. That was called *Pies and Prejudice* and I turn, somewhat sheepishly in casc I'm spotted, to the end of the book which found me in another wonderful northern watering hole; the transport café on Hartside Pass in the Pennines. It was late spring, and it felt more like early summer. April 2007; the sky thick with larks, the dusk gentle and lambent. I was in a romantic, reflective mood. A year or two of research for *Pies and Prejudice* was ending, researches and travels that had taken me all over northern England and had rekindled my complicated love affair with the north, its landscape, its people and its hard, wild, gorgeous history. I wrote then about the view from that spot, the top of Hartside Pass and was forgivably lyrical I hope about 'the gathering blue dusk' and 'that silvery stream of twinkling light along the mighty tributary of the M6'. Kindled for that first book which came out in 2008, love raged on, as complex and intoxicating as ever, as difficult and as wonderful.

'Write about what you know' is the timeworn, oft-repeated advice given to budding authors. There's some truth in this, although it would leave the sci-fi and fantasy shelves of your local bookshop looking pretty threadbare. (That's even if you have a local bookshop.) 'Write about what you care about' strikes me as better advice. In 2007–8, I wrote that book about the north of England because I knew a fair bit about it and I cared a good deal too. I didn't know or care as much as I thought I did, though, which was why the book, and what TV talent shows and celebrity baking programmes call 'the journey', became so important and enjoyable to me.

I fancy making those kinds of journey again. To the heart and the hubbub of working Britain to see what folks are up to. I am in search of what a long-running BBC radio show called 'workers' playtime'. It ran for 24 years, between 1921 and 1964, and came three times a week from a different factory, bringing music and comedy to the shop floor from top entertainers of the day. With its venues chosen by the Ministry of Labour, exhortations to increased production and its regular catch phrase of 'Good luck, all workers!', it sounds positively North Korean now, or at least rather quaint and paternalistic. A little patronising, yes, but in the age of *Benefit Street* and Jeremy Kyle, when working-class people and their lives are routinely offered up contemptuously as a freak show, *Workers' Playtime* now seems rather sweet and warm. In fact, *Workers' Playtime* might have been an alternative title for this book had *The Pie at Night* not suggested itself first, as a nod to its predecessor and to the notion of clocking off and enjoying leisure. Not all the activities here are actually exclusively nocturnal, but whether the play is at night or day, this is a book about love and work and the debatable land between.

'Love and work are the cornerstones of our humanness' said Sigmund Freud, a truth that Johnny Marr of The Smiths once quoted to me during an interview. While I've long been a fan of Johnny's, I've never been the most ardent disciple of Sigmund, especially not of his cockeyed (literally) dream theories. I've always believed that sometimes when you dream about a snake, it may be that snakes are on your mind for some reason best known to yourself. You may have been watching re-runs of *Animal Magic* or *Snakes on a Plane* or *The Jungle Book*. You may work in the reptile house of Chester Zoo. Similarly, I've always held that our dreams are merely a random nocturnal whizz through the mental Rolodex of the day's events.

(Hence, in one of my more vivid and memorable recent dreams, I went to see the American alt rock band The National at a village hall in Yorkshire. I alighted at a station called (implausibly) Catterick Hat Shop. A local family took me back to their house for tea, which consisted of a vast oleaginous fry-up. When I got to the gig, I was by now, and for reasons unclear, carrying a large roll of stair carpet which the band kindly let me leave backstage. I then watched the show on the shoulders of the radio broadcaster Marc Riley, who subsequently dropped me on the pool table.)

But this axiom of Freud's from Johnny struck me as an insight of an entirely different order; more than that, a kind of mantra or philosophy that offered truth, inspiration, consolation even. Love and work are the pillars and the poles of life that we navigate between. To be human is to love and work, and what we cannot get from one, we can hopefully find in the other. The Beatles had it slightly wrong. Love and work are all you need.

Love gets the better press. There are no pop songs called everlasting work, whole lotta work, are you ready for work, work is a many splendored thing or I've got my work to keep me warm. Not even work train, I'm not in work or the work of the common people (although there should be). Similarly, there are no songs extolling the virtues of loving in a coalmine, which I think is a real pity. It sounds intriguing.

But there are songs and plenty of them that either imply or come straight out and say that, hey man, work is a drain and a drudge, a shackle and a sentence, something that gets in the way of the proper stuff of life, which generally in the popular song is love.

There is a marked and telling difference between us and the Americans here. From Springsteen to Jimmy Webb, American songwriters have regularly and passionately lionised the working man/woman and the blue-collar life. In Britain, from the Kinks to The Jam to Cat Stevens' 'Matthew & Son', our pop musicians have tended to sneer at the supposed banality of the average working life. There are a few honourable exceptions to this. In fact, Johnny's old band mate Morrissey wrote about the friction between freedom, boredom, unemployment and work as well and wittily and mordantly as anyone. His early lyrics are full of ambivalence towards what Phillip Larkin called 'the toad work'. In 'Still Ill', he's never had a job because he's 'too shy' and he's 'never wanted one' and if you must go to work tomorrow, well, if he were you, he wouldn't bother.

Less glumly than Moz but still evincing no great enthusiasm, there are lots of adages and axioms about work, most of them wry. 'I like work: it fascinates me. I can sit and look at it for hours' said Jerome

K Jerome in loafer's bible *Three Men in a Boat*. It's the 'curse of the drinking classes' according to the old T-shirt gag. Cilla Black sang 'Work is a Four-Letter Word' (covered by The Smiths, funnily enough).

There are lots of earnest and pious homilies about the virtues and values of hard work. But for most working people they ring a little hollow and smack of a lecture from the boss. But if Freud's love and work are two poles, two extremes, then surely between them lies play. In a sense, it is where the two come together and have a good time. Play is work invested and enriched by love, it's love bolstered with the seriousness and dedication of work. At this point, Mark Twain can usually be relied upon to say something smart and he did; 'work and play are words used to describe the same thing under differing conditions'.

Here comes the science bit. In 1938, the Dutch cultural historian Johan Huizinga wrote perhaps the definitive text on play, *Homo Ludens*, or 'man the player'. In it he claimed that not only was an element of play necessary for the health and transmission of human culture and ideas, play was in fact pretty much all that culture was. When we weren't digging, building, reaping or sowing (or teaching, marketing or graphic designing) in order to put food on the table and shoes on our feet, we were playing.

J S Bach, *Hamlet*, Chief Wiggum from *The Simpsons*, 'The Waste Land', Crewe Alexandra, hopscotch, *Citizen Kane*, *Beowulf*, The Rubettes, *Finnegans Wake*, ten-pin bowling, Guernica, *Look Back in Anger*, 'Don't Look Back in Anger', Oedipus Rex, *A Brief History Of Time*, The Incredible String Band, *Middlemarch*, the collected works of Don Estelle and Windsor Davis – and for that matter Don DeLillo and Peter Maxwell Davies – Ingmar Bergman, orienteering, the novels of Alan Titchmarsh … the entire gaudy, profound, dazzling tapestry of our culture was woven from play. It was what defined us, what made us.

From the Puritans to the Taliban, spoilsports of every creed, class and colour have tried to put a stop to it. But they all failed and will always fail because it is at the heart of who we are and what we do.

Banning Christmas (by the former) or ridding life of music (the latter) were probably some of the smaller of those two ideologues barbarities. But they were significant ones. More to the point, they failed. You can't keep a good man the player, *Homo ludens* down.

Huizinga was a sociologist of a sort; a subject that has been getting a bad press for years. In fact, sociologists were probably delighted when media studies came along to take some of the heat of them. Sociology is a Mickey Mouse subject comprised of left-wing claptrap, as we all know, and I am proud to say I taught it for several years at colleges in the north of England before getting involved in this crazy business we call 'show'. Some bits of sociological research always engendered heated debate among the single mums, recently made redundant factory workers and unemployed scallies of Skelmersdale and Wigan. One such was Goldthorpe and Lockwood's Embourgeoisement Theory.

In the early 1960s, John Lockwood and David Goldthorpe survey- ed a sample of the workforce at Vauxhall Cars, Skefco Engineering and La Porte Chemicals in Luton. In the subsequent book, *The Affluent Worker*, they put forward the idea that these manual workers were becoming 'privatised', more middle class if you will. They were more family focused, less driven by notions of class. Other theorists disagreed, claiming that these workers didn't see themselves as middle class and still voted Labour. What it actually seemed to boil down to was that they were spending more time watching *Double Your Money* and less in the Boltmakers Arms, Keighley.

Whether Goldthorpe and Lockwood's theories were ever really true is highly contentious. And even if they were true of Luton in the 1960s, years of economic upheavals, the death of our manufacturing industry, the financial big bang, Thatcherism, New Labour and all the other seismic shocks to the British system seem to have knocked the Embourgeoisement Theory on the head. Yes, working-class people stay in and watch *X Factor* and *Doctor Who* with their spouses and families sometimes. But as I found out over a very enjoyable year of research, they also go to speedway, visit museums, play bingo, climb up hills, eat out, play crown green bowls, go to comedy clubs, join brass bands and take part in large-scale zombie apocalypse enactments.

Television may have insinuated itself into our lives but it is nowhere near as important to us as the commissioning editors think it is. En passant, pretty much none of the things I went along to in my year of days and nights out would look good on television, with the possible exception of football, and even that is much more fun in the raw. You can't convey on the gogglebox the feel of wind and rain on your face on a brisk walk up Dovestones or Cat Bells, the methanol tang of the speedway, the overpowering aroma of coriander and garlic on Rusholme's curry mile, the sweat and lager cocktail of a gig at The Ritz, Manchester or the Brudenell Club, Leeds.

Technology is said to have revolutionised work and play. But, where leisure's concerned, that revolution has been more about organisation and information than the activities itself. Sure, bored commuters play Angry Birds and Kandy Krush to numb the passing miles and kids (and me) do spend hours in front of Assassin's Creed and Call of Duty on the Xbox. But, from text messages and email to Snapchat and Grindr, we are using the internet simply to make it easier to hang out. Social media is just that, media that helps us be more social.

During the course of my researches I read an interview with Janet Street Porter where, while singing the praises of affluent Whitstable, she shared with us that she's 'not a big fan of Manchester, to be honest. It's just not my kind of town. It's a bit flashy and vulgar. All those women dressed up to the nines on a Friday night. I just can't cope with it.' Janet presents a programme called *Loose Women* on ITV at the moment, which tells you everything you need to know about the sincerity of television and how it views its audience.

I love Manchester, I love the fact that its women (and men) like to dress up on a Friday night. I love that, as you shall see, from the tapas bars of Halifax to the pubs of Berwick-upon-Tweed, from the bowling greens of Chorlton to the grand hotels of Hull, from dodgems at Silloth to the Women's Institute meetings of Carlisle, my north still puts its coat on and goes out, makes an effort, gets dressed up, refuses to stay at home mortgaged, munching and passively consuming dire telly shows.

I was out of work for about six months in the mid-1980s. I hated it. I was by no means, and by no one's reckoning, a driven careerist or nascent workaholic. But I felt that I had become unmoored, becalmed, that life was passing me by and being lived elsewhere. Then I got an office job with Courtaulds that was even worse. But at least it kick-started in me the desire to be somewhere else. Getting the bus to Bolton every day to work in the peculiarly hateful environs of a male office in the eighties made me realise how awful, how genuinely soul-destroying it is to have a job you hate, and how grateful one should be to have one you like. Saul Bellow wrote that 'death is the dark backing a mirror needs if it is to see anything'. I think I know what he means, and I think the same applies to work. Work is the grit in the oyster that makes the pearl of life.

Polly Wiessner is one of the anthropologists who's explored the relationship between humans and leisure and its roots in that mastery of fire. She has been studying Kalahari Bushmen for years and it's her theory that the camp fire gave us culture, art and play. In the journal *Proceedings of the National Academy of Sciences* she wrote 'there is something about fire in the middle of the darkness that bonds, mellows and also excites people. It's intimate. Night-time around a fire is universally time for bonding, for telling social information, for entertaining, for a lot of shared emotions.' All of this still rings true, as I found out in these travels; fairgrounds at night, floodlit football matches, Blackpool illuminations – the thrill never leaves you.

The great American film critic Roger Ebert called *Annie Hall* 'just about everyone's favourite Woody Allen movie'. My favourite scene takes place in the cinema queue, when a cultural studies blowhard is boring his date with an exposition of the works of Canadian media theorist Marshall McLuhan. Allen, forced to overhear all this too, drags the real Marshall McLuhan out from behind a hoarding who berates the bore by telling him 'you know nothing of my work'. 'Oh if only real life were like this,' says Allen ruefully to camera.

McLuhan is best known for his 'medium is the message' mantra which you'll be familiar with if you've even as much as accidentally wandered into a media studies class – essentially, McLuhan thinks the whole environment and weight of TV, radio and other modern media is more powerful than any individual bit of content. Less well known is his work 'Guaranteed Income in the Electric Age'.

In the future – the near future, he thought, writing in 1965 – technology and automation will free us from the drudgery of much labour and the result will be a society where individuals, liberated from work, will be free to pursue other interests and lead meaningful lives. The new, vibrant technologically driven economy will produce enough wealth to pay people to live like this in a new, non-competitive kind of society.

The relative affluence and peace of the fifties and sixties and a certain naive Panglossian faith in progress led intellectuals like McLuhan to make all sorts of pronouncements about the future. Don Marler, Robert Theobald and Eric Fromm all wrote soothingly of the elimination of work and how unemployment was not a scourge but a victory for society. All we needed to soften the blow and have us all using our new found leisure to learn Mandarin Chinese and master the lute was that old 'guaranteed income'.

Ken Dodd once disparaged Freud's theories of humour by saying 'the trouble with Sigmund Freud is that he never played second house at the Glasgow Empire after both halves of the old firm had just lost'. Similarly, while I have a lot of time for Marshall McLuhan, he never had to outline the blissful future predicted in 'Guaranteed Income in the Electric Age' to unconvinced, unemployed teenagers and the laid off languishing on the scrapheap in a ravaged, northern new town. In a way, it had come to pass, if you counted dole money and Jobseeker's

Allowance as 'guaranteed income'. Those rich and meaningful lives, and those robot butlers, seemed a long way off though when I walked through the ravaged, concrete concourse of Skem, with its packs of wild dogs, tributaries of piss and boarded-up shops.

Those once fashionable theories emerged from the book-lined, lamp-lit study rather than the dole queue, and they pre-suppose a view of the world, like the functionalist sociologists, like Fukuyama's End of History theory, like *Star Trek* if you will, where class conflict, self-interest and corruption have all disappeared, and we stroll around ornamental gardens in long silver robes listening to harp music all day, while unseen automatons dig coal, clean the bathroom and rustle up risottos. It didn't turn out quite like that, obviously. This distant academic view of the workers and their fun has always been either innocent, patronising or just plain wrong. Alan Sillitoe's fabulous creation, factory worker and full-time hedonist Arthur Seaton, put it brilliantly in *Saturday Night and Sunday Morning*.

> I'm a fighting pit prop that wants a pint of beer, that's me. But if any knowing bastard says that's me I'll tell them I'm a dynamite dealer waiting to blow the factory to kingdom come. Whatever people say I am, that's what I'm not because they don't know a bloody thing about me! God knows what I am.

So I spent a year travelling and thinking about what working Britain does now when the hooter – metaphorical or not – goes and it's time to clock off. The focus of my travel and thinking was still primarily northern, and in some cases I did follow in my own footsteps from *Pies and Prejudice*. But times change quickly and in the end this is more a companion piece than a sequel. The view from the terrace and the stalls, from mountain top and seaside, from the bingo hall and the chip shop, the concert hall and the best table in the Michelin-starred house.

In the heady world of sociology, sixties totems like Goldthorpe and Lockwood are now wildly unfashionable. They belong to an era of 'polytechnics', Nelson Mandela bars and pear drop collars on Open University programmes in the small hours. An era before that even; duffle coats and skiffle and Aldermaston marches. These days, a growth area in sociology is leisure studies. Once this largely meant training graduates in how to run sports centres à la Gordon Brittas. Now, though, it's a fast-growing area of critical post-Marxist sociology, dealing with leisure as a 'cultural space' within global capitalism.

Determined to put the hours in on your behalf, dear readers, I picked up a couple of books and listened to a few very earnest podcasts. Even I, long inured and even mildly affectionate for the kinds of top quality flummery at the highest levels of the social sciences, found these pretty indigestible. Many of the commentators were keen to make the point that modern leisure was a global and corporatist phenomenon, usually regulated and commodified by capitalism. Well, yes, I suppose. But the people I met and hung out with, and the things I did over my year or so of research, didn't smack remotely of being dupes or playthings of 'the man', even if they did sometimes have to buy a ticket or a hot dog.

It felt, naively maybe, much more like freedom than sitting passively in front of the telly. Or, for that matter, a lecture on the sociology of leisure. I prefer to think of what I was trying to get at – when I visited the Rochdale United's Spotlands ground, the Weardale moors, the Gala Bingo at Salford, the fairground at Silloth or the bars of Manchester – as maybe trying to do what John Updike said he wanted on his tombstone; that he was someone who had tried 'to give the mundane its beautiful due'.

Just as my year of research was ending and I was settling down to the serious business of writing, Johnny Marr came into my radio studio again with a new record to promote. He asked me what I'd been up to and I told him about this book and how it had been partly inspired by his quoting of Freud to me and, more to the point, about how it had got me thinking about love and work and play. And coincidentally Johnny's new album was called *Playland*.

'Oh yes. I've been thinking a lot about that too. I've been reading this book by a guy called Huizinga. Dutch bloke. It's a bit obscure so you may not know it. But it's called *Homo Ludens …*'

Back in the buffet bar at Stalybridge railway station, the evening is starting to blossom as the sun dips behind the hills. In the conservatory, a gang of young people are chatting amiably, one wearing a Ghost B.C. T-shirt, my favourite Scandinavian death metal band. A glamorous Afro-Caribbean woman sits alone and relaxed at the bar reading a magazine. A young couple come in and perch by her on stools, he orders a pint, she a large Baileys with ice. Apropos of not much, the barman enquires out loud, 'Right, name me the three pale blue monopoly properties.' The Afro-Caribbean lady raises a perfect eyebrow and laughs but almost instantly the lad with the Baileys-and-ice girlfriend offers, 'Euston Road.' The lad in the Ghost B.C. T-shirt, who turns out to be Paul the landlord's grandson, chirps up, 'Angel Islington.' From the knitters room comes the shout 'Pentonville Road!'

Later I have a drink in the ladies' first-class waiting room, now a kind of secret back-room sanctum, with the chatty members of the knitting circle, one of whom gives me a jar of home-made chutney and honey. Outside, on the darkened platform, my train was pulling in, and so I thanked her, and shoved preserves and book into my manbag, and made reluctantly for the door. 'Don't miss it,' shouts a knitter, 'it's a long walk to anywhere from here.'

I just made the last train from Stalyvegas. This time I had the carriage to myself, plus the odd rolling beer can and scrunched up *Yorkshire Post* and *Manchester Evening News*, as the northern night enfolded me like the hills. As the old railway guards at Euston and Kings Cross used to say, 'We are for the north' and we have work to do.

Or maybe not.

CHAPTER 1

PLAYING AT WORK

Rotherham, Beamish and a Diversion to Swindon

In a high, girdered, cavernous hall, part of a cluster of hulking industrial remains on the outskirts of Rotherham, a man is singing sweetly in the liquid glow of a spotlight. A full symphony orchestra sits behind him and before him a thousand people are listening, rapt in an echoing, sepulchral space that would once have been a cauldron of flames and noise. Thirty years ago, this would have been no place for sweet melodies, but rather a cacophony of struck metal, a miasma of sweat and flames, and that glow on his face would have come from a 10,000 tonne electric forge made by Sheffield Forgemasters International.

Welcome to the Big Hall at Magna, a £46 million visitor attraction that has won design awards around the world and become one of the landmark structures of South Yorkshire. It's truly enormous; the length of ten football pitches and a dizzying 30 metres high. Even so, it's only a fraction of the size this site was a few decades ago, when this huge building, now standing alone in its majestic enormity, was surrounded by similarly sizeable siblings, cogging mills and cooling beds, vast tracts of land and machinery.

This was once the melting shop of the Templeborough steel works owned by the company of Steel, Peech and Tozer, one of the region's major employers. Massive and massively productive, they called it 'the anvil of South Yorkshire'. Built in 1917 to produce steel for artillery shells used in the First World War, it was a prime target for the Luftwaffe in the Second World War – it saw them off naturally – before being modernised in the 1950s with the introduction of electric arc furnaces that produced molten steel at a temperature of 1630°C. They'll tell you in these parts – and, for once, it's no Yorkshire exaggeration – that passengers on the buses passing between Sheffield and Rotherham could actually feel the heat pulse through the windows. Those buses would have to turn on their headlights as they passed through the thick orange smog drifting from the melting shop.

As 1978 gave way to 1979, workers at the Templeborough melting shop received their very own Christmas card from then prime minister James Callaghan. That was how powerful and how valued these workers and their labour was. No one could have known when they received that festive card how close the end was. Just one polling day away, in fact. Back then the works employed 10,000 men in conditions of unthinkable clamour and heat; one of them was the father of the man now singing on stage.

Richard Hawley, Sheffield based singer and songwriter and a friend of mine, is something of a local hero; tonight he plays a homecoming concert here with the BBC Philharmonic orchestra. He talks of his dad, and how amazed and proud he would have been to see his son perform here. Son like father earning a living in this potently symbolic living relic of the region's industrial might, although in very different ways. He falters a little as he speaks, and everyone in the capacity audience understands why. It is a moment completely without senti-ment but one of real emotion. There is a lump in our communal throat; something in our collective eye.

So much so that Richard and I have to stay up drinking in the bar of the Leopold Hotel, Sheffield, till three o'clock in the morning to fully process the evening's events. I scribbled some notes in my Moleskine notebook. But, written in a shaky hand at a pavement table buoyed with fine wines and spirits, they now are about as intelligible to me as the Rosetta Stone or a Latvian verse drama. But I know what the gist of those thoughts were. Nothing could symbolise more sweetly, more sadly, more perfectly, the change in how we live and work and have fun than this heady night; a man singing beautiful and romantic songs of love and home and loss in the vast churchlike space where his dad once hammered and forged in a thunderous crucible of industry.

There are ironies galore in stories like that of Templeborough/ Magna, stories that have been repeated all over post-industrial Britain. Make no mistake; the nation that was the cradle of the industrial revolution is now a post-industrial country. Walk through the pedestrianised centres of our old industrial towns and cities, once 'a world of great noise and much dirt' as the Tyneside historian Paul Kennedy put it, you will now hear nothing, except maybe the tapping of a keyboard, the whoosh of a PowerPoint presentation, the jabber of an overloud mobile phone conversation. Look around – you'll see offices and 'outlets', not foundries or factories. Look through the windows and what you glimpse is not bright cascades of sparks or the flickers of flames but row upon row of PC terminals; slack, tired faces; and suit jackets hung casually behind doors in strip-lit 'workspaces'.

When did all this happen? Not that long ago. I don't regard myself as quite in the 'sere and yellow leaf' yet but I remember as a child of a world of men in overalls and factory hooters, the air being full of smoke and coal dust, and the smell of oil and engines. The sixties and seventies were still largely this kind of world; a crowded world, a noisy world, a dirty world; tough times but exciting ones. Paul Kennedy goes on:

> There was a deep satisfaction about making things ... a deep satisfaction among all of those that had supplied the services, whether it was the local bankers with credit; whether it was the local design firms. When a ship was launched at Swan Hunter all the kids at the local school went to see the thing our fathers had put together and when we looked down from the cross-wired fence, tried to find Uncle Mick, Uncle Jim or your dad, this notion of an integrated, productive community.

Then, about 30 years ago, began what's been called the 'De-Industrial Revolution'. Prime Minister Margaret Thatcher, a shop-keeper's daughter from what some might even call the north, had a keen tribal distrust of manual labour, manufacturing industries and their burly, powerful unions. Whether practical or ideological, she favoured policies that were not so much laissez-faire as let them 'all go hang'. The job of government with regard to industry was not to intervene or protect their own, but to encourage competition, stand back and let the best, or at least the cheapest, man win. They did, from the sweatshops of Taiwan to the dangerous coal mines of Argentina.

The 1980s saw Britain de-industrialised on a scale and at a speed unheard of anywhere else in Europe, possibly the world. Scant regard was given to the communities and classes destroyed by it; it was the law of the free market. All this time, Germany and Scandinavia were husbanding their economies and industries. And look where it got them.

Britain became a financial clearinghouse and manufacturing industry was starved and ground down. Jobs in that sector were replaced by more precarious, short-term work in retail, services and the production of luxury goods. A new class of worker was identified by the theorist Guy Standing; where once there had been a proletariat, now there was the 'precariat', people, both local and migrant, skilled and unskilled, whose work was characterised as short term, unreliable, zero-hour contracted and certainly not for life.

Oddly, the eminent leek-wielding sociologist and light entertainer Max Boyce had predicted this turn of events in the 1970s in his melancholic lament 'Duw It's Hard'. Boyce had actually worked underground for eight years and his song from the album *Live At Treorchy*, which was in practically every Welsh home in the 1970s, is a more poignant and insightful study of the coming of the post-industrial world than a thousand academic treatises.

In our little valley
They closed the colliery down,
And the pithead baths is a supermarket now …
They came down here from England
Because our output's low.
Briefcases full of bank clerks
That had never been below.

Lest you think this mawkish tosh, and that's tempting, consider Cortonwood Colliery, South Yorkshire, where the shower block and baths is now a branch of Morrisons. In Boyce's song, the ex-miner gets a new job counting buttons in a factory. At Cortonwood, one bitter ex-miner told the BBC on a news programme in the nineties, 'Oh aye, we've all got jobs again. Selling sandwiches to one another.'

When Labour ousted the Tories in 1997, the last thing they wanted to dirty their hands with was anything as grubby and potentially problematic as the manual working class or their noisy, unpleasant manufacturing industries. Echoing the 'we know best' optimism of McLuhan and the US theorists, what had been a harsh, unpalatable tenet of Thatcherism was re-branded as an improvement. We would no longer have to get dirty or injured working in filthy conditions.

New Labour and its prime movers had an unshakeable belief in what they called the 'knowledge economy'. Infatuated with Silicon Valley and Bill Gates, they claimed they'd make Britain the e-commerce capital of the world within three years. Aditya Chakrabortty in a *Guardian* piece, 'Why doesn't Britain make things any more?', based on his 2011 Radio 3 talk on de-industrialisation, summed it up nicely:

The future lay in coming up with the ideas, the software, and most of all, the brands. Once the British had sold cars and ships to the rest of the world; now they could flog culture and tourism and Lara Croft.

The odd thing is that all this techno-utopianism came from men who would struggle to order a book off Amazon. Alastair Campbell tells a story about how Blair got his first-ever mobile phone after stepping down as prime minister in 2007. His first text to Campbell read: 'This is amazing, you can send words on a phone.'

As you may have guessed, I am something of a romantic about the way things used to be. I come from a part of the world which owes its civic riches, its streets and parks, even the might of its football teams, to the former glories of its manufacturing industries. Every member of my family, up to and including me, worked in factories or foundries, mills or mines. But I'm a romantic with a fairly hard head. I hated my brief time working in the textile trade in the mid-eighties. I hated the desperately blokey milieu of the office, with its bullish moustaches and what would now be called 'banter'. I liked the actual mill better; its bracing atmosphere was more brisk and convivial. There were young and old there, male and female. But the physical labour left me wrung out like a dishrag. The carding room of a textile mill is a back-breaking, soul-sapping place, and at the end of a day lugging the heavy spindles around (bales were they? Doffs? I seem to have excised it from my memory) I was streaked with dirt and sweat and frankly knackered. But I am sorry they have gone. Without its heavy industry, Britain is a cleaner and quieter place. But it's also in many ways duller and poorer.

The one place British industry lives on splendidly, and goes from strength to strength, is in its recreation as a heritage tourist attraction for today's worker, which is where I thought my look at modern leisure in post-industrial Britain should begin. Overseas, you can visit the cheesemongers of Alkmaar and Gouda, the vineyards of the Douro, even take a sip with the good ol' boys at the Jack Daniels distillery in Lynchburg. But these are all going concerns and the tours are sidelines.

Britain is the world leader in post-industrialism and post-industrial heritage tourism. As writer Richard James put it, 'Britain now lavishes the same care on its industrial heritage as it once reserved for its castles and cathedrals.' How have we turned these pits of sweat and toil, these dangerous, dark, noisy spaces, into places where the former workers' kids can now go for a nice day out, have a baguette and do some interacting?

With Magna (Or the Magna Science Adventure Centre, to give it its full name), the designers took the wise decision to leave the exterior of the huge buildings just as they were, and merely colonise and smarten up the interior space. That now holds a concert hall, a banqueting suite and an exhibition that brings to life the shop's incendiary and incandescent heyday. At Magna, on the hour, they have something they call Big Melt. Quite a thing it is too. You can see and hear it from every part of the building. Essentially, it's a massive modern *son et lumière* type show with pyrotechnics and robotics. The idea is to replace the look, sound and feel of 'E' furnace, one of Templeborough's original gigantic (and back then thrillingly futuristic) arc furnaces of the 1950s. It's an impressive 12 or so minutes, tension ratcheted up by the doomy background sound, mood lighting, a voice-over that's richly local but gruffly dramatic, and naturally the massive furnaces themselves.

A phalanx of little kids were milling about expectantly when I was there, in outsized hard hats with clipboards and big novelty pens. They were being herded with difficulty by a harassed looking young female teacher, herded like cats, but cats in a massive noisy foundry, which is even harder than the proverbial. As turbines thrummed and machines of unknowable function rolled along great gantries above, a little Indian lad was very carefully drawing a dog on his mate's forehead, skilfully taking advantage of the noise and clamour as cover. Then there came a whoosh of sparks and a hot garland of flame from below.

Go along yourself. Take some kids; they may not follow exactly the sections of exposition about how burgeoning demand for cars created a need for cheap steel which in turn led to the demise of the open-hearth system in favour of electric arc furnaces. But they will have a ball. It's hard not to. The Big Melt is enough to bring out the little kid in anyone with its arcing showers of sparks, flashes of electric light and tongues and tributaries of fire. Who wouldn't enjoy the rumblings and shakings below and overhead and the narration's splendidly, reassuringly macho talk of 'lowering five metre long graphite electrodes', 'giant casting pots' and 'doing in 90 minutes what took volcanic eras'. There will be 'oohs' and 'aahs' and possibly the odd whimper.

Of course, Sheffield and Rotherham being what they were, some of the little 'uns granddads will have worked here in what the voice-over calls 'the sweltering heat all day'. Jarvis Cocker, son of Sheffield, made a documentary film called *The Big Melt* about how steel shaped the character of the city, and it was this point about the work itself, the daily routine in these extraordinary conditions, that stayed with him. 'It was just super-intense extreme conditions. The idea of even being in a place with a massive ball of flame coming at you most of the day, with an ear-piercing noise. That was your working environment. That's just crazy.'

The process by which Templeborough became Magna, of how the 'swords' of industry were beaten into the 'ploughshares' of leisure, is one that's been echoed and mirrored all across industrial and post-industrial Britain. In Blaenavon, South Wales, there's Pwll Mawr, the Big Pit. If you've seen the cover of the Manic Street Preachers *National Treasures* album, that's the Big Pit's main shaft and winding wheel there on the cover. A working colliery from 1860 to 1980, it's now the Big Pit National Coal Museum.

Museum is slightly misleading though; the idea is to give the feel of what a working pit was like. My dad made pit props in an engineering works called Gullick Dobson and he will tell you that the ones in the Big Pit are not there for show but to stop the mine roof falling in on you as you take your tour underground. In fact, just like a working pit, it's covered by the regulations of Her Majesty's Inspectorate of Mines. This can disconcert some visitors when they find they must wear a hard hat, safety lamp and battery, and on their belt a carbon-monoxide filtering Rebreather which will buy them an hour and a chance of survival in the event that the mine fills with toxic air. Mobile phones or battery devices are not allowed or, rather, 'contraband'. (This reminds me of the time I made a TV film in the disused nuclear reactor at Sellafield. During the intensive security briefing I was told to surrender any bottled water, food, cigarettes or snuff. 'Blimey, I've lost so much snuff at nuclear reactors this way,' I quipped. No one laughed.)

At the Bradford Industrial Museum, I have taken wine and cheese with the J B Priestley Society and admired his amateur watercolours in a building that was once known as Moorside Mills. In the town's considerable commercial heyday, it used to be a thriving mill where they spun worsted, the fine smooth yarn that made the city rich and powerful. In Saltaire, the old mill houses some rather more celebrated art works by another local lad, David Hockney. There's some ironic consolation to be had in the fact that, though the industries themselves have been killed off by neglect or malice, they have spawned a new sector of the economy, a new market; the heritage industry. If its unwitting mother was Mrs T, its father is a Yorkshireman called Frank Atkinson.

Frank Atkinson was born on 13 April 1924, the son of a labourer and a schoolteacher. An inquisitive child, he was obsessed with fossils and museums and soon became the youngest member of The Museum of Barnsley Naturalists and Scientific Society. Later he was appointed director at Wakefield Museum and Art Gallery. In 1952, Frank toured Scandinavia and was struck by their 'folk museums', demotic, unstuffy, 'living' museums dedicated to enshrining and preserving a record of disappearing ways of life. In Sweden and Norway, these were chiefly rural communities. But Atkinson decided that England, specifically the industrial north, ought to have a similar museum devoted to its heritage. Atkinson knew that the communities and ways of life associated with mining and shipbuilding were declining. He said, 'It is essential that collecting be carried out quickly and on as big a scale as possible. It is now almost too late.'

After decades of collecting, sourcing and wrangling with various county councils, the Beamish museum was opened in 1971 on 300 acres that had once belonged to the family of former prime minister Sir Anthony Eden. It's a fine spot, a wooded river valley, in a peaceful corner of County Durham. The wood is called Hell Hole Wood and a nearby village is called No Place, but these are complete misnomers, particularly on an unseasonably balmy late October morning with the sun blazing down from a cloudless sky on woods of copper, amber and russet. Some will say, rightly, that something clearly cannot be quite right for it to feel like a day in high summer when it's nearly Bonfire Night. I decide to put my climatic fears for the planet to one side, take my coat off and enjoy it.

The entrance arch, though I didn't notice this at first, is no decorative construction but a bright red steam hammer the size of a house. Through it, the site stretches away, though there's no way of taking it all in or getting any clear idea of how big and rich and various it is from here. Pretty much everything you can see from this ridge to the wooded hills in the distance is Beamish, farmsteads and towns, crannies and pockets, each celebrating and enshrining a different era of northern life and work.

Almost immediately a tram appears, chugging along the rutted track just below the entrance. I decide to join the small waiting queue. It mainly comprises a big family group headed and marshalled by a bustling, genial kind of dad in what seem to me insanely optimistic white pumps for a day late in the year on the County Durham coalfield. His lad of about ten is dancing around with suppressed anticipation. 'Have you ever been so excited about anything?' Dad asks me with a smile. Well, to be honest, yes. But I take his point.

Small boys of all ages will find oily, smoky delight in Beamish's handsome fleet of trams and buses. They include the Sunderland 16, an open top vehicle that, after Sunderland's tramways closed in 1954, had been a football changing room and a farmyard apple store before being lovingly restored to the job it does best. There's a 'Blackpool Balloon' that plied its trade on the Golden Mile in the 1930s and the Oporto 196, born in the Boavista motorworks of Portugal's second city and now a stunner in South Shields' blue and primrose livery; the Jose Mourinho, the Special One, if you will, of trams.

Ours pulls to a gentle stop before us, we embark and I head for the top deck of Newcastle 114, the actual tram that ran from the 'Toon to Gosforth circa 1902, as its snowy-haired and luxuriantly moustachioed Geordie driver tells me with evident pride. This occasions among my neighbours, two middle aged ladies with small dogs, a similarly warm assessment of Newcastle's current Metro system, its speed, convenience and handiness for the shops of the Metro Centre. One day, perhaps, centuries hence, we will wax nostalgic for that as we look at a Prototype Metro-Cammell Metrocar of the current system in a future museum, but today, as we roll down the hill by the waggoners' station, we ride through the County Durham of a century ago.

Eerily so, when, at one point when the tram reaches the halt at The Town, a small group of men in khaki meet us as we disembark. They chat, they show the kids their rifles and bullet belts, and they gently cajole and sport with the male passengers. At the time I visited, scenes like this were being enacted all over Britain, as the nation remembered the outbreak of the First World War on its hundredth anniversary. We did this nationally in a variety of ways, from the sublime to the less so, from Paul Cummins and Tom Piper's blood-red tide of a million poppies at the Tower Of London to a Sainsbury's ad that somehow strove to equate the horrors of the Somme and the Christmas truce of 1914 to BOGOF Baked Beans and Taste The Difference Streaky Bacon.

Once regarded as the ultimate folly and the last word in futile carnage, newer perspectives on the Great War are starting to see that as a primarily English view, encouraged by our First World War poets.

Certainly, their influence has been pervasive – when the Beamish chaps in their puttees and neat trimmed 'tashes lean on their rifles in the main street and tell us of the Bosche and our brave boys at Mons and Ypres, the echoes are all of Owen and Sassoon, of bugles calling from sad shadows, and at each slow dusk a drawing down of blinds.

The main street is where the commercial bustle at the heart of the town lies, a fug, reeking of horses and coal smoke, echoing to the clattering trams and hooves and wheels on cobbles. When I first saw the documentary films of Sagar Mitchell and James Kenyon, made at the turn of the twentieth century and rescued from a Blackburn shop basement after a hundred years to be shown on BBC TV as the *Lost World Of Mitchell & Kenyon*, one of the many things than stunned and delighted me was how crowded and alive the town streets of England of the 1900s were. Even at their busiest now, on maybe a hot summer Saturday or the last working day before Christmas, the Lancashire towns they filmed in like Wigan, Blackburn are Preston are like ghost towns compared to what you see here. Mitchell and Kenyon's streets are thronged with folk, horses, barrows, traders, vendors, kids, dogs, trams and trolleybuses. It's an invigorating mayhem. Life was not the privatised and domestic affair it is today, conducted under fluorescent lights in offices and cubicles, on out of town estates and shopping centres. It was lived communally and al fresco and must have been maddening and thrilling at the same time. Beamish's Town, thanks to its stream of visitors and parade of actors, has some of that same vibrant feel.

Watching the Briton of today in the urban townscape of a century ago prompts a few thoughts from your ever vigilant observer; chiefly that eating or at least snacking seems to have become our national sport. Scores of kids are milling around, all are eating constantly in that remorseless, slightly hypnotic way that sheep on the high fells do. I watch a tiny girl on a bench in Redman Park wrestling with a family size bag of Pickled Onion Monster Munch as big as herself. Everywhere you look small children are brandishing and cradling pasties, toffees, Pringles, Mars bars and the occasional banana. To be fair to them, this is not of their own volition. Legions of fussing parents are watching them like hawks, except no hawk was ever so worried about his or her fledgling's food intake. It's like the movie *Speed*, if it were called Nosh. At no point must your calorie intake fall before 50 kilojoules a minute or you will die a hideous death from starvation.

Also, here's a serious question. When did we become so hung up on flipping hydration? I never heard the word till I was about 20. Now you hear old ladies in the hairdressers under those big hairdryers saying, 'Are you keeping yourself hydrated, Doreen?' and blokes down the bowling green carrying plastic sacks with tubes bottles designed for endurance runners. If you're crossing the Serengeti on foot in the dry season or smelting in a foundry, I can see the need for having a small bottle of water to hand. But everyone here at Beamish – toddlers, football dads, young mums, gormless youths, elderly ladies – are laden with gallon bottles of Highland Spring that they suck from constantly like Joe Frazier during the 'Rumble in the Jungle'.

Funny how our attitude to water has changed. Now it's seen as a sophisticated lifestyle accoutrement, like a smartphone or an avocado. It used to be something boring that came out of the tap. When I was a kid, dashing in from a ten-hour, forty-a-side football game during the summer holidays, desperate for a glug of Barr's Cream Soda or Corona Limeade, I was told dispiritingly to drink 'corporation pop' or 'Adam's Ale'. Or even tea, which was supposed to be most thirst quenching of all. A huge money-saving fib, and I knew it then as I know now, because I have never seen anyone with a teapot running alongside Paula Radcliffe at the London Marathon.

Speaking of gormless youths, which I think you'll find I was, I bump into a particularly fine example on my way across the square. His faded jeans are cut off at the bony knees and he wears a presumably ironic Rolling Stones T-shirt and has Kurt Cobain's Vileda supermop hair. There is none of the doomed Nirvana singer's nihilistic intensity here, though, as he chews vacantly on something unidentified and smirks at his mate. Both have spots and languid Home Counties' drawls, and I fight hard against ingrained prejudice. Let us be generous and say that he may well be stumbling down the dark and enclosing tunnel of adolescence, soon to emerge a model citizen and go off to work with Médecins Sans Frontières in Eritrea.

The residential street at Beamish's Town is called Ravensworth Terrace, saved from demolition in the 1970s and rebuilt brick by brick here from its original site in Gateshead. The houses have been beautifully recreated as various dwellings. Number 2 represents the home of music teacher Miss Florence Smith. There is manuscript paper on the stand and a love token of a glass rolling pin on the dresser. The Budget Kurt Cobain follows me in with his mum in tow. She looks at the neat back room with its blackened range and charming wallpaper, a small, neat much loved domicile, and pronounces it 'creepy' before going out for a fag.

I can't agree with her there. But young and old, gormless and smart, we all get the creeps at Nos 3 and 4 Ravensworth Terrace. This belongs to J Jones, a dentist in Edwardian Hartlepool, and whose chilling surgery is now also relocated to Beamish. Free dentistry didn't arrive till the coming of the NHS. Before that you would have your teeth pulled at travelling fairs, markets or, if you were lucky enough to live in a town, at grisly establishments like J Jones. Preventative dentistry was largely unknown – you went to the dentist when you were in pain – although it was not uncommon for young women to get a set of false teeth for their twenty-first birthday and for them to have teeth pulled needlessly to save future husbands the expense of buying dentures later on. Apparently this was standard in County Durham till the mid-fifties. Dentistry even in my seventies' youth was primitive too, as I found to my cost when, not that long ago, I had to have work done on mine that could have bought me a BMW and was in no way commensurate with the pleasure I got from my childhood diet of Tooty Frooties. My friend's dad actually did his own dentistry, removing a loose and painful tooth by facing himself in the mirror with pliers poised, gripping said tooth and then 'waiting until I least expected it' before yanking it out.

As you head upstairs at Number 3 Ravensworth Terrace, with shrinking trepidation, upsetting childhood memories fill one's head along with the Proustian scent of the chloroform and the Nitrous Oxide or 'laughing gas'. A dentist once told me that, at dental school parties, they would sometimes let a little 'nitrous' leak gently into the room to improve the mood. They could certainly do with some in here. The room is crammed and bristling with various nightmarish instruments, leather pipes and tubes, vicious looking clamps and I remember that reclining green leather chair from my school dentist and from many subsequent bad dreams. In here, the dentist and his nurse are showing a traumatised little girl the large pincers used for tugging out teeth. 'Then I'll put a cotton wool ball in to soak up the blood and help it clot,' he says gently and terrifyingly. He asks her how often she brushes her teeth. 'Twice a day,' she answers weakly. 'Oh no! Once a week is more than enough,' he replies.

After all this I am glad to be out on the street with my new friends The Purples. I have christened them thus because dad and son are both resplendent in eye-watering violet football tops and matching quiffs. Maybe it's the new Newcastle United away strip, though not the quiffs, obviously. Anyway, they are loud and jovial and after some initial reservations – they really are loud – I decide I like them, not least for the fact that they've chosen to spend their precious leisure hours immersing themselves in their own history and culture rather than sit watching some berk in a spotted bowtie pricing up Delft china.

We walk past the Town Stables and the big yard reeking of lanolin and leather. There are several horses in there and The Purples (and me too, to be honest) are unsure whether they are real or not. They seem very still but their eyes occasionally flicker. 'Are they robots?' Purple senior asks me thoughtfully. He may well be right but I wonder where one would buy a robot horse. If they were readily available, Kanye West would surely have one. Eventually we decide they are sleeping. A career in equestrian journalism does not beckon for me or him, I fancy.

At the end of Ravensworth Terrace are the shops and institutions of the town. There's a sweet shop called Jubilee Confectioners which is doing a predictably brisk trade in pineapple chunks, black bullets and Tyne mints, for which they are queuing out of the door. Next door is the newspaper office and upstairs is a print shop. In it, the printer is explaining, with great patience and pride, the technicalities of his craft and the workings of the Jack Ascough's Printing Press of Barnard Castle. He is setting the type for a brass band concert poster and trying to get all the alignments, font sizes and justifications exactly right. 'One band is playing twice, which makes it a little awkward,' he says tinkering with bits of iron and pots of ink. A family watches him, crunching humbugs with the mechanised precision and regularity of a robot horse.

The bank, moved here from Gateshead too like the houses, is an imposing edifice in Swedish Imperial granite; its dignity, stolidity even, designed to give confidence to its customers. I wonder how many working folk from the pit villages or farms of County Durham and Northumberland have stood within these walls, awkward and apprehensive, twisting their caps in their hands, waiting for a mortgage, a loan or withdrawing savings for some red letter day. A young teller in glasses and wing collar is putting up a poster from the period explaining why nationalisation of the banks is absolutely necessary. *Plus ça change*, I think.

There is also a Co-op at Beamish, transplanted from Annfield Plain, a nearby ex-mining village. It is wonderful. The Co-op began in Rochdale, in 1844. Twenty-eight textile weavers from the town, poor and desperate and blacklisted for striking for better conditions, pooled £140 to buy a small dry goods store stocked with oatmeal, sugar, butter, flour and a handful of candles. Ten years later, with a fine reputation for quality, the British co-operative movement had grown to nearly 1,000 co-operatives. That first little shop at 31 Toad Lane, Rochdale, is now a museum, but in its heyday it would have looked a lot like the one I mooch about now.

Two older ladies are reminiscing about their 'divi' numbers – the Co-op's very own pioneering dividend loyalty card system – and I admire the marble slabs for keeping the cheeses cool and fresh, the wooden butter pats, the hams and pipes and snuff, and the Dainty Dinah Toffee tins. I marvel at the elaborate nature of the Lamson-Paragon cash carrying system, which whizzed payments and change inside hollow wooden balls along overhead tracks. It is delightful and more than a little nuts. I chuckle at the ad for 'Mekumfat', a feed guaranteed to give you 'plump poultry' and showing a rubicund, breathless farmhand chasing some huge, crazed chickens around a barn. I ask the nice assistant in the pinafore dress where the bacon slicer is and she tells me gently but firmly that, 'They weren't invented till 1920 and in this shop it's 1913.' This reminds me of the time at a similar attraction, Dudley's Black Country Living Museum, when a customer in the pub asked for a Diet Coke and some prawn cocktail crisps only to be told sharply 'It's 1932 in here chum. You can have a Sarsaparilla and a cheese and onion bap.'

There is so much of Beamish that to cover it all would take the rest of this book; farms, churches, a fairground and railway, the entire Georgian village of Pockerley. So let me take you to a couple more places nearer our own time. The trolleybus up the hill to Home Farm and Orchard Cottage is driven by a young Asian man who is openly covetous of the disabled ramp/lift of a fellow driver. 'I'm hoping to get one in the New Year,' he says, wistfully, as if it were a Maserati. Thus conveyed, I arrive at the cottage with The Purples whom I am starting to like more and more.

'Aunty Jen's house was like this, she had her cooker there,' says Ma Purple, as the householder played by an actor sits silently, playing solitaire ludo (somehow) and listening to *ITMA* on the wireless.

A newspaper lying nearby tells us that we are in *Warship Week*. It is now 1940. Orchard Cottage is intended to represent the home of a family of evacuees escaping urban bombing raids. There's anti-blast tapes on the windows and an Anderson shelter in the garden. But inside, it is small and neat and homely; pastel blues and warm creams, utilitarian but cosy. It reminds me of my Irish grandmother 'Granma Coney's' little house in Haydock near Wigan.

It also reminds me of a conversation I once had with Laurence Llewelyn-Bowen, the design expert. Sometimes dismissed as an arch televisual fop, I found him engaging, intelligent company. The Second World War and the supercharged vibrancy, danger and urgency it gave to daily life fascinate him as they do me. For Bowen, it was a sexy time, a time of glamour in the face of darkness. 'When you know that every night, the Luftwaffe might blow up your house and kill you in your bed, you get on with today.' I grew up adoring Richmal Crompton's Just William books and would lie in bed at night on a seventies' council estate absorbed in the doings of a fictional 12-year-old from the Home Counties, his ration books, gas mask and dealings with the ARP warden. This, and *Dad's Army*, made kids like me and Laurence pine to have lived in these fabulous times. That may have been trivial but, for me, it's deepened into real respect for the generation of Britons who found and forged a national voice and character back then; who, whether fighting in the skies or sitting stoically with ludo and *ITMA* at kitchen tables, defied a ravenous, spreading evil and then built a better fairer Britain from the wreckage and ruins.

I also really like the clothes. How cool did Land Girls look? Those tank tops and hair piled up in scarves, the rolled-up sleeves, the jumpers and plaid shirts. My Auntie Mag never married and stayed at home to look after Granma Coney. In the war, though, she'd been a teenage Land Girl and you knew from the way she talked about it – the camaraderie, the work, the sense of youthful vigour and purpose – that it was the greatest time of her life. I'll bet. Who wouldn't want to spend summer in Devon or Kent mucking about in haycarts and barns with all your mates, a gang of hardworking, fun-loving young women, and give international Fascism a bloody nose at the same time?

I have my lunch in the British Kitchen. It's 'Allotment Soup', a hearty stew 'made from everything in the allotment except the greenhouse' and served to me by a smiling woman in full Land Girl gear. The next lady in the queue just wants a paper bag and asks how much. Slightly baffled, the man behind the counter says, 'You can have a paper bag for nothing, missus, we're not the National Trust.'

The British Kitchen is an example of a British Restaurant, institutions set up in 1940 to provide cheap, wholesome fare for people bombed out of their homes or otherwise in need. At the height of the war, there were several thousand of them serving over half a million cheap and much needed meals a day. They were originally called Community Feeding Centres, but Churchill disliked the drab, functional, faintly socialistic sound of that so re-named them British Restaurants. There was undoubtedly a political element to them. Labour liked their egalitarian impulse and when they came to power post-war thought they might become a permanent feature of life, guaranteeing a nourishing diet for the poor. However, they were disbanded in 1947.

I meet the man from the British Restaurant outside as he's coming out after his shift behind the counter. He points me in the direction of Home Farm, once part of Sir Anthony Eden's family estate and full of the high-tech gear and innovations that would never have been lavished on the estate's ordinary tenant farmers. 'Look at that water boiler,' he says, indicating what looks like a small U Boat in a nearby field. 'That was the boiler for the steam engine. Can you imagine getting all that water to boil? And of course it was deadly. Loads of people were killed and maimed by the bloody things. But of course, they were only farm workers so it didn't matter ...'

At the farm itself, I am greeted by a compelling sight. The biggest pig I have ever seen. I'm no huge pig enthusiast so I realise this statement lacks real authority, but boy, was it ever gigantic, and standing on its hind legs leaning over a stone wall seemingly addressing a small crowd of people. It's all a bit *Animal Farm* and, to tell you the truth, it freaked me out. As I get closer I see that the pig is, in fact, leaning over to eat a proffered bit of sausage roll (which seems in poor taste to me though not, I have to say, to the pig) and, obligingly, to have his picture taken. Or her. I was in no hurry to find out.

At the centre of the knot of onlookers are, predictably, The Purples. Pa Purple and youngest daughter – and writing this has instantly made me think of *Ask the Family*. Ask your dad – are having an earnest and thoughtful discussion about how effective a pig would be in the disposal of a body.

Pa Purple: 'The thing about a pig, y'naa, is it will eat any part of a human except the bones.'

Daughter Purple: 'What about teeth?'

Pa Purple: 'Well, OK, yes, you're right. It can't eat the teeth. But that's still a canny way of getting rid of a body.'

Daughter Purple: 'Not really, Dad. They could still identify you from your dental records, like.'

Just then another family arrive, led by an efficient-looking young blonde woman in her early thirties. She turns to the others with a look of stern admonition and barks, 'This is where we lost Darren,' before entering the farm. Possibly it's a search party.

Inside, there's no sign of the elusive Darren but the farm is lovely and homely. Vera Lynn's singing on the radio and a little girl in pigtails (I'm not sure if she's a visitor or an extra) warms her hands in front of the fire. There is Glory Roll to eat, a stodgy forties' teatime favourite and a tiny plate of bacon, eggs, cheese and such which represented an adult's weekly ration for the week. It looks minuscule. It wouldn't feed the average Beamish visitor for 20 minutes let alone a week. No wonder no one was fat. As I stand round the back of the farm making these notes, I look up into the doleful eyes of yet another gigantic pig, leering over the wall at me from about six inches away. If I close my eyes, I can see it still. I probably will forever.

*

Beamish is a delight. Go there. Make a day of it. Make a night of it. At the risk of sounding like an over-enthusiastic ad voice-over, it's fun, it's educational, it's different. But my favourite part of Beamish also carries an undertow of wistfulness, a bottom note of pride and sadness, an elegy for a vanished way of life that recognises the hardships of that life as well as its joys.

Hetton Silver Band Hall stands at the entrance to the early 1900s Pit Village, Beamish's beautiful, brilliant recreation of life in the County Durham coalfields at the beginning of the last century. At its peak in 1913, when again this village is set, they dug 56.5 million tons of coal a year out of the ground. Towns and villages like this, like Esh Winning, Bedlington, Annfield Plain, Seaham, Ushaw Park and Langley Park, came into existence just to work the seams, deep dark seams with resonant names: Maudlin, Five-Quarter, Ganister Clay, Brass Thill.

The band hall was moved here brick-by-brick from South Market Street, Hetton-le-Hole on Wearside with the help of that community. I picked up a little grizzling on social media about the relocation, saying it was a pity. Possibly. But I can't help thinking it's far, far better than it becoming a poundshop or nail bar which was a far from unlikely fate. Inside, pride of place is given to a huge Durham Miners banner with a quote from *Das Kapital* unapologetically emblazoned upon it: 'Workers of the world unite. You have nothing to lose but your chains.'

Karl wasn't long dead, and his ideas were just about to transform the world, when the original of this Edwardian pit village was booming. That boom made these men and their families the aristocrats of the working class; they earned three times as much as agricultural workers. But they earned it, as we're about to see, in conditions scarcely believable today.

As you wander down Francis Street with its tiny neat cottages, each little house with a shed for racing pigeons or plant potting, you get the feeling that, however hard the life, the sense of community here must have been extraordinary; hundreds of families living side by side, men working side by side underground, kids going to the same school. This must have had its darker side, of insularity and claustrophobia, but it must also have fostered strong ties of solidarity and belonging. There was even a communal bread oven down the back alley for making 'stotties' and sweet treats. Inside the little colliery-owned houses, families slept cheek by jowl. Mum and dad in the front room, grandma and grandpa in the Dress Bed, stored folded in a cupboard, the kids all in the one tiny upstairs room accessed via a ladder. Staircases arrived just before the First World War. Down the road in the Methodist chapel, Sunday school would be held, and the occasional magic lantern show.

Popping into the school reminds me of how close that older world was in the north I grew up in. It's as if little changed apart from hemlines and hairstyles until the early 1990s, when seemingly overnight we went from being an essentially Victorian milieu to one of 24-hour Peruvian street food vendors, craft microbreweries and boutique hotels. The classroom reminds me a little of my first primary school, St Joseph's just off Wigan's Miry Lane, a name with something of the Thomas Hardy about it. It had these same antiquated posters of skeletons and nations of the world, the same A is for Apple, B is for Ball sequences, the tiny wooden-framed slates for the children to practise their handwriting. We didn't have hoops and sticks, although I would often hear my Lancastrian nana talk of them and threaten us with one for Christmas. Here in the yard, a few baffled kids of today are trying them out, trundling the steel rims across the yard with varying degrees of competence and clatter. Now a relic from another era, in their day these were as techy, flash and ubiquitous as Kandy Krush, Tumblr or Snapchat, which of course are terms that might be as outré and outmoded as Omo and Bournvita by the time you read this.

Not far from the schoolyard is the very reason that villages like this existed. To get there, you take a walk past Davy's Fried Fish and Chip Shop (the queue is, naturally, phenomenal) and there it is; a small, damp, blackly forbidding entrance into the hillside itself. This is the Mahogany Drift Mine; a real working mine between 1855 and 1958, and the memory that will linger longest from my trip to Beamish.

You pick up a lamp and wait your turn, and for the previous tour to emerge, bent backed and blinking. A guide in period gear (older readers, think Brian and Michael on *Top of the Pops*) then leads you to the dark mouth of the mine entrance. He picks out a small boy in front of me and asks him how old he is. 'Seven,' comes the self-conscious answer from the tiny lad. 'Well then, in six months' time you'll be ready to go in here.'

There's palpable shock in the queue. But the guide is absolutely right. That was the age of the youngest lad to be found working as what was called a trapper boy, a young lad who squatted at the swinging wooden doors and opened them for the passing trucks laden with coal. Each trapper boy was given a candle, an expensive commodity, and hence a poor kid who wasn't up to the job was said to be 'not worth the candle'.

'Ready?' asks the kindly guide, and we, including the fearful looking little lad, enter the Mahogany Drift Mine. By the time I've gone about 20 paces, I'm hurting. Badly. The low roof of the mine entrance tunnel means that you must walk bent double, like a very old man, which is how I feel very quickly. The alternative is to crack your head on the rock ceiling and the rafters. Alternating between these two equally painful activities, I make my slow way through the tight, echoing tunnel, ankle deep in chilly, mucky water.

Try it. Stoop down now and walk across the room a couple of times. Every time you feel like stretching a little to ease your aching back, get a friend to hit you on the top of the head with a brick. This was a Mahogany Drift miner's commute to work for a mile-and-a-half each way. That's like walking between Manchester's Piccadilly and Victoria stations. If you're in Birmingham, like walking from Five Ways to the Bull Ring. Or, if you're in the sticks, from Tottenham Court Road tube to Harrods. Crooked backed, feet sloshing through cold, dirty water in the dark. We complain if the escalators are out of order.

Mahogany Drift Mine was what was called a 'pillar and stall mine', a precarious way of working shallow seams with low corridors, the coal face being held up by wooden stakes and props. The hydraulic pit props that my dad made at the Gullick Dobson factory were a long way off and, by the time they came, Mahogany Drift had gone the way that all our mines soon would.

When you got to the end of the tunnel you could stand up a little and maybe walk a mile along the seam to your stall. Once there, there were a couple of methods by which you could get the coal that would comprise your wages, since all the miners were on piecework. Most preferred lying down on their side and lighting a small charge of dynamite under the face thus causing it to collapse. You ran the risk of bringing the whole face down on you or blowing your own hand off, of course, but most miners preferred that to the hated Widowmaker, a rock drill that used a hammering motion to pound the face and created clouds of noxious gas and dust. Tobacco and snuff were needed to try and clear the lungs and throat and fend off silicosis and 'black lung'. After a year or two of this, many were unable to work and often died within six months or so. The Widowmaker had been as good as its name.

This they did for eight hours a day, six days a week, lying in dirt and water and a candlelit cloud of choking filth filling the trucks – by hand with a shovel – with the coal they'd hewed. Ten trucks if you were good (and lucky); four tons in an eight-hour shift, and then walking back the mile-and-a-half to what, even in the depths of winter, into rain and snow, but particularly on a long summer evening or a cool moonlit autumn, must have felt like heaven. Till tomorrow.

As I leave Beamish, I feel very fortunate in being born when I was. That was their life. We're just playing at it.

The Industrial Revolution re-drew the map of Britain swiftly and enduringly. Even in this post-industrial era, we still live on and in that map by and large. After industrialisation, places that had once had great power and significance – Canterbury, for instance, or Winchester – became dormitory towns or tourist destinations, as cattle markets, courts and ecclesiastical seats became less important than muck and brass. Manchester is your classic example here. Cotton saw it expand explosively from a small Lancashire town to the richest city in the world in just a few decades. Other backwaters grew into crowded, bustling cities too, often powered by specific industries. In Glasgow and Barrow it was shipbuilding. In Sheffield it was steel, as we have seen.

In Swindon it was a man in a stovepipe hat that Jeremy Clarkson thinks is the greatest ever Briton. Don't hold that against him though.

A slight, unmistakeable but largely unfair whiff of comedy hangs around Wiltshire's largest town. For a place of its size and history, it has few famous sons or daughters. Quirky popsters XTC spring to mind, as do comic Mark Lamarr and pint size glamour puss Melinda Messenger, but I had to resort to Google to find out about Billy Piper, Diana Dors and some of the members of Supertramp. Don Rogers, whose winning goal gave the town its moment of football glory when they beat Arsenal to win the League Cup in 1968, was actually from Somerset, though he runs a sports shop in his spiritual home. Jasper Fforde's comic novels are set here, as well as Mark Haddon's *The Curious Incident Of The Dog In the Night-Time*. Python Terry Jones wrote a short story called 'The Lift that Took People to Places They Didn't Want to Go' which delivers people to Swindon.

When I tweeted to the effect that I was Swindon bound, many of the replies had a mocking ring. One asked me to find out in advance 'if it was shut', a remarkable slur when you consider that the correspondent came from Devizes, hardly itself the city that never sleeps.

Now then, Swindon is not by anyone's definition the north I agree. But I had been tipped off that, if I wanted to see how the labour of yesterday is the leisure of today, I should take a diversion south for a few hundred words or so. I wanted to include a mention of maybe the best example in Britain of how a one-industry town is now trying to turn a largely vanished enterprise, the one it was founded on, into a twenty-first century leisure destination, built on workers' memories and the burnished iron vestiges of a vanished Britain.

In 1842, Isambard Kingdom Brunel chose the little market town as the site for his new railway works that would build and service the locos for his new Great Western Railway, or GWR. It was a remarkable story of rapid, explosive expansion and the classic tale of benevolent corporate capitalism and a paternalistic employer building a community. Swindon was a company town back in the days when there were such things.

One can argue about Marxist Dialectics and False Consciousness until you're blue (or rather red) in the face. But it would be hard to argue that GWR was bad for Swindon. The company built a neat, pretty little railway village to house the workers. It had what must have been one of the first ever 'health centres', with a clinic, a hospital, a pharmacy, swimming pool and Turkish baths. Each week, GWR workers paid a small portion of their wages into a healthcare fund and in return they and their families received free cradle-to-grave medical treatment and dentistry. Those unfortunates who lost limbs in war or at the works could have new ones custom built free in the carriage shop of the works. This pioneering system was used by Nye Bevan as a blueprint for the NHS.

Swindon had the UK's first public lending library and thanks to its Mechanics Institute and their ambitious New Swindon Improvement Company, the town had probably the best-educated manual workers in Britain who could avail themselves, free, of night classes on everything from first aid to playing the xylophone. Ideologues might dismiss these notions as quaintly patronising paternalism, but from the viewpoint of the early twentieth century, isn't there something rather admirable and touching about working people (and it has to be said, their employers) wanting to use their free time to 'better themselves', not just in the sense of improving their material status but in the sense of broadening their minds and expanding their horizons. They bettered themselves in a more practical sense too. Swindon had powerful trade unions and thriving local democracy.

I think about this in the queue at the Tesco Metro. It is a swelteringly hot summer day, and the young chubby lad on the till is red-faced and sweating profusely in his thick black work fleece. (Note to self: does anything else happen 'profusely' except 'sweating'?) He has a soft Wiltshire accent and a kindly manner thrown into a kind of melancholy relief by his acne, his piercings and his many and varied tattoos; a kind of floral motif on his neck, a tendril emerging from the fleece's collar and on his forearm, in florid italics, 'You Only Live Once'.

The Tesco Metro is in the modern part of the New Town, the Swindon that the GWR built. The old New Town (if you catch my drift) is the part around the original works, which I'm going to be visiting and I'm told is pleasant. The new development though, with the Holiday Inn and the shopping area, is as unlovely as these places always are. It's crowded in a kind of aimless way, with milling shoppers who seem more stupefied than energised by the magnetic lure of retail. Here we can marvel anew at how Britain has become a nation obsessed by coffee. Every other shop in Swindon's shopping precinct is devoted to the sale of it, and everyone from toddlers to old ladies on Zimmer frames seems to be slurping a skinny hazelnut latte from a corrugated plastic cup the size of a milk churn. Outside each of these, on metal chairs, a few smokers puff on the most expensive cigarettes in Europe, some furtive and sheepish, some voluble and cheery in their habit.

Steam is the museum of the Great Western Railway, and stands on the wonderfully named Fire Fly Avenue on the site of the old GWR works, which it shares with the HQ of the National Trust. It is a very popular attraction though 'it won't be so busy on a glorious day like today' a guide tells me, as he directs me through the impressive hallway over which loom the letters GWR, an acronym indissolubly knit with another, less-used one: IKB. Isambard Kingdom Brunel.

The good burghers of Bristol had long been fearful of being eclipsed by an upstart called Liverpool as an Atlantic port. They realised that a fast, efficient rail link from the West Country to London was vital. To get it, they needed an engineer of prodigious talent. They found it in a 20-something with no previous experience of railway construction or design and with an extraordinary name even by Victorian standards.

There are several tall-ish tales about how the Great Western Railway works came to Swindon. Some say that Brunel and his engineer Daniel Gooch were out surveying in the countryside round about one day and Brunel dropped his lunchtime sandwich on the ground. Declaring it an omen, he said that this would be the site of his works. But Gooch, disappointingly, leaves this out of his account:

> I was called to report upon the best situation to build these works and, on full consideration, I reported in favour of Swindon, it being the junction with the Cheltenham branch and also a convenient division of the Great Western Line for the engine working. Mr Brunel and I went to look at the ground, then only green fields, and he agreed with me as to its being the best place.

The story of Swindon is the story of the railways, and that story is told brilliantly at Steam. In its heyday, the works were a citadel within a little Wiltshire town. It had its own gasworks, its own laboratories, its own fire station, its own doctors and nurses. A watercolour on Steam's wall shows what New Swindon was like in 1849 and it's essentially a pastoral scene with a few houses dotted around meadows through which run lazy streams. Within a few years of this painting, though, the GWR works had mushroomed from nothing and dragged little Swindon into the modern age with it as it created it. The pretty and compact streets around the works were known as the railway village; 300 homes whose workers, swelled by thousands of others from elsewhere, would pour down the dedicated subway tunnel each morning and night to the blare of the klaxon by which the town kept time.

Everyone in the town had a connection with the works. Many of those workers' stories are told vividly on recordings throughout the museum. According to these testimonies, working here was actually lively and invigorating, if tough. It was work undertaken with pride by a workforce who knew just how good they were, as they produced three state of the art locomotives a week. As one worker recalls: 'You learned from "the old sweats" who weren't afraid to give you a clip round the ear. There was a real pride in working in the machine shop, if you did job badly it wouldn't be the boss who told you off but the bloke at the side of you.'

Making a train, as of course I'd never considered before, involves a whole range of associated crafts and workshops. There's the oily, smoky miasma of the engineering shop. There's the clamour of the boiler room, which those in the know avoided for its noise. (In Swindon, it's still said that if you see two men in the street talking, one with his nose in the other's ear, 'they must work in the boiler room'). But also there was the quiet concentration of the seamstresses in 'upholstery' and the detailed craftsmanship of the carpentry shop. In the main halls, you can see the result of their labours; trains so huge, imperious and beautiful, like the GWR 4073 Class Caerphilly Castle and the GWR 4000 Class 4003 Lode Star, that you start to understand how people fall in love with them, even if you'd never write down those numbers in a little book. You begin to appreciate why, from the *Night Mail* film to Sherlock Holmes with his Bradshaw to Celia Johnson and Trevor Howard, trains and railways loom so large in our national culture, especially the Age of Steam. The noise, glamour and mystery of major stations then must have been incredible. No one with blood in their veins would set their thriller or romance around Southampton Airport Parkway, or the Northern Trains Sprinter to Westhoughton.

Even the 1930s diesel looks fabulously chic and streamlined. Nicknamed the 'Flying Banana' it dashed from Birmingham to Cardiff just as quickly as the train does now, and while I don't want to wade into the HS2 argument, it's worth pointing out that Stephenson's first ever passenger service of 1830 went from Liverpool to Manchester faster than today's equivalent service. The buffet bar is fabulous; 12 or 13 green leather stools and a long, sleek counter with a glass and metal cake display. The effect is like Hopper's 'Nighthawks' meets *Brief Encounter*. Interactivity, the holy grail of modern museums, is used judiciously here without everything having to be reduced to toddler-friendly games. One such game appeals though, a 'Could you run a railway as efficiently as Brunel?' type of thing. In my case, the answer would seem to be 'no', since every time I become quickly bankrupt after a major tunnel fire, although this probably wouldn't disbar me from being CEO of one of our privatised franchises.

Isambard Kingdom Brunel and George Stephenson died within weeks of each other. They were kindred spirits but keen rivals to the end. Brunel thought he was right to reject Stephenson's narrow gauge of four feet eight-and-a-half inches for the 'broad' gauge of seven feet, which could accommodate bigger engines and faster trains. But he was wrong, as he often could be. He was brilliant, capricious, energetic, but sometimes impetuous. He was popular with his gangers certainly. 'The little giant' would often roll up his sleeves and work alongside the men, particularly when the work became more difficult or dangerous. After a force of 4,000 men and 300 horses had been working day and night from opposite ends of the Box Tunnel, Brunel was on the spot when the two drills broke through the rock and met. Ecstatic and grateful, Brunel took a gold ring from his finger and presented it to the ganger in charge. But when Brunel was shown a list of more than a hundred navvies injured in this project and admitted to Bath Hospital he commented, 'I think it is a small list considering the very heavy works and the immense amount of powder used.'

I was told all this by someone who studied at the university that now bears his name. That university is in London. But Swindon celebrates Brunel too, if rather differently, in the Brunel shopping mall with its Brunel Plaza and Brunel Arcade. Isambard Kingdom himself would have enjoyed having a seat of learning named after himself, but equally would have had no quarrel with being commemorated in the retail outlets either. The profit motive ran as thick, dark and treacly as engine oil through Brunel's innovations and adventures. It was as powerful an incentive for him as any scientific zeal or quest for immortality. Victorians like him, unburdened by our modern squeamishness about industry and class and their nexus, had no trouble yoking all these notions together in one superheated whole.

Though places like Magna, Beamish and Swindon's Steam are celebrations of Britain's industrial past, commodified as leisure, their relationship with the past is tricky and nuanced. In a Manchester museum of working life, the forerunner to its wonderful People's History Museum, I once had my ticket stamped by a man who'd worked there decades before when it was the Pump House on Water Street, a hydraulic pumping station for the city centre. He was proud of his new job, but a little wry and rueful about how his working life had panned out. When Mark E Smith of The Fall came to the BBC's new Salford studios to be interviewed by me for a radio show, he was greatly amused to be finishing his working life in the place he started it, except back in the 1970s, he'd been a messenger boy riding a moped along the rutted tracks between the long vanished dock offices where now there are concert halls and museums.

So the working past becomes a part of our future leisure, but which bits we take forward into that future is a matter of choice and emphasis. When popular entertainer Paul O'Grady made a TV series exploring such issues in 2013, it was originally to be called 'Paul O'Grady's Working Class'. This title gave an attack of the vapours to the then BBC One controller who insisted it couldn't have the word 'class' in the title. So *Paul O'Grady's Working Britain*, as it became,

went out as a very different beast, cut from three episodes to two
thanks to the excision of a 'contentious' section on council housing,
and so changed that two academics from the Open University who
worked on it asked for their names to be removed from the credits.
The OU's Jason Toynbee concluded, 'When it comes to social issues
I'm just not satisfied that the corporation is capable of taking an
informed and critical line any longer. The urge to rely on celebrities
and a tabloid narrative seems irresistible.'

Celebrity and tabloidism is blamed for infecting another great
passion of the working north. The Labour historian Daryl Leeworthy
said of sport in industrial Britain that it was 'an articulation of working
class self-awareness ... [and] a mechanism through which working
class desires and visions could be expressed'. Whether you take this
view, or feel it was always only a game, I couldn't go any further
without living the sporting life.

CHAPTER 2
LIVING THE SPORTING LIFE

Scrumming down in Warrington and bikes
and bowls in Gorton and Chorlton

North and South, our north and south, are creations of each other. They were forged in the same white heat and are looking-glass reflections seen through the grimy mirror of industrialisation. For long millennia of Ancient Britons, Romans, Vikings, Normans and more, north and south meant nothing more than compass points. London was no grander than York, and Essex was far less civilised than Durham. Chelmsford can argue otherwise till it is woad blue in the face.

But by the time Mrs Gaskell wrote the book of that name, North and South were as heavy as soot with meaning, their identities shaped by the Industrial Revolution and the coming of the factories. Proper, prosperous and respectable as opposed to dark, saturnine and unknowable, the south became Jekyll to the north's Hyde, an analogy that would be even more satisfying if there were a place in the south called Jekyll as there is one in the north named Hyde.

The historian Richard Holt sees sport as fundamental to this:

The North and the South reinvented each other in the nineteenth century. Beyond the broad geographical boundaries of the Wash and the Trent, deeper cultural territories were carved out as the pace and scale of Northern industrial growth left the South behind … This was a new country with a new culture and professional team sports were a key male component of it.

Sporting heroes gradually came to represent a distinctive idea of the North, of how Northern men saw themselves and how they were seen by others, including Northern women.

This to me is a self-evident truth, and it's why sport was always going to make its noisy claim early in this book.

The best of sport has something of the night about it. The drama and romance of floodlit nights, wintry terraces, bosky parks and tracks, stamping feet, flapping arms, nocturnes of clouded breath and mauve sunsets, hipflasks and Bovril, sizzling sonatas of hot dogs and frying onions, the bowl of gold in the distance, cradled in the arms of the night, the crowd surging down rain-lit streets or roaring like the unchained sea beneath a darkened heaven dotted with stars.

I can go on like this for a while, to be honest. Do you want a go on this hipflask?

But I do mean every florid word. When I conjure up a classic sporting Saturday, that high holy day of the sporting week, the romance is not of perfect, clement afternoons on rollered, manicured greensward or balmy days on a gently eddying river. It's raw winter dusks, the floodlights coming on at four at the end of another year, the great twilit final movement of the Grandstand symphony, the chattering of the teleprinter, David Coleman, Tony Gubba, sheepskin coats and muddied men under glowering skies, chips and fish, sausage butties, the Football Pink, smeared and blurry, still inky from the press rollers.

Back in the day, the good old, funny old days, there were even dedicated TV shows that elevated the commonplaces of after-work industrial sport into something glamorous of their own. *Midweek Sports Special*, a mainstay of my school nights, tried, gamely, to make Wednesday the new Saturday, and a cup replay at a freezing Roker Park or waterlogged Deepdale as glamorous as a trip to the Maracanã or Bernabéu. Still, it was well worth staying up for, if Mum would let you and if you'd 'looked away now' during *News at Ten*.

But 'appointment viewing' in my town was BBC 2's Rugby League *Floodlit Trophy*. It featured the legendary Eddie Waring whose unhinged Doppler-effect delivery ('Aaand the Castleford scrum HAALF got AAAWAAY with A VERRRRRY VERRRY bad TAAACKLE there …') made him ripe for mockery and impersonation, something Mike Yarwood did every week. The show ran from 1965 till 1980, and I vividly remember the day when Stephen Hankin used a rude word at St Jude's Juniors and, in blushing defence, claimed to have learned it from ITV's coarse sitcom *The Dustbinmen*. Unimpressed, a stern-faced Mr Unsworth informed him he'd 'do better to watch *Floodlit Trophy*' on the other side. There were many sage nods of approval, including one from notorious crawler David Hughes.

Posh sport tends to happen by day. This may have a whiff of sweeping generalisation about it, but think. It stands to reason, as the famous West Ham supporter Alf Garnett used to say. Long sunlit afternoons at the wicket or the outfield, days on the court or the lawn, are only really viable if you don't have a job you need to go to, and a country house you can. Henley, Ascot, Cheltenham, Cowes, all of these have major elements, either big days or famous competitions, that take place on a weekday afternoon. Imagine if the FA Cup final were held on a Tuesday mid-morning? In order to get the most out of 'the sport of kings', or rowing or eventing or shooting or any other of the sports of the gentry, you have to have a hell of a lot of free time and a pretty flexible job spec.

This would definitely have applied to Sir Henry Newbolt. Like Black Forest gateau, the music of Richard Clayderman and embroidered loo roll covers, the poetic works of Sir Henry are seen these days as a bit naff. But in his day – the mid-Victorian era – his stirring, patriotic verse, with its emphasis on stiff upper-lipped masculinity and the glories of empire, was quite the thing. If he is known at all today, it is for his ripping yarn 'Vitaï Lampada', the much parodied but well-loved tale of how lessons learned on the playing fields of Eton – or Harrow or in Newbolt's case Clifton College, Bristol – could be transferred successfully to the battlefields of Waterloo, Ypres or Normandy.

> *There's a breathless hush in the Close to-night –*
> *Ten to make and the match to win –*
> *A bumping pitch and a blinding light,*
> *An hour to play and the last man in.*
> *And it's not for the sake of a ribboned coat,*
> *Or the selfish hope of a season's fame,*
> *But his Captain's hand on his shoulder smote*
> *'Play up! play up! and play the game!'*
>
> *The sand of the desert is sodden red, –*
> *Red with the wreck of a square that broke; –*
> *The Gatling's jammed and the colonel dead,*
> *And the regiment blind with dust and smoke.*
> *The river of death has brimmed his banks,*
> *And England's far, and Honour a name.*
> *But the voice of schoolboy rallies the ranks,*
> *'Play up! play up! and play the game!'*

The poem's essential thrust – experiences gained in childhood play form the character of the later war hero – was turned into a popular Edwardian music hall song entitled 'Two Little Boys' sung by Harry Lauder, and which brought a distinctly un-swinging end to the 1960s when it was an unexpected number one for the now-disgraced TV entertainer Rolf Harris.

Many decades after Newbolt, another English public schoolboy, this time an old Etonian called Eric Blair, took a rather different view of the virtues of sport. In the mid-1940s, the Soviet football giants Dynamo Moscow made a visit to the UK to play some exhibition matches. In these days of the Champions League, and saturation TV coverage when the Sporting Lisbon back four are as familiar to the armchair footie fan as their own immediate family, it is impossible to really understand the excitement this occasioned. Capacity crowds filled the stadia, and press and politicians alike frothed and fomented. George Orwell though was not so thrilled.

> Now that the brief visit of the Dynamo football team has come to an end, it is possible to say publicly what many thinking people were saying privately before the Dynamos ever arrived. That is, that sport is an unfailing cause of ill-will, and that if such a visit as this had any effect at all on Anglo-Soviet relations, it could only be to make them slightly worse than before.

That 'thinking people' phrase is telling here. He means people like George Orwell, of course. For all his genuine socialist sympathies, Orwell could be something of a snob and his contempt – or at least bafflement – here for the average football fan is thinly veiled. He talks of 'the vicious passions that football provokes'. He goes on:

> Serious sport has nothing to do with fair play. It is bound up with hatred, jealousy, boastfulness, disregard of all rules and sadistic pleasure in witnessing violence: in other words it is war minus the shooting ... There are quite enough real causes of trouble already, and we need not add to them by encouraging young men to kick each other on the shins amid the roars of infuriated spectators.

Whether you take the Newbolt line or the Orwell one; whether you think that sport is a powerful force for good and an instiller of healthy virtues, or a mindless orgy of petty divisions and naked aggression, it is certainly about much more than lobbing some kind of ball about or running around a track. People often bleat about 'keeping politics out of sport'. From Jesse Owens' humiliation of Hitler at the 1936

Olympics to the sporting boycott of Apartheid-era South Africa, you cannot keep it out. Nor should you.

Sport – watching it, playing it, talking about it, betting on it – may be the first thing that springs to mind when we think of what working people have done for fun in their off-duty hours. But sport as we know it is a relatively modern phenomenon. The growth of sport and the rise of industrialisation go hand in hand. The Romans and Greeks languidly threw the odd discus about, all the while eyeing each other's glistening haunches hungrily we're told, but between the fall of the Roman Empire and the start of the nineteenth century, sport doesn't seem to have been taken very seriously or occupied much of our time. Orwell had a theory about this naturally:

> … organised games are more likely to flourish in urban communities where the average human being lives a sedentary or at least a confined life, and does not get much opportunity for creative labour. In a rustic community a boy or young man works off a good deal of his surplus energy by walking, swimming, snowballing, climbing trees, riding horses, and by various sports involving cruelty to animals, such as fishing, cock-fighting and ferreting for rats. In a big town one must indulge in group activities if one wants an outlet for one's physical strength or for one's sadistic impulses.

I think it's fair to say that when down and out in Paris, London or Wigan, Orwell couldn't often be found at the Parc de Prince, White Hart Lane or the DW Stadium.

There was sport of a kind before industrialisation. Drake finished his game of bowls before seeing off the Spanish Armada, and some think that a form of football called Harpastum – perhaps using a non-regulation human head – had been practised by the Roman legions. Women played sport alongside and against men. In *Richard III* and *Love's Labour's Lost* Shakespeare has women playing bowls with men.

Pepys' Diary records men and women playing against each other at the bowling alley and running races for bets. Women archers were often the biggest prize winners and big crowds would turn out for all-female boxing bouts until the coming of the Victorian era. But modern sport as we know it rises alongside the rise of an industrial working class and the changes in the way they worked.

The establishment of regular if scant-paid holidays, weekend free time and the coming of the Bank Holidays Act in 1871, was the harbinger of the Leisure Age. Workers' rights to time off became enshrined in law. This made some people a little jumpy. Middle class fears over the latent energies and stirrings of the workers in our industrial towns and cities led to the encouragement of what was called 'rational recreation' and the rise of sports clubs, parks, baths, etc. The thinking ran that if the workers were burning off their excess energies kicking balls about and panting round tracks they would be less likely to ferment violent revolution and overthrow the bourgeoisie. So was born the 'sports and social' club where many of our oldest and most famous football teams have their roots. Aston Villa and Everton football clubs are examples of teams that were linked to local churches, and there were work-based clubs, such as those in the railway towns of Swindon and Crewe. Saturday began to become accepted as a half-day holiday for the urban worker, giving more time for attending and participating in sport.

Not always the sports you'd think of either. Though you wouldn't guess from the gear of the committee of the Royal and Ancient club, St Andrews, golf had a pretty egalitarian start in Scotland. Tobias Smollett went to a golf 'field' in Leith in 1766 and observed, 'Of this diversion the Scots are so fond, that when the weather will permit you may see a multitude of all ranks, from the senator of justice to the lowest tradesman mingling together in their shirts, and following the balls with the utmost eagerness.' But it soon became established and viewed as the preserve of the rich male. Sports historian Dennis Brailsford has observed that 'the only role for the worker was as club servant'. Municipal golf clubs and the rise of the game on TV has meant more popularity among the lower orders, but it still carries a bourgeois air, even if the plus fours have now been replaced by lemon pastel cashmere sweaters.

Back in the 1980s I remember reading an earnest newspaper article that predicted the rise of a new golfing generation drawn from the urban unemployed, who would hone their drives and short game at municipal clubs during the almost limitless leisure hours afforded them by Margaret Thatcher's economic policies. We still await, however, our first Open Champion called Darren from Chorley. Similarly there are periodic efforts to make the game hip and funky rather than something for accountants from Stevenage to fall asleep in front of on Sky Sports 4. In 2004, former lad-mag stalwart Tim Southwell and my old *NME* colleague Iestyn George launched a magazine called *GolfPunk*, designed for a trendier new golfer. It was, ultimately, a brave failure though that may be due to the downturn in magazine publishing rather than the publication itself. (It survives online.)

Cricket is a tricky one and apt to bowl you a googly. Like golf it looks and feels like a posh pastime. There is costly and awkward equipment and club membership to negotiate, it takes forever to play and, as far as the sport's establishment goes, a prevailing aura of flannels and panamas, tea breaks and Tanqueray. Status division rears its head with every delivery though, with the squire and the blacksmith bringing class struggle to the village green. A political reading of the infamous Bodyline series of the 1930s between England and Australia casts working-class bowler Harold Larwood as doing the dirty work of the aristocratic and (literally) imperious team captain Douglas Jardine. Larwood was furious when he was asked to apologise for his aggressive bowling, pointing out he had been ordered to do so by Jardine who loathed the upstart colonials.

The contradictions in cricket are part of its lore, and maybe even its vague claim to be our national sport. It can stir passions that are more rough than refined, and surprisingly regional. Brian Sellers once remarked of spin bowler Johnny Wardle, 'He may be good enough for England, but not for Yorkshire.' And here's something from a *Guardian* TV column by Martin Kelner.

> 'We were invited ... to reassess two great northern monsters, in *'Myra, The Making Of A Monster'* on Five, and *'The Real Geoff Boycott'* on Channel 4. A key difference between the two programmes was that obviously it was easier to find people prepared to speak up for Myra Hindley than it was to find anyone with a good word for Boycs.'

In the summer that I was researching this book, England's cricket team lurched from mishap to mishap under the beleaguered stewardship of the ineffectual *Boy's Own* figure of Alastair Cook. The few bright spots came with a couple of drubbings dished out to the Indian cricket team. This was widely seen though as evidence of how poor the Indians had become rather than any great resurgence on our part. Here again was evidence that our working lives impact and shape our leisure time. The Indian historian Ramachandra Guha observed in his book *A Corner of a Foreign Field* that

> Cricket fits in easily with the rhythms of what is still – in its essence – an agrarian culture, accustomed to thinking in calendric rather than clock time. Indians have no difficulty aimlessly filling up the hours ... Five days or 30 hours: an unconscionably long time for an industrial and industrious American, but a bare wink of eye to the Indian.

Some speculated then that Indian cricketing decline as a test playing nation – but improvement as a one day and limited over side – was down to the fact that the thrusting and aspirational young and growing middle classes of Delhi and Mumbai were working harder and faster in order to escape their rural, poverty stricken past and become more

American. Similarly, the decisive, results-driven American society finds itself baffled by the languid, labyrinthine nature of test cricket. As the *New York Times* put it:

> Americans have about as much use for cricket as Lapps have for beachwear. The fact that elsewhere in the civilised world grown men dress up like poor relations of Gatsby and venture hopefully into the drizzle clutching their bats invariably mystifies … And the notion that anyone would watch a game that, in its highest form, could take five days and still end in a draw provokes widespread disbelief …

Tennis remains a literal private club as far as most working-class people are concerned. In theory, there's no reason why this should be the case. The equipment is basic and relatively cheap, but until well into the twentieth century the courts were almost exclusively in private, genteel clubs and the sport thus did not catch on among the workers. Tennis and cricket was also riven for decades by absurd division between 'gentlemen' and 'players', i.e. people doing it skilfully and properly for money, as in the latter, and poshos mucking about, the former. Fred Perry, our greatest ever tennis champion, was a working-class lad whose dad was active in Labour politics, and who learned the game on the public courts near his family's terraced house in Stockport. Because of this, he was shunned by the tennis establishment and treated disgracefully. When he won Wimbledon for the first time, the administrators couldn't bring themselves to congratulate him and left his winner's tie on a chair in the dressing room. Understandably, sick of the snobbery and ingratitude of the so-called All England Club, Perry moved to the USA and became a naturalised American.

There are some pastimes that feel emblematically, definitively, even comedically, working class. I've never kept a racing pigeon; nor has anyone in my family or anyone I've ever known. If they are, they've been doing it pretty furtively and hiding it marvellously well. But as a teenager I did used to take part in the other great proletarian time killer – coarse fishing. Again, class runs like a fissure even through the gentle world of Izaak Walton and rod and reel. Coarse fishing has always had a faintly socialistic cast (sorry) and early coarse fishermen would call each other 'brothers'. By contrast, fly or game fishing was and is clearly for the likes of tweedy aristo J R Hartley. My mate Nigel had a creel (the little wicker manbag thing fly fisherman wear at the hip) and would sometimes cast his lure – always unsuccessfully – on some sleepy trout stream. But then his dad was a telecoms engineer and they lived in a bungalow in the nice bit of Shevington. So he was practically from Downton Abbey.

I didn't go fly fishing. I would go angling with another mate, John, in pursuit of perch, tench and carp in canals, gravel-pits and the like across Lancashire and Cumbria. Sometimes we would go straight from Bluto's night club in our best post-punk finery and arrive at the water's edge just as it was coming light. Then, around nine, we would fall fast asleep on the bank and wake up hungover, sunburned and starving in the early afternoon. We would make nocturnal visits to dark and silent Lake District tarns (after closing time) to catch eels, and then silently take them back through the woods to cook them up for campfire breakfasts when to be honest we'd have preferred a bacon bap or a Pot Noodle.

Eel fishing was great fun to participate in but would have been deadly dull to watch. The essentially static/somnolent/furtive nature of the angler's art has meant that it has never been a great spectator sport either live or on telly. Now, though, the proliferation of niche channels and the need to fill them up has meant that you do get the occasional fishing programme. This largely consists of Robson Green and a man in a beany hat going 'Isn't she a beauty', while disgorging a hook from the enormous, blubbery, frightening mouth of some cold-eyed denizen of the deep.

One activity more than any other though epitomises division in British leisure. In 1895, an iron curtain was drawn across the sport of rugby, creating a class and regional split that endures. Essentially, working class equals rugby league, middle class equals rugby union. North = league, south and Midlands = union. (Don't bring Wales into it. It confuses matters.) Just before the turn of the twentieth century, a body called the Northern League threw off the yoke of administrative bullying by an elite who'd run the game since William Webb Ellis first ruined a perfectly good game of football at Rugby School by picking up the ball and running with it, according to the sport's creation myth. Even before the schism, the game was largely working class in the north, middle class in the south. But matters came to a head at the end of the 1800s, with the sport now drawing big crowds in industrial Lancashire and Yorkshire. The players however were denied any of the benefits of this burgeoning sport. They were forbidden from being paid by the ruling body's ban on professionalism. They lost wages taking time off work to play and they had to pay their own treatment bills for frequent injuries.

So, 22 clubs got together in the George Hotel, Huddersfield, and in effect told the boss to shove it. Rugby league was born and over the next few years evolved into a different sport; faster, less reliant on kicking and mauling, generally more skilful and entertaining. But then I would say that. I'm from Wigan, one of those 22 original rebels and, of course, the greatest club side in the history of the sport.

So here's an illustrative vignette from my own largely non-existent rugby career. At primary and junior school I played rugby league, badly and at scrum half if memory serves (it was a bit of a concussed daze). This was perfectly natural. Not only was I growing up in the sport's capital and powerhouse – with all due respect to Leeds, Widnes, Castleford, etc. – but my school, St Jude's, was a feeder club for the pro side, with a crack amateur team which fostered many future England internationals.

Then I passed my 11-plus exam and went to a grammar school on the outskirts of Wigan run by the Irish Christian Brothers. There, in line with its slavish adoption of the trappings of a minor public school, such as daft little caps and housemasters, and out of step with the culture and history of the town, we were forbidden to play rugby league and forced to hoof it up in the air and collapse on each other union style. It didn't help that my dad brought me up with an ingrained lack of respect for union, believing that 30 people was an absurd amount for one pitch and union was essentially devised to occupy as many public school boys as possible on a wet Wednesday afternoon.

Rugby league – fast, violent and skilful in equal measure – can baffle even people who call themselves sports fans. Sometimes it baffles even me, who grew up with it. I settled down in great anticipation to watch last year's Grand Final, featuring my team Wigan Warriors against deadly rivals St Helens. Held at a packed Old Trafford, it was to be a grand occasion. Except that within a few minutes of the kick off, Wigan's Ben Flowers was sent off for punching Saints' Lance Hohaia twice in the face, the second time after his opponent lay stunned and prone on the deck from the first blow.

It was one of the most stupid and malicious things I've ever seen on a sports pitch, maybe even anywhere. It ruined the game, and our chances of winning. Flowers was banned for six months and at one point almost faced criminal charges. I'd have sacked him on the spot, making sure he never played for Wigan again, so badly had he let down the town and its people. I still feel like that. Worse, maybe, it reinforced a prejudice held by many in the sporting elite and the media that rugby league is a game for thick, aggressive proles while union is for gentlemen. Nothing could be further from the truth. But thanks to Ben Flowers, that message is just that little bit harder to get across. (As I write, Flowers is set to return to the game. The Wigan Coach has enjoined him to 'be more aggressive' this time. You could not, as they say, make it up.)

My dad still watches league, though these days not from the terraces he took me to as a youth, but from the comfort of his armchair with a whisky; largely thanks to Rupert Murdoch, who seemingly is good for something. In 1996, he pumped £87 million into the sport in return for TV rights and sizeable control over the sport. It changed from a winter to a summer game and some muttered darkly about a clause that gave Sky sway over who played for who and the nature of player contracts. Teams were rebranded with silly US sport style ad agency names. St Helen's resisted this (for which even this staunchly rival Wiganer respects them) and Bradford, with its links with the woollen trade, nearly went for Bradford Sheep before settling on Bulls. Purists and sections of the press were sceptical, not to say hostile, but that soon dissipated as the game thrived. There are many reasons to dislike Rupert Murdoch. But Super League is probably not one of them.

For all Sky's money, the game is still rooted in the industrial heartlands of the north and the support of the working classes. They even end the games with a factory hooter for goodness' sake. Many of the original professional clubs, like Castleford, had mill owners and other local entrepreneurs as early patrons. Lindsay Anderson's bleak movie of David Storey's novel *This Sporting Life*, in which Richard Harris undergoes a sexual and existential crisis in Wakefield, has further enshrined the idea of the game's quintessential grimness. But the slick new names are an attempt to bring some transatlantic razzmatazz to a sport that is still wreathed in smoke from factory chimneys, winter fog and stinging rain on raw November evenings in Halifax. Wigan are now Wigan Warriors. Keighley are the Keighley Cougars. Oldham are the Roughyeds, which is brilliant, and Wakefield Trinity are now Wakefield Trinity Wildcats, which is just stupid.

Warrington are the Warrington Wolves. Another change for the Cheshire club – although nothing about Warrington is Cheshire excepts its map co-ordinates, it should be said – is its move a few years ago from the beautifully named Wilderspool Stadium, the club's home for over a century and which once boasted a Kerry Katona stand that burned down, to the Halliwell Jones Stadium, named after a local car dealership. If the new name is less evocative, the new stadium is a huge improvement on its decrepit predecessor from which I was once chased by some Warrington bootboys in the late 1970s after one of our fiercely contested, on and off the field, local derbies. Conjure a rugby league club owner or chairman in one's mind and the picture will be of a fat, bluff man in a car coat; someone pompous and aldermanly, a civic grandee or the boss of a discount supermarket or plant hire firm. It will probably not be someone like Simon Moran who owns Warrington Wolves. Warrington born and bred, and a life long fan of the club, he took charge shortly after their move to the new stadium. I first met him (I've just worked out, appalled) a quarter of a century ago when, at the height of the 'Madchester' music fad, he could always be found backstage at local gigs, either as fan or promoter. I have relied on my 'SJM Promotions Access All Areas' sticky pass or laminate to get me backstage, on tour and into all sorts of scrapes with the Happy Mondays, New Order, James, The Charlatans, The Beautiful South, Inspiral Carpets and many many more. I've watched him go from indie kid hustler to the man the *Guardian* called 'the most influential music executive of the Noughties'. So when I decided that I should pay my first visit to rugby league in Warrington since I was a terrified teen, I knew who I was going to call.

I am one of a few thousand passing through Warrington Central station on this warm autumn evening, here for a top of the table fixture between Warrington and Huddersfield, or Wolves against Giants if you insist. I ask the community support officer, a small, unsmiling blonde girl with a 'Wigan facelift' (hair pulled back so tightly that blinking is impossible) where the 'new' rugby ground is. Tersely, without making eye contact, she tells me she doesn't know, which causes me to wonder which community she's supporting and in what way. Fortunately, the Scouse ticket collector is more helpful. 'Just follow the shirts, love,' she says, and I do. I follow a river of blue and white that flows and surges down Mike Gregory Way, named after a Warrington and Great Britain stalwart who died tragically young of Motor Neurone Disease.

The two main pubs by the ground are The Rodney and the Kings Head, and punters have spilt out of their doors to enjoy their pints in the evening air. From the colours, it seems that most of the home fans go to The Rodney and the away ones to the Kings Head, nearer the station. But there's much mixing. You could throw a glass from one to the other, but no one will. Rugby prides itself hugely on not being football or doing things that football does, a game for overpaid nancy boys, and this includes hooliganism. This is not entirely accurate and we should be careful. As mentioned above I got chased several times at rugby league games in my youth, and at one especially violent Boxing Day fixture between Wigan and 'Wires', my mate Brownie was thrown over a ten-foot wall into an industrial bin. That was the seventies though, when sporadic hand-to-hand fighting used to break out during *Songs of Praise*.

A word about that nickname. Warrington are known as Wires or The Wire because of the town's wire-pulling industry. That craft became the centre of its economy after the decline in its previous staple, sailmaking. I have no real idea what wire pulling is, so I look it up online. The first site I come to begins 'Have you ever seen a wire-pull become a disaster? This doesn't need to happen. Several wire pulling tools and methods exist, but 'pull by fishtape' is the most common.' So that clears that up.

I meet Simon in the new stadium reception, where he sweeps in straight from the London train to Warrington Bank Quay. Simon's big new project of the autumn is the Kate Bush comeback concerts at the Hammersmith Odeon, her first since 1979. Everyone in 'the biz' is in a flap about it. I loved Kate Bush's early albums, but she seems to have disowned these in favour of her slicker and for me less interesting later stuff which is all she plays at the shows so I don't bother even trying to get a ticket. I keep this to myself though, as pretty much everyone I know has become Moonie-like in their gush of approbation.

It's quite a day of contrasts I imagine for Simon; afternoon rehearsals of hippie drama tableaux with Kate, and then an evening on the terraces watching Warrington and Huddersfield play rugby league. Of his time in London, Simon is too discreet to give away much in the way of gossip beyond saying that Kate likes spaghetti bolognaise. He asks immediately for a copy of the *Warrington Guardian* which carries an 'open letter to Simon Moran' and has some mild criticism of him. He tosses it aside with a laugh and we head upstairs to the Platinum Lounge where we are surrounded by glitzy Warrington ladies sipping Sauvignon Blanc before we make our way through the backstage 'corridors of power'. Simon introduces me to a young man in a smart suit called Stefan. 'Hey Stuart, Stefan's from Wigan too. We just signed him from under your noses.' Stefan isn't playing tonight and in between chatting about pubs and streets we have in common – he's from Pemberton, about half a mile from where I grew up and an old stamping ground of mine – he tells me about his injury. He's torn the muscle that ties the rib to the ligament. 'I get bloody knocked out and knocked about all the time and I do this just stretching for summat.'

When we've moved on, Simon tells me that Stefan is a very hot prospect indeed and there's been interest from Australia, but Simon's negotiating new terms for him here. I ask him why he doesn't delegate. After all he has a full-time job as one of Britain's biggest concert promoters. 'I don't trust anyone else not to fuck it up,' he says, smiling thinly, as we head for the terraces.

Yes, the terraces. No prawn sandwiches in an executive box for Simon. We stand with the fans on the terrace, some of whom nod to him as he goes by, but to whom he is clearly just another fan. He eats a Holland's pie from the tinfoil as we chat about the game. I can't imagine standing with Roman Abramovich in the shed end with a bag of chips. But this is the exact equivalent of that. Except I'm not sure that Roman Abramovich – or the Glazers or the Manchester City sheikhs or any of the other owners of big football clubs – had any pre-existing (or indeed existing) emotional attachment to the clubs they own. I like this scenario. If we must have capitalist moguls (which is by no means proven) then let them eat smoky bacon crisps and pies and stand on terraces of the local rugby clubs they clearly love and have supported since they were 11. In the stands opposite, Simon points out an older couple sitting together – 'Ian Brown's mum and dad,' he says indicating the lifelong Wire-supporting parents of the Stone Roses singer.

As well as owners who stand with the fans, there are other things that may baffle the football fan or the rugby league virgin. Chris Hill's job, as prop forward, appears to be to run directly at opponents as a kind of human battering ram and then fall down. The ref and his assistants are all dressed in pink and sponsored by Specsavers, which seems to me a deliberate and hilarious attempt to undermine them. More significantly, giant screens show video replays of disputed tries, which are judged on by a video official in a secret chamber somewhere (and by everyone in the ground of course). There is music too; brilliantly, a try for opposition Huddersfield is accompanied by the theme from *The Good, The Bad and The Ugly*.

For much of the first half Huddersfield are under pressure and pushed back into their own half. Three young women in replica tops at the side of us are in high-pitched high spirits. A thin man with glasses says, 'It's all us, isn't it?' But then things begin to change. Huddersfield snatch a couple of tries and go into the lead. Soon after, there's a bad accident involving Warrington's Welsh international Rhys Evans over in the far corner, when he lands on his head attempting to score a try. It's obvious from his stillness, the reactions of the other players and the speed with which the medical staff dash across the pitch that something is very wrong. The game is held up for eight long anxious minutes, and then he is carried off to loud applause. Happily we hear that he came round in the dressing rooms. Later on, after a similar incident, an opposition player staggers from the pitch clutching a bloodied head. 'You're shit,' shouts a bald man on the touchline, supportively. It's all Huddersfield now. Their 600-strong travelling support who've come over the Pennines start singing incomprehensible songs. 'We' retaliate with loud chants of 'Wire! Wire!'

Simon introduces me to an Australian agent who's over here scouting new talent. He's a thick-set chap in a tweed jacket and jeans who actually uses the expression 'fair dinkum'. He tells me that Wigan, though a big club, have never really had any top French players because of the language difficulty. Even the ones whose English is good find Wigan English perplexing. He disappears at half time and then turns up pitchside with the legendary Alex Murphy. 'Murphy the Mouth' or 'Yapper' is a legend, the cocky, loquacious former Saints and Warrington player who was never trusted in Wigan even when he was our coach, and who left us after punching the chairman in the face in an argument over a 20 quid bonus. Classy. Today he's on his best behaviour in front of a crowd who clearly adore him. The Aussie agent hops over the touchside fence and comes back to us and I buy him a half of lager. 'That's fair dinkum,' he says.

Warrington, egged on by the partisan crown, louder and lairier after their half-time beer, try and make a good fist of it. Partisan they may be, but not blinkered. 'They are playing well,' says one of the young women grudgingly of Huddersfield. When one of the Yorkshire team's stars intercepts a pass and begins a breathtaking run chased in vain by a Warrington full back, head in hands, the thin man with glasses says, 'Goodbye. Give up son. You won't catch Jody Broughton.' He doesn't. In the end, Wire lose. Simon slips away to his car and his Kate Bush emails, and I stroll back down Mike Gregory Way.

I pop into a couple of the pubs, diligent as ever in my investigations and research. In The Rodney, a DJ is playing a selection of nineties northern lad rock, The Verve, Oasis, Stone Roses (maybe Ian Brown's mum and dad are in), and in the corner on a huge screen, a cluster of drinkers are watching Sky Sports coverage of the game we've just come from. The trailers and credits feature huge, bulky animated and armoured robots playing rugby. This may go down well with the kids, but would seem to me to entirely miss the point. It's the fact that the blokes playing tonight weren't steel-plated automata but regular blokes who bled when you cut them (and got told they were 'shit' for their pains) that makes the game so visceral and compelling. We can feel their pain.

As I can of player Danny Brough who is subjected to a touchline interview as he trudges from the pitch. 'Two games left Danny? Where do you think you are?' I have no idea what this question means, and I'm in a warm pub with a Jameson's and haven't spent the last hour-and-a-half running several miles, lungs burning and being battered and bludgeoned into the damp northern turf by massive blokes. 'Steady,' says Danny, which is better than I'd have managed under the circumstances.

You also realise that the game is very different watched on TV and experienced from the touchline. Both perceptions are valid, but they are really entirely separate events and one must understand this. I realise that often when the crowd were most passionate, most vehement, most secure in the certainty of their judgement and the incompetence of the officials, they (we) were wrong; completely, laughably wrong. The thin man with the glasses, the girls in the replica tops and the whole terrace behind me bayed for the ref's blood when he disallowed a try by Warrington's Ben Harrison. But on screen, it's clear that several players were miles offside. There's no debate from the pundits, no controversy at all. But that doesn't mean that the supporters were wrong. They were watching a different game, a different beast.

Trying to find the gents at the back of the Kings Head I wander into a huge, almost empty room in which some kind of disco is happening. A very odd kind, though, held in what seems to be the garden furniture bit of B&Q and where some vaguely soft porn animations are playing on a huge screen to 'December, 1963 (Oh, What A Night)' by the Four Seasons. Like much of the north's nocturnal entertainment, it is both exhilarating and nightmarish.

Back in the main bar, two gangs of supporters of either team are chatting amicably about, for some reason, taxi firms. 'Back in Huddersfield, none of the taxi drivers are English.' 'No, none of ours are either,' says a Warringtonian. You brace yourself for some racist jibe or slur. But it doesn't come. They move on. It was just a statement of fact, offered for information, and I remember that the greatest hero in the history of the sport in my town is a mixed race Welshman called Billy Boston, the sixth of 11 children born to an Irish–Welsh mother and a Sierra Leonian seaman and, arguably, the greatest player to ever play the sport; swift, skilled, powerful, and the first black player to be picked by the British Lions. He later ran pubs in the town, though he himself, now 80, will never have to buy a pint in Wigan or indeed the north ever again. A year or two back, he and I were both given civic awards by the town. It was a genuine privilege for me to be classed in that company. Also, seeing my dad reduced to a star-struck groupie in Boston's presence was wonderful.

The station platform is thronged with Huddersfield fans heading home. There's a young geeky looking lad with a poster that says 'Huddersfield, home of Rugby League'. There are students and old timers and, on the other platform, four glam girls in black micro-skirts are giggling and teetering, surely headed for late night revels in Manchester. The atmosphere is warm and beery, lively and welcoming, and I realise that these are my people. Whereas others might find it dull or intimidating, tacky or incomprehensible I'm at home here in the raw northern night with these hardy folk.

I remember once watching Jonathan Miller, then one of the geniuses of *Beyond the Fringe* now an opera director, being very funny on Parkinson about Motocross. Having watched it often on *Grandstand*, he said words to the effect that it was as a sport the very dictionary definition of the word 'lugubrious'; filthy, wretched blokes riding bikes around in the mud of godforsaken northern quagmires, watched in a continuous sheeting rain, by other men in pacamacs and rain hats. To me, this would be vastly preferable any day to sitting through Verdi's *Otello* again but, hey, I like Jonathan Miller. And if he and Alan Bennett want a really exciting northern night out, Motocross without the lugubriousness, they should come with me to Belle Vue Speedway.

*

Belle Vue. Just the name starts a ripple of nervous anticipation somewhere deep down, brings out the excitable child in anyone who remembers it from anywhere near my patch. Depending which bit you recall, which night you remember, which exact vintage you are, Belle Vue meant Lions, Tigers, the Firework Lake, the Wall Of Death, the Caterpillar – Ride in the Dark, elephant poo, motorboats, a chimpanzees' tea party, the Lake Hotel, a scenic railway, a toboggan, Peggy the Leopard, the helter-skelter, even The Clash playing live in its Elizabethan Suite. For generations of thrill seekers across the north-west, it made Kubla Khan's pleasure dome look like a Godalming Harvester. It was danger, romance, ludicrously transplanted wild animals, furtive sex, punk rock, music hall, motorbikes, parrots, booze and light orchestral music. I adhere very strongly to the dictum that there is no such thing as 'fun for all the family'. But Belle Vue's decades of random madness delivered something irresistibly like it. It certainly got a lot nearer than Euro Disney.

It was the brainchild of an enterprising gardener called John Jennison from Stockport. Originally a pub, Jennison developed the unpromising site in Gorton, Manchester into firstly an aviary, then a zoo, then added a racecourse, a concert arena, a funfair and finally everything else imaginable. When I was a kid if you told me Belle Vue was going to open a Cape Kennedy-style rocket launch pad, a convent, or a robot controlled abattoir-cum-prison, I'd have believed you, so breathtakingly nuts was its scope and variety.

Belle Vue originally wanted to cater to the gentility, but it soon became a magnet for the pleasure-hungry shift workers. In 1848, there were complaints about 'local roughs' trying to dance with the middle-class ladies on the dancing platform – which sounds brilliant – and then soon after, further complaints of said roughs dancing with each other. You can't win if you're a rough, can you?

For 150 years, the park was a Mecca for northerners, except unlike the actual Mecca you could get hammered there and have a bacon buttie, so it was way better. 'The Playground of the North' it styled itself, and for once maybe the adman's hype was true. Crowds flocked to it, lured by attractions like the 'Siege Of Delhi Firework Display', more pyrotechnics on the lake, much-loved roller-coaster 'The Bobs' and monkeys boxing each other.

Later, sport and pop music and food and fairground fun made it a magical place for we sixties and seventies kids. I made the trip several times back then either as a toddler in my dad's sleek, racy second-hand Ford Capri GT1 (we graduated to this, weirdly, from a Wolseley Hornet) or as a teen on the number 32 bus painted in the famous 'fried egg' livery of the Greater Manchester Passenger Transport Executive. However I arrived, I had rarely been so excited in my young life. Music, food, girls, darkness, mystery, what boy would not be enthralled? But, struggling to compete with trendier, flashier and, let's face it, probably safer attractions, crippling debts closed it in 1982. But the memory lives on. Actually, more than the memory lives on. A large part of the site lives on, and the Belle Vue Aces live on, swaggering romantic buccaneers of the wonderful thing that is Speedway.

The first customers to Belle Vue came by horse-drawn omnibus from Piccadilly, the last departure coinciding with the 6pm shift finish for most Manchester workers. These days you can come by your own horseless carriage, or make the five-minute journey from town to Belle Vue station, built for the park's heyday and still just about operative.

Just down the road, through an autumn haze, I can make out New Belle Vue, which in its blue-and-yellow colour scheme looks like a maximum security Ikea or a militaristic Gala Bingo, perhaps a Chechen Gala Bingo that has been occupied by anti-government rebels. That afternoon I'd tweeted to the effect that I was making my first trip to Speedway at Belle Vue and had solicited any sage advice out there. A lady called Suzanna Cruikshank replied, 'As a lifelong attendee of speedway, I recommend low expectations and a warm coat …' Not a great night out then, I mused disappointed but, no, she was teasing. 'No, you must go! The smell, the sound, ahhh I miss it. They are against my childhood team Coventry. But do take a warm coat.'

So I did, and paid my £7 to watch the Belle Vue Aces versus Coventry Bees in the Elite League of British Speedway. In case you've heard of speedway without knowing exactly what it is, put simply, it's a motorcycle race on an oval track of dirt or shale usually over four laps. But, as I'm about to find out, this doesn't really convey its unique appeal and ambience. This is going to be my first live experience of it, although when I was a student I nearly went with some friends who had a memorable night out. As the bikes rounded the first corner, bringing up a wave of shale, one of my mates was struck on the head and knocked out by a piece of flying rock and everyone spent the evening in A&E.

Before that, when I was very young, somewhere at the blurry edge of memory, I recall that *Sportsnight With Coleman* would sometimes, on a thin football week I imagine, bring us speedway highlights from Wolverhampton, Scunthorpe or Workington. It seemed to me even as a child that as a TV spectacular it was somehow lacking; gloomily monochrome and a tad predictable in that whoever was in the lead at the first corner stayed there all race. Overtaking was rare, if not unheard of. There are names from this time that ring vaguely, yes, lugubrious midweek bells – Peter Collins, Ole Olsen, Barry Briggs, Anders Michanek and others. But the undoubted star in this muddy firmament, the one speedway rider that most non-devotees can name, was Ivan Mauger. A Christchurch born Kiwi, Mauger came to a one-bedroom flat in south London as a 17-year-old with his even younger bride to become speedway's greatest star. He rode for Belle Vue Aces as well as Exeter, Hull, Wimbledon and Newcastle. Six times world champion, he was awarded the MBE and, much more importantly, the accolade of being a *Desert Island Discs* castaway where he picked two Herb Alperts, a Jim Reeves, a Roger Whittaker, some selections from *Oliver!* and a Maori choir. He and Raye are still together half a century on, and now live in contented retirement on Australia's Gold Coast.

It must be a lot warmer there than it is here. I'm in the queue for the chippie van, since greasy foodstuffs eaten al fresco is one of the great delights of outdoor sport at night, and it affords a good vantage point to take in the sights. The crowd are a fabulous spectacle in themselves. No boring uniformed ranks of replica tops or corporate logos here. On display are yards of battered leather and frayed denim, big coats, the odd 'sheepie', loads of retro embroidered patches and much flashy bike gear, as you'd imagine. Plus beanie hats. Lots of beanie hats. If not a beanie hat, then a cap covered in enamel badges, clearly the mark of the real aficionado.

It is primarily male, as you might think, but not exclusively so. Some girls cling, maybe long sufferingly, to the arms of intense boy-friends, but there are gangs of girls here, too, laughing and blowing on their chips. It feels like a very northern translation of an American sporting night out; quirky, full of offbeat, budget razzmatazz and ritual, part cup final, part bonfire night. Speedway is not exclusively northern, of course. Though Belle Vue Aces are one of the sport's glamour clubs, Poole and Kings Lynn are the current top dogs. But the place it holds in local affections can be seen from the fact that a nearby street on the housing estate is named after legendary Aussie manager of the Aces Johnny Hoskins.

Munching thoughtfully on doner meat, chips and curry sauce, I soak up the atmosphere. The crackling PA is playing a great selection of vintage disco records interrupted by the odd cryptic announcement that doesn't make much sense to the uninitiated. One of the races seems to be sponsored by 'George Heartthrob Dental Boss' but I decide this must be a mishearing. Chip poised midway to mouth, it is in this unflattering posture that, naturally, I get recognised. Sometimes on book researches, this can be a bind – the loss of anonymity can compromise the author's independence and also make me feel less glamorously like a spy. But the upside is when you meet someone like Ian, who turns out to be heavily involved with the running of the Aces on a voluntary basis (as, like so many minority sports, Speedway survives on passion and enthusiasm).

Suavely ignoring the aroma of chip shop curry sauces, Ian gives me a crash course on the protocols of speedway. It consists of several rounds of races, each of which lasts four laps and takes roughly a minute on a track of shale, gravel or brick dust. It is not, in the words of famous cycling cheat Lance Armstrong 'all about the bike', but the pared down simplicity of the cycle is a large element of the thrill. 'No brakes. No gears' is the sport's manta, its cri de cœur, its motto, and it is absolutely true. A speedway bike is essentially a steerable engine running on methanol, the fuel whose rich deep tang gives the stadium that characteristic smell. With no brakes, the rider negotiates the turns at speed using just the steering handles turned against the curve and by dragging his inside foot in the dirt. This explains the weighty, Frankenstein-style metal boot worn on one foot; it's like an anchor. You do get the odd punch-up between riders, but they are rare which is just as well. You wouldn't want to get kicked with one of those.

There's a buzz in the crowd as the first riders emerge. These young men, some British, many East European and Scandinavian, ride for clubs all over the world and travel nearly every day for a race somewhere. Aces rider Matej Žagar is about to race every night for the next 12 at stadia across Europe, getting by on snatched sleep in cheap airport hotels. 'They fly EasyJet every day of their lives almost,' says Ian, 'and in Eastern Europe they're superstars.'

Speedway is massive in Poland where it's essentially the national sport and races take place in huge arenas that are regularly full. Thousands will turn out for a midweek club meeting in the Polish Ekstraliga, the richest and most popular speedway league in the world, and since the fall of communism now luring the best riders from all over the world. Some of these are here tonight; revving up their bikes here on this damp, grey night in Gorton. 'They couldn't walk down the street unmolested in Gdańsk or Warsaw, these lads. They might get 15,000 quid for a meeting there. You could say it's not bad for five minutes work. But then you're not the one on the bike.'

It is, Ian thinks, less dangerous than it was, chiefly because of the introduction of the 'air fences'; chunky, padded barriers on the corners. If you watch footage of 1960s races from Belle Vue, you can see players regularly ending up in the dirt and almost in the crowd as they careen over the rope fence after a bad turn and a slide. But the effect of the fences has been to make the sport more exciting as riders are more willing to take chances. It is still gutsy, volatile and dangerous. Even with the better padding and safety improvements, several players have plates and bolts in their bodies that play hell with airport security scanners. Few get away unscathed. 2013 World Champion Tai Woffinden broke his collarbone twice in that glory season, the second time severely bending the metal bar that had been put in following the first break. Aces legend Chris Morton had an undiagnosed broken neck for two decades and some mornings had to literally lift his head off the pillow. Worst of all, the former Aces rider Alan Wilkinson's career came to a sudden, horrible end on Saturday, 1 July 1978, when a crash during a match against Swindon consigned him to a wheelchair for the rest of his life.

A draft system operates with the riders, rather like the one in American football, whereby the lowest ranking teams get first pick of the best players. Thus this season, a young rising star from 'down the road' in Gorton has ended up riding up for Coventry who were last year's worst team. Tonight there'll be eight races, each with four riders, and points from four to one are awarded to each rider depending on placement. Ian asks us if I want to watch the race from 'the centre green'. As I have no idea what this means, I mumble and stall politely until some nearby enthusiasts intervene. 'You absolutely have to do this. This would be a lifetime's dream come true for lots of speedway fans.' Humbled and a little sheepish, the tardiest of Johnny-come-latelys is thus led through the diehards, over the perimeter fence, across the red shale and into the grassy area in the centre of the track. There's a small knot of us here, including 17 times Isle Of Man TT champion John McGuiness who is a speedway nut and diehard Aces fan.

The Brolly Dollies, four young women with umbrellas in the riders' colours who usher out the riders and herald the start of every race, are an anachronism that's more quaint than offensive. They are doughty northern young women in sensible padded jackets, jeans and boots, and their function is more informative than decorative. They stand at the start, displaying to the crowd (who seem to write everything down in their programmes or little battered notebooks) which lane the different riders are in. Then they exit, leaving the riders revving and lurching their bikes backwards and forwards in the loose dirt. The aim is to gouge a furrow from which they can get vital purchase, the start being hugely important and advantageous in speedway. Powered by the almost-pure alcohol 'rocket fuel' in their tanks, they can pull away from the start as fast as a Formula One car. Nosing the tape, edging forward, rocking backward, they watch for a flicker from the starter. He waits until, walking away with seemingly blithe unconcern, the tape rises and they're off.

Though it shares some of the appeal for fans of statistics, speedway is at the other end of the sporting spectrum from test cricket. In place of the long contemplative stretches of ambient torpor, that delightfully textured boredom, is a compacted minute of crazed activity, a roaring whirlwind of helmets, shale and mud. The other spectators are right. The best view you can have is this one; close up, surrounded by noise and action, spinning around to catch the bikes as they circle you at speed. In this way, with the odd dash to the shed for lager, the next couple of hours pass in a hugely entertaining blur.

Coventry may have been the worst in the league last year but tonight they eventually beat the Aces and take a little lap of honour, waving, in a sort of big tractor. This is definitely a protocol I would love to see adopted in the effete world of football. People write up the scores in notebooks, the riders disappear, and in spite of this mildly downbeat ending to the evening, my hosts are still wonderfully enthusiastic and hospitable.

They give me a tour of the pits where the Coventry team is celebrating, high fiving, laughing and chatting in a quickfire blend of accents: Scandinavian, Black Country, northern. They are all on the small side, which could just be chance or perhaps, like jockeys, it's an advantage. Are there big brawny speedway riders? Like any backstage environment, but particularly one that reeks of methanol and echoes with roaring engines, the pits are quite exciting for what are basically a couple of tin shacks with stalls for the home team and one for the visitors. There's a reporter from Sky and the odd Brolly Dolly. The Aces pit staff are all volunteers. Ian tells us that he's never been paid. 'None of these guys get paid, it's all lads and dads really.' One turns out to have been one of the security staff on duty when a crazed gunman tried to abduct Princess Anne in the Mall in 1973, and was wounded in the process of saving her. He didn't get a reward but a few months later, following a vague phone call from the security services, he found that his mortgage had been paid off.

This is a fascinating story but, best of all, they let me sit on a bike. They show me the Dead Man's Handle, a string and a peg attached to the arm basically, which cuts the bike engine should you fall off. 'Think you could manage a few laps?' says Ian, and I answer instantly in the negative. Give me a ball and I can hit it, head it or kick it reasonably well. But I know that even if I could rev the thing properly and then cool the throttle, even if I could make that groove in the shale for purchase and let the bike thrum against the tape, I know that once I had to loose that left hand throttle, feel the bike rear with latent power, I would either a) plough a slow and wobbly furrow through the red loam of Lancashire at a snail's pace, or more likely b) bolt as if riding a deranged horse right off the tracks, into the barriers, scattering the crowd as bike and I somersault straight into the merchandise stall where that hairy guy is selling old speedway magazines for 5p. Instead, I buy a Belle Vue Aces scarf which is hanging on the wall above my desk as I write these words. The new season starts in a month. I can't wait.

At the other end of the scale in almost every way from both rugby league and speedway is crown green bowls. If rugby league is all about the crunch of bone and the clamour of crowds, and speedway the rasp and roar of engines and the heady tang of burning fuel, bowls is the gentle click of polished wood and low murmurs of appreciation. While rugby league is pretty much all physical contact, bowls has none. At least it shouldn't have, and I have yet to find any evidence of a great bowls brawl.

It may be more genteel but it is a great, great deal older. In his twelfth-century biography of turbulent priest Thomas Becket, William Fitzstephen mentions, for some odd reason, young men indulging in an early version of the sport; the world's oldest surviving bowling green dates from 1299. Disliked by Henry VIII and the establishment for its appeal to the lower orders, in 1541 an act of parliament forbade labourers, servants and apprentices from playing 'Bowls at any time except Christmas, and then only in their master's house and presence'.

But then, as the centuries rolled on, bowls went through a schism with odd parallels of rugby's class and geographical fissure. The flat green bowling that Sir Francis Drake had indulged in while the Spanish Armada approached stayed right there on Plymouth Hoe, and the south in general. In the north, a more complicated version, crown green, developed on greens with a raised hump or 'crown' in the middle. This was said to be an accommodation of the north's hillier and more rugged geography. Crown greens were often at the back of licensed premises and it developed into a predominantly working-class sport in the north. As a teenager, I heard the funniest, and possibly the only, bowls joke I've ever heard. We were having a pint and a few 'ends' at the green behind The Bowling Green pub in Wigan (it's a common pub name in the north). Nearby, a doubles match was going on. The protocol here is that when one of the pair has bowled, the other will run down to the other end to survey the scene around the jack – the small target ball – in detail and state the position. 'You're a foot in front!' shouted one chap to his partner, who then turned to me and asked, 'What did he call me?'

The pubs and inns of Lancashire became the crucible of what became an unlikely big money 'glamour' sport from the 1830s onwards. Top bowlers began to command the kinds of earnings that we associate today with professional footballers, Formula 1 drivers, tennis players and golfers. Sports historian Peter Swain has uncovered the stories of bowling 'celebs' like Gerard Hart from Blackrod or Tom Taylor (known as 'Owd Toss') from Bolton.

> As the century wore on the triangle between Bolton, Westhoughton and Chorley produced most of the outstanding professional crown green bowlers of the day culminating in the heyday of professional crown green bowling around 1900. A top bowler at that time would earn around £800 a year in prize money which is worth about £300,000 today.

That lucrative and high profile heyday is long gone. When then Labour MP for Sheffield, Helen Jackson, criticised Sport England's 2004 decision not to award Lottery Funding to the sport, she pointed to bowls' deep community roots and its high levels of voluntary support: 'Clubs exist in every village and community, located in local parks, working men's clubs, behind pubs and in the grounds of steel and factory premises.' While her tone was measured, her message was clear. Crown green bowls, like coarse fishing, despite enjoying one of the highest levels of active participation of any British sport (including disabled players), was losing out because of prejudice, ageism and regionalism.

In Australia, bowls was the sport traditionally taken up by sports mad Aussies when their days of playing more energetic, high impact sports were over. It grew through the late twentieth century, peaking in 1990 when there were 50,000 registered players making it the country's fourth biggest participant sport. The numbers were huge but the image was fustian, and after that heyday the sport went into a decline for want of new players.

But noughties hipsters changed all that. There's been an influx of what are known to the Aussies as 'barefoot bowlers', cool kids who took up the sport ironically at first but have grown to love it and rejuvenated the ailing sport, generating a comedy movie about the phenomenon called *Crackerjack* and was featured in early epsiodes of hit TV show *The Secret Life Of Us*. Hundreds of barefoot bowlers began to show up at the clubs (every town has one) at weekends and new ones catering for the barefoots have sprung up. At Paddington Lawn Bowls Club in Sydney's Eastern Suburb the club motto is, rather odiously, 'bowls without the olds', and they cater almost exclusively to the under forties.

If bearded barefoot bowling ironists were to blossom anywhere in the north, it would surely be Chorlton, Manchester's hipster enclave of bobble hats, craft breweries and vegan co-operatives. The Lloyd Hotel though seems to be cheerfully resisting this trend.

The beautiful crown green at the Lloyd Hotel Bowling Club was laid in 1870, the year of the first ever international football match (England v. Scotland) and the death of Charles Dickens. This local landmark on Wilbraham Road, Chorlton-cum-Hardy is perhaps the oldest and most successful club in the history of crown green bowling. They have been champions often and they are home to the second largest youth bowling competition in the country, which regularly attracts a field of over 50 players of under 18, giving the lie to the geriatric stereotype of the sport.

The pleasant young barman is genially vague about when or whether tonight's fixture will begin. 'Oh they're usually out there,' offers a gravel-voiced woman nursing a blue WKD at the bar. The pub, newly refurbished, is almost in the nature of a deluxe corporate executive hospitality box for bowls-mad billionaires if only such things existed. One side of the pub is a huge window that overlooks the (deserted) green, and at the de rigueur stripped pine table, a young couple are getting to grips with two teetering overloaded burgers and a cairn of filled potato skins. I have a pint of Peddler and wait.

Soon enough, there's activity. Men of all shapes and sizes begin to emerge and congregate in the glorious evening sun, not in whites and flat caps but those billowy untucked sports shirts that corpulent darts players favour. A clutch of people begin to assemble at the perimeter with pens and books and the grave and responsible air of officialdom, like the Supreme Court. Time to get out there, I think.

Taking my pint out onto the edge of the green and lifting my face to the late, soothing sun, I meet a 'character'. He's a fit looking pensioner in powder blue Manchester City shirt and a gold skull tie. He looks kindly yet seasoned, a bloke I fancy you wouldn't have mucked about back in the seventies. He's the kind of bloke you still find often in our urban working communities; genial, matey, but with an edge that means you are never fully at ease in case the handshake turns into a headlock.

He spots this ingénue with unerring savvy and homes in, telling me at once without a shred of false humility, that he is 'a legend'. Eric the Blue Legend, in fact. 'Everyone here knows me.' Bowls is his joint love, along with 'City'. He is, he offers thoughtfully, 'probably the greatest Manchester City fan in the world ... I slept in a freezing, lorry at 15 to go up to Middlesbrough and it's been love ever since.' He is 68, been to a thousand City games, and yet managed to miss all five of City's FA Cup Finals in his lifetime of fandom. One of these, in 2013, was their defeat to the mighty Wigan Athletic. This is my cue, of course, to tell him that I'm from Wigan and I was there to see his pampered, overpaid Galácticos get squarely beaten. He takes it in good part, and he is gracious in defeat. He may even have ruffled my hair.

Eric becomes my chaperone and guide through a sunlit evening of bowls while offering a great many insights into his own life, sometimes almost poetically. 'As a high profile blue, I've taken many a ribbing, goading and verbal battering. But I'm a tough old so and so. My father did his paper round in his bare feet so I know where I'm coming from. I was born on Halloween and I believe in fate. What brings you here? You look a bit official to me but then you have the casual style of the modern era.'

This is a West Cheshire Premier League clash between the Lloyd Hotel and arch local rivals Buddenburg. They don't sound that local, I say. I find out that they are in fact the works team of a German engineering firm based in leafy Altrincham. Having recently moved into a new half a million pound sports and social club home, Buddenbrook resemble Chelsea – or indeed Manchester City; wealthy aristocrats of the game and a further example of Teuton sporting prowess. We will all be reminded forcibly of this later that night when Germany beat hosts Brazil 7–1 in the semi-finals of the football World Cup, a scoreline I thought had to be a typo when I saw it on my phone later.

The match here, if not quite as gripping as that one, is now on in earnest. Several different pairings and games seem to be going on concurrently at a fair lick, the bowls criss-crossing at speed, the choreography bewildering. Obscure remarks and bizarre observations rend the summer night – 'Bowling, mon!' 'That's won it!' 'You're two feet away!' '4–7, Pete!' 'Short as a carrot!' 'Drop yer sand!' At one quiet and terrifically tense moment, a hearty belch rings out across the greensward accompanied soon afterwards by low chuckles. At precisely this moment, enormous pizzas arrive for the scorers, the cue for a great deal of wonderful 'Whose was the Meat Feast with extra olives?' palaver and debate. Would that this happened with the officials at Wimbledon. 'Advantage, Federer. Oh and mine was the Thin and Crispy American Hot, Dennis …'

Eric, who has himself acquired a passing slice of Quattro Formaggi, explains that while tonight's Tuesday match is a significant fixture, 'Wednesday is the big Premier League night, certainly as far as Yorks and North Lancs is concerned. The pub'll put a buffet on for that.' In these days of gastro-pub gentrification, apparently, landlords are not always thrilled with or supportive of an association with a pastime as proudly and defiantly 'flat cap' as crown green bowling. 'You know the sort of pub. The ones where they'll put the tennis on the big screen but not the football. There's plenty of them round here. This has always been a bowls pub but one landlord here, he used to boast he'd close the green down. But we have a 20 year lease. We saw him off.'

The current owners are tolerant. But the sport itself has receded much from the public eye since the 1970s when the Waterloo Cup at Blackpool's Waterloo Hotel, the FA Cup Final of the Sport, was shown on terrestrial TV. (It's being streamed live on the internet these days.) In truth, Eric thinks that bowls has never really worked on the telly. 'If you're playing end to end across a big, difficult green, being a yard away from the jack is bloody good bowling. But on the box it looks miles off. It looks rubbish.' Waterloo's prize money is £2,000, while the World Championship's is £20,000, probably equivalent to Wimbledon's barley water bill. But still the game is a part of the fabric of British sporting life in its quiet, dogged, homespun way. Attendance for decent handicap tournaments at a pub or club will be between 50 to a 100, but three or four times that for big matches. Tonight about 30 or so – including the pizza-munching volunteer judges and scorers – have gathered around the sunlit green. Among them are a family in matching leisurewear, two spectacularly elegant ladies in their late sixties, the retired, flat capped elderly men you might imagine and an interesting pairing of a steely-haired short cropped grandma with a pint of Stella and her granddaughter with an iPad and Beats wireless headphones.

The sun drops behind the sheltered housing, the lager foam slides down the sides of a hundred glasses and Buddenburg pull away from the home team with every end. Eric, known to all it seems, drifts away to chat with judges and the warm Chorlton night fills with sounds and smells, from the curry houses and tapas bars, to the old school boozers, to the trendy brew shops where the hipsters tap at laptops.

A few months later, I am sitting at mine one chilly January typing up my notes and posting the odd tweet about how the researches are going. I mention enjoying my warm summer evening at the bowls.

Several replies ask me about the evening, wonder if the terminology is still the same as they remember from watching the old men at the municipal park, some even think they know Eric. One, though, piques my interest more than the rest.

'You should go to the Panel in Westhoughton. The only one left.' Of what? I wonder. 'Professional crown green bowling. The best players in the world. Playing for money. With betting. Every week day. Whatever the weather. Unbelievable but true. Best kept secret in sport.'

I look out of the window, at the snowflakes drifting under the street lights, turning to sleet, glassing the pavements, and I check the times of the trains to Westhoughton.

CHAPTER 3

HAVING A FLUTTER

Bowls with the 'Keawyeds' of Westhoughton, races with Wolves, going to the dogs in Perry Barr and eyes down in Salford

I grew up in houses full of women. This was the case for many northern men of my background, though usually of an earlier generation. If it wasn't foreign wars or frothing lungs or collapsing coal seams, it was gelatinous pies, best bitter and ready rubbed that did for all our granddads early. They lingered on stern-faced and blurry in photos on mantelpieces, standing proudly outside churches in wedding albums or tanned and uniformed in foreign ports. They were still there in the dark suits kept at the back of wardrobes, in watches and cufflinks and lighters kept in musical boxes.

I never knew either of my grandfathers. But stories about them filled the house like pipe smoke when I was a kid. There was my Scottish granddad, Granma Coney's husband, born in a tiny house in Edinburgh behind Holyrood Palace on a street with the wonderful name of Croft-an-righ Wynd. (I fully intend to write a series of period detective novels featuring ace sleuth Croftanrigh Wynd one day.) He once came home drunk on rum and cooked himself an impractical late snack of a rabbit acquired from a poacher mate but which rapidly 're-appeared', shall we say. My terrified grandma apparently thought that, in his cups, he had managed to violently expel his own liver and ran down the street for an ambulance.

There were fewer rakish or oddball tales about my maternal granddad. From the pronouncements of his that were handed down, he seemed drearily upright, severe even. But from time to time, if I were to toss a coin or play with a deck of cards, it wouldn't be long before Nana told the story of the day Granddad got chased by the 'bobbies' for playing pitch and toss. It was told with a mixture of shame and illicit thrill. My granddad, the sober suited Methodist miner on the mantelpiece, a maverick backstreet gambler on the run from the law.

'Pitch and toss' or 'pitching pennies' or 'liney' or 'jingles', depending where you're from, was getting blokes into trouble a long time before my granddad. The Ancient Greeks played it with bronze coins; some think it was played at the earliest Olympics. It's simplicity itself. Players throw coins at a wall from an agreed distance. The one whose coin lands nearest the wall wins all of them. In some variants, the coins must hit the wall first and some play an extra round where the coins are chucked up in the air and guesses made as to how they'll fall are made, but basically that's it. It's not the world's most riveting spectator sport. It's all about the winning of money.

And it was illegal. This seems ludicrous now. Wagers in gentleman's clubs such as the one that sent Phileas Fogg around the world were seen as gallant and sporting. Not so coal miners lobbing money around in the street apparently. Pitch and toss, played fiercely and furtively, seems to have been a facet of working-class life in nearly every corner of urban Britain, up throughout the nineteenth and the first half of the twentieth century. Its heyday was relatively recently, the 1950s in fact, which I guess is when my granddad got busted for it, and its decline came only with the growth of TV and the coming of modern legal bookmakers following the Betting and Gaming Act of 1960.

Sometimes the game would be played by just a few in a back alley, as was the case with my granddad and his mates, who sprinted away when the local bobby surprised them. But often the pitch and toss schools were huge, organised and bloody rough. The sites of these schools were known to all. In Glasgow, they played in huge numbers by the canal in Port Dundas, and witnesses recall hundreds of pounds changing hands on the fall of the coins. A 'copboy' would yell when he saw the police and then came the scatter. Some of the gamblers would escape the police by jumping into the canal and swimming to the opposite bank. In Sheffield, the biggest 'Pitching' site was on 'Sky Edge', a promontory looking over the city immortalised in a Richard Hawley song. In northern England, the lookouts were known as 'crows' and took high vantage points where they could spot trouble from afar. A 'towler' or 'toller' took a cut of all bets placed and 'pikers' would patrol carrying sticks and breaking up fights. In Seaham, County Durham, local metal detectorists regularly turn up old coins left in the undergrowth or buried after 'scatters' on a famous rough ground site.

Pitch and toss has all but disappeared now. But gambling or gaming thrives and the laws surrounding it are detailed and complex. Until that 1960 legislation, off-course betting on any sport in person was illegal, and 'bookies runners' dashing from pubs and callboxes to the bookmakers, taking surreptitious illegal bets, were a common sight and fixture of industrial towns. Until 2005, the 'betting and the passing of betting slips' on licensed premises was illegal except for six specific games – pool, cribbage, darts, bar billiards, shove ha'penny and dominoes – which could be 'played for small stakes on those parts of the premises open to the public', but only if a notice to this effect was displayed prominently. Nowadays, dire adverts for bookmakers punctuate every Sky TV football match, and we gamble openly on our phones and our laptops with not a copboy, towler or piker to be seen.

Culturally, gambling hovers somewhere between the toxic and the trivial. My friend Lydia won 50 quid on this year's Grand National. She bought herself some felt pens and stationery with her winnings. She's just turned ten. Some people might be scandalised by this, but most seem to think it's cute and funny. On the other hand, the haggard men in the harsh light of the late-night bookies seem anything but.

Money and class frame our feelings towards gambling too. The free-spending rich man is seen as a 'playboy', carefree and glamorous.

The poor man at the fruit machine is merely a 'gambler', a sap and an addict. The playboy is assumed to have no dependents. The gambler conjures in the imagination something from an Edwardian illustration; the empty table, the hungry child, the weeping wife. When New Labour announced that they were going to build projected 'super casinos' with £1 million jackpots in blighted Blackpool and run-down east Manchester, critics painted pictures like this and talked of the human and social cost of gambling addiction.

A University of Illinois Policy Forum magazine of 2000 claimed that a third of all the money spent in US super casinos came from addicts and the associated problems and debt led to assault, rape, robberies, burglary, car theft, embezzlement, fraud, lost productivity, unemployment, bankruptcy, anxiety, depression, heart attacks, wife beating, child neglect, child abuse and suicide. It concluded that problem gambling in the US cost the nation about $54 billion a year.

Minister Tessa Jowell said that such objections had the 'whiff of snobbery' about them. Political commentator Nick Cohen, writing in the *Guardian*, thought differently though:

> If you believe that people should be free to spend their money how they choose, then you will doubtless shrug your shoulders and say these prices are worth paying.
>
> Still, even the most committed libertarian should retain a sense of the ironies of political history and marvel at the spectacle of the Labour party encouraging the poor to redistribute what wealth they have to the rich.

But I did not know that any of these concerns could apply conceivably to crown green bowling, which is why I take an empty, freezing, ramshackle train to Westhoughton on a cold, hard January afternoon.

The snow had become sleet as I detrained at Westhoughton station. This small Lancashire town is about five minutes from where I grew up but was as alien as Neptune to me. We can be terribly insular up here, you know. When my Uncle John married a girl from Westhoughton and moved here in the 1960s, my family seemed to think that he was going to live in Albania. When I mentioned to my mum that I was going to a bowling green in Westhoughton, she said, 'Your Uncle John will know it,' in the same way that New York cab drivers will ask if you know their cousin in London.

Westhoughton is a somnolent industrial suburb now, but it has a lurid past. It was the scene of a bloody civil war battle where Lord Derby's Cavaliers from the Wigan garrison clashed with Parliamentarians. In 1812, 12 Luddites burned Westhoughton Mill down and were publicly hanged for their actions.

Wigan folk tell a story about their less sophisticated Westhoughton neighbours to explain their local nickname of 'Keawyeds' (cow heads). Apparently a Wiganer once came across a Westhoughton farmer whose cow had got its head stuck fast in a five bar gate. 'I have a hacksaw you can use,' offered the Wiganer helpfully. Gratefully accepting it, the farmer promptly sawed the cow's head off. Depending which town you come from, you read this implausible tale differently. Wiganers cite it as an evidence of the none-too-bright nature of Westhoughton residents. But the Keawyeds themselves claim that, as the gate was worth more than the cow, the tale just shows how shrewd and canny Westhoughtoners are.

The station is on the border with Wingates, home of one of the world's best and most celebrated brass bands who recorded an album with Michael Nyman recently. But I'm pretty sure I need Westhoughton proper, and that's down the hill. I pop into a general store across the road for directions. The proprietor and his sole customer are engrossed in the latest edition of the *Bolton News* with its striking headline 'Skirt Fetish Voyeur Jailed'. Tearing themselves away from this, the customer, a younger, heavily tanned man, says, 'Ah, tha wants Panel, Red Lion pub, just walk darnt streyt, than carn't miss it, they're knockin it dairn, tha'll see all't scaffolding.' Normally, I hate phonetic transcriptions of local speech. It's usually employed by a snob to patronise. But the dialect of Westhoughton and Bolton is so distinct, with its rolling almost West Country cadences, that it needs to be at least approximated.

The street I'm told to walk down is Wigan Road, a melancholy thoroughfare with a handful of shuttered and derelict pubs (one called, with hollow irony, 'The Commercial'), Compensation 4 U lawyers, a fruiterers that has had to close after several decades 'because of illness' and one sleepy pie shop where I buy my lunch, a hot meat and potato pasty. I know you would be disappointed in me, dear reader, had I passed it by.

At the bottom of the lane, just past the war memorial, is the Red Lion pub. Half of it has become a dementia care home, half of it is decrepit and boarded up. Across the street from this, beside a wrecker's yard, is an ugly patch of waste ground that's being used as a car park. Beyond that, on a concrete wall, is a fading sign that reads: 'This is the home of the Professional Crown Green Bowling Association. Welcome to the Panel.' Beneath it is a shabby green door. As homes of sport go, it is some way from St Andrews, Lords or Wimbledon. But this is indeed the home of the Panel, a mysterious name I never quite get to the bottom of but which is the designation of the only version of Crown Green bowls for which money, and quite a lot of it, changes hands.

I knock on the green door. It opens and behind it is a well-kept green and a collection of men in their fifties upwards, mufflered and overcoated against the winter afternoon. 'Who's tha looking for, son?' asks one, in a not unfriendly way. Well, no one really, I shrug, I've just come for the bowls. 'Oh, you've come to the right place then, come in.'

The green is surrounded by a high wall, and beyond it stands a row of houses from whose upper windows I guess you'd get a good view of the action; quite the des res if you're a bowls nut looking for bedroom action, as it were. On our side is a covered gallery with a little heated glass enclosure promising hot drinks, and a few sheds and outbuildings of obscure purpose. Clearly, everyone here knows everyone else and has been coming for years, so a newcomer like me is naturally the object of some curiosity. I'm asked a few good-natured questions which I fend with some vague noises about 'writing a book'. I offer to pay but Ian, a club official, waves my money aside.

'Your first visit is buckshee. Keep your eyes and ears open and you'll get a good article.' He turns out to be right, though I should say that reported verbatim it would be a largely unprintable one. Bowling may sound awfully genteel, particularly if you've seen those nice old chaps down Hampshire way in their white flannels and caps on BBC2. But crown green is different and the all-male environs of the panel are like many all-male working-class environs, that is to say a Lancashire *Goodfellas*, the air thick and blue with colourful profanity. One man in particular seems to be in some kind of sponsored Swearathon. Ian, by contrast, is calm and genial. He introduces me to some of the regulars who are unfailingly helpful and informative. There's Roy, who patiently answers my daft newbie questions, and one nice bloke turns out to be Jackie Edwards, dad of former England rugby league captain Shaun and a legendary player himself for Warrington. I mention that I once 'hung out' with Shaun in Vienna and Hull on tour with M People, when he was married to singer Heather Small. Edwards senior says he'll remind him of this when he calls that night from South Africa, where Shaun's currently working. 'Write your name down there,' he says, then, 'No, no, not on my bets!'

More of the betting in a moment, since that is why we've made a second visit to a bowling green. The panel used to be played all across this area, with eight greens in Wigan and Bolton with licensed greenside betting. The daily papers would carry fixtures and results in columns such as the *Mail*'s 'Bowler's Diary'. Now only this one venue remains where it is legal to bet, the players are pros and where they play every weekday whatever the weather. There's a Polaroid on the noticeboard of two men shovelling a trench of snow exposing a track of green just wide enough to bowl on. Jackie has helped clear thigh

high snow to get matches on. Roy can only recall two cancellations in the last five years, for blizzards.

The two men on the green at the moment are Noel Burrows and Chris Morrison. They are unremarkable blokes in cagoules and trainers, the sort you might see in the car park of B&Q loading some planks into an estate car. However, they happen to be the two greatest crown green bowlers in the world. 'And that chap there,' says Jackie Edwards, indicating a man in his sixties in a waterproof jacket leaning on the rail and chatting casually, 'is Brian Duncan. In most sports, you get debates about who's the greatest player ever. But in bowls, there's no argument. He is the greatest crown green bowler there has ever been.' Yes, that fellow there in the anorak and woolly hat smiling shyly over to us. It occurs to me that, in footballing terms, I am watching Ronaldo and Messi in competition while standing next to Pelé. Here, between a dementia home and a scrapyard in Westhoughton.

Friday is the big day here. 'We'll have a good time today,' says Roy. 'All the big betters come down today. That bloke there,' and he indicates a younger chap with a Scouse accent, craggy,, padded jacket and a thick Bible-sized notebook, 'he's a professional gambler … bowls, dogs … he'll be looking to win or lose three or four hundred pounds today.' Jackie just wants to win a fiver. That's his daily target. It might take him two pages of bets to get there, but he'll usually do it.

The match ends when the first player reaches 41 on the board. Actually its 31, since numbers were reduced to shorten the games for the players and spectators who'd come long distances and had to travel home. However, since 41 is so ingrained in the panel player's mind as the winning total, they start with ten on the board and still play to 41. 'So they don't get confused,' says Jackie, with a smile, as if talking of a much-loved but slightly senile old Labrador. The 'professional' tag is 'really more historic than anything. They used to get paid to play but now they pay a tenner and the winner takes home 40 pounds.'

I mention to Roy my recent visit to the Lloyd Arms match in Manchester. 'The Lloyd Hotel,' he corrects gently. 'I play for Sale

Excelsior. The Lloyds are our deadly rivals,' he informs, with a hint of steely sangfroid beneath the soft Lancashire burr.

It's not the sport, though, but the betting that is the real revelation. I went to Chorlton to watch them bowl. I've come here to watch them bet. If you become a member of the Professional Crown Green Bowling Association, you are entitled to place bets here, the only place left in Britain where you can wager by the side of the green on a game of bowls. I, being naive, had come expecting official bookmakers, tic-tac-toe men and chalkboards of odds. The truth is odder and much more complex. Everyone here is betting with everyone else. They watch the play, make snap decisions and wagers, lay their bets off against each other in an ad hoc way. To the uninitiated, maybe even to the initiated, it is dizzyingly complicated. In full earshot of the players, the spectators offer odds to each other. 'Burrows to win, lay you 5 to 4', 'I'll take 5 to 4', 'I'll go two tenners', 'I'm offering fives'.

It's bamboozling and mightily impressive. Shouts are coming from all corners of the green and the gallery, but only once do I hear the query, 'Who said that?' It goes without saying that I do not understand a word of it. In the middle of it all, the bowlers seem unfazed, even though as well as the bewildering chorus of arithmetic and odds, comments are offered about the game and their own performance. 'That's miles off, Noel', 'No, Chris, you'll have to do better than that'.

The lure of being able to have a bet is still strong, although clearly the numbers are in decline. 'It's the internet. If it's a cold day, some people are tempted to gamble online.' But the hardcore still come for the thrill of the flutter and the social element. One regular called Stan Stafford died last week. He was 92 and had been coming to this unprepossessing spot for 70 years.

No one's writing anything down, I say to Roy. 'No, they do it all on trust. If you're new, they will ask if anyone knows you and if they can vouch for you. If not, they will put you down as "Glasses" or "Pipe" or "Yellow Hat" or, if it's a woman, "Lady".' (I get the impression this last doesn't happen very often.)

Then, at the end, they settle up. They mingle, Soho art gallery opening style, except instead of bearing canapés and plastic glasses of fizz, they bear rolled bunches of fivers, tens and twenties, which pass between them quickly and unshowily. Even if I was a member, or could be vouched for, I would no more have risked a bet than I would have got on the green and bowled a few ends myself, so confusing and arcane was it, and done at such speed with such fluency. At the side of me, as they count their winnings, two men are having a hugely entertaining conversation about spouses and holidays (which in the original was a lot more colourful, believe me).

'My wife's Thai, I didn't meet her in Thailand. I met her in Hull. We went to Dubai last year – 6k for two weeks. Outrageous. One night in the restaurant we had this sweet chili prawn starter … four shrimps on a piece o' lettuce on a plate this big.' (Indicates with hands, an object the size and shape of a manhole cover.) 'She had two glasses o' beer. I had a glass of the house red. We both had fillet steak and chips. Guess how much? Guess how much? 172 pound!! 172 pound!! My house red were 32 quid, and it were Asda shit!'

In Dubai, I doubt this to be honest but say nothing. Dusk falls, the sky darkens and a few flakes of snow begin to float across the green. There's a rumour that there's been a big smash on the motorway, 'the 62', and in ones and twos, the crowd, which has never really been much of a crowd, begin to slip away. As the punters drift away like the snow, the two bowlers continue to criss-cross the green in the fading light, and Jackie, his fiver (and a little more) pocketed, bids me goodnight.

Westhoughton is ur-north, uber-north, the north in excelsis. But the north can sometimes seem a moveable feast, a matter more of mood than latitude. The Black Country lies a little south of Cheshire, but Dudley and Tipton feel grittier than Wilmslow and Prestbury and from my experience the people there think of themselves as vaguely northern and certainly not Brummies, which they are often lazily conflated with.

The sprawl of the Midlands, once lit by flickering foundries and ringing to the sound of jackhammers, was the model for Tolkien's Mordor. It has a distinctly northern industrial cast. But it was more than that that sent me there on my next gambling excursion. I knew that people will bet on the fall of coins and risk the wrath of the law for it, as my own family had 'form' in the matter. I'd discovered that even the supposedly sedate world of the manicured green and the rolling jack can tempt men into parting with their wages. But for the working man and woman, it is generally other living things that they normally pin their money to.

Horse sense, said W C Fields, is the thing a horse has which keeps it from betting on people. If you want to spoil the joke, you could say that it's that plus lack of sentience, opposable thumbs, language, bank accounts and the rest. But the point of W C's remark is that betting on races between horses is mad really, and should have no part in a sensible society. Yet it has, and has for millennia. There are horse races between the gods in Norse mythology and across the ancient world from North Africa to the Steppes. Thanks to Charlton Heston, we all know the chariot races of Rome.

During Henry VIII's reign, stables specifically for the training of racehorses were established and the world's oldest horse race as we know it. The Kiplingcotes Derby took place in Yorkshire in 1509. Racing declined under Elizabeth I but then when out with his hawk, James I chanced upon a village called Newmarket and decided it was the perfect place to race horses. He became so keen that parliament rebuked him for neglecting his kingly duties. From the seventeenth century onwards, English aristocrats crossbred native mares with Arab and Barb stallions, to create 'thoroughbreds' of great speed and stamina ability in order to race them for wagers. Thus did horse racing become known as the Sport of Kings. This, though, can seem a strange and inappropriate name if you've ever been in a grimy William Hills in a winter dusk surrounded by sallow defeated men throwing down their pencils at the end of last race from Uttoxeter or Thirsk.

I grew up with neither a fear nor a fever for the horses. I never saw men in my family come home skint and murderous after a bad session, nor laden with flowers and champagne and buoyed by a rare success. In this I guess we were pretty typical. We were the once a year gamblers, beloved of the bookies, who each year would follow the same Grand National ritual. *Daily Mirror* on the big Saturday morning. Nana and me and mum picking horses whose names we liked, to the despair of Dad and Uncle Brian who would tell us to study the form and that there was no point going each way on a 3–1 favourite. In the similar way that we are the only country in the world where, once a year, children can demand money in the street to buy explosives with which to commemorate a failed political assassination, the Grand National is still the only occasion where kids are not just allowed, but encouraged, to gamble with money, as we saw with my friend Lydia.

The names of all the gee-gees who earned me a few childhood bob are still there: Red Alligator, Highland Wedding, L'Escargot, Rag Trade, the legendary Red Rum, who was trained by pounding the beaches at Ainsdale where we would sometimes go for a drive out on a summer Sunday. I spent the occasional few bob I made on them on a Corgi Thunderbird 4 or James Bond Aston Martin, which of course would now be worth a fortune had I kept them in their box and looked at them admiringly rather than throw them off the roof during heated re-enactments.

But it was the early nineties before I ever actually went to the races.

Granada TV, with whom I'd done some work, invited me to Ladies Day at Aintree – the day before the Grand National when the well-heeled and fun-loving ladies (and their squires) would teeter down to the course in miraculous gravity defying fascinators and astonishing dresses to have a flutter and get blissfully hammered. That day it poured down all morning and the course was a quagmire but spirits were undampened. I took my place in a special box of invitees who included snooker ace and *Question of Sport* stalwart John Parrott and scouse scriptwriting legend Jimmy McGovern.

I had decided that I would allow myself a £10 bet on each race of the nine-race meeting. So at the very worst I'd be less than a hundred quid out of pocket. But that would be at the very worst, and I was sure to do better than that. Wasn't I? In fact, I wasn't. Whatever luck or sixth sense I'd had as the child tipster who'd cleaned up on Highland Wedding and bought a Spectrum Pursuit Vehicle with my winnings had deserted me. Rain fell pitilessly from a leaden sky, the fascinators drooped, and I lost and lost and lost. To make matters worse, quietly and unshowily McGovern and Parrott were both on winning streaks. They knew what they were doing, and after every race I would watch them secrete another plump wad of notes into their inside pocket while I was drinking (on tick) in the last chance saloon. Just before the final race, I stood up (itself something of a feat by this time) and addressed my fellow gamblers, telling them that I thought it only fair of me to say which horse I was going to put my money on so that they might avoid it. Everyone laughed and Jimmy slapped me on the back. Then we settled down to watch the final race of the day. I lost.

So I went to my second race with no great expectation of riches but in anticipation of all the fun of not a day but a night at the races. This is something you have not been able to say for very long. Wolverhampton Racecourse hosted the first floodlit regular night-time horseracing meetings in Britain and is still the most famous, one of four all-weather tracks in the UK, and a good pace to wrap up warm on a cold winter night and watch the gee-gees. The course is reached, unusually, through the entrance to a Holiday Inn that would seem largely for the benefit of race-goers judging by the large statue of a horse in the lobby. By this token, it occurs to me, every Travelodge in Britain should have a statue of three girls in tiny skirts drinking from a bottle of Sambuca in reception.

I'm ushered upstairs into a large, well-lit room, full of dining tables and floor to ceiling windows. It is nothing like the scene I imagined, which was of men standing on orange boxes shouting and making incomprehensible gestures, bookies' runners smoking roll-ups, looking hunted and furtive, and burly men in sheepskin jackets barking orders at homunculi in garish pantaloons. No, this is more like, well, the restaurant of a midrange Midlands hotel that happens to overlook a race track. Quite a view, too, the bright sodium white of the floodlights illuminating the sandy ochre carpet of the all-weather track. I order a glass of something nice and red and take in my surroundings.

Each table has a little TV terminal. I am childishly impressed, even though the technology to do such a thing has been with us decades. It offers different screens worth of betting info, coverage of this and other meetings, and so on. Instantly, I manage to switch it off and can't switch it back on again, and several young members of the waiting staff have to come and help me in the way you might help your aged grannie to send her first tweet. Gratifyingly they are no better at it than me, and we resort to pushing every button in every available permutation and hitting it with a soup spoon until it flickers back into life.

The young male waiter is conscientious and eager but seems a little nervous in his work. Perhaps he is new. He defers, sensibly, to his colleague Rosie who is just ace, a sweet Black Country girl with a touch of Emo Goth. I admit that I am baffled by the racecard and she smiles sheepishly, 'You really don't want to ask me. I know all about the menu but I know nothing about racing. They have free racing for the staff in January and I lost so much this year that I had to work every day in February to make my money up.'

There's a mildly raucous, curiously cosmopolitan gang on the next table. Half of them look like typical Brit office workers on a boozy, 'spendy' night out; a very British mixture of 'bling' and gauche. One is dressed in a beautiful charcoal Armani suit but he staggers out of the gents hoicking up the trousers as if they were trackie bottoms. The other half of the party look more tanned, more chic, less loud. A small dark man wears a pale blue cashmere sweater loosely knotted around his shoulders. I form the scenario that a Black Country precision engineering firm have been bought by a large Italian concern and these Latin types are from the head office in Turin. This is an impression reinforced when one, a small pneumatic lady with vibrant green eye make-up and lustrous black hair, starts to tell the table in her glorious accent about her favourite wine which is 'made in a leetel village just outside Montepulciano'. There is a moment's thoughtful silence before the fellow with the troublesome trousers offers, 'Steve loves a Malbec, din't ya, Steve?'

A race is imminent. Out of nowhere, one horse bounds away out on his own and starts to gallop around the track. I decide that this poor creature is frisky and unreliable and make a note of his name the better to avoid him: Desert Ranger. The brochure for the evening begins promisingly: 'Whether you're a first time visitor or a seasoned racing enthusiast, we hope that you have an enjoyable experience today...' – but rapidly becomes unfathomable to this first time visitor. This is entirely my fault. I don't seem to be able to get past the horses' names and trying to work out their rationale. Is Doo Wah Diddy Diddy owned by a former member of Manfred Mann? Has Madonna got shares in Like A Prayer? What on earth is Shiftin Bobbins all about? Also, many of the races are sponsored, which thus lumbers them with the most dreadful and stupid titles. Even I, no 'seasoned racing enthusiast', can see the allure and romance of the Oaks, the St Ledger or the Two Thousand Guineas. I doubt that anyone's heart would beat faster at the thought of the 'Download The Free App At Bookies Dot Com Handicap'.

As the race begins and the horses thunder away from me in the chill night, I realise that I have completely misunderstood the arcane symbolism of the formbook and that the horse I have bet on, Chester Aristocrat, is the rank outsider. It comes in last. With hilarious inevitability, the unhinged Desert Ranger wins. After this inauspicious start, though, I hit a rich vein of form and get placed – or rather my chosen horses do – in the next three races. One of these is, astonishingly, a 33–1 shot with a little beauty called Bittern. The on-course commentator emphasises the 'tern' bit of his name so for a little while it doesn't dawn on me that I've had a bloody good win. When it does, my elation is tempered by the fact that I have lost my ticket. Seeing my discomfiture, Rosie and her young assistant waiter come to my aid. We all start to go through the many bins in the restaurant. After ten minutes of excavations through half-eaten bread rolls, corks and bottles of Stevie's Malbec, I find it in my pocket.

Before the next race, as the horses and riders assemble at the gate, it becomes apparent that one particular steed, Steel River, really doesn't want to go in there. Several men and a host of small boys – they could, I suppose, be jockeys – seem to be employed about his flanks and hindquarters, shoving the recalcitrant beast into the pen. 'One more heave and he'll be in,' says the commentator. I think this shows a reluctance to race and decide to avoid it. Naturally, it wins. My horse 'pulls up', which is horse for 'sod this for a lark'.

There is consolation in the form of the food. I overhear a crackling intercom message telling the staff that there are only two twice-baked vanilla cheescakes left and the meal become a race against time. But then, pausing midway through my duck rillette, gnocchi and minted pea puree, I begin to think I may not be getting the authentic tang of a winter race meeting and decide I should go 'trackside'.

The people thronging about out here are a colourful mixed bag. There are lots of girls in Hunter wellies and jodhpurs with broad Black Country accents. Four middle-aged ladies are huddled intently around a couple of *Racing Posts* (racing has its own dedicated national daily newspaper. Beat that, Premier League and F1). I fall into conversation with them as we both make a few bob on Delightful Sleep, runner up in the 8.30 race, the relatively soberly named Betting Tips Galore Handicap Stakes. 'Did you have a swinger on that?' one asks me, to which I can only shrug. They clearly know their stuff and chuckle at me a little pityingly.

The paddock area is quite bizarre. It is rather like a little fashion parade where the horses are led around by awkward looking stable hands. (Stable 'lads', by the way, can be any age.) People crowd around the rails, studying the horses intently. Up close the horses are beautiful creatures, glossy and chestnut with glistening flanks and noble heads, wreathed in their steaming breath. One is of particular interest to a bossy looking woman by me in tweeds with a notebook. 'Is it a boy or a girl?' she asks, weirdly. 'It was a boy last time I looked,' returns the hand, a mischievous girl in a ponytail.

There is some mildly pervy sounding chit chat about Tongue Straps and Blinkers, but I am more mesmerised by the jockeys. They really are funny little guys. If any jockeys are reading this, I should say that this is not meant offensively. I'm genuinely fascinated. Not like children at all, or young boys, as I'd sometimes wrongly thought. But adult men sort of scaled down. A little light googling showed that I was not alone in my curiosity.

'Jockeys – What The Fuck Are They?' was one of the first sites I came across. Here's a typical post:

> … men weighing under 50 kgs are extremely uncommon, also horseriding isn't accessible to everyone, it's fairly exclusive really. Yet the horse racing industry always manages to have tiny athletes who've grown up riding horses. You couldn't even tell if a kid was going to grow into a tiny man, so could they really be scouting kids and prepping them? No. How many men as small as jockeys have you seen in other proffessions [sic]? It would be striking to see a jockey-sized man changing the oil in your car. You'd be alarmed I think.

It's a reasonable point. I used to go into a Cumbrian pub that was frequented by jockeys. In the end I had to drink elsewhere. I was freaked out constantly by the fact that, at five foot nine, I stood goliath-like at the bar and could have rested my pint on their heads, though that would have been unwise as they were pretty rowdy after a few pints. Anyway, out come the jockeys to the paddock area and it's fair to say that their essential strangeness is not tempered by their garb. Silks. What is all that about? How have jockeys ended up wearing clobber that makes them look like camp paramilitary clowns? Why silk? Why the bizarre colours? The guy on Like A Prayer is wearing a pale cerise blouse with mustard polka dots and a matching cap. You could probably see him from the moon.

In the week before coming to the races I'd listened to a sort of *Any Horseracing Questions* podcast – yes, I know how to live – and someone asked retiring champion jockey A P McCoy what the toughest part of the sport was. I'd expected him to say falling off or getting up at first light in midwinter, but in fact he replied instantly that it was the dieting. 'It's when you're 10 stone 6 on a Sunday night and you have to make 10 stone dead by the morning. So you have nothing to eat all day and you go for a run at bedtime. Still not there. So you get up at the crack of dawn and go for another run. It's OK if you're riding a favourite but if you're on a 25–1 outsider, you do think, "Is it worth it?"'

In 1990, Marcus Armytage won the Grand National in less than nine minutes on Mr Frisk. Six years later, he tried again and fell at the first fence. He'd lost so much weight to try and make the race that he was simply too weak to control his mount, Bachelor's Hall. It took a fence wildly, careered off, over-jumped and threw Armytage onto the track. As he lay stunned, the aroma of a nearby burger van wafted over him. 'If I had any money in my breeches,' he said, 'I would have bought one. By the end of the day I must have put on 10lb, I consumed so much food.' Dr Rachel Edwards-Stuart, a food scientist, came up with a 294 calorie meal especially for jockeys to eat for their Christmas dinner. It included turkey gel, dehydrated Brussels sprouts, potato foam and cranberry air. Because it just isn't Christmas without second helpings of Cranberry Air, is it?

Riddled with jockey guilt, I skip the twice-baked vanilla cheesecake and decide to cash in and go home. 'Going to spend it on something nice?' asks the lady who'd floored me with the query about 'swingers'. 'Chips,' I reply, truthfully, as I pocket a few fivers and head out into the chill Black Country night. There are a clutch of little prefab shacks by the car park, overnight quarters for the jockeys. Most though will try and get back to their stables or to another town for tomorrow's races. I see a van headed for a stables in North Yorkshire, four or so hours' drive away, and I think of the little men inside, heading up the M1, stomachs rumbling, for a late night Ribena and some potato foam, if they're lucky.

However small and emaciated the jockey, they're never going to fit on a greyhound. In greyhound racing, the little guy is in the crowd and at the heart of the sport. If horse racing is the sport of kings, greyhound racing is the sport of blokes. Far less glamorous than its haughty equine counterpart, it has hardly any opportunities for dressing up, wearing ludicrous hats or quaffing champagne in the Cotswolds, and because of this is firmly on my radar from the beginning. Greyhound racing is the poor relation of horse racing, literally. There is considerably less money in the game and far less coverage and cultural clout. But its roots are resolutely urban and proletarian. The tracks are in the hearts of our industrial cities, and the races happen at night so are not just the preserve of the fanatic, the wealthy or the leisured oddball such as John McCririck and Prince Philip. Working (and not working) men have traditionally watched the horses on a pub telly or in a cheerless bookmakers on a drab provincial high street. But we can all go to the dogs.

I had, once. It was in the mid-nineties when the beat group Blur released a record called *Park Life*. The group had been on their uppers for a while, although their second album *Modern Life Is Rubbish* should have alerted anyone with ears to their promise. With *Park Life*, they fulfilled that promise and made the record of the decade. In fact, they made the record that made the decade, one that would invent the nineties and, for better or worse, usher in Britpop, by extension Cool Britannia and by even further extension, New Labour.

Blur's new sound was defiantly English in the face of a dreary tide of American grunge rock that had swamped pop music here for several tuneless years. *Park Life* was a whirlwind tour though several Golden Ages of British Popular Song, from music hall to Morrissey, parlour ballads to punk. So what better place to launch it in a blaze of new found patriotic confidence than Walthamstow Dog Track, a setting as chipper and proley as they come. My memories of the evening are a little vague. It was that kind of era. I remember trying to explain what 'each way' meant to Jarvis Cocker and I recall an all pervasive, and at the time radical, sense of Britishness, a funny kind of wry affectionate melange of Elgar and jellied eels, dimple beer mugs and mod scooters, *Hancock's Half Hour*, *Python* and punk.

Ironic then that modern greyhound racing is an American invention. Commoners and kings had 'coursed' for centuries, that is, chased terrified game such as rabbits and hares with packs of dogs. But it was an American Owen Patrick Smith who, revolted by the killing of the defenceless prey, turned the hunt into a race in 1919 by opening the first professional dog-racing track in Emeryville, California. O P Smith's innovations, like the oval track and the mechanical hare were introduced to Britain in 1926 by another American, Charles Munn. Within a year, attracted by its cheapness and the opportunity to pop down to night-time meetings, 40 tracks were operating in Britain, mainly in the industrial north, Midlands and London. The people who came were almost exclusively male and working class and, by 1946, there were 34 million punters and hundreds of tracks.

Those glory days are long gone. In 2013, the BBC homepage carried a story gloomily headlined 'Is the end nigh for dog racing?' It reported how the closure of the Oxford track meant that the sport was officially dead in central southern England with all four of its once popular courses gone. In the last 65 years, the number of stadiums had dropped from 80 to just 25. The once famous White City track in London is now the offices of the BBC. The piece concluded by wondering if greyhound racing would make it to its centenary in 2026, a hundred years after Britain's first greyhound race. That race was at Belle Vue in Manchester, naturally, since Belle Vue had everything as we have seen, but I wanted to see if the decline of the British 'dogs' that had seen it gone from the home counties, the Thames Valley and the south coast had spread as far north as Birmingham.

This is how a beautiful Indian summer evening finds me under the amethyst skies and basking in the tropical heat of a Friday night in Brum's Perry Barr. From all around, the sizzle and scent of barbecues and baltis is overpowering and hard to resist. But I am going to the dogs, a rough and vulgar pursuit of the lower orders, sure to end in ruin. Now that's my kind of Friday night.

Appropriately then, Perry Barr Greyhound Racing Stadium is built on a former rubbish tip on the Aldridge Road. In the late twenties, it was turned into an athletics stadium for the famous Birchfield Harriers athletics club, venerable home of many an Olympian, from Diane Leather, who ran the first female five minute mile here in 1954, to world-beating heptathlete Denise Lewis. Then in their centenary year of 1977 the Harriers moved out, and left the stadium to the greyhounds and the Birmingham Brummies speedway team.

On the stairs as I enter the grandstand, I pause to mop my sopping brow and take in the pictures of famous Birmingham Brummies down the years in the speedway hall of fame. Having been to two speedway meetings, I am now something of an expert and connoisseur of the sport and pause thoughtfully, head to one side, in that way people do when they are examining someone else's bookshelves. The gallery is just brilliant, row upon row of intense, muddied men with ratty hair and Viking sideburns, looking for all the world like Uriah Heep after a rainlashed festival in a sodden Lincolnshire field circa 1971.

Like Mark Twain's famous remark upon seeing his own obituary, reports of greyhound racing's death would seem to have been greatly exaggerated. The grandstand is packed and I can see through the floor to ceiling window that trackside is bustling too. There's a healthy amount of young people, women and groups drawn from Brum's rich mix of ethnic minorities. It feels bright and airy and still solidly working class, like Butlins or Alton Towers. It may be that this lovely

Friday night has drawn the crowds and is not representative at all. Maybe most meetings are run in front of the proverbial three men and a dog – well, several dogs but you know what I mean – but apparently not. Though afternoon greyhound racing run by BAGS (Bookmakers Afternoon Greyhound Service racing) is done daily in empty stadiums purely for the sake of gambling and subsidised by the bookmakers, weekend meetings can still regularly draw well over a thousand people in the sport's northern and Midland heartland. It is still, amazingly, the fourth biggest spectator sport in Britain, after football, horse racing and rugby.

I head for the bar for something cool and long. A man with his arm in a sling and a bottle of WKD nods at me, 'Not seen you here for a bit.' As I've never been before, it's hard to know what to say at this point. While I'm formulating my strategy he carries on, 'Did you hear about how I did this?' he nods at his sling. 'Fell off Terry's car. Sober as a judge too.' At just the point when I am going to have to come clean, the barman asks me what I'm having and my new mate wanders off to put a bet on. Here inside the grandstand they are playing that 'Stay the Night' record that has blighted my summer, so I am driven by its horrible sexless stormtrooper 'dance' beats down the stairs and out into the sunlit trackside.

Strolling aimlessly but contentedly around, I go into a reverie about how much I would have loved this as a kid. A sticky Friday night in late summer, the floodlights burnished and white hot in the gathering dusk, the sweet cloying scent of frying onions, the warm laughter of your own people, the literal buzz of electricity in the air, the silly, sexy, trashy glamour of the tinny piped music. Here we are all kids again, and the real kids here are among grown-ups they know and love who are taking their fun with the relish of their class. Three young girls of around ten, sucking on ice pops, are squealing with delight at the sheer joy of being here, and of a first glimpse of the dogs in their little jackets. Like all the kids here, of whom there are many, they know they are safe and happy in the warm, beating heart of their world. A little further along, by the first bend in the shale track, stand two Japanese girls with colourful outsize backpacks. They look both mystified and delighted by the unfolding evening.

I go into the trackside bar and order a glass of wine without thinking where I am. Standing there with my teeny effete Merlot makes me feel like Quentin Crisp at a … well, at a dog track. There's a different vibe here down here, sweatier, noisier, a bit lower rent really, burgers and beer bellies and gold chains, and it's just as much fun in a slightly different way. A massive, deeply tanned, muscular chap in a polo shirt that shows off his huge brown forearms and the gold ingot nestling in his steel grey chest hairs, trundles between trackside and the bar in a mobility scooter that I can only describe as 'pimped'. It has a little tray for snacks and a holster for his umbrella. It has wing mirrors. It may even have a machine gun emplacement round the back for a rear gunner. The people he leaves in his wake, me included, smile in wonderment and admiration. There appears nothing wrong with his mobility. He's just making life a little sweeter for himself. Some, made fearful and angry by an innutritious tabloid diet of suspicion and jealousy, might find this appalling: I raise a metaphorical glass to him. He could pick me up in one of his mighty fists and chuck me from here into the centre circle at Villa Park. He is as fit as an ox. He just fancies riding around a stadium on a sunny evening on a customised mobility scooter. Who wouldn't?

I go back inside to the grandstand restaurant for the meal that comes as part of my ticket. This being Birmingham it is quite properly a balti with samosas for starters and, when it comes, my balti chicken is perfectly serviceable – with its top notes of curry powder and monosodium glutamate it makes me nostalgic with its echoes of the rehydrated Vesta meals of my youth, if not up to the city's best. Some years ago, I was taken to a venerable, much lauded Indian restaurant on Regent Street by some nice media people who assured me of its world-class reputation and flair. Had it been slightly better, it would have been average. I realised that I had perhaps been spoiled by my time in Birmingham, where on every street in every district, chic or shabby, you can get a meal that knocks the spots off anything in the West End for a quarter of the price.

Along with your dinner, you are given a fantastically helpful booklet, which outlines the many and varied ways you can lose all your money. These include placing it on 'Totalisator', a crime against English that makes my head hurt a little. The grandstand is almost full. Next to me, a table of several families arrive, laughing. One little man in light blue slacks is labouring under the misapprehension that he is hilarious and does a range of funny voices and walks. His kids, bless 'em, exchange meaningful looks and roll their eyes indulgently. Over by the window, the shale track below them, two young, smartly dressed guys sit at a table, chatting and laughing a little nervously. Is this a gay first date, I wonder? If so, well done lads for refusing to be slaves to convention and choosing Perry Barr dog track. They should put this in their literature as well as great for birthdays, anniversaries and works Christmas parties.

When it comes to betting, in the absence of a shred of knowledge about the world of greyhounds, I go for names that I like. Romeo Militia stands out a mile, being the kind of name I might choose if I'd been in a Midlands glam rock band of the seventies. (Incidentally, racing dogs can only have three words in their name.) On the little screen at my table, I notice that Romeo Militia's odds, indeed all of the odds, are changing and flickering constantly: 11/8, 5/2, 2/1. It's extraordinarily confusing and hard to follow, especially when a young Afro-Caribbean woman, laughing uproariously, is ladling hot pungent curry from a tureen at the side of you as you're trying to tot it all up and place your bets.

Down below in the honeyed sun, beyond the short-sleeved men with their lagers and their families with hot dogs and cokes, the dogs limber up (or whatever dogs do), with white-coated owners who look disturbingly like vivisectionists. So with that thought in mind, we should address the darker side of greyhound racing. When I tweeted that I was writing about greyhound racing, one correspondent replied instantly: 'Hope it's all about how many are killed inhumanely just because they don't win at something they have no choice in'. I replied as speedily that I would certainly address this side of the sport and could he point me in the direction of some hard evidence. He never replied.

These allegations have, and I rue the weak pun here, dogged the sport for years. This book doesn't have the scope and I don't have the expertise to do those issues justice. There is lots of literature that does, both pro and con, and I'd point you there. The welfare of the animals has been a hot and contentious topic inside and outside the dog racing world for some time, with exposés and allegations about euthanasia, maltreatment and the sale of retired dogs to animal labs. In return, the sport is at pains to point out how this has been and is being tackled, and how well the dogs are treated these days. Around the track and in the programme are a great many adverts for canine charities, dogs' homes and schemes for adopting greyhounds. From the side of the track, I have to say that they look healthy and happy enough, but then I am aware that this is what Shirley Maclaine famously said about the people of China after her visit in 1973, and wound up looking like the worst kind of dopey stooge.

I spot a dog called Mr Fahrenheit in Race 3. This was a refrain bellowed by Freddie Mercury in 'Don't Stop Me Now', and having a cordial but enduring dislike for the music of Queen, I decide to back it. It comes last. Next up on the programme is the strikingly titled Usain Bolt Handicap. 'Unfortunately, Usain can't be with us tonight,' says the laconic Brummie announcer down on the track. 'So we have a lookalike, our general manager Dave.' Dave, standing glumly by him, is a fat bald white bloke. This makes me laugh a lot, as I do again when the joke is repeated for both the Mo Farah and Jessica Ennis stakes later in the evening.

As for 'going to the dogs', well, it didn't feel like it. There are ways of destroying yourself and gambling your life away for sure, but probably not with the balti meal deal at Perry Barr stadium on a Friday night. There are six dogs in every race, so if six of you come and bet on a different dog each time, one of you will always win and you'll pay for your drinks if nothing else. At Perry Barr I saw some old neighbours of mine, Dave the roofer, his wife Mandy, Rob and Dawn. Mandy won £36 straight off for a quid stake and then sailed through the rest of the evening making fivers here and there with little surprised giggles. You can get a lot of tiny effete glasses of Merlot for that.

The night I went to Perry Barr the papers and the scrolling tickers on the sleepless rolling news networks were full of a report that said the economy was on the upturn. Blather, of course, but even I could have believed it, as the fivers were counted and the small plastic bottles of Merlot uncorked, well unscrewed. But a week later, by the time my flutterings had taken me to the Gala Bingo Salford, the Indian summer was still sweltering on but the mood was chillier.

Bingo is the proletarian *Casino Royale*. Bond sipping his martini at the gaming tables of the Côte D'Azur may seem a long way away from housey-housey on the seafront, but they are in essence the same; games of chance for money. There is no more skill in roulette than bingo. It just looks that way when dressed up in a dinner jacket, and when the prize is a few thousand euros rather than a large pink teddy bear. Neither one holds any appeal for me, and never has. There is nothing to watch, no skill, no art, no human drama. Just greed and luck, however sexy Daniel Craig may be. I've found, on the very rare occasions I've been inside one, that casinos are simply upscale bingo halls, with the same undercurrent of sadness and desperation. The stakes are higher in Monte Carlo and the locale is easier on the eye than Ordsall, Salford, but the impulse is surely the same, the thrill of something for nothing.

In *Casino Royale*, Bond ends up I recall being tied to a wicker chair and having his testicles thrashed by a surly Eastern European man. Ordsall has a reputation for being a little rough but at no point did this seem likely on my visit to the bingo. In fact, the people at the Gala Bingo hall were supremely helpful, sensing I think that I didn't go to bingo every night. Actually, I'd never been before, unless watching my mum slide the little plastic shutters across on the ones at the Pleasure Beach at Blackpool counts. I had somewhat naively expected to hand over a small amount of cash and then go in and play bingo. I had forgotten of course that nothing is like this in the modern world. The modern world requires passwords, registration, mothers' maiden names and first pets, the writing down of reference numbers, the skilful copying down of weirdly drawn numbers that look like you're having an LSD trip, and nonsensical words in little boxes. Not even the Ordsall Gala Bingo, a bastion you would think of the Old Britain of postal orders and Chestnut Mild and whooping cough, not even they are immune to this. Eventually, after a rigmarole that would seem involved for gaining security clearance for the Pentagon, I am given a blue plastic wallet with my Gala Bingo card inside it. But it's not over yet. Now I have to choose which of the many playing options I want.

'Would you like the Salford Special?' asks a kindly lady behind a counter. Having no idea what this might entail and more than a little nervous, I plead to be given the simplest option possible. 'Ah, OK love,' she smiles sympathetically. She reaches beneath the counter where I assume she keeps the books of tickets, before handing me an electronic tablet. I gaze at it mutely for a moment, rather like the chimps looked at the monolith in *2001: A Space Odyssey* and then go inside the hall.

Eric Morley, the oleaginous fellow familiar to my generation from his appearance at the end of every Miss World contest, once claimed to have invented bingo. He's a fibber, though his outfit Mecca did make it a mass commercial venture after the Gaming Act of 1960 which extended the legality of wagers and gambling for money beyond the confines of the race track. But evidence of something like a set of ancient bingo balls was unearthed in Mexico in the 1830s, and bingo's recorded history dates back to 1530 to an Italian lottery called *Lo Giuoco del Lotto d'Italia*. Lotto is still bingo's fancy name and what they probably call it at the Palace. In Britain, bingo-like lotteries were held from the time of Queen Anne onwards, usually as a means of raising revenue for foreign wars. Appropriately, bingo has always been popular with the British military. The Germans played a version of the game in the 1800s, but, with characteristic flippancy and sense of fun, they used it primarily as a maths aid. It was the Americans who gave us the modern version, originally played at travelling fairs and called beano.

Bingo became a craze in Britain in the mid-twentieth century. Newspaper headlines of the early 1960s suggest there was even a mild moral panic about it. *The Times* fretted over 'Bingo's hold on womenfolk' while the *Daily Mirror* told of 'Woman's Bingo Bonanza' and how 'Wife's bingo led to divorce'. During the sixties, bingo or lotto or housey-housey was regularly played by hundreds of thousands of people, a far cry from this large and largely deserted hall on a weeknight in Salford.

Times are tough in the bingo industry, and the decline has been sharp. Bingo peaked later than you'd think, in 2003 when it made £122 million, but it's been downhill ever since. In the last decade, the number of clubs has dropped from 600 to fewer than 400. (Think, where's your local bingo hall?) There have been 6,500 jobs lost in the past decade. Visits are down from 80 million in 2005 to 43 million today. The 2007 smoking ban and the advent of online gambling have made a night at the bingo a less attractive option than it was back in the day when my grandma and aunties would go at least a couple of times a week.

But it is trying to fight back. In 2014, the chancellor George Osborne halved the taxes on bingo taking a swipe at Labour as he did. ('Labour decimated the bingo industry,' he said, possibly fighting back tears.) Brian Binley, Conservative MP for Northampton South and chairman of the All Party Parliamentary Bingo has said: 'Of all forms of gambling, bingo is the most socially welcomed … I say that because

I go once a year to my own local bingo centre and I see many people, many of them elderly, who find comfort and friendship – a hot meal at a low price in a warm and happy environment. And if that isn't social services, I don't know what is.' Stirring words, though my immediate reaction was, 'There's an all party parliamentary bingo group?'

To be brutally honest, the ambience here tonight is more last chance saloon than drop-in centre, though in mitigation it is the hottest night of the year and every beer garden in Lancashire will be full. There are a few people in though, dotted at tables across the cavernous hall. The staff are lovely, ushering me to my table and talking me through my iPad thing with the same patience and pain as you would perhaps show a bushman of the Serengeti how to use a washing machine. A pitcher of lager is six quid and several tables are adorned with one, as well as the books and dabber pens that the hardcore players use.

On each table, there's another bit of kit, a kind of plastic kids' toy involving numbers and sliding panels that turns out to be used for the first couple of games, a kind of warm-up. Except that even this entry level loosener leaves me gawping and flipping the little windows randomly while a neutral almost robotic voice, apparently on tape, intones, 'Gold 43, Blue 5, White 17, White 39.' The effect is disorientating and stressful, like listening to those number station espionage broadcasts that used to come out of East Germany through a blizzard of shortwave static. On an adjoining table, a man with an enormous neck goitre chuckles dementedly as his fingers fly, all blurs and lines like one of those Futurist paintings that are meant to convey speed.

Eventually, it's over. Damp and wrung out, I drain half of my pitcher in one go and slump. Within seconds, Gavin, the personable and flamboyantly camp general manager leaps to his feet and takes the stage.

'Evening everyone!! What a lovely day it's been and it's going to get even better because ...' – what fresh hell is this I think – '... now it's time for the Diamond Deal!' There's a peal of thunder and a sudden explosion of that insanely, nightmarishly cheery music you get on afternoon game shows, a kind of ersatz Vegas mania that trembles on the verge of a nervous breakdown. This is probably 'an innovation'. Bingo is keen on innovation. You use tablets that mean you don't even have to mark your own card. You can have your hen party here. You can enjoy a 'multi-zone gaming experience'.

But beneath all this is the game itself, largely unchanged this half millennia and strangely restful. In fact a realisation begins to dawn on me. Underneath the cheesy glamour and the razzmatazz of the prizes, the appeal of bingo may be that it's actually quite restful. The steady rhythmic intonation of the numbers has the same soothing regularity as the shipping forecast. The numbers and repetition have the same contemplative calm as the music of Philip Glass or Morton Feldman. Next to me, someone is reading a book while playing. The gameplay itself is thoughtful and unhurried. It's a bit like playing collective sudoku.

The bingo caller is nothing like the manic and tortured titular character of The Fall's 'Bingo Master's Break Out'. He is actually rather suave, in a daytime TV show host way. He is well spoken, in that strange, over-modulated melisma that some people have – Richard Hammond, Paul McKenna or those Sky Sports presenters with unplaceable accents. But the real disappointment is that the traditional lingo has gone. There's no fat ladies or little ducks, no Kelly's eye or clickety-click. There's a bit of desultory whistling from the players for 'legs eleven' but that's it. Maybe it was only ever there to buy time so that people could cross off the numbers with unwieldy, massive pens. In the age of the tablet, there's no need for it all, and a little gaiety has gone out of the world.

It's still baffling, though. Various games with various odd names come and go. Every now and again, the suave voice will say, 'The top left square is now free,' and all the people who know what they're doing – which is largely everyone except me – busies themselves with their tablets and dabbers. I just sit and randomly mark things off. The lady who's selling the pitchers of lager takes pity at one point and comes over and gives me a sort of tutorial. But I'm still floundering. It doesn't help that my tablet keeps randomly flashing up adverts for Mini Cheddars.

The next game is another weird perplexing variant on the simple, honest bingo I learned at my mother's knee. It probably had a name like the 'Super Electric Topaz Flyer' but I don't seem to have written it down. Gavin bounds back onto the stage to explain, 'Now for this next game, a full house in less than 50 numbers wins a hundred pounds ...' There's some faint 'ooh-ing' at this, some of it from me, '... and if you do it in less than 40, it's £20,000.'

BLOODY HELL! I nearly drop my iPad. TWENTY THOUSAND QUID? No one else seems bothered. They clearly know how rare this eventuality is. A screen behind Gavin's coiffured head tells us that 211 people are playing this game. We play for a few minutes and then comes the news that someone in a Gala Bingo in Chorley has won. I'm surprised we didn't hear them shout from here.

It was still light when I left and strolled along the Manchester Ship Canal in the last of the throbbing summer heat. Though it was no fault of anyone at Gala Bingo, I don't think I'll be back. Unlike the bowls or the dogs or the horses, there was no drama or spectacle to distract you from the fact that this was simply about trying to win money. It felt grim and mercantile and more than a little melancholy. But I guess it would have been different if I'd won the 20 grand. In that case, I'd be using my nice new Gala Bingo member's card a great deal. As it is, I put it in my wallet behind my library cards and set my mind on higher things.

CHAPTER 4

GETTING A BIT
OF CULTURE

*To Hull and Berwick with Larkin and Lowry,
and getting arty in Wakefield with Hitler*

Anyone who writes about the north, its people and their culture, will find a small but imposing cluster of giants standing at their shoulders, company that is both inspiring and daunting. Priestley, Orwell, Alan Bennett and, first among equals some would say, Richard Hoggart. In 1957, Hoggart wrote a book called *The Uses of Literacy* which was the first serious study of working-class cultural life and the mass media's effect on it. Whole university departments were built upon it, and the entire discipline of cultural studies. Its influence has been profound, sometimes in the quirkiest ways. Persuaded by lawyers not to use the real titles of pulp crime novels in the book for fear of libel, Hoggart invented some he thought were typical, like the brilliant *Death Cab for Cutie*. A decade later, the Bonzo Dog Doo-Dah Band took that name for a song, and several decades after that, a dour American indie rock band named themselves after it.

I love *The Uses of Literacy* for many, sound reasons, not least for the fact that, while it is rooted in Northern working-class life, it neither sentimentalises nor sneers at it. It is generally and penetratingly on the money, as you'd expect from a man of Hoggart's intellect and sensitivity who grew up on the terraced streets of Hunslet. He reserved some of his sternest words of rebuke for those metropolitan critics and newspapermen who claimed to speak for the working classes, particularly those who used a supposed identification with 'common folk' as an excuse for philistinism and crassness, for an attack on:

> … the debased world of Bohemia. Modern art will only be mentioned if someone has given an excuse for trouncing the odd. The Arts Council is a 'fiddle' by a lot of 'sissies' who despise the pursuits of the plain Englishman; and the BBC is little better. Any University Extension lecturer is a stodgy 'do-gooder' and his students spotty and thin-blooded …
>
> Hence the aggressive 'plain man', the embattled lowbrow tone of many columnists and leader writers.

Hoggart wrote that in 1957 but that same tone of belligerently bullying 'common sense' is still heard from the Clarksons and Kelvin Mackenzies of this world.

In fact, as Hoggart pointed out '"Highbrow-hating" … is not strong among working-class people'. The opposite may well be true. Though it might not seem like it if you watch the nastier end of daytime TV, working-class people have always been voracious in their appetite for high culture as well as low. 'Improving oneself' smacks of Hyacinth Bucket and crocheted toilet-roll covers. But self-improvement in a different sense has always been the goal of 'ordinary' people. Not just in the sense of acquiring a bigger house or flashier car, but in getting an education and by seeking out the best in art, music, literature and culture generally.

If you do a cursory trawl for 'improving oneself', through magazines, books or the web these days, you will by and large unearth fad diets of varying weirdness and clickbait lists of self-help mumbo jumbo. It was not ever thus. Self-improvement in the Victorian era was a matter of moral and intellectual growth, and was often handed down from on high to working people.

One winter evening I wandered Manchester following a walk you can find in a leaflet put out by the Royal Geographical Society called 'Slums, squalor and salvation; Discover how religious organisations helped the poor in Victorian Manchester'. In 2015, it is deeply unfashionable among the chatterati to give religion and religious people (or at least Christians) an even break. The dominant tenor of our age is 'scepticism', brandished as a torch of honour by 'satirical' comedians and the like, normally in the thrall of the self-aggrandising Richard Dawkins. I am a confirmed agnostic. I find fundamentalists of all kinds, atheist or apostle, boring and small-minded. If Einstein wasn't sure whether there was a God or not (and he wasn't), I'm pretty sure it's an issue that's too large and complex for someone who wisecracks on panel shows.

But more to the point, the new breed of high volume atheist get on my nerves because they're not much use to anyone. It is a very teenage kind of stance; self-regarding and full of haughty opinion but feeble. The humour website The Onion made this point beautifully with a spoof article entitled 'Local Church Full Of Brainwashed Idiots Feeds Town's Poor Every Week' and containing lines like 'As of press time, the brainless, unthinking lemmings had donated winter clothing they no longer wore to several needy families and still hadn't opened their eyes to reality.'

I thought about this as I followed the walk from Victoria Station down to the Charter Street Ragged School and Working Girls Home. It's a fine Victorian building built by those well-meaning lemmings back in the day as 'a place of meeting by any temperance society or societies and for any other purpose or purposes of a religious, moral, scientific, literary or educational nature.' From the moral high ground of our self-assured time, it's easy to mock such efforts as paternalistic or patronising. The benefactors of the day though were in no mood for moral relativism. They didn't worry about not respecting the 'distinctive culture' of the girls. They just thought they should be fed, protected and educated.

The Methodist Men's Hostel on Hood Street didn't let its residents go out in the evening. They provided pastimes for the men instead. Intolerably prescriptive by our delicate standards, perhaps, but it was meant well and much appreciated. The walk ends at the Methodist Hall on Oldham Street, in the heart of that hipster enclave, Manchester's Northern Quarter. A century-and-a-half ago, it was built thanks to fundraising by suburban Wesleyans and depended for its day-to-day running on the efforts of 2,000 volunteers. Inside there was a large main hall for worship and entertainment and the alcohol-free Saturday night concert provided popular family entertainment intended to compete with the local music halls and pubs. The basement café, offering cheap sustenance to the poor, is still there. As I walk past in a murky winter drizzle, two young lads are emerging after their meal, both with the cheap leisurewear and pimply pallor of the gluehead or junkie. They shake hands with a smartly dressed young African man of about their age who sends them on their way with a smile; brainwashed idiot that he is of course.

God helps those who help themselves, though, and the growing industrial working class of the Victorian era was also busy improving its own lot without charity, however well meant. Alongside the bastion of the Methodist Hall in the towns of northern England and Wales was the miners' institute or 'Stute, as it was often known. Miners would contribute a percentage of their wage towards their building and upkeep, places of education and relaxation with a library, reading and meeting rooms, a bar and a billiard table, so that all manner of healthy appetites could be provided for. Nye Bevan said that his intellectual development was all down to time spent among the volumes of the Tredegar Workmen's Institute. The night I watched the Manic Street Preachers play a homecoming show in their hometown miners' institute in Blackwood near Cardiff was an unforgettable occasion, full of pride and passion and community and other such outdated notions.

As a concept, the miners' or mechanics' institute was never entirely disinterested and airy in motive. They were also there to fill the gaps in technical and science education needed by the modern skilled workforce. Those gaps were often substantial. Until 1870, there was no legal compulsion to send children to school, and even the most basic of those schools charged fees ('school pence') which meant that most working-class kids got a sketchy education at best, further constrained by the need to go to work as soon as possible to earn a wage. Well-meant and undeniably a force for good as they were, mechanics' institutes were normally managed and run by churchmen, landowners or local middle-class entrepreneurs, who made no secret of what they were there for.

Yorkshire historian David Pickersgill writing on the Langentian blog cites local bottle manufacturer William Breffit, who in a letter to the *Castleford Gazette* in 1878, wrote: 'to spread among our workers, and the boys and girls of our workers a knowledge of the true principles of political economy [was] the surest method of preventing strikes and their numerous attendant evils [and of] securing to them those blessings which attend provident habits and an economical expenditure of wages'. Pickersgill concludes, 'in other words, that the purpose of educating the working classes was to make them compliant employees at work, upright citizens at home and to instill in them a passive acceptance of the economic and social order.'

Working men's clubs had a similar genesis, developing in Northern England, Wales and the Midlands in the late nineteenth century as places where men – and only men – could attend lectures, read and play games. They arose from the temperance movement and in the beginning didn't serve alcohol. They soon evolved though into that curious beast of my youth that was part pub, part music hall, part leisure and community centre. Being allowed to go to 'the club', Poolstock Labour, Newtown 'Workers', was always a huge thrill. Although by anyone's standards, they must have been Spartan and basic, even the Formica and cigarette smoke, snooker tables, silvery stage curtains and the rest had a kind of secret, elusive glamour to a child.

The Reverend Henry Solly founded the Working Men's Club and Institute Union (CIU) in 1862 and, though their heyday is gone, you will see the CIU logo on – and use your CIU card for admittance to – many such clubs all across the north. To be part of the CIU was to be 'affiliated', a catchphrase said with oozing northern relish by Colin Crompton as club secretary on TV's fictional *The Wheeltappers and Shunters Social Club*. That an affectionate parody-cum-full-scale-recreation of a night out at a northern working man's club could be a primetime seventies TV mainstay shows just how socially significant these clubs were, as well as just how much TV has changed.

In the background at the Wheeltappers lurked the shadowy cabal called 'the committee', a politburo of men who met in rooms choked with blue smoke to discuss club business. Wedded to the democratic principles of those old lefty founding fathers, or perhaps because it mirrors the power structures of their bosses and is a sort of 'dressing up', the workers have always loved a committee, and like nothing more than convening meetings, taking minutes or making a 'point of order, Mr Chairman'.

There were only two people at the inaugural meeting of the Association to Promote the Higher Education of Working Men on 16 May 1903. Albert Mansbridge and Frances, his wife, met in their terraced house in Battersea with Frances famously contributing 2s 6d from her housekeeping money as a working fund. In what can't have been a close fought election, Albert was voted 'Hon. Secretary *pro tem*'. Two years later, there were a thousand people at a meeting in Birmingham in which the organisation was renamed the rather more progressive sounding Workers' Educational Association.

Down the years, the WEA has had its critics. It's been loathed by the right, naturally, as it seeks to empower working people. But it's also been lambasted by more po-faced elements of the left for filling the heads of the proletariat with useless bourgeois book learning. It seeks to integrate them into society as it stands, in all its inequality, and distracts them from the proper business of barricade building and brick lobbing. I always think that if you can manage to annoy zealots of both persuasions you must be doing something right. But then I am probably biased. When I was out of a job in the mid-1980s, the WEA put some work my way and thus I spent several mornings a week in a cheap suit telling redundant textile workers about the joys of R D Laing and Philip Larkin.

Larkin probably hated the WEA; or he would at least have pretended to. He'd have written obscene and vituperative letters to Kingsley Amis about it. I think – and I realise that this is what is called being an 'apologist' – several of Larkin's more unpalatable 'opinions' were probably affected to annoy Terry Eagleton and the Marxist critics who held academic sway in the eighties, or at least exaggerated after a couple of stiff gins just to amuse himself and Kingsley. Clive James put it another way, and more beautifully, when he said that he probably 'disliked multiculturalism because it altered his bolt-hole version of England, and that he could no more stand alteration than an institutionalized prisoner can stand being issued with a new cup.'

But, assembled together between two covers – as they were by Anthony Thwaite in 1992 – those many, many letters offered us a lurid picture of a 'hang em and flog em' reactionary, closet racist and splenetic Thatcherite. Odd, then, that he should spend most of his productive life in Hull, a tough northern town famed for its fish and chips, rugby league and pugnacious socialist politics, literally on the glorious occasion when Hullite John Prescott thumped that Tory farmer with the mullet who threw an egg at him.

Larkin didn't automatically take to the place. After three weeks there, he wrote to a friend, 'Yes, I'm settling down in Hull all right. Each day I sink a little further.' Four months later, he was even more forthright, 'God, what a hole, what witless crapulous people, delivered over gagged and bound to TV, motoring and Mackeson's stout ... a frightful dump.' But slowly he began to love it, or at least to respect it, and would offer up occasional and muted praise; 'as good a place to write in as any' he wrote in the foreword to an anthology of Hull poets and continued 'Hull has its own sudden elegancies'.

In 2013, Hull was named UK City of Culture for 2017, provoking the expected snickering in some quarters. The leader of the campaign of rival bidder Swansea was cheap and ungracious, saying the people of Hull would 'at last have something to look forward to' and even those you'd have thought would be sympathetic, like Prestonian cricket legend Andrew Flintoff, tweeted, 'It's not April Fool's Day is it?'

What Larkin would have made of it, we will never know. Neither can we know whether we would have been amused, delighted or horrified by one of Hull's latest cultural attractions, the Philip Larkin trail. This is, to quote the literature, 'not only a literary journey, but also journeys through diverse landscapes and rich architecture and, seeing the city through a poet's eyes, to gain a philosophical view of the place where Larkin lived and worked for three decades.' He came here at 32 and was Hull's university librarian from 1955 until his death in 1985. Hull was also home to another great post-war poet, Douglas Dunn. Stevie Smith was born and raised here, and both Roger McGough and former poet laureate Andrew Motion studied at the university in the Larkin era. Peter Porter, the great Australian verse-smith (yes, I know but there's only so many times I can say 'poet') said Hull was 'the most poetic city in England'.

It's appropriate that it was the need to earn a crust that brought Larkin here, since no one has ever written better about the daily routines and strictures of work. As one of his many biographers James Booth said of him 'Larkin is virtually alone among 20th-century poets in writing in a natural, first-hand way about work in the sense of paid employment'. He wrote about it with a kind of grudging tenderness in poems like the famous 'Toads', although in a scribbled verse in one of his letters to lover Monica Jones, he was less equivocal:

Morning, noon & bloody night,
Seven sodding days a week,
I slave at filthy WORK, that might
Be done by any book-drunk freak.
This goes on until I kick the bucket.
FUCK IT FUCK IT FUCK IT FUCK IT.

Of his adopted city, Larkin seems to have liked the fact that Hull was a city that rolled its sleeves up 'a working city, yet one neither clenched in the blackened grip of the industrial revolution nor hiding behind a cathedral to pretend it is York or Canterbury'. Hull has no beauteous cathedral but it has something to my mind just as gorgeous and stately, the Humber Bridge.

I arrive in the city at dusk, and the magnificent span is stark and monumental against the darkening sky, a ribbon of lights and passing traffic. When it opened in 1981 it was the longest bridge of its kind in the world, linking some of the most remote and inaccessible areas of England. Larkin relished Hull's isolation, famously saying that when journalists decided to venture up to doorstep him, once they'd seen how awkward it was to get to Hull, they'd stay on the train and bother fellow poet Basil Bunting in Newcastle instead.

Larkin's first volume of poems was published by a DIY publishing house called Marvell Press, run by a couple of twentysomethings from a terraced in Hessle, a small ferry port now in the shadow of the Humber Bridge. On the opposite bank, at the actual foot of the bridge, south of the estuary in Barton upon Humber, is another fabulous example of what can be done with the dereliction left by retreating industry and political neglect – if you have talented and hardworking people determined not to let their towns stagnate. Barton is a fine town anyway, once a major medieval port, and prosperous and busy throughout the Georgian and Victorian period as you can see from the architecture. But one of its pride and joys (and major employers) was Hall's Barton Ropery down in Waterside. They sent ropes all over the world from here – to the shipping lines, then as vital equipment in two world wars and then to the mining industry, until that was destroyed in the 1980s. After that, the ropeworks struggled and was finally bought and asset-stripped by a competitor.

The ropeworks languished until, in 1999, an artist called Liz Bennet and some likeminded souls turned it into what is now: artists' studios, venue, theatre school, museum, exhibition space and a brilliant café in what is a truly unique place. Ropes can't be made round corners so they needed space. The Ropewalk at Barton is the longest listed building in Britain, a quarter of a mile long but just 30 feet wide; rope-shaped, in fact. If you're in the area, drop in. Over the bridge from Hessle to Barton, turn right into Waterside, you can't miss it.

Several legions of French folk are enjoying a trip across the Humber on the night I come to town. Supporters of the Catalan Dragons from Perpignan, the only team from outside England in the English rugby Super League, are trooping down Clive Sullivan Way, named after a former Hull player of legend. Hull itself has two Super League teams, Hull and Hull Kingston Rovers, or Hull K R as they are known. The existence of two big teams in the one town tells you how serious the north takes its rugby league. But it's also simply a fascinating quirk, throwing up the questions all local derbies in the ball sports do for me. Who supports who? Why? What informs the choice? Family? The part of town you grew up in? Religion? Class even? Is the Hull rivalry cordial like Liverpool's or corrosive like Glasgow's? One of the fiercest, not to say poisonous football rivalries I know of is between Witton Albion and Northwich Victoria, next door neighbours in a little Cheshire town. No, me neither.

I'm headed for the Royal Station Hotel because, well, I like old school railway hotels in our industrial cities, and also what better place to base myself for my Larkin Trail than a hotel he wrote a poem about. 'Friday Night At The Royal Station Hotel' is about work, about transience and boredom, and the melancholy passing of time in our cities.

... the dining-room declares
A larger loneliness of knives and glass
And silence laid like carpet. A porter reads
An unsold evening paper. Hours pass,
And all the salesmen have gone back to Leeds,
Leaving full ashtrays in the Conference Room.

The tone is morose and everyday, typically Larkin, but it concludes with a flourish that is Larkin too, an image that pulls you up short with its mystery and grandeur.

Night comes on. Waves fold behind villages.

Larkin described this old Hull landmark as 'isolated ... like a fort', but tonight it glitters. The salesmen may have gone back to Leeds but the well-heeled of Hull have come out to what used to be rather quaintly called a 'dinner dance'. The bar is filling up with couples in tuxedos and cocktail frocks. Most are middle-aged, striking women with Friday hairdos, husbands pulling at their tightened collars or fiddling with unfamiliar and constricting dickie bows. One or two though are in their twenties. Perhaps he is trying to impress her with adult sophistication, to woo her with his easy familiarity with the wine list and the fish knives, while other suitors stick to Nando's. Good luck to him, I think. One woman in sheer satin and clicking heels slips past me and out through the revolving doors to have a smoke on the glistening pavements on what has become a filthy night. It takes commitment to be a smoker (or a vaper) in the north these days. In my smoking day, you could do it anywhere. Now it is as proscribed and furtive as drinking meths or sniffing glue.

As the night is foul, but I don't fancy the dinner dancing crowds in the restaurant, I dash across the road to an Indian restaurant. I get the last table in the house, which is actually for ten people. Ludicrously, I sit there at the head of the restaurant, alone and splendidly isolated, like some seventeenth-century monarch at Versailles or a nutty dictator or the King of Hull. The service moves at glacial speed with the waiter occasionally lapsing into both French and Spanish for no reason I can fathom. The whole thing feels like one of Buñuel's craziest movies.

Dabbing the last of the distinctly average bhuna from my lips, I re-enter the Royal Hotel. The mood is more raucous now, the volume higher, the ties askew and the pinching shoes kicked off. The lady who slipped out for the smoke is looking decidedly out of it, slumped on a banquette, eyes rolling wildly. Is she ill or just hammered? It's hard to say. Paramedics have arrived and one, a small balding man in black paramilitary outfit with red scissors tucked into his armband, is being infinitely patient and gentle, stroking her cheek, looking into her eyes, one imagines to see whether it's just alcohol that's the problem. Eventually they steer her protectively out to the ambulance and I am once again glad to be part of a nanny state. It occurs now that the kindly paramedic and his skilful colleagues may soon be out of a job.

It's the dregs of the evening, the foamy end of the pint. Everyone is florid and unfocused, blurry and boozy. The men are shouting and the ladies are shrill. The prim choreography of earlier is now a scrum of staggering and wobbling, unsteady men holding out winter coats for ladies who miss the sleeve every time in burlesque drunk fashion. When the African cleaners start to arrive, models of melancholy poise by contrast, I decide it's time to take my well-thumbed copy of Larkin's *High Windows* to bed and bring my Friday night in the Royal Station Hotel to a close.

Next day I breakfast at Café M, a classic greasy spoon of the kind I have much time for. Sundry generations pile in for Saturday breakfast, and one old chap in flat cap and muffler seems to be the Don Corleone of the place. People stop by his table to pass on well-wishes, grasp his hand, pat his shoulder, as he works his way steadily through the Pensioner Special Full English Breakfast (£3.95). Some even crouch by the table to confer with him. I once sat next to Terry

Wogan at the Sony Awards and it was a bit like this. All the black clad waitresses are Polish, naturally. Mine is from the shipyards of Gdańsk. She must feel at home in the fresh salt air and harbours of Hull, where the townsfolk call themselves Codheads.

I've decided to use the Larkin Trail roughly rather than religiously, and let it lead me around Hull as I see fit. Walking down the street as I leave Café M, a man comes out of a lighting store with a large pink elephant under his arm. This naturally grabs my attention. 'I'm not stealing it,' he shouts across the road to me. 'It's my shop. It's pink to distinguish it from all the bloody white ones I've got in there.' I take it trade has been better.

In 2003, in a poll conducted in a book called *Crap Towns*, Hull was deemed the crappest. Being partisan – come on, you'd noticed, hadn't you – I'm always looking for metropolitan snobbery in such stuff, the same snooty disdain that fills the restaurant review pages of the posh papers when Aubrey can't get decent meze or gravadlax in Crewe when he's changing trains. Well maybe it was crap in 2003 but it certainly isn't now. The Hull I'm playing the poetry flaneur in this crisp Saturday morning is a handsome town with wide streets, big, bold squares and little cobbled alleyways called staithes. The Museum Quarter has branded itself MQ and has eight free galleries. I am much taken by the giant mosaic toad, a nod to Larkin's classic poem 'Toads', outside the Streetlife Museum. A plaque by the sculpture says 'initial concept' by Sue Meritt. Hmm, initial concept by Philip Larkin surely?

The museum is a powerful reminder of something I touched on earlier; how lively our streets once were. The attendant says to me, 'Funny the things we once took for granted,' and I know exactly what he means. The craftsmanship and care invested in these everyday accoutrements of a bygone age are evident. The trolleybus and steam trains are works of art, especially a mahogany and teak one with carvings of grapes known as the Grapes bus. The Morris Minor van, even the tins in the shop window, glow with a patina that's more than just nostalgia – Merrills Custard Power, Grenville blancmange, the buttered Brazils. All of it reminds me of something Larkin once said about his work: 'I don't want to transcend the commonplace, I love the commonplace. Everyday things are lovely to me.'

There's a great picture gallery of Hull through the ages. In this one, two kids loll on a doorstep. It's taken in 1977 but it could have come from the thirties. Here's one of Hull's most famous and best-loved sons, the late Mick Ronson of Bowie's Spiders from Mars, in pear drop collar and floral jacket. A little girl comes up to me as I'm making notes and her mum intervenes, 'Don't disturb him, cuddles, he's working.' She gives the child a handful of sweets and then says, 'Blood sugar levels having been restored, we shall go on our way.'

Outside the museum is one of Hull's signature sights, a cream phone box. When all the UK's other exchanges and private telephony companies were absorbed into British Telecom, Hull's municipally owned provider, Kingston Communications, remained obstinately and curiously independent. Thus it has its own exchange, its distinctive phone boxes and 'really shit internet', as one disgruntled local told me. He told me this in the bar of the Ye Olde Black Boy, part of the Larkin trail and one of the Hull pubs he liked an occasional drink in. Ye Olde Black Boy is a dark and intimate cave of a place where Larkin, a huge jazz fan, would come and talk music with his Hull mates, and where he once gave a talk in the back room on one of his heroes, the clarinettist Pee Wee Russell. The pale, sullen girl behind the counter can't do me a coffee and so, even though it's the middle of the day, I make do with a single malt. She brightens when a lanky boy comes in and hands her a catering pack of Twix. 'You're a star,' she says breathlessly and with wholly unnecessary gratitude. I detect a subtext. 'Did you have a good night?' he asks taking up position alongside her behind the bar. She rolls her eyes. 'Don't ask!' I wish he would, at least while I'm in earshot.

A man comes in and tells Twix Boy (who is quite posh and I guess a student supplementing his non-existent grant) a very long and involved anecdote about how he once appeared fondling some root vegetables in a Sainsbury's advert. The boy, I have to say, does an admirable job of feigning rapt absorption in the tale. I wonder what Larkin, an old school trad jazz buff with conservative tastes, would have made of the wildly eclectic selection of music: Arcade Fire, Chuck Berry, old Motown, Roxy Music and Barbra Streisand. Two couples come in muffled against the cold. 'We don't want a drink,' they say apologetically. 'We're just old students reminiscing.' I picture them 40 years before, shaggy haired and cheese-clothed, smoking roll-ups, and putting Zep and Carole King on the jukebox.

On my travels, I visit a few more significant Larkin spots such as the branch of M&S, a slick modern wonder in the early sixties, that inspired his poem 'The Large Cool Store'. A plaque by the lifts near the lingerie features the text. As the afternoon turns towards dusk, and the lights come on at four, and the streets ebb and flow with shoppers and workers, I conclude that I like Hull a lot. It's bold and characterful with that air of self-sufficiency and rakishness that ports often have. Alexei Sayle once said of it 'it doesn't feel like an English city, or like anywhere else, at all. It feels like an enclave of itself … It's a fascinating city, on the road to nowhere and at the end of the line – it's isolated and self-contained without being insular or unwelcoming.' I know exactly what he means. Like Liverpool, with which it has much in common, it doesn't seek to blend in. It's very much its own place.

I liked the Land of Green Ginger and Pearson Park. I liked the pubs and the cranes and the boats. I liked the landscape. If you follow the longer version of the Larkin Trail, you'll end up in the more isolated landscape to the west, where Larkin enjoyed cycling around the scattered villages along the Humber estuary, such as Broomfleet.

In the end, you'll come to the 'unfenced existence' of Holderness plain and the striking, desolate peninsula of Spurn Point, where Larkin would sometimes come to look back at the town and find the words to sing its praises in that Eeyorish voice. In 1399, the usurping

Henry IV landed here from France en route to dethrone Richard II, who he later imprisoned and starved to death. There's nothing to mark this historic event since the entire port of Ravenspurn has disappeared, claimed by the North Sea. But Larkin has fared better.

Leaving Hull by train, you pass a statue of him on the concourse, looking like a cross between Jean-Paul Sartre and Eric Morecambe, comic and melancholic in his owlish glasses and drab raincoat. On the train I chat to a nice chap called John whose hands, marked with various little nicks and wounds, suggest that he's a carpenter which, pleasingly for my detective skills, he turns out to be (OK, a picture framer and wood turner, close enough). But his passion is board games and he enthuses to me about one he's invented. It's called Iceflow, it won best British board game five years ago and he's now trying to sell around the world. 'The French loved it. They talked of its *mouvement perpétuelle*. They loved it at the Essen games show. But we've had some setbacks. We lost a container full of them en route from Chicago. There's 150,000 blue plastic icebergs somewhere on the seven seas. Tiny ones obviously.'

He's now working on a game about money and dynasties in the Middle Ages. 'There was no credit creation then, so there was a finite amount of money in the world. And it'll play out just like the real history did. Every five years something will happen so you have to plan for that. You know, Jerusalem will fall so if you're king of Jerusalem you have to plan for it. You know the Mongols will sack Baghdad. You're just going to have to deal with it.'

We look out across the flat Eastern plain and Larkin's 'shining gull-marked mud' to the Humber estuary and inland to Beverley and Goole. Larkin loved its flatness because he loved to cycle its deserted lanes. 'Hull is so flat,' says John, 'that they say the only exercise the Codheads get is visiting their elderly relatives on the ninth floor of the Royal Infirmary where they put the oldies.' He says that, though the town was once rich, money is ebbing away from the centre out to the suburbs and that there are only ten higher rate tax players within the city boundaries. 'Hull's an island … and sometimes being an island is good for you, and sometimes it's not.'

Encouraging people to come and visit post-industrial northern towns, and alerting townspeople to the cultural heritage on their doorstep, is what initiatives like the Larkin Trail is all about. The Pennine village of Haworth boasts several Brontë trails, of course, and for 3,000 bucks or so, one American firm will even take you on a Brontë tour of England. Walkabout Leeds shows off the city's superb civic architecture.

You could have made an educated guess that the Larkin Trail would be in the poet's adopted Yorkshire home. But you'd probably not put the L S Lowry Trail in Northumberland's Berwick-upon-Tweed, he being the visual laureate of the streets and people of industrial Lancashire. But Berwick is where The Lowry Trail is and, not least because I never got quite this far north in *Pies and Prejudice*, I set forth for this town on the Tweed.

Berwick has had divided loyalties and ownership for centuries, its place on the border between England and Scotland has meant that its history has been complex, shifting and extremely bloody. It has changed hands between England and Scotland 13 times, sometimes peacefully (as in when Richard III sold it to fund the Crusades) but usually with a great deal of associated violence. According to legend, it was the devil's own holiday bolthole. When he was tempting Christ by showing him all the treasures of the earth that could be his if he'd just lighten up a little, 'he kept Berwick hidden beneath his thumb, wishing to reserve it as his own little nook.'

I could see at once why the old rascal might want to keep it to himself. One's feelings for a place are often coloured by how one arrives. People tell me that Worksop is a nice town but when I was a kid we once drove into town behind a stinking dustcart and then had a grim sandwich in an awful backstreet boozer. So I've never been back. (Happy to rectify this, Worksop Tourist Board!) Arriving in Berwick in the crimson of a winter dusk, the silver moon large and low over the majestic ink-black Tweed, which swirls and eddies under ancient bridges, I am instantly enchanted and a little spooked.

The town feels sweet, somnolent and slightly weird. Gulls cry and church bells peal, and interiors are being lit against the coming dark. I spot a shadowy figure in the lamp-lit back alcove of a bookshop and a tired looking waitress blowing out the last of the candles in a tea shop. The pubs of the town are all very different. The Brown Bear has several tellies, bawling kids standing on chairs and shaven-headed men smoking sourly in the little alley by the side. It doesn't exactly exude a hearty welcome. The Barrels is funkier and more genteel. The pine is scrubbed, the fire is lit and couples in Gore-Tex cradle real ales and Soaves as they pore over OS maps in the window seat. Someone – a friend of the owner surely at this hour – is getting her hair cut in the Saddlery while two young lads on bikes practise wheelies by a tugboat. Some of the streets are as ghostly as the grave but a couple of cafés are still selling hot crab sandwiches and soup. It reminds me of the seaside town in Robert Aickman's unsettling short story 'Ringing the Changes' which I urge you to read (after you've finished this book, of course), and for that and other reasons I decide I'm going to like it.

Two of our great cultural touchstones, The Beatles and Charles Dickens, have both stayed here in Berwick, according to the plaques on my hotel wall on Hide Hill. 'Dickens gave a reading out there apparently,' says the rather sleepy lad from Newcastle pointing into a small tidy garden. How long has this place been here? 'Hundreds of years. Me? Three months.' Are you going to stay? 'I don't know. It's very quiet after Newcastle …' and he drifts into a reverie, perhaps of giddy nights in the Bigg Market and crates of 'Newkie Brown'.

Many people have a special place that lures them back year after year, their own kind of magical anchor in the turning year. For some it's an event like Glastonbury, the Hay literary festival or the TT Races, or it may be a haunt from your childhood still beloved – a favourite Cumbrian lake or Cotswold village. Writer Caitlin Moran goes to Aberystwyth for a week every summer and stays in the same place and eats in the same cafés on the same days. For the great English painter L S Lowry, it was Berwick.

The fact that, like Larkin, Lowry had a day job and rooted his art in working communities led the salon mandarins of the art world to dismiss him as an unschooled amateur. This irritated him. 'If people call me a Sunday painter I'm a Sunday painter who paints every day of the week!' Much of the hostility to his work came and still comes from his subject matter; the grimy streets and hovels of urban Lancashire were not thought of as worthy of artistic repesentation by some critics, especially not in such a seemingly spare and untutored way …

Others were more far-sighted. Art critic Herbert Read said, 'No one else to my knowledge has been so sensitively aware of the poetry of the English industrial landscape.' Once a year though Lowry would leave those bleak, urban wastelands, those cramped and cobbled streets and looming factories that he immortalised, and take himself even further north. Every summer, from early 1932 till he died in 1976, he would pack his easel and oils and come for his week in Berwick. Lowry loved the sea and found this little historic town charming. He stayed at the Castle Hotel by the railway station and produced about 30 paintings and drawings of Berwick during his visits. Now there is a Lowry Trail, which takes in the scenes from most of these, marked by interpretive boards. Armed with my Lowry Trail leaflet, I seek out a café to plot my route.

Thistle Do Nicely! How horribly twee I thought your name was when I came across it on Trip Advisor, and how blinkered and wrong I was. I love your haggis and cheese toastie, your delicious apple crumble and your even more delicious staff, whose accents, pitched between gentle lowland Scots and rough, warm Geordie, are as welcoming as the food. A young mum is feeding a massive BLT to her little girl, who in turn feeds bits to her tiny stuffed animal. John, dapper in his cap and cardie, says he's chipped his tooth and he'll have his scone 'here today rather than to take out', and is given it with solicitous, loving care from beneath the Perspex cake cover. Two prim but elegant Scots ladies have asked for apple crumble. 'Large or small?' the owner asks. 'Small … but not too small,' comes the reply. When one nips to the loo, the other puts on some lippy beneath a poster with Berwick Rangers fixtures. They are known as the 'Wee Gers', in unnecessary deference to the louder Glaswegian namesakes whom they famously beat in the Scottish Cup of 1967 (remembered still in The Barrels and The Black Bull I bet). And as every pub quiz veteran knows, the Wee Gers are unique, the only English team to play in the Scottish League.

Lowry, it seems, loved, drew or painted every aspect of the town, from bustling street and yard scenes to eerie seascapes, from austere architectural compositions to busy evocations of fun on the beaches. His first painting of the town was the High Street in 1935, and was included in his first London exhibition. Even by then, his standing was such that it was priced at 30 guineas, about £1,000 today. The painting is reproduced on a board up on the city walls overlooking Marygate. The scene has hardly changed in the last century or so, although in this and other pictures he made of the scene, Lowry distorts reality and exaggerates dimensions slightly but unnervingly. The Spire with its clock like a Cyclops eye is higher than in reality, and the famous stick figures seem to be lured irresistibly towards it for some obscure purpose.

In Lowry's paintings, there are often monoliths, towers, lamp-posts and other solitary symbols, which naturally commentators claim reflect his own isolated existence. Lowry was a strange man all right. Withdrawn and blunt to the point of rudeness, he nonetheless loathed snobbery ('All my life I have felt most strongly against social distinction of any kind,' he wrote to Harold Wilson, turning down his offer of a knighthood). He was cagey, capricious, flirtatious even, which in turn brings up the murky matter of sex. Lowry is assumed to have died virgo intacta and once said, 'I have never know passion.' But his close Lewis Carroll-ish friendships with teenage girls and the paintings of doll-like women in restrictive and fetishistic clothing that came to light after his death, suppressed like Goya's Black Paintings, throw up unanswered questions, some of a disquieting nature.

A walk along the ramparts to the sea is the perfect way to clear the head of all this. As well as L S Lowry, and its tiny dual-citizenship football club and the fact that technically it's still at war with Russia over the Crimea (Berwick was accidently left off the peace treaty, as one might leave Marmite off a shopping list), Berwick has another claim to fame. Six hundred years ago, Berwick was the most fortified town in Europe, thanks to the series of bastions and ramparts built by the Virgin Queen. Now a playground for tourists and walkers, then these were the most sophisticated defence technology in the world, costing more than every other civil project of Elizabeth I's reign altogether. Walking these ramparts and moats, you achieve a sense of how Lowry saw the town in his day with the views across the roofs and spires and cloistered squares, down Castlegate and Marygate, into the picture postcard town centre. But also how the soldiers of the sixteenth century and beyond would have seen it as they crisscrossed the walls in gales and rain, manning the gun emplacements, peering into the North Sea murk for successive enemies, the French, the Scots, the Jacobites.

Nowadays it's much quieter. I find a couple of beer cans and Alcopops bottles which suggest that it's a nocturnal hang out for what gets awkwardly referred to as 'the youth' on phone-ins. Here, where they may once have poured boiling oil on French corsairs or Scottish raiders, a woman with a buggy is chatting to her neighbour in the street below, near the Co-op. I drop down to where they are and turn up by the sign that says 'To The Cliffs' just by the shop selling Edinburgh Rock, Irn-Bru and 'See You Jimmy!' hats which seems both ludicrously dated and pretty courageous this close to the border. I walk up past the Women's Institute whose array of coming attractions dazzles – a Pie and Peas supper, 'Relax and Unwind With Aromatherapy', 'Scott Weightman talks about his Russian travels', 'Cheese making workshop', 'Argentinean tango and Alzheimer's café'. The WI have shed some of their genteel image since they mildly savaged a hapless Tony Blair a few years back. I gave a talk to the Eden Valley WI last year and had a lot of fun, although oddly I can't remember now a word of what I said. This may have been because of the anxiety brought on when I realised that, in order not to offend, I would have to sample each of the 30 or so buffet items hand cooked by the ladies. It was hell.

Across Golden Square and up Walkergate onto Wallace Green. This seems to be the ecclesiastical centre of town with churches to suit all tastes; a tiny, unpretentious Methodist one, a big Church of Scotland, a Catholic and even a Cromwellian Church, which bills itself 'the most northerly Church Of England' and 'one of the first and only English churches in the unadorned Presbyterian style'. I expect if I looked hard enough I'd find a ziggurat and a Shinto temple.

In her excellent biography of Lowry, Shelley Rohde suggests that his affection for Berwick was not just artistic. He claimed to have 'got to know some people' here, which hints to me at a romantic infatuation, and thought about moving here permanently. But Rohde also thinks he'd also just had his fill of cobbles and chimneys, and had seen a nice house he liked by the sea he was fascinated with. I'm standing in front of it now. It's called The Lions and while I can see that the views across beach and ramparts and waves must have been stunning, especially at sunrise and sunset, the house itself is more than a little creepy – a melancholic, isolated structure on the Elizabethan wall that had fallen derelict in the last years of Lowry's life. In fact, it came to resemble one of my favourite of Lowry's paintings, 'The Empty House', a work so pregnant with gloom and regret that you wonder if critics of the Brian Sewell school who snigger at Lowry's 'ineptness' and 'tedium' can have ever seen it, or indeed any of his paintings.

Lowry said of his own work, I think with a hint of Morrissey's self-mythologising irony, 'Poverty and gloom. Never a joyous picture of mine … I never do a jolly picture.' But the beach scenes he painted at Berwick seem full of simple delight. 'Spittal Sands' is thronged with brightly clothed children having fun, errant dogs and sandcastles.

But look a little closer, and the washed out figures look spectral, like wraiths, and walk a little further, drawn by the sea as Lowry was, and the mood alters. At the end of the long, unadorned, stone pier is a lighthouse which becomes in Lowry's composition no longer the maritime decoration you see in the prints on Cornish pub walls but a lonely and inscrutable sentinel. Beyond that is the sea itself.

'Once you have seen a Lowry painting of the sea, you will then never see the sea again in the same way,' said Ian McKellen in 2004. He's right, and you will also never see Lowry in the same way. Vast, haunting and somehow monumental, they have something of an obsession about them, as if the artist were compelled to paint these scenes almost beyond his own understanding. He said it was simply boredom but he is being mischievous again. Friends testify to his habit of sitting for hours staring out to sea.

Seemingly empty of meaning, his seascapes in fact teem with philosophical weight. Like the silences of Ingmar Bergman or Harold Pinter, or the stillness of Frederic Mompou's piano pieces, the very absence of incident and detail is what speaks so profoundly. They compel you to view them and Lowry in a different way. Shelley Rohde commented that they are 'of such power that to look at them is to risk drowning in the depth of their mystery. The sea' she continued:

> ... absorbed and thrilled him. It was something he remem-
> bered, with a fascination bordering on obsession, all his life.
> He saw in the inexorable ebb and flow of the tides the same
> vain struggle for survival that possessed the people among
> whom he was to live and work. It was a theme to which he
> would return, and return again, all his life.

L S Lowry himself said:

> It's the battle of life – the turbulence of the sea – and life's
> pretty turbulent, isn't it? I am very fond of the sea; how

wonderful it is, yet how terrible it is. But I often think …
what if it suddenly changed its mind and didn't turn the tide?
And came straight on? If it didn't stop and came on and on
and on and on. That would be the end of it all.

So, the sea is calling. I'm heading up over the Elizabethan walls to the
cliffs that face its huge indifference. On the ridge, there's a golf course
where a few bedraggled men are whacking balls about. Tiny figures
absorbed in their funny game on the fifteenth green, dwarfed by the
sheer and eroded cliffs and the grey immensity of the North Sea.
There's something profound here to speculate on, but my attention
is distracted by a man with a huge Alsatian dog. He's throwing a ball
for the beast using one of those plastic ball holder things that stop you
having to bend down. But he's throwing the whole thing, not just
the ball, thus defeating the whole object of the bloody contraption. I
wonder if I should tell him, but he might take it the wrong way, and
he does have an Alsatian.

After the northernmost tee, the course gives out, just as the day
is starting to give out – the last of the weak sun failing to penetrate
the gloomy sheltered bays scalloped in the cliffs above the beach,
that's deserted today. The forlorn golf club house has a couple of cars
parked outside, maybe someone nursing a cheering whisky. Looking
back to the town, you see the higher buildings peeping up above
ramparts. In the other direction is a sheltered little beach which must
ring with kids' voices in high summer. But today it is all spray and
white horses and looking at the grey and indistinct skyline you don't
think of sundaes or beach balls but the prows of longships coming
over the horizon.

With rain in the breeze, I head back to town through the faux
streets and avenues of a deserted caravan park. The storms have
scattered the bins around, leaving a flotsam of foam chip trays and
cans of Irn-Bru and chocolate bar wrappers. 'There are no valuables
in this caravan and the alarm is on' says a sign outside 'Rio'. It's

maintenance season; a young man in blue overalls is taking away the Calor gas heaters and his mate with a roller tray of white paint nods as he passes me. Two girls are filming what must be some college project or arthouse short, and I walk up past to the basketball court and back into the outskirts of Berwick past a huge stone structure where a plaque reads 'Sounding the Alarm' and tells me that here Elizabeth's armies and the good burghers of Berwick would scan the seas for the approaching enemy. It was built 1577, last rung in 1683, and is the only example of Elizabethan tower like this in Britain.

Lowry would spend hours just wandering around Berwick. 'My recreation seems to have developed into drifting among all the back streets etc I can come across,' he said. In honour of my esteemed Lancashire forbearer, I do the same, ending up in a separate part of town called the Greenses with its own little harbour. This was home to the sea fishermen of the Greenses and their families and, until the First World War, was cut off from the rest of Berwick-upon-Tweed by the Elizabethan Walls and formed a separate neighbourhood. The intermingling of locals with Flemish, Portuguese, French and Spanish sailors meant that people from this little enclave, bearded and swarthy, were known as the Greenses Arabs, as the Sunday League football team still is according to the fixture list in the Pilot Inn. I pop in but don't stay long, just in time for a quick Laphroaig at the bar where three men, silent and sullen, sip their pints and are watching some Swiss Bobsleigh race meeting, presumably on Sky Sports 18, on a giant screen.

When I leave, the lights are coming on in Berwick, and the gulls are wheeling overhead and the sea mist is turning to rain. It would be the time of day when Laurence Stephen Lowry would pack up his easel and head back to the Castle Hotel for a glass of something warming, and maybe an evening with that mysterious person 'that he had got to know'.

It has taken a long time for that bastion of British art, the Tate, to lose its prejudices again Lowry. Was it that they feared nothing that was so loved by ordinary folk could truly be any good? Is he really no good? Or is that those cripples, strikes, evictions, football matches, factory chimneys and fever vans baffled and disturbed them, speaking of a world far beyond Francis Bacon's Soho, the French House and the Coach and Horses? The world I like to think of as the Old Weird North.

Though it's never easy for a Lancastrian to acknowledge Yorkshire broadmindedness and generosity, Yorkshire has had no petty Trans-Pennine prejudices here. Lowrys have always been welcomed into its major galleries to sit alongside its favourite sons and daughters such as Barbara Hepworth and Henry Moore. They may be miserable buggers but they know a thing or two about art. I'm joking of course. Of course I am.

In this, they've been nurtured down the years by an admirable civic attitude to culture. Alan Bennett has written warmly of his early visits to Armley Public Library and Leeds City Art Gallery where he first came across Sickert and the Camden Town Group and of Leeds Central Library's grand old reference section. Opera North in Leeds and Huddersfield's support for contemporary and experimental music are subjects we'll return to, and from adopted tyke P Larkin to Simon Armitage to Helen Mort to Peter Sansom, the county has bloody poets coming out of its ears.

One of them is Ian McMillan. It was he who told me about Sir Alec Clegg, Chief Education Officer of the West Riding County Council from 1945–74. It was a long, distinguished reign in which he helped raise several generations of Yorkshire writers, musicians and painters, teachers, doctors, sportsmen and administrators as well as miners, butchers, bakers and candlestick makers to know and care about the arts and not think it a world 'not for them'.

Clegg oversaw an education system that completely rejected the notion that urban kids were nothing more than factory fodder. It placed art, craft, music, drama and sport at the heart of the curriculum. He also encouraged an interest in social history, and a belief that their own communities' past was as relevant and significant as the doing of kings and queens. He wasn't afraid of the avant-garde and wanted kids introduced to modern art, experimental music, challenging literature. Clegg's achievements were many but one of the most justly celebrated was the creation of Bretton Hall. This was maybe the centre of alternative and creative thought in the north, a teacher training college with innovative courses in design, music and the visual and performance arts that eventually spawned the world renowned Yorkshire Sculpture Park and whose alumni include John Godber, Colin Welland, Kay Mellor and three of the four *League of Gentlemen*, Mark Gatiss, Steve Pemberton and Reece Shearsmith.

Clegg's office, its walls festooned with children's art, was in Wakefield, the administrative capital of the West Riding of Yorkshire. The name would probably fall like a stone into polite southern company. It sounds defiantly northern, like a factory hooter or a Viking curse. Even though it has given its name to Oliver Goldsmith's genial vicar and a lovely New England town, it still evokes scrums and mills and collars turned up against the wind. And hopefully modern art.

Barbara Hepworth, probably the greatest female British artist of the twentieth century, was born and raised in Wakefield where her dad was a civil engineer. She went to the girls' high school in the town and then Leeds School of Art where she met friend (and cordial rival) Henry Moore, alongside whom she would forge a new modernist style of sculpture. After the Royal College of Art, the 21-year-old Hepworth travelled to Florence to work and study. She had no wealthy patron, no trust funds, no rich family (though she did possess an accent that the Queen would have thought 'cut glass'). What she had was a West Riding Travel Scholarship. This was in 1924 when Britain was a great deal poorer and more ravaged than it is today, and yet somehow more civilised.

I'm reading up on Dame Barbara, as she became (none of Lowry's egalitarian misgivings here), on the train from Manchester to Wakefield. I've certainly got enough time. There's much debate, heated and knotty, about the pros and cons of the controversial HS2 rail 'improvements' to north and central England. Discretion being the better part of valour, I've no intention of wading into this, but it does seem bizarre that you can reach Wakefield from the centre of London in a little over two hours, but it takes an hour and 20 – with a change in Leeds – to make the hop across the Pennines from Manchester. This mostly on trains that are Soviet era exercises in misery and dilapidation. Fortunately, for the last 15 minutes of the journey, I bunk into the snug, caramel warmth of the first class section of the East Coast Mainline. Sadly, this isn't going to be long enough for the penne arrabbiata, Thai green chicken curry or 150ml bottle of Merlot. I do try, however, to enjoy the short trip through the Yorkshire heartlands but with every swish and thrum of the rain on the glass I think, I'm going to be walking round Wakefield in this later.

My destination this evening is the Wakefield Artwalk, a bi-monthly nocturnal ramble intended to show off the city's growing status as a creative hub for the visual arts. That's evident from The Hepworth Gallery, the glittering brutalist trapezoidal structure on the banks of the Calder that has divided the town about its beauty but not its significance. When the Sage in Gateshead opened, they were queuing round the block at midnight to get in, cocking a lively snook (whatever that is) at the suspicions of London critics that it's all woad and philistinism up here. Similarly, the Hepworth packed in 100,000 visitors in its first month, and half a million within six. One quote I saw trumpeted that 'about to take its place on the country's map of significant art destinations is the Yorkshire town of Wakefield'. Admittedly that was the company who built the Hepworth, but I think their pride is entirely justified. Brutalism divides people, and there will always be some who prefer colonades and velvet ropes behind which hang pastels of bowls of fruit and fat babies, but whatever your stance, The Hepworth is a bold statement of a town who are serious about the business, in every sense, of art.

Part of this is Artwalk – a peripatetic mobile museum, if you will, and an idea brought back from the Pacific Northwest by local artist Richard William Wheater. He lived in Seattle for a while, and then set up a Wakefield version of their 'First Thursday' monthly walks in 2008 while working at Westgate Studios. Wakefield's happens on the last Wednesday of every other month and the blurb trills winningly 'You don't need to enjoy art to enjoy Wakefield Artwalk. If you like meeting new people, have an inquisitive mind and want to experience an alternative night out by yourself or with friends, give it a try. It's informal, friendly and a good opportunity to meet the city's creative community.' That's all true of course, but seems unnecessarily coy about the actual art which is great. That's at the core of it, and to be applauded, even if it also comes in handy to meet new friends, pull, and eat cake; possibly simultaneously.

I fear Wakefield may never appeal to well-heeled art tourists in the way that Florence or Venice does. Old DHSS buildings in Yorkshire will never have the same sublime cachet as the Uffizi or the Doge's Palace. But you can't get in the Uffizi after teatime usually, and the whole point of the Artwalk is that it is there for people who can't fill their afternoons sauntering around galleries – i.e. most of us. The walk celebrates Wakefield's supportive attitude to the arts by basically flinging open the studios, shops, cafés, building societies, old council buildings of the town, filling them with painting, sculpture, lithographs, etchings, gouache, etc., etc., and encouraging you to mooch. There's no route, no itinerary and no specific walk. But there is a map and lots of advice, particularly if you're lucky enough to get spotted by some of the Artwalk team, as I was, and taken to the Art House for a glass of wine, a piece of drizzle cake and a bit of a warm. The Art House is at the heart of what Wakefield are trying to do for their burgeoning art community. There are 14 studios which will have risen to more than 40 by summer 2015. The artists have 24-hour access to the building should they be struck by inspiration after last orders. The artists are all different, working in different media, with different things to say. The very first one I walk into is full of intense etchings of imagined cityscapes, the next home to a smiling potter with clay up to her elbows and something wobbling on the wheel.

Activity is everywhere and mostly the artists are there too, paint-flecked and happy to chat about the technique and craft which have always been a mystery to me, by common consent one of the worst artists these islands have ever produced. (I used to think this was unique to me but pinned to the wall above my desk is a drawing of an owl done by my Dad during a game of Pictionary one Christmas. Freakish and distressing, the head of a suicidal Pilsbury dough boy stuck on a grotesque sausage of a body, it suggests that real artistic incompetence may be genetic.)

We walk down cobbled streets slick with drizzle, past the tempting lights of the Bollywood Lounge curry house and the Boccaccio pizzeria – both packed – and down to Westgate Studios, which shares a name with the town's ultra-modern 'interchange' railway system. A stolidly Victorian structure in the middle of town, it hides a warren of artists' studios. I like the blurry TV snapshots of Viv Owen and I love the one-woman outfit of Timid Elk, whose studio door is daubed with niche art jokes ('Joseph Beuys Felt Me Up!') and who makes standard lamps out of recycled rail tickets, which I like so much I buy one.

On the next corner is Unity House. Since Bretton Hall stopped using it a dozen years ago, this old landmark building on the corner of the main drag had fallen into disuse and disrepair. But thanks to Wakefield's vibrant underdog civic groundswell (I want to say 'plucky' but I don't want to patronise), and the efforts of local indie rock heroes The Cribs, a trio of brothers with accents as flat as the Calder valley and the haircuts of medieval serfs, life is being breathed back into a Grade II listed building where from the music hall era onwards Wakefield folk have supped and snogged and been entertained. Tonight a kind of guerrilla event is taking place, an evening of short experimental films corralled from around the world by two impossibly young women and projected onto an immense sheet draped on one wall. There's an impromptu bar in the corner where I buy the organisers a drink (crates of wine and beer are bought in from the cash and carry) and the whole thing has the thrilling samizdat feel of some secret underground free jazz club in late sixties Prague.

Appropriate then that our next port of call, through puddles and cheerless streets, bleared by sodium streetlights, should be Fell House. Fell House is the sort of place where you'd queue up to be humiliated when you signed on the dole in the early eighties. Wigan's was called Brocol House and was a classic of the genre. It looked, as this does, like a place where the Stasi would take you for interrogation if you were a troublesome intellectual in the Leipzig of the same era – an ugly, squat, concrete block; strip-lit, pre-stressed and chilling. It was in its previous life, in fact, something in between. Something both as seedily British as DCI Gene Hunt in *Life on Mars* and as totalitarian as Honecker's East Germany; namely the headquarters of the West Yorkshire obscene publications squad. It was, as one of my guides says as we enter the grim basement, 'the sort of place you expect to find a table, an overturned chair and a full ashtray.' Yes, and perhaps the odd bloodstain. But in a brilliant move that both subverts and echoes the building's original function, during the walk it becomes a modern art venue. Upstairs, there's woodcuts and pastels and rosy-cheeked artisans, pieces full of craft and care and love. Down here, there's a lot of yellow police tape and bare metal, the kind of art that you can get mixed up with the security fittings.

I know this because I nearly blunder into one room and thus almost destroy the mesmeric installation piece it contains. 'In Time', by an artist-in-residence called Jaimini Patel, consists of hundreds of carpet tacks placed in geometric grids and rows across the floor of a bare cell-like space. I manage to grab the door jamb and stop myself before I bowl in kicking the nails everywhere. This is just the sort of thing some people think is the correct critical response to conceptual art, but not me. I get as much from the thoughts and ideas that pieces like this seed and trigger in my head as I ever will staring at one of

Corot's landscapes. What they are is different, and difference not convention is the great engine that drives our culture on, otherwise the 'The Hay Wain' would never have crossed that sluggish stream and moved on to 'Guernica'.

I don't claim to arrive at a comprehensive analysis. But it provokes thoughts about the painstaking nature of work and devotion to a task and the fundamental absurdity of art. Furthermore, it just looks great; strange, cold, serene. It lingers in the mind as I leave the gloomy bowels of Fell House and take in more of Wakefield's night of art. The Bradford & Bingley has some thought-provoking watercolours and collages, and the artist, a quite posh and forceful lady in her fifties, gives me a brisk sales pitch. I explain though that I've already bought a standard lamp made from old rail tickets and that I have to get it back on the train.

I end up repairing to the pub with some of the staff and volunteers involved in the walk and the Art House. Internecine politics rears its head sporadically over the pints. One bloke is getting quite voluble about some of the organisers of the Artwalk and how they have 'hijacked' the creative spirit of the town. It's a story I've heard before in many a northern boozer; I grew up with it. I know the type because, hey, once maybe I was it. The angry free-spirited small town maverick, always working on that experimental novel/political poetry/radical theatre group who refuses to 'sell out'. That is, refuses to do any real work, get anything finished or risk the curt rejections of the cruel, real world. We can't all be real geniuses, but we can all be the kind of helpful person who puts themselves on a rota and offers to wash up. Community art probably needs these people more than it needs geniuses, and certainly more than it needs free spirits or mavericks who can often be real pains in the arse to be around, and usually forget to bring their tea and biscuit money.

By chance, the resident artist whose installation of tacks I admired at Fell House, Jaimini, pops in. I buy her a drink and tell her how much I liked the piece. She tells me about the long, awkward days of kneeling, squatting and sitting on the cold concrete floor involved in setting the work up (there's a video of the process at the Art House website). Wryly, she tells me how she lost a couple of days' work when she realised that she was going to 'paint' herself into a corner and hem herself in with a floor of tacks that stopped her getting to the door. One of the most useful tools she had was a long stick for turning the lights on and off from a distance. We coyly dance around the matter of what the piece was 'about' and I start to see that we don't have the same opinions. 'Well, you're the artist, so you're obviously right,' I concede smiling. 'Hmm, I don't know about that,' she replies, and I realise she is quite serious.

Later, I find my hotel, ordered online, and check in. 'Ah, the nicest room in the whole hotel,' says the darkly handsome Middle European owner. 'What a waste that you are on your own … maybe not next time …' he says meaningfully, and I half think he will tap his nose or nudge me like a Romanian Eric Idle. A little nervously I take the lift up to the second floor and then to perhaps the strangest hotel room I have ever encountered. It is the size of a basketball court and nearly as empty, stripped to the irreducible; a bed, a lamp and, oddly, a leather chesterfield couch. It is also clearly in the process of being re-decorated; a process that looks and smells as if it was paused about five minutes before I put my key in the door. The tang of fresh paint in a hotel room is simultaneously the most reassuring and upsetting of all the odours you can come across; it shows they're making an effort to keep things spruce, but it guarantees that you'll spend the night alternately weeping and coughing. I hatch a plan.

Back out onto the rainy high street and, from the all-night curry and kebab house, I buy a lamb dupiaza for £4.50, because a) I am hungry and still regretting not finding a window in my evening for the Bollywood Lounge and b) I want something as smelly as possible to take the overpowering aroma of Cornflower Blue away. In what I think is an excellent deal, it comes with three chapattis and a carton of raita, but no fork, an omission I don't spot until I'm back on the second floor of my hotel. I sit for a while in my gigantic, partly painted room, me and the three pieces of furniture, wondering whether I could eat my curry with my toothbrush or maybe a coathanger, until I end up trying to eat it with the plastic lid of the raita carton sitting in the windowsill with dark, glistening Wakefield stretched out below me. Perhaps this is how Modigliani dined in his Montmartre garret; eating snails out of the shell with a golf tee. Repast over, I fall asleep after my night of art in a very fitting state, in a room flecked with fresh paint, reeking of turps and emulsion, and randomly smeared with turmeric.

A postscript. Not long after Artwalk, I came back to Wakefield as performer at the literary festival. 'Lit Fests' are things I associate more with the gentle south than the workers' north. Pluck a letter from the A–Z list at literaryfestivals.co.uk, 'B' in my case, and you'll still find many more Baths, Banburys, Brightons, Bournemouths, Burnham Markets and Budleigh Saltertons than you will Bradfords and Berwicks. But this is changing, as all things are. Over the last year or two, I've circuited the Lit Fests of the north, sometimes just looking, sometimes performing. In Hexham, I was the support act to Germaine Greer, where a man in the pub later told me I 'blew her off' which was flattering if a little disturbing to hear. This year I'm going to Derby's first one. So I came back a few weeks after the Artwalk to play a show at the lovely Victorian Theatre Royal as part of Wakefield's literary festival, delighted that Wakey's getting arty again. A tweet I receive blusters 'A Lit Fest in Wakefield is a contradiction in terms', which gets my back right up until I realise the tweeter is from Leeds and thus horribly partisan of course.

After the show, which is great fun, the excellent curator Robert Powell asks if I need to be looked after and fed and watered, but I say (and this is genuine) that after the show you quite often just want to do your own thing and be your own boss without having to be social. I ask him if this sounds miserable of me and he tells me Will Self said exactly the same thing. I am reminded of Alan Bennett's explanation as to why he gave up on readings and festival appearances. He said he had enough of feeling awkward eating Chinese banquets in the back streets of unfamiliar towns at midnight with complete strangers.

Robert understands all this and tells me the room booked for me should be fine he hopes, at least the aforementioned Will Self and Roger McGough said it was when they stayed in it recently (and separately I should add). I set off armed with the address and, yes, it is exactly the same room in the same hotel as before and I get exactly the same response from exactly the same gentleman on reception. 'You're alone … what a shame … it's a very nice room … we've just had it decorated …'

So, something of an old hand at this routine now, off out I go to grab a late meal. Down darkened streets I head purposefully with but one destination in mind, and arrive at the Bollywood Lounge just too late for their 10.30 last dinner order. A real shame as I liked their advertising billboard in the doorway. It featured recent celebrity diners such as Cliff Richard who apparently came in with mates Freda Payne, Lamont Dozier, Jaki Graham and (the late) Percy Sledge and the MPs Frank Dobson and 'Eric Prickles' (sic). They all look contented and well fed (especially 'Prickles', obviously), unlike I who trudge back to the very same kebab emporium that catered to me the last time I was here. Determined to carry back all the requisite cutlery and appurtenances this time, I produce a small fabric bag I have with me that I picked up in the Paris book shop Shakespeare & Co. On it is a large reproduction of the iconic picture of the immortal bard himself.

'Nice bag,' says the Indian proprietor, as he places my pakora and doner with salad and extra chili in it.

'Is that Hitler?' he asks cheerily.

What can he possibly have thought? I wonder, as I eat by the open window – the room still stinks like a Dulux factory – listening to the deafeningly loud thumping music from a club that seems empty, but has three girls outside smoking with the bouncers in the misty rain that is rolling in over West Yorkshire. I eat my kebab with 'Hitler/ Shakespeare' on my lap as a napkin, looking longingly out across the rooftops of Wakefield at the laughing, sated revellers leaving the Bollywood Lounge and the pizza parlour. Do the smoking girls and the laughing burly bouncers ever take the Wakefield Artwalk? Do the drinkers in the Brown Bear and The Pilot Inn in Berwick ever tear themselves away from the giant television screens and wander the headland in the footsteps of Lowry? Maybe. Maybe not. But that is to miss the point. Both are there for them should they wish and these encouragements to culture make these towns richer and more full, confounding those who might see working class leisure as a matter of frenzied hedonism, of drinking and eating to roaring excess.

But that said, this too has its place in the downtime and free time of the north. The road of excess leads to the palace of wisdom and I was happy to be led there by my stomach.

CHAPTER 5

HAVING A GOOD FEED

Chips and tapas in Tod and Halifax,
Michelin stars in Lancashire

I dined out most evenings as a teenager, and somewhere different every night. My fellow gourmets and I were adventurous, curious and willing to travel but like all connoisseurs, we had our favoured haunts. There was Bentham's by Alexandra Park in Newton, conservative in scope but always tremendously good; classically prepared traditional cuisine, served by excellent and knowledgeable staff under the stewardship of a first rate lady maître d', who would however insist on shouting, 'Do you want a Jubbly lolly with that love?' rather too loudly when the establishment was crowded. If we happened to have business uptown, there was Jimmy's on Wigan Lane. This was always busy with discerning regulars, but they would normally fit us in. Renowned for its gravy and pies, latterly they did venture into a sort of oriental fusion cuisine which was popular with younger diners – chop suey rolls, spare ribs, etc. – but wisely maintained signature dishes for the longstanding clientele.

In the centre of Wigan was The Millgate, something of an oldschool downtown institution *à la* the Gay Hussar or the Ivy. Its cachet rested on an intimate back room with very few covers but exceptionally good food, freshly cooked (hence some waiting at busy periods), a cellar of chilled Vimto and always bread and butter. If we were nearer our own patch but craving variety or we were particularly 'clemt', there was always Greasy Lil's on Warrington Road, Pemberton. Here the resident chefs would often experiment with the menu and, to be candid, not always entirely successfully; saveloys, faggots and the like are not regional staples of the north and here they could be woefully hit and miss. But the steak puddings were always superb and the curry, gravy and 'pea wet' were clearly the work of a skilled saucier.

Chippies apart, and we shall return to them, or the dining room at various Butlins, I didn't 'eat out' in the accepted sense until I was in my twenties. In my town back then, one just didn't do it unless your folks were wildly aspirational – the type who had 'carports' and Mateus Rosé in the drinks cupboard – or it was a very special occasion. I can vividly recall my first instance of 'going out for a meal'. Terry Stokes, brother of the aforementioned food critic Jeff, and myself had given up a week of our summer holidays demolishing an old garage used by his caterer dad to store pop and crisps. It was filthy, back-breaking work and our reward at the end of the week was a 'meal out' at a pub; a nice pub, mind you, with decent food. Not a spit and sawdust boozer, the kind where the dining options were either a gelatinous pie or a packet of Big D peanuts taken from many on a card hanging behind the bar, removal of which would reveal progressively more of an unclad young woman's alluring frame.

No, the Cross Keys in Wigan's fashionably chi-chi Standishgate district was an epicure's playground by comparison. There were various cooked animals on offer, probably even an omelette for Wigan's very few and presumably emaciated vegetarians of the day. But like suburban swingers making small talk over the Matchmakers, we all knew what we were here for. Steak.

Steak in my house was just steak; a once a week treat and always reliably tasty, as procedurally it came with onions and gravy and had been in 'the slow cooker' all day while we were all out in school and factory. But here, in this faux-rustic 'olde worlde' dining room with dimple mugs and horse brasses, steak could be ribeye or T-Bone, porterhouse or tenderloin, rump or minute or chuck or fillet. Not only that, but (for a small supplementary charge) you could have it with a little ramekin of sauce, mustard or Provençal or blue cheese. Blue cheese sauce! Mental! Almost as mental as the onion rings which claimed to be 'beer battered'. Would life ever be the same again? What was it the old song said? 'How you gonna keep 'em down on the farm now that they've seen Paris?' Having eaten a beer battered onion ring AND a grilled half tomato cut in a special jagged way, would I ever be content with rehydrating a Pot Noodle again?

In my lack of dining experience, I was not unique or enormously disadvantaged. I was fairly typical of my kind. Until relatively recently, working-class people would no more have gone out of the house to sit in a formal setting just to eat than they would have to have gone someplace special to iron their clothes. Food was fuel, elevated to a domestic treat on Sunday dinners or Christmas day, but otherwise not to be made an activity of, least of all a palaver, unlike going out to drink or dance or be entertained, none of which could be easily done in your own front room.

Chips were different though. A source of comfort and joy for decades and, we contend, another brilliant northern innovation such as the computer, female suffrage and nuclear fission. Fried fish was introduced to Britain by Jewish refugees from the continent. It was initially sold by street sellers from a tray around their neck, 'ice cream at the pictures' style, or from a 'fried fish warehouse' as mentioned by Dickens in *Oliver Twist*. But it was a northern entrepreneur called John Lees who in 1863 began selling fried fish with chipped potatoes out of a wooden hut at Mossley market in the heart of industrial Lancashire. Like Lennon meeting McCartney at Woolton fete, Rolls having lunch with Royce at the Midland Hotel, Manchester, or Burton and Taylor's eyes meeting for the first time in Rome on the set of Antony and Cleopatra, this was surely one of history's most significant bunk-ups.

At a time when tripe was regarded as exotic fare, and ordinary diets were bland, grim and unvaried, this new pairing was a sensation. Orwell thought that fish and chips 'averted revolution' in Britain, and in his academic tome *Fish and Chips and the British Working Class*,

Professor John Walton argues that fish and chips helped win the Great War. He told the BBC, 'The cabinet knew it was vital to keep families on the home front in good heart … unlike the German regime that failed to keep its people well fed and that was one reason why they were defeated.' We longer think of Fish and Chips as a healthy diet of course, but we had more pressing concerns then than saturated fats. Fish and chips were packed with calories, filled our bellies and lifted our spirits, and this kind of reading was firing my imagination, making my mind race and stomach rumble as I made my way through a drenching East Lancashire fog to Grandma Pollards.

I'd been doing my homework, asked around, made some enquiries down at the counters, drooled over the keyboard as I scanned forums dedicated to the subject, and had finally found a handful of names that were by common consent the best chippies in the north. But I was in for a shock when I looked at the posh media. *The Times* restaurant critic boasted that 'all the best chip shops are in London', a statement as dense as it is inflammatory. In their 2013 'Best Traditional Chippies in Britain' feature, *Esquire* chose just one northern chip shop and concentrated on London and Suffolk. Feigned or not, this was the kind of madness that got my considerable dander up. There is more to a 'chippie' than its fresh locally sourced fish, you foodies. It is a rare and mysterious ambient blend of location, vibe, trappings, mushy peas, lighting, curry sauce, forks, staff, smell. Each has its own stamp, its own sizzling music, its own terroir. The place I wanted, said the word on the streets, was Grandma Pollards.

Crawling through Milnrow in the late rush hour on a freezing night of murk and sleet, I pitied those who make this commute daily. (I once made a TV film round these parts in which we set a keen runner against a motorist on a notorious four-mile stretch. The runner won.) I pass the dark watery bowl of Hollingworth Lake and see that the famous old Italian restaurant Del Lago has closed and become a bar called Marina. Sad. Del Lago was properly, wonderfully old school; Chianti bottles in wicker holders, gigantic phallic pepper pots, trolleys of extravagant gateaux stacked and layered like Venetian palazzi. All around the walls were signed photos of celebrity diners, mainly male TV hosts, comedians and kids' presenters of the seventies. Maybe that's why it's closed down. Maybe all their regular clientele are in prison.

As I pass through Littleborough at the back of a line of cars moving slowly enough to make out the famous, enigmatic graffiti on the station wall – 'Mark Owen 93' – the night is getting worse, becoming a thick drenching clag as I reach the darkened hills of Todmorden and eventually the little 'Tod' suburb of Walsden. In a blaze of light and people in an otherwise dark and deserted street, Grandma Pollards looks fabulously welcoming. 'You Can Park Here' says a sign by a big yellow *Simpson*'s style school bus with a weird dummy in the driver's seat. Even on such a foul night, Grandma P's is doing a brisk trade. In the takeaway section, there's a queue and, here in the café area, many of the tables are occupied. I am instantly confronted with what some theorists – not usually with regard to chip shops it has to be said – call the 'tyranny of choice'. There is every kind of fish in every kind of format. I wouldn't have been surprised to see mini barracuda and chips or battered ichthyosaurus on the menu. There's a flummoxing offer of specials and deals. Under a glass counter lounges a glistening, calorific selection of home-made sweet pies – bilberry, apple, raspberry – sugary tarts and vanilla slices, the most sybaritic and irresistible of all the cheap cake treats. With all this choice I feel a bit bad for Emma behind the counter for ordering 'off the menu', but she seems sweetly unphased by my request for steak pudding, chips and curry sauce. This Lancashire classic was, according to Victoria Wood, the only meal she still missed as a vegetarian and it had been my default chippy order since my teenage years, when it was mainly eaten in bus shelters with a can of Vimto and, if lucky, Anne Thomas.

Grandma Pollards, 'arguably the best chippie in the world' as their lively website will tell you, has been here since 1957 when the titular baking matriarch branched out into fish and chips. Youngest son

Tony is still in charge here, five days a week. 'But don't forget we are closed Saturday & Sunday. Tony's little legs need a rest.' Tony is here tonight, not doing much in the way of cooking, but generally 'being around' chatting, joking with customers, teasing the staff. I have no problem with this maître d' concept. One of the reasons I liked and miss the above mentioned Del Lago was that it met in every regard my requirements of the perfect traditional Italian restaurant. For me, they must have a) zucchini fritti, b) 'semplice' tomato and red onion salad and c) a silver-haired gentleman of obscure role in a smart suit fiddling with his expensive watch, who you know could have someone quietly and expertly drowned for you in a nearby reservoir.

I take a seat and almost instantly my bread and butter arrives, a mixture of brown and white; daringly cosmopolitan but unsettling. A chip butty with brown bread feels wrong to me at some deep-seated, pre-logical level. Nostalgic music blasts out at impressive volume. First it's 'songs from the shows', *Joseph* and *The Sound of Music*, then Elaine Page warbling something dire, then chirpy Tommy Steel and a clutch of early sixties teen idols. Next we have a bit of wartime stuff, like The Andrews Sisters and Glenn Miller before moving onto Sinatra and Tony Bennett, and in passing the worst version of 'My Funny Valentine' I have ever heard. Behind me sits a cheery, rotund family of three. 'Eat your sausage,' says mum to a girl of about four, while Dean Martin slurs woozily 'when the sun hits your eye like a big pizza pie, that's amore'.

They like their signage at Grandma Pollards, and they like it bamboozling. An entire wall is taken up with pictures of Tony and staff with a variety of customers, and with shots of various diners accompanied by fabulously literal captions. There's a picture of a man and woman tucking in to their dinner, he with peas, she without. The caption reads: 'What, no peas lady?' There's a picture of some empty plates (caption: 'empty plates'), an elderly man holding up a sign saying 'I am 91 and a Dunkirk Man' ('We Are So Proud Of Him') and my particular favourite, a cheery fellow caught opening a sachet of tomato ketchup ('Time For Tomato Ketchup'). Another adjoining board is headed 'Celebrity Collage' and features Tony with Ken Dodd (caption: 'His Idol') and, less predictably, Prunella Scales and Timothy West tucking into pie and peas with some gusto. Emma brings me a vanilla slice as big as four desserts in Knightsbridge, and quite heavenly.

Reluctantly leaving Emma and the warmth of Grandma Pollards for the wild night coming in over the Pennines, I stop for a whisky at the White Horse, a pub on the moors that is as boisterous and warm inside as it looks chill and deserted from the exterior. 'Which one would you like?' asks the barmaid. 'Thank god,' she says when I ask for Laphroaig, 'it's the only one I can pronounce' – which seems somewhat weird on many levels. As I leave I notice a van in the car park bearing the legend 'Equine Dentist'. How does one arrive at that line of work? Who in that crowded bar was the equine dentist, looking for some simple human warmth after a raw day on the hills (possibly) staring gift horses quite literally in the mouth with not even the consolation of asking them where they were going for their holidays.

The simple, enduring glories of fish and chips aside, working Britain has always been playing catch up in the foodie stakes. The church basically dreamt up the sin of gluttony during the Middle Ages to make the poor feel better about having nothing to eat. Centuries passed, and the notion of eating out in establishments dedicated to just that took hold in Britain, with the indulgent mood of the post-Cromwell Restoration a tipping point. But it was still largely the wealthy who could afford the time and money required to spend an evening living it up over several courses.

The early Edwardian era was a boom time for dining out, when the modern restaurant as we know it began to emerge. Even so, most people's experience of a dining establishment was the new-fangled and very welcome works canteen. The enlightened Titus Salt of Saltaire was a pioneer here, as was Thomas Adams, lace makers of

Nottingham, where 'girls leave their counters and refresh themselves with a bun and a glass of milk from four to half past six'. Alongside these were 'ordinaries'; working men's taverns and chop houses where you could get an 'ordinary'; a basic sustaining meal at a cheap fixed price. (Incidentally, here's a tourist tip; in Berlin, anyone can eat in a works canteen. They're completely open to the public so you can enjoy the great views and exalted company at, for instance, the Berlin Philharmonic or the Ministry of Defence plus rump steak 'with herb butter, beans and croquette potatoes' for about 7 euros.)

Looking back, the pub-cum-restaurant I was taken to by the Stokes for that impossibly glamorous and adult excursion was perhaps one a chain of establishments that revolutionised the British night out in the seventies, thanks to two brothers from Italy. Frank and Aldo Berni came from a tiny village high in the Apennines where they went to school on skis. In 1929, like many of their countrymen, the family moved to the valleys of south Wales and opened a café. During the war, the brothers were interned as enemy aliens but this didn't turn them off their adopted country. After the war, they visited America and were impressed by the slick restaurant chains with their reasonable prices and good service, but not by the bland and flavourless food. They decided to try something similar but tastier here.

They opened their first restaurant in Bristol's oldest pub The Rummer in 1952. Through that decade and the next their eating houses became enormously popular firstly in the West Country and then throughout the UK. Berni Inns had a simple, set menu requiring only a grill and a deep fat fryer in the kitchen and no trained chefs. The manager was key. He or she worked from a detailed operational manual known as 'The Bible' which covered everything from presentation, place settings, cooking procedures and complaints, which the diner was encouraged to make rather than go away seething and spreading bad 'word of mouth'.

They were clever chaps. They used place mats instead of tablecloths, a gesture towards informality that also saved on laundry. Portions were strictly controlled by weight; an idea which critics claimed had been borrowed from the prison system but kept costs standard and diners happy. Berni's grills cooked at far higher temperatures than was usual so the meat was sealed instantly and far juicier than we were used to; five minutes rare, seven minutes medium, ten minutes well done. A competent grill chef could turn out 300 steaks a night.

Their ads were ubiquitous; in one a smiling, sympathetic husband is consoling a wife standing glum-faced over a smouldering chip pan. 'We'd be better off at a Berni' runs the tagline. In 1970, they sold up to Grand Metropolitan, who wisely kept the Berni Inn name and gave Britain its definitive seventies meal out: prawn cocktail, steak and chips and Black Forest gateau. After the sale, Frank retired to Jersey (£14.5 million better off) by which time the chain had 147 restaurants in Britain and several in, of all places, Japan.

But fashions change. The lure of the exotic and the dread rise of *nouvelle cuisine* alongside hollow eighties snobbery did for the homespun Berni. In 1990, Berni Inns were sold off to the brewers Whitbread, who immediately dumped the name and re-launched them as Beefeaters. As the food writer David Smith put it, 'Berni Inns had become a bit like a teenager's parents. They had taught the British how to eat out at restaurants but were an uncomfortable reminder of who we used to be not who we are now.' This slightly squirming sense of affection and nostalgia was nailed perfectly in a number in Victoria Wood's musical *That Day We Sang* entitled 'Berni Inn' with lyrics like, 'Would you like to grapple/with gammon and pineapple' and 'It's wrong to brag/It's just cake in drag/But it's gâteau at the Berni Inn'.

Just around the time that Berni Inn was dwindling in status, receding into memory to become a seventies' cipher like Space Hoppers and skyjackings, another nosh behemoth was inexorably rising. It was moving across the Atlantic like those unstoppable predecessors Ford, Coca-Cola and Walt Disney. Resistance would be futile. I remember well the first McDonald's opening in Wigan. It was around 1984, a particularly grim period in the town's history and an appropriately

Orwellian one, at least if you're one of those types who wears a Guy Fawkes mask and thinks fast food is at the very least imperialist and at the worst probably something to do with the Illuminati. I'm neither but I didn't go in McDonald's often.

At the time Wigan still had a Wimpy, and to this day I have a deep vestigial loyalty to Britain's original burger chain, whose first branch grew out of a Lyons Corner House on London's Coventry Street. Wimpys, with their chunky, idiosyncratic hand-assembled burgers and rough chopped salads are now as rare as hen's teeth, and never to be passed by anyone with taste buds and a feel for tradition. From a peak of 500, there are now just 89, maybe less by the time you read this. If you have one near you, patronise it. Preserve it. It is in its own way a cherishable national culinary oddity like Spud U Like. A chain of potato outlets for people who find fish and chips too flamboyant, and once owned by the British School Of Motoring. Yes, really.

Anyway, 'Maccie D's' never became the treat or hang out for me that it did for some teenagers. Perhaps it was that first experience in Wigan, when scanning the illuminated menu boards and trying to decode and disentangle the Big Macs from the Quarter Pounders, musing on whether McDonald's actually thought a grown person would ever ask for a 'Fillet-O-Fish', the man in the queue in front of me asked for a 'beefburger … and I don't want any of that fucking shit on it' thus brusquely dismissing the finest pickles and condiments of Ray Kroc's devising.

In the same way, I seem to have been missed out on the generational food cult that is Nando's. To call Nando's a phenomenon is to damn it with faint praise. Like text messaging and selfies, it is one of those new notions that seem boring and unappealing – in this case a new restaurant selling the dullest of all meats – until young people with their massive cultural muscle and consumer soft power made them into 'a thing'. No, make that 'the thing'. Nando's is the most popular food outlet among British teenagers. It's particularly big with young black Britons, and about 50 of its 333 restaurants in the UK are halal, which makes a hit with Muslim diners. My Sikh friend Gary, who can't eat halal, takes his children there for their favourite dish, chicken livers. Any restaurant that can make liver palatable, let alone irresistible, to kids wields a terrifying power.

Quite how it got here is a bit of a mystery, like much about the Nando's cult. Sometime in the mid-nineties, there grew a backlash against the perceived tackiness of McDonald's. Nando's was in the forefront of what retail jargon calls 'the fast casual chicken space'. It's not haute cuisine, and you have to queue up to order, but at seven quid-ish for a chicken leg and some sides (an average meal spend is nine quid plus) it's not Greggs either. Its demographic is huge, its appeal genuinely classless. You are equally likely to spot a gang of hip-hop youths in there as a middle-class family, a young couple on date night or grannie and granddad having a bite after shopping. This makes it catnip to politicians. David Cameron has stopped off several times in various Nando's for selfies with customers when on the campaign trail. Prince Harry has been seen tucking in at the Fulham branch. Ambulance, police, fire services, Army, Navy, RAF and NHS workers all get a 20 per cent discount, a neat PR move. During the summer disturbances of 2011, a Facebook group called The Nando's Defence League sprang up, demanding that rioters and looters leave Nando's alone. If Nando's were to launch a political party, their spicy Reich would last a thousand years.

But the most enigmatic element of all Nando lore is the 'Black Card', or the Nando's High Five Card. This fabled object is the Bilderberg Group of fried chicken retail, shrouded in secrecy and power, a sliver of metal that makes a platinum Amex look like my Gala Bingo membership. Ownership guarantees the holder free chicken for themselves and four friends for life. Like the minutes of the Bilderberg Group, Nando's are hugely coy on the matter of the card. But rumour has it that David Beckham and Lewis Hamilton have one. Rapper Tinchy Stryder says he has one. Ed Sheeran has been pictured with one. What gives here? Perhaps we will only know when the saucers come to hover over every one of the 333 branches – something odd about that number, isn't there? – and the walls start to revolve, revealing the blinking lights of the subterranean control rooms, as Nando's move into the final glorious phase of their project.

Nando's proclaims itself 'the home of the legendary Portuguese flame-grilled peri-peri chicken'. Peri-peri is Swahili for 'pepper-pepper', which in fact comes from Mozambique and the company's majority shareholders are from South Africa. So it definitely qualifies as foreign food – of which of course myths and prejudices were once rife. My friend's tiny and permanently suspicious grannie eschewed curry on the grounds that it would 'thin your blood' and 'make you sexy', admirable functions both, I would have thought, unless you wanted to be a sexless dolt with clotted blood. Similarly Chinese food was OK but there was something in it that would make you want another one two hours later. There is actually; monosodium glutamate, 'MSG taste powder' as it's known in the trade, and the sort of thing middle-class people regarded as only slightly better than putting powdered weapons-grade plutonium in your sweet-and-sour sauce.

But look a little deeper and you'll find we have always been more adventurous in our tastes than our self-image suggests. It's customary at this point to refer to the chicken recipe from the Middle Ages that called for 40 cloves of garlic (it's called, brilliantly, 'Chicken With 40 Cloves of Garlic'), or to the fact that Saik Deen Mahomad opened the Hindostanee Dinner and Hooka Smoking Club in London in 1810 which offered 'Indian dishes, in the highest perfection'. He even offered to have dishes delivered to his customers' houses. Crazy! That'll never catch on.

We have never been as dull as we think. A Tudor recipe for a picnic salad instructs 'take parse, sawge, garlic, chibllas, oynons, leek, borage, myntes, porrectes, fenel and ton tressis, rew, rosemarye, purslayne, lave, and waisshe hem clene. Poke hem, pluck hem small with thyn hond and myng hem with rawe oile. Lay on vinegar and salt and serve it forth.' It certainly sounds more adventurous than some Hellman's on a hard-boiled egg.

Hybrids abound in our eating landscape. There's 'the Chinese chippy', offering fish and chips as well as Chinese dishes; 'the full Muslim', a whopping traditional English breakfast without the pork. Chicken tikka masala, said to be our national dish these days, is rumoured to have been invented one rainy night in Glasgow in 1971 when a curry house customer moaned that his chicken curry was too dry and the chef improvised with a tin of Heinz Tomato Soup. In 2010, a survey by Cauldron foods found that six out of ten meals prepared in British households were derived from foreign culinary traditions. Of our five English Chinatowns, four are in the industrial north or Midlands: Manchester, Birmingham, Liverpool and Nottingham. The first two of those cities also boast Curry Quarters or Miles and I know both well, too well some might say. In Brum, it's also known as the Balti triangle (from the Urdu Balty for Bucket, referring to the metal bowl the food is served in). It's a crowded corner of the city where Sparkbrook, Balsall Heath and Moseley meet in the crowded, buzzing streets of Stoney Lane, Ladypool Road and Stratford Road. Every other building is a curry house or Indian sweet centre.

When I first wandered this street in the late 1980s it was not uncommon to see Roy Hattersley, then MP for Sparkbrook, tearing his chapatti in one of them. None were remotely smart but all were unique; menus under glass on the table tops, cutlery 'liberated' from ancient British rail buffet cars, and in one famed establishment chained to the table. Whole extended Asian families would sit in them for an entire Sunday afternoon, laughing and chatting noisily, the women and children dazzling in scarlet, lemon and turquoise, deftly scooping the dahls and sambars one-handed with scraps torn from the enormous karack, or 'family' naan breads the size of dustbin lids.

Somehow all stayed in business, prospered even, each with its own hardcore fan base who came for the specialties of the house; fresh naans folded over those little tea towel covered domes and stuck on the side of the tandoor ovens, seasonal bel puri and papri chat. On a roadside stall or two, you could find a snack so rare and prized that even today I know Asian friends from Prestwich and Didsbury who will drive to the Midlands to get the prized ones from the Ladypool Road. This is panipuri or golgoppa which means roughly 'all in one mouthful', the best way to eat this delicious street food of Kashmir and Nepal, crisp spheres of bread filled with scented liquid, tamarind and chick peas. Once you would have had to go to the roof of the world for such delights, to the backstreets of Lucknow, Chittagong or Kathmandu. Now you can get it on the 8A bus route to Aston via Five Ways.

In Manchester, the curry mile runs along Wilmslow Road, the main drag of Rusholme. There is nothing quite like it on a summer night, when Pakistani hip-hop and Lollywood soundtracks blare from the shops offering mobile phone unlocking, and the air is heady and sizzling with cumin and coriander. My two favourite curry houses here are busy enough, thank you, without me making my life harder by naming them. I'm sure you understand. One is the only place on the curry mile where you can get dhosa pancakes and good bel puri and something of an insider's secret. I remember the little swell of pride I got once when jumping in a cab at Piccadilly station and asking to be taken to it, the Asian cab driver turned around and gave me an admiring look and said, 'You know your food I see, my friend.'

Somewhat disloyally, Somerset Maugham once said 'to eat well in England, you must have breakfast three times a day'. The warmth and zeal with which we've embraced the food of the subcontinent, as well as the Orient, the Mediterranean and the Middle East, is sometimes reckoned to be proportional to the blandness, wretchedness even, of traditional British cooking. I have some sympathy with this view, raised as I was on a grim diet of haslet, tongue, brawn, corned beef and other vague, translucent, grisly pressed meats of every hue, flaccid pies and vegetables boiled to within an inch of their lives (I drew the line at tripe, which looked exactly like what it was, the rubbery lining of a dead ruminant's stomach).

My first encounters with foreign food – not counting Vesta chow mein or ravioli in a tin – with Chinese (sweet and sour chicken, back of Anne Thomas's car, Hindley, circa 1978), proper curry (lamb pathia, Oriental Grill, Southport, 1980) or Italian (penne amatriciana, Bolton Last Drop Village, 1981) were all life-changing moments; the realisation that eating could be fun, delicious and companionable, not just the joyless taking on of calorific fuel to ward off starvation. Over the last few years, though, British or more correctly English food has been fighting a rearguard action and re-asserting itself, thanks to some high profile restaurants and celebrity chefs.

Now, rather like the food critic, of whom more shortly, the celebrity chef is a tricky beast. I like good food but I have no desire to eat it beneath pictures of the proprietor sulking in a bandana, which is why I tend to avoid Marco Pierre White's places. I agree with the singer Paul Heaton, who remarked recently, 'women have been cooking for a thousand years and no one ever mentioned it. Men have been cooking for ten minutes and they never stop bloody going on about it'.

But they're not all cut from this cloth, and some chefs have been robust in their championing and rehabilitation of British food. Gary Rhodes of the sticky up hair was the pioneer here, winning a Michelin star at The Greenhouse in London for his braised oxtail, fishcakes, faggots, and bread and butter pudding. Then St John in Clerkenwell made sucking on bone marrow trendy rather than disgusting. Steven Doherty, in various Cumbrian dining rooms, has continued the trend for good English food made with our own seasonal specialities – asparagus, rhubarb and cabbage in spring; salads, strawberries and peaches in summer; in autumn, mushrooms, figs and game; and, in winter, root veg, russet apples and venison.

During the height of Britpop, that slightly hysterical, speed-fuelled re-discovery of all things home-grown, there was a café in Camden that everyone on 'the scene' frequented. Most lunchtimes, you would find pale, dishevelled members of Menswear or Elastica in there, as well as journos like myself, getting over their hangovers with fish fingers, steak pie or jam roly-poly. It was known to all, in a deliberate reclamation of a maligned institution, as 'School Dinners', and it was loved partly out of nostalgia for childhood and partly because the food hit the spot. There are times when a spinach and ricotta parcel just will not do. 'School Dinners' was ahead of a coming curve. So it came to pass that the chalkboards of hip boozers throughout the land had their confits and roulades wiped away and fish finger sandwiches and bangers and mash chalked up. Or maybe even 'crispy squirrel and Vimto trifle'.

That was the name of a cookbook written by Robert Owen Brown, the chef most associated in the north-west with the defiantly, deliberately quirky, embracing of the north's curious food heritage. He is a pioneer of what became the foodie mantra of 'top to toe eating' – the kind of food that my iron-stomached Lancastrian grandmother would have revelled in: tripe and 'lights', lungs and testicles. He has also, for four years, served the most original pub grub in Manchester.

The pub's called the Mark Addy, who you may recall as the genial, well-upholstered actor from *The Full Monty*. But he took his stage name from a famous Salford pub landlord and boatman of the Victorian era who was, it seems, always leaping in the filthy Irwell to save people from drowning. He saved 50 people, it's said, and won the Albert Medal, the precursor to the George Cross. The pub named after him stands on the bank where Addy often launched himself into the river. In fact, you could be forgiven for thinking, at first glance, that it was a roadside pissoir, tucked away under an arch on a bridge across Manchester's treacly parent river, the Irwell, or the Sewage Canal as it was jokingly once known.

Christmas is coming and there are skaters on the ice rink in Spinningfield, a scene that's Rockefeller Plaza meets Brueghel, as we head across a glistening, frosty Manchester for something warming at the Mark Addy. Though Scrooges may cry 'humbug', it takes a hard heart not to enjoy the way that northern cities, indeed cities throughout Britain, have started to copy their continental neighbours as Christmas approaches. The crowds may be oppressive but having a Glühwein and a bratwurst in a chilly market square is surely a nicer way to spend the week before Christmas than queuing up for a dressing gown in Marks and Spencer's.

There are tents like Inuit settlements in the centre of town, booming with smoke and laughter, and a huge shack of a bar that resembles an old arctic encampment at Spitsbergen. Inside, though, rather than bearded men in parkas (not counting the hipsters) with rime clinging to their whiskers and bloodied harpoons, there are girls dressed up to the nines, sipping champagne and hot cider by flaming braziers.

Walking along the icy river Irwell, this reborn city feels like Oslo or Copenhagen, modern, white, gleaming, cold, with a slightly sixties sense of urban optimism and space-age cool. Like the now stunning downtown Newcastle riverscape, 25 years ago, no sensible person would have wandered down here unless you wanted to score drugs, or women, or rob an abandoned boatyard. Nowadays, although it maintains an air of darkness and mystery, and will never be cosy like the Cotswolds, it is a place to wander and be impressed by both the civic and commercial renaissance of 'Cottonopolis'. On one side, the great white edifice of the modern courthouse, guarded by pillars of light along the colonnades, and on the other, the great modernist cliff of Manchester's only five-star hotel, the Lowry. When not painting his Berwick seascapes this is where the artist painted a different Salford, one of cripples and rickets and haunted ginnels. At the Lowry Hotel you can recline on a red leather chaise longue in your Mies van der Rohe style room and sip an Earl Grey martini from room service above the streets.

Down some steps that Lowry would have loved, wonky and crepuscular, and into the pub itself. One disgruntled online reviewer said that it smacked of a '1980s social club' and I know what they mean; there is a certain faded quality to the interior, particularly the drab, municipal entrance, a relic indeed of the design-addled eighties.

But the staff are as warm as the night and the Perspex receptions are cold. I order a bottle of Shiraz and he commends, 'Good choice ... would you like to taste it?' Seeing that it's a screw top, I say there's no need, as it won't be corked. 'Oh I know, but some people like to test the temperature,' and at this he rolls his eyes good-naturedly. I like this about northern waiters. Some people don't think they're obsequious and fawning enough, but their impish cheekiness adds a bit of seasoning to the dish, I think.

The food is, as I believe some people say, 'to die for'. I go for everything that smacks of Brown's signature spit-and-sawdust style, the 'Manchester thingymabobs' he's become known for. One of these is crispy battered spam fritters, which are properly sensational. Yes, you can feel your arteries fur and thicken just by looking at them, but the memory of that crunching crust and that warm pink savoury slab of meat will remain with you as a wonderful memory in the hospital bed.

Then there is the Manchester egg, a creation of this city to rank with better known inventions. It was dreamed up in a pub on the other side of town, The Castle in the Northern Quarter when, while eating Seabrook's salt and vinegar crisps and a pickled egg, web designer and amateur cook Ben Holden was inspired to create a distinctly northern riff on the slightly underwhelming picnic staple of the scotch egg; a pickled egg encased in black pudding, with crunched crisps as the shell, served warm with a liquescent yolk. I want one so much right now I would steal one from an old lady's handbag if the occasion presented itself. I ordered a boxful once when the Manic Street Preachers played live on my last radio show from the Beeb's old Oxford Road studio. They went in seconds in a flurry of hands and mouths. I think drummer Sean had six.

Hollywood A-lister Donnie Wahlberg loved these, and doubtless he also loved the Lancashire hotpot, ribeye steak with duck-fat chips, bread and butter pudding, if not the shabby carpet. Intimate and candlelit, with the odd adventurous rower or goose gliding by on the inky Irwell, I couldn't help but notice that there were only two occupied tables, which was criminal for food this good. That was just before Christmas 2013 and after the festive break it never re-opened. Robert Owen Brown decamped to a gourmet dining club in Didsbury and the contentious view about Manchester's attitude to good food, i.e that it doesn't appreciate it, gained more credence.

There's a Manchester drinkers' saying, oft repeated by the excellent Guy Garvey of Elbow, that goes 'eating's cheating'. Roughly, it means that it's wrong to waste a moment of the evening's boozing time on something as needless and potentially sobering as food. It's a joke, of course, but at its heart it does seem to bear out a longstanding opinion of Manchester, namely that it loves its clothes, its football, its music and its partying, but it isn't that fussed about food. While brethren cities like Birmingham have four Michelin-starred restaurants and Birkenhead, Sheffield and Newcastle have a smattering, Manchester – Britain's second city, it likes to think – has none and hasn't had one for 40 years. Nottingham has. Hunstanton has. Abergavenny has. Even the kind of northern town Manchester swaggeringly looks down on – Blackburn, Ilkley and Birkenhead, can take the wind out of pimp rolling, swaggering Manchester's sails here. They've all got starred establishments. Cock of the north it may be, cook of the north it certainly isn't.

It isn't for want of trying. Raymond Blanc and Marco Pierre White both tried and failed, which must have made Marco even crosser than he looks in his promo shots. More recently, two of Britain's best chefs have been fighting a very public battle, with each other and with the imperious, mysterious Michelin judges, to get that long lusted-after star.

Aiden Byrne is that rarity, a Scouser working for the good of Manchester (and, of course, for the good of his employers the powerful, glitzy Living Ventures whose bar and restaurant chain has colonised many a downtown space). Byrne's restaurant is the self-consciously stylish Manchester House, located in a functional glass eyrie above the city centre. 'It looks like a very normal city tower, but don't be fooled. Inside lies a very special experience for both food lovers and lovers of a life with a view' runs the blurb, a little meaninglessly. You can glean quite a bit of the restaurant's outlook by the fact that the staff are almost exclusively drawn from the city's elite MAWs, as they are known in the dismissive vernacular – model, actress, whatever – hired on the basis of youthful beauty rather than skill in shelling a langoustine, and that on opening night one of the starters seemed to be a kind of large edible white pill, presumably to remind the now mature and well-heeled diners of their youthful indiscretions on the dancefloor. (Manchester trades unashamedly and rather tackily on all this history. When the Haçienda nightclub, the city's musical fulcrum in the 1980s and 90s, was turned into upscale city centre flats, a huge promotional poster adorning the building said 'The Party's Over, It's Time To Come Home' much to the groans of Manchester's cooler residents.)

Byrne has had to reconcile this vibe of slightly gimmicky aspirational trendiness with his undoubted skills in the kitchen and the purism of his cooking. We know this because it was the subject of a TV show in 2014 called *Restaurant Wars* which pitted Byrne, a little contrivedly, against his rival in the race for Manchester's first Michelin star, Simon Rogan.

Rogan is a boy from the south coast who has been helping improve the north's reputation for food this past decade, starting with his restaurant L'Enclume in the tiny north Lancashire village of Cartmel. With two stars there, he was lured to Manchester for a new challenge, one he seemed to relish. 'I have always loved Manchester – it's like being in London, but on a smaller scale,' he said, innocently risking the wrath of every proud Mancunian (except the ones who moved to London as soon as they could. You, and they, know who they are). 'It's trendy and dynamic, but very accessible and friendly. Overall, the Manchester dining scene has been quite casual and bar-driven, but this is a great opportunity to set the trend for luxury dining, and the city is definitely ready for it.' Was it? Some weren't sure and still aren't.

Restaurant Wars found Rogan having taken over a city dining institution, The French restaurant at the Midland Hotel, and trying to drag it, and its stolid regular clientele, into the twenty-first century. When the very first Michelin guide was produced in the UK in 1974, The French was awarded a star. But not for long, and since then it is seen to have been left behind by changes in food fashion and styles, a place that is forever a boozy lunchtime in the late sixties, where Anthony Burgess, Bill Grundy and Matt Busby are finishing the turbot and chateaubriand and moving onto the port. In the TV series, Rogan was seen trying exasperatedly to win over both old staff and regulars such as Mr and Mrs Best, who have been coming every Wednesday for decades and spending about 25 grand a year. Mrs Best has only ever had the omelette and smoked salmon, which even by my mother's standards is conservative. Rogan's task is to get them to try a 12-course tasting menu with not a well-done steak or a coq au vin in sight.

Well, I tried it, Mrs Best. And I loved it. I have to be honest here and say that I can't really recall much of what I ate, as my last clear memory of the evening seems to have been the prosecco I had in the lounge served by a very suave, accomplished, old-school maître d'-cum-waiter. That's the way I like it. Call me old-fashioned but I don't want to think that my waiter might leave at any moment to join *Hollyoaks*. Oh, and I remember the room too; the old sickly, ornate, mirrored dining room that felt like you were eating inside a giant meringue has been stripped down, with Skandi-style rustic green natural fabrics and wood. It's more Ikea than the Ivy and it won't be to everyone's taste but I liked its crisp, relaxed informality.

The meal passed by in a fragrant and delicious blur of hake and foam and tiny balls of clotted stocks and fronds and drizzles and mouth-watering morsels of meat and vegetables (from other planets, I assume) that I couldn't place but tasted insanely good. The canapés were mind-blowing: parsnip crisps with pork fat and smoked eel, a wooden tray of black pebbles that looked like something from a Shinto shrine but held two pickle-poached mussels on the half shell. There was some raw ox in coal oil, which sounds like something you'd eat in a ruined power plant after a nuclear war has destroyed civilisation, but was, in fact, wonderful.

If I'm a little vague, forgive me. It was a lovely night and I didn't want to spoil it by scribbling throughout it. I should have taken notes I suppose but I didn't want to look like a food critic. Restaurateurs live in fear of food critics and their reviews, bowing and scraping and doing their best to please them but secretly they despise them, think they know nothing about food and want to skewer them to the table with the fish knives and lobster picks. Well, that's what I think anyway, even if Simon Rogan didn't, actually, say this when I worked alongside him.

Yes, that's right. I was Simon Rogan's sous chef once. Just for a day; an insight into the backstage world of the kitchens as part of a stay and dinner at L'Enclume, a dinner that I helped prepare. It was a fascinating experience, not least because it exploded pretty much every myth that TV has helped to create and foster about chefs and kitchens these past couple of decades. If your experience of restaurant kitchens is limited to watching Gordon Ramsay through splayed fingers, you will imagine them to be a Fight Club held in an Inner Circle of Hell; a horrible bear pit of overcooked, saggy male egos, where a dislikeable, foulmouthed bully barks at younger men and reduces them to tears over a collapsed soufflé or lumpy coulis; a preening macho world of sweat and anger.

Well, take it from me, the sweat is all glycerine and the anger is as staged as an Albert Square Christmas dinner. The kitchen at L'Enclume was a model of well-ordered calm and efficiency, and for good reason: it's a place of work not a boxing ring. Simon told me, while making me the best omelette I'd ever had, that you simply could not run a decent restaurant in the odious, grandstanding way that the Ramsays and Whites ham up for the cameras.

'See that guy there,' said Simon, indicating a young blond man julienning a courgette. 'He's been with me four years and I'm training him up to be my second in command. I've invested a lot in him, and he with me. If I spent my time screaming and f-ing and blinding at my staff, the food would be shit because people don't work well under those conditions, and my staff turnover would be phenomenal. I'd lose good staff like him as they'd be coming and going all the time. Shouting at people … it's all macho bollocks for the telly.' He added that in Ferran Adrià's elBulli in Spain, for many years the world's greatest restaurant and a place still spoken of with reverence by gourmets, there were highly prized tables downstairs in the kitchen, and from these you could see the staff glide around in silence and Zen-like calm under Adrià's patient but critical eye. 'It was like a bloody temple.'

I deconstructed a tequila sunrise dessert and helped with the smoking, billowing flasks of liquid nitrogen. I skinned some cow tongues – that wasn't that great to be honest – and I filled the hypo-dermic syringes with the egg yolk mixture that, later that evening, diners would, with childlike glee, squirt into their hot clear Chinese soup and would instantly become a noodle. 'Isn't this great?' I wanted to shout across the dining room, 'I filled those syringes,' thrilled to be part of the whole theatrical experience.

I also got an insight into how patient and forgiving a restaurateur must be with diners. When the cheese trolley arrived, laden with a hundred or so local cheeses of every flavour and hue and texture, a loud and very blokey bloke at the next table boomed, 'Got any Cheddar? I'm not into all this fancy stuff,' hoping that his regular guy 'bantz' would impress the ladies at the table. An intense wave of misery descended and time expanded sideways. The ladies looked like they wanted to crawl under the table and weep.

L'Enclume has two Michelin stars, and naturally I personally take a great deal of the credit for this. The French hasn't got one yet, and neither has Manchester House. Some people think that the TV series, didn't help, alienating the aloof and inscrutable Michelin judges with its reality telly brashness and naked human-interest angle. I watched a couple of them. I loved the moment when the hard and unyielding Mrs Best, determined not to like the new gastronomy at The French, snarkily asked her sated and smiling husband over the dessert he was clearly loving, 'Well, would you come here again?' 'Not with you,' he replied, his eyes liquid with delight, his mouth full of something obscenely pleasurable.

A word about restaurant critics. Apart from the ones who are my friends, and until such time as someone sees fit to employ me as one, I generally regard restaurant critics as scoundrels who in any decently organised society would be put to work on collective farms, or shot, depending upon my mood on the day (the day being 'the glorious day', obviously). This will seem harsh to some, but I fancy others will be nodding sagely in agreement and perhaps even unlocking the gun cabinet. Brian Eno once said to me that he could never be a critic, as he couldn't imagine spending his time 'trying to persuade people not to like things'. I coloured and winced at the time as I think he probably meant rock critics. But rock critics are creatures of Solomon, with wisdom and fairness and Mother Teresa levels of patient saintliness, compared to food critics. Effete, indulged fops of no use to anyone, these spiteful cry babies, having never known true hardship, will ruin some poor sod's livelihood over an underdone blini or a thin jus. They are nearly as bad as motoring journalists, and that is saying something.

Yes, I'm joking. But only a bit, and through gritted teeth. Reading the weekend papers, especially the thin, glib magazines that fall from them like snow sliding from a winter roof, I am always suffused with the same very particular emotions. I imagine that the fashion advice and tips on which cocktail bar 'to be seen' in and reviews of small, implausibly exclusive, St John's Wood trattorias, are meant to make one feel aspiration and chic, or faintly dissatisfied and imbued with what we now call 'FOMO' or fear of missing out. They have a slightly different effect on me, in that they make me want to form a UK branch of the Shining Path Peruvian Maoist Guerrilla Group and institute a brisk form of workers' dictatorship in which London-based restaurant critics toil on giant treadmills to generate electricity for the city of Doncaster.

Harsh I know. But in so many other ways, fair. What really bugs me about them, and I fancy you may know what's coming here, loyal reader, is their pride in their cosseted and blinkered London metrocentrism. A football writer who wouldn't come to Anfield or Old Trafford because he didn't fancy the train journey would soon be given his or her marching orders. A theatre critic who didn't bother with Stratford or the West Yorkshire Playhouse or Hull Truck or the Royal Exchange would soon find himself or herself similarly under-employed. Food critics, though, for whom a trip to Streatham is like scaling Annapurna without oxygen, wear their laziness and prejudice as a badge of honour, which is why, from my experience, most general readers outside the M25 despise them.

So my interest was piqued when the restaurant critic of *The Times* gave a rave review to a tapas bar in, astonishingly, Halifax. I had to check the page several times in case it was in Halifax, Nova Scotia; it's far more likely that a North London based foodie would head there on expenses than West Yorkshire. But no. Obviously the trip had taken it out of the poor thing, since he wrote as much about the various train changes he had 'had' to make, as he did the food. But the latter he did find grudgingly good, and his review was admirably positive, if littered with watery and patronising asides in the vein of Samuel Johnson's 'like a dog's walking on his hind legs. It is not done well; but you are surprised to find it done at all':

> Mini chorizo cooked in cider were a bit old-school, in the sense of Anglo-Spanish cooking before the London tapas boom, but the tortilla of the day was nice and sloppy … and a juicy slab of garlic-roasted ibérico suckling pig was more good value at only £7.90 (it's cute to see pence at all on a

menu, frankly, when you're used to London menus which have been rounded up to the nearest pound for years, and lately to the nearest five).

Nonetheless credit where it is due. Our fearless epicure (who later claimed that all the best restaurants in England were within half an hour of his London home and he only ventured further to appease his editor and the darkly muttering troglodytes beyond Potters Bar) had actually made the effort, even if he had never stopped going on about it. If he could manage the impossibly difficult, fraught and possibly dangerous trip from London to Halifax, surely I could manage to cross the Pennines, if clearly always on the lookout for brigands around Rochdale.

The approach to Halifax at dusk from the sprawl of Manchester, over England's highest motorway, the fabled, feared M62, and into the chill blue gloom of the Pennines, will either put you off your dinner or whet your appetite on the blade of your senses, depending on your temperament. For me, it was the perfect *hors d'oeuvre*.

Of course, no one from the north passes over Saddleworth Moor without an involuntary shudder, as this is where the Moors Murderers Brady and Hindley buried their young victims, and their last, Keith Bennett, lies here still, undiscovered but not forgotten. Before and beyond these sorrows, though, this is a beautiful if bleak place, and for centuries a place for the people from the nearby towns to come and stretch the legs and 'blow t'stink' of the factory off them.

Tonight, snow lies pale under a cold moon, and the moors rise dark like waves behind each ridge. In the gloaming, I pass one of the north's most treasurable oddities, and a Calderdale landmark – Stott Hall Farm has stood 1,100 feet up on this exposed Pennine flank near Scammonden since 1737. For two centuries, all there was to break the upland silence was the cry of birds and the bleating of sheep, the howling of the wind and the whisper of rain.

Then, in 1972, the men from the ministry of transport came, with their retinue of bulldozers, to clear a path for the new motorway. But the doughty farmer Ken Wilde refused to budge. Wilde had lived there since he was five and refused to move or accept the value which had been placed on the land under the terms of a compulsory purchase order. Eventually, the engineers decided it was possible to divide the east and west-bound carriageways and leave the farm intact between them on the high Lancashire–Yorkshire border. Tunnels were built underneath the motorway, allowing Wilde and his dogs to reach the open fell and tend the flock. And though Ken has gone and there's a tenant farmer now (who sometimes acts as unofficial service station to stricken drivers), Stott Hall remains a working concern, proudly marooned on its thin strip of grass while on each side the traffic roars on.

Past the farm and there lies Halifax, cast like a sparkling electric net across the landscape, like a web of silver light left by some giant spider across the Calder valley. Like Carlisle, Halifax is a border town, but like Carlisle disputation and proximity to 'the other side' has made it even more partisan. Halifax is as Yorkshire as Yorkshire gets, as Yorkshire as curry and wool. I tried googling for Halifax and Lancashire, hoping for some dissent or debate, but all I got was page after page about the wonderful Sarah Lancashire, one of the stars of *Last Tango in Halifax*, one of the acclaimed TV dramas of recent years and set in the town.

Maybe, like nearby Holmfirth and the long-running *Last of the Summer Wine*, this will become a TV tourist draw for the town like another recent development, the Eureka! science park. The Calder Valley may not be Silicon Valley, but it has claims to scientific and engineering fame. The man who discovered Uranus, William Herschel, was church organist here, and Halifax boasts the tallest folly in the world, the 275 foot Wainhouse Tower. It was designed by Isaac Booth for John Wainhouse as a chimney for his dye works. But this seems to be the last part of the story anyone agrees on. Some accounts say it was never paid for, so Booth kept it for himself. Others say Booth quit and Wainhouse got someone else to finish it, putting on the decorative cap with an observation platform reached by an interior spiral staircase containing 403 stairs. You can still go up there, if you have the puff, but only on public holidays.

Wool made Halifax rich, rich enough to have a handsome town hall built by the same man, Charles Barry, who built the Houses of Parliament. There is, literally, nothing like wool. No other material, natural or synthetic, can match its range of attributes and qualities – its warmth, durability, texture. Human ingenuity though can tweak and improve and fashion it, and we have been doing that since the Bronze Age. Wool-making took hold in West Yorkshire due to the terrain of the Pennines; too tough and coarse for crops or cattle but perfect for those hardy little buggers, sheep, and the steep streams of the Halifax hills meant plenty of water and steam power for the mill machinery. But then, the twentieth century brought steady decline and the mills fell into disrepair and dereliction.

Over the last few years, though, things have changed. Quality is ageless and British wool is popular once more with designers and rich customers. Even when the mills themselves no longer spin, no longer ring to the clatter of looms, they have found new purposes and are now lit again at night, great edifices of stone and light in the Yorkshire gloom.

Dean Clough sounds like he should have played for Bradford City or Leeds United in the early nineties – a small, stocky midfielder, quick and skilful but prone to rash challenges and indiscipline, and now running the youth team at Sheffield Wednesday or a bar in Fuengirola. In fact, Dean Clough is a part of Halifax (a clough being a sort of stream), and here in 1802, John Crossley, his brother Thomas, and James Travis started a mill. It boomed, employing 5,000 people by 1900 with a Kidderminster branch and warehouses in London and Manchester.

But times change and it closed as a mill in 1982 to be reborn shortly after as a successful commercial and cultural hub, watched over by a giant aluminium sheep by artist Frank Darnley, which wittily reflects the grand old building's former life. Now it houses the brilliant Northern Broadsides Theatre Company and some 150 other companies, studios, art galleries, a radio station (Phoenix Radio 96.7 FM!) and a couple of restaurants, one of which is so alluring that it can apparently even tempt the plump-lipped gourmands of Islington down the west coast mainline or the M6.

I get to Dean Clough Mill and Ricci's early, nearly an hour early, and, before I kick my heels around the bars of Halifax in the sleety rain, I pop in and see if they can fit me in. The tiny waitress fixes me with her huge brown eyes in a look of cod-exasperation that suddenly blooms into a smile. 'Oh I think we can fit you in and get you sat down, I'm sure,' she says, vowels rich as the smells from the kitchen, and she points me to one free table in the place.

I'm the only bloke here, except for a chap nursing an early evening cerveza at the bar. The place is packed with Halifax ladies ending or beginning their day or night, bags of shopping and big white wines to hand. Over the coming hour, it will fill and flow with other diners of every kind; nervous couples, laughing families, old friends, cute kids, change-jingling businessmen, clusters of tipsy, happy girls.

I like the fact that, in the teeth of economic adversity, and Michelin starred or not, the north eats out, shows it face, dresses up, flashes a bit of cash. I love that story about Nye Bevan, who when challenged that his taste for good wine and champagne sat uneasily with his supposed allegiances, said 'nothing but the best for the working class'. I will raise a glass to that, Nye.

I'm seated next to a couple of nice, garrulous, late forties women – one blonde, gritty, severe in that Yorkshire way that normally hides a lovely disposition; her friend more Beatrix Potter, twinkly in glasses and a lemon fleecy cardie. They shoo me towards the menu, and I fancy everything on it, except maybe the spicy lentil and cardomom dahl. Who orders lentil dahl in a Spanish restaurant, eh? It turns out my blonde neighbour has done just that. 'It's lovely,' she asserts and her friend explains, 'We've just been to see that film, *The Second Best Marigold Hotel*, and it's all set in India and so we fancied something like that, spicy, you know.'

We fall further into conversation. 'Have you come far?' asks the sharp, blonde one. Hmm, a little way, yes. 'Ah,' she says, 'you saw the review then? How far?' When I reply 'Manchester' she asks, 'Do you know Noel Gallagher?' Well, yes, a bit but that's not important. Tell me about you. What do they do in Halifax? The other lady replies, sheepishly, 'We own a tapas bar.'

If they have come to check out the competition, the menu must have made daunting reading. Aside from the maverick non-Iberian stuff, the spicy lentil dahl, spiced cauliflower fritters with rosemary, thyme & garlic roasted tomato & lemon chutney, there are tons of alluring riffs on classic tapas and chicetti, its Italian cousin – ox cheek spring roll with cauliflower purée, cooked Italian rustego ham marinated in wild herbs, with watercress and walnuts, whipped goats cheese and jamon Iberico stuffed piquillo peppers … In something of a daze, clouded further by a bloody lovely if totally unseasonal chilled Amontillado, I order pretty much at random and watch the sleet pulse in over the hills and the roofs of Halifax.

I quite like the ad hoc, even random, nature of the choreography of courses in tapas restaurants; you are never quite sure what will come, if it will come and when. I sat once getting gnawingly hungrier in a tapas bar on the Carmarthenshire coast with the poet Simon Armitage for an hour, and got through a couple of bottles of wine with nary a pitted olive emerging from the kitchen when, all at once, scurrying legions of small children arrived at our table laden with plates of food, most of which we hadn't ordered but fell upon like starving men, which we were. Later recounting the tale Simon said, 'The food came with all the suddenness with which it previously hadn't', which I thought was a rather beautiful gnomic haiku.

In Ricci's it came quickly and kept on coming; a dish of powerful, almost disturbingly porky pigs' head croquetas, scallops on a lemon quenelle, zingy green beans. But best of all, and still haunting my dreams weeks later, is a pork and chorizo scotch duck egg with celeriac remoulade and apple puree draped in strands of saffron.

My young waitress came back to check everything was alright, perhaps because I was lying under the table sobbing. I imagine she gets this all the time. When she finds out I've come over from Salford way, she's excited and curious. She's 18 and headed to Salford uni in the autumn for a degree in psychotherapy and counselling, and you can see in her face the anticipation of embarking on life's great adventure. I tell her she'll have an ace time and I mean it.

Because of some very minor mix-up with the order, the owner – transatlantic, young, on the case – is hugely apologetic and insists it's on the house. Minutes later our brown-eyed future psychotherapist announces, a little disturbingly, 'Grandpa's balls!' as she proffers pudding, two spherical churros-type offerings served with an espresso cup of bitter chocolate and orange sauce, the lovely comforting fattiness undercut by a rapier swish of citrusy orange. Blissful. I couldn't manage more than about eight though.

In line with Simon Rogan's observations, the kitchen, glimpsed at the end of the long bar with circular stools – my favourite kind – seems calm and breezy. 'Not on a Saturday, it isn't!' she tells me. 'They're queuing up from five to get a seat to eat at the bar. Even worse on bank holidays … well, I mean better of course.'

Those bank holidays come six times a year, as Blur sang on their track 'Bank Holiday', 'Days of enjoyment to which everyone cheers. Bank holiday comes with a six pack of beer … then it's back to work AGAIN.' If I was going to write about work and leisure, then I would need to write about this institution. These, and a handful of other red letter days, were how we plot the passing of the working year, how we mark it, in charcoal briquettes and multi-packs of lager, in trick or treat bags and gift cards, in traffic jams and record fairs, in lie-ins and days out …

CHAPTER 6

MAKING A DAY OF IT

Bank holidays in Silloth and Southport
and a trip to see the 'Lights'

Only virgins and generals keep diaries, they say. Samuel Pepys, Adrian Mole, Alan Bennett, Michael Palin, Bridget Jones and other diarists of note notwithstanding, that may still be true. But everyone used to have one, if not keep it. Nowadays, when the future is swiped into view with a finger, giving a child a 'day to day diary' for Christmas would maybe seem a little weird, like buying them a cummerbund or purchase ledger or a book of log tables; an oddly adult, formal gift, a queer relic of an era before phones were smarter than their owners.

Back in the days before Apps and Apple, schoolkids even had their own diaries, little leatherette volumes in burgundy or green, crammed with stuff which the stern implication was would surely come in handy one day though it never did: avoirdupois and troy weights and the differing grains thereof, chains and furlongs, pecks and bushels, nautical miles and the Beaufort scale. Its tiny printed pages told you that today was the second Sunday after Septuagesima, whatever that was, and how many more weeks of Advent and Lent, or more importantly chocolate and no chocolate, there were.

To a child these markings meant little. But once they had been signposts to navigate the year by. Before electric light and fridges and central heating tamed the seasons, smoothed out the jagged edges and rising ridges of passing time, this was how we charted our progress round the sun and round the working year, from pole to festive pole. Wakes and Whitsuntide, Candlemas and Michaelmas; a kid nowadays would probably assume that they were minor characters from *Game of Thrones* rather than old red letter days. In Macclesfield, they have their own special holiday for the silk workers called, fabulously, Barnaby.

High days and holidays; even in our sleepless 24/7 world, we still keep them though we give them different names. What my mum calls Whit Monday is now Spring Bank Holiday but the meaning holds. It's a day away from the normal round, one of those six times a year Blur identified that we refuse to let the toad Work squat on our lives. The need for days like this, days when we lie in, kick back, slope off, dress up, have fun, can be seen in the enthusiasm with which we cultivate and embrace new ones; Halloween and trick or treat, Valentine's and Mother's Day, Red Nose Day, Pudsey, Wogan and baths of beans. What is the fuss about Transfer Deadline Day by Sky Sports if not the childish need for special days dressed up as news?

For working people, precious days of paid holiday were rare, hard won and to be celebrated fiercely and without restraint. Leisure in the pre-industrial world is sometimes rather rosily seen as an idyllic sunlit parade of maypole dancing, cider quaffing, Morris dancing and cricket on the village green in a Merrie England theme park, a Pop Larkin vision of rural life as full of plump, buxom and bucolic pleasure. Then along comes the Industrial Revolution with its dark satanic mills and we're all condemned to be sooty-faced factory fodder. In fact, for most people, the myth of the pre-industrial golden age was just that – a myth, and one sadly encouraged by well-meaning types like folk music collector Cecil Sharp and a casual acquaintance with *Cider with Rosie*. Rural life, for those not lucky enough to belong to the landed gentry, was fairly grim and circumscribed. Holidays and free time were strictly rationed. Apart from the odd hiring fair or rare afternoon spent rush-bearing, cheese-rolling, well-dressing or the like, life for the agricultural worker was more *Tess of the D'Urbervilles* than *Darling Buds of May*.

The Factory Act of 1833 prohibited the employment of children under nine in cotton mills and restricted the hours that older children could work. It also prohibited night work for youngsters and made educational provisions. Further acts improved the lot of children and women and eventually in 1847 the full Ten-Hour Act, as it was known, became law for workers of both sexes and all ages. It was patchy in its coverage and far from exhaustive or ideal in its provisions but it was the beginning of a turning of the tide toward workers' rights and employers' responsibility, of a recognition that welfare and safety as well as profit and productivity needed to be borne in mind (a trend in working conditions that seemed irreversible until the 1980s). For many ordinary British people, it offered a new, richer life in which education, self-improvement, sport and pastimes became not just the preserve of the rich. Workers' playtime had begun, at least for men. For as Dennis Brailsford puts it in his book *Sport Time and Society*, 'working class women, though they might nominally have the same free time as their menfolk, had the harder bargain. The meals still had to be on the table even on holidays.'

From there on, the rest of the nineteenth century brought forth what's been described as a 'leisure revolution'. As people crowded together in the big, bustling new Victorian towns and cities, as their jobs become more intense and their hours more regular, so the appetite for recreation – often noisy, wild, hedonistic recreation as release from their arduous, private, silent work – grew. A French politician called Léon Faucher who came to northern England at the time claimed in his *Studies Of The English* that the urban working class 'cannot partake of anything in moderation'. In the north we like to say, 'all things in moderation … including moderation'.

Zero-hours contracts, erosion of union power and more fluid and flexible working hours have meant that the formal paid holiday is not quite the social institution it once was, when the whole of Britain would seemingly down tools and put on a knotted handkerchief. But you only have to drive on an English motorway on Easter Sunday

or hear the sorrow and regret in the weather forecaster's voice on
August Bank Holiday Monday or try to buy a drink in Ireland on
Good Friday to see that, in these islands, the bank holiday is still a
cherished national institution.

As a youth, as I kicked a football about with Brownie, Nidge
and Mike Tyrer, or went to Knowsley Safari Park and watched
monkeys pull my dad's windscreen wipers off (off his Ford Capri.
He didn't have windscreen wipers) or eat a 99 on Ainsdale Beach, I
could see just why Good Friday was good to me, but less so Jesus.
But then Easter was a funny business all round. The logic by which
the gruesome and brutal execution of mankind's saviour should be
commemorated by eating chocolate eggs filled with Smarties eluded
me, but I wasn't complaining.

I wasn't complaining either as I made my way in 2014, along with
a goodly proportion of Cumbria, on the most glorious Good Friday
in years, to the north-west coast of England. All morning, weather
presenters had beamed and made elaborate sweeping hand gestures
in front of maps covered in egg-yolk suns and beetling isobars. It was
going to be a beautiful day and while some in this part of England
were heading for the high cloudless fells, a great mass of humanity had
packed its bucket and spade and Factor 50 and was heading for Silloth.

Like some people, Silloth was built for fun really. The pretty
town, nestling on the wide Solway Firth, eight miles across the water
from Scotland at a terminus of the railway from Carlisle, grew quickly
as a place of recreation for the factory workers of the great Border
city and its workers. Famed for its shrimps and sunsets, its long sandy
beaches, mild winters, hot summers and pleasant airy streets, it is one
of the very finest examples of a Victorian seaside town in England. Its
heyday may have been a century or so ago, but even now in this age
of budget air travel and stag weekends in Riga, a hot bank holiday will
find its streets and beaches crowded with the workers of Cumbria, and
its population of 3,000 more than doubles in the summer months.
Golf courses and caravan parks abound.

The glittering blue Solway, which can make the promenade as cold and inhospitable as a Baltic naval base in winter, is a powerful draw on a day like this, when Dumfries and its parent mountain Criffel look just a stone skim away across the glinting water. I have heard Silloth sneered at by clots who've never been but assume it will be some decrepit resort that time forgot, when it fact it is just shy, easy to miss and very easy in its own skin; sweet and likeable but without the brashness or the air of seediness that can hang around parts of Blackpool or Morecambe.

That said, it's good I didn't come yesterday as all roads into town were closed because of an armed robbery at the bank. And, true, if you arrive like I do from the north via Skinburness, you can glimpse a sad side of the town. This lonely hamlet is a haven for birdwatchers and the raised shingle spur of Grune Point is a fabulous spot. It's a Site of Special Scientific Interest with the Solway on one side and the bleak, alluring saltmarshes on the other, rich in sandwort, sea holly and sand couch-grass, haunted by fast-rising tides than can snare the unwary. But the Skinburness hotel looks forlorn; shuttered and creepy like somewhere that Scooby-Doo and the gang might investigate to discover that Old Man Rogers was deliberately scaring customers away from so that he could build a new supermarket there and, yes, he would have gotten away with it too, if it hadn't been for those pesky kids. 'Gas Off' says a chalked sign hanging limply in the doorway, the 3 RAC and AA Rosettes now covered in dust and mildew.

Spirits improve though as you stroll into town along the cobbled main drag. This is called Criffel Street, named after the bold, shapely mountain that faces you across the water. The day is heating up and there's lively trade and some deft aerobatics at the Silloth Town Council BMX Track, tucked in a wood overlooking the sea. Down the road at the RAFA club, there's 'Live Big Screen Sky Sports' and a sign exhorting you to 'Be Part Of Something Special Every Day', although it would have to be monumentally special to keep me in a sepulchral interior on a day like today. To get you in the mood for relaxed fun, there's a large pictorial chart in the doorway, explaining the specifications of various fighter aircraft; the thrust of the AV-8 Harrier, the wingspan and machine gun capabilities of the Eurofighter Typhoon. All the fun stuff.

Silloth is justly proud of its green. It has its own website, its own Facebook page and its own Twitter feed. Here you will learn that it is 'one of the largest and longest village Greens in England and forms a grassy link between the Silloth townscape and the sea front promenade, complementing the grand regency style buildings on Criffel Street, which runs along the opposite side of the broad cobbled road.' Today it's overflowing with lads and dads playing football, toddlers toddling, dogs chasing drifting Frisbees and young women in sunglasses stretching out in the sun. Squat and proud in the midst of all this is a cute feature; a clay millennium disc with various elements of the town illustrated – the convalescent home, the aerodrome and the tennis club – like something from a giant's plasticine playbox.

Further down Criffel Street, the Queen's Hotel looks smart in biscuit and white and, next to it, I am drawn to investigate the sprawling warren of the Queen's Court Charity Shop. Despite, or maybe because of the sun outside, scores of bargain hunters are leafing absently through old bri-nylon shirts, seventies board games and laminate place mats featuring hunting scenes. A large pleading sign in the doorway says 'No More Videos Please'. The last word in desirable tech chic in my youth is now a sorry bit of aged tat. There is a cassette section, too, featuring a breathtaking range of artists: Bruckner, Suzanne Vega, Harry Secombe, The Royal Scots Dragoon Guards, Slayer. In the CD section are six different Billie Piper albums. Someone has clearly gone off Billie very suddenly and irrevocably, ditching the lot in one fell swoop in one of those moves that must have a story behind it – a divorce, a move, perhaps just a tale of growing up and moving on, to Slayer maybe. Wondrous items abound; literally hundreds of jigsaws, each with a tale to tell of rainy static caravan holidays in North Wales. There's a pristine copy of the MB games classic Frustration 'with the Pop-o-matic dice', a child's glow-in-the-dark skeleton suit and a knitted toilet-roll cosy in the shape of an Edwardian lady. No wonder both Paul McCartney and Tom Waits have written superbly sad and creepy songs ('Junk' and 'Soldier's Things') that are essentially simply inventories of the items you find in these places.

The toy soldier museum is just about to open but a glance at the leaflet makes me wonder how many rows of small lead figures I could want to look at before I think myself sated. Four perhaps. I put the leaflet back in the arms of the giant guardsman outside – not real – and head over to another part of the green and that most oddly English and variable of things, the craft fair. By the wildly inconsistent standards of the enterprise, this is quite a good one. There are some actually half decent carved wooden sculptures, a perfectly edible Guinness chutney and some coasters of owls that are only mildly disturbing. There is certainly nothing here as poor as the crude plywood cat's face with googly eyes and legend 'You're No-One Till You've Been Ignored By A CAT!!!' that adorns my fridge, bought from a craft fair in the north Lakes in a moment of irony. But the best thing about the fair is the strange and particular ambience in the tent. The air is beginning to gently congeal, the white canvas walls throb with light, and from underfoot comes that sweet, musty aroma of grass gently cooking under sunlit tarpaulin that may be the signature scent of an English summer.

Outside at the end of the green an enormous queue snakes its sunburned way out of the chip shop, scarlet of arm and mustard of shorts. The obscure and confusing 'two door' queuing system is causing some confusion and not a little simmering tension in this hungry high noon. The accents are mainly Cumbrian but the specifically local lady ahead of me is starting to get a tad vexed at our ineptitude with the procedures. I give her a sheepish smile and she softens and her son tells me that he's a local musician and plays on 'Frank's new album'. In this part of the county, Frank is not Sinatra, but Dunnery, the prodigiously gifted guitar prodigy who with his band It Bites, had a hit that readers of an eighties vintage will remember with 'Calling All The Heroes'.

Once the queuing has been mastered, there is to come the complexities of the menu and noticeboard. The choice, as it was in Grandma Pollards, is enormous and bewildering. Skate, rollmops, black pudding, haggis, 'shrek kebab one pound', turkey sticks, scallops, breakfast baps. Pinned behind the counter are several cuttings and pictures. A page from a newspaper shows a young girl offering some chips to the camera and the caption, 'The girl who can finally eat fish and chips', a nice human interest tale from the local paper one assumes. By this is a blurred photocopied picture of two burly shirtless men with shaven heads. Before them another man in a white shirt is crouching in what seems to be supplication. From the bunting and vague crowds in the background of the shot, they seem to be at some kind of fete. Below it, there's a caption which may explain things. It says, in thick marker pen, 'Soup and a roll one pound'.

Armed with the banker choice of chips and curry sauce and an icy perspiring cream soda straight from the fridge, I head for the fairground. As I near it, I can hear that over the crackling boomy tannoy, they're playing pre-Beatle rock and roll standards: Del Shannon's 'Runaway', Johnny Tillotson's 'Poetry In Motion'. These are perfectly acceptable fairground soundtrack selections I'd say. I would also allow glam pop, disco and 'The Boys Are Back In Town' by Thin Lizzy. Nothing hip or clever or too modern. No one wants to hear some sensitive young man blubbing a ballad when you're trying to snog or fight on the waltzer, be it Nick Drake or Ed Sheeran.

I lurk by the dodgems. The dodgems fascinate me. Long before an electric car was something that Guardianistas approved of, it meant slow mo gladiatorial combat in these little vehicles showering sparks. What is the etiquette here? Can you go after a stranger without motive or mercy, like the truck did in Steven Spielberg's early classic *Duel*? Who can you not ram? Breastfeeding women? OAPs, people carrying fragile crystal ornaments? I think there should be signs that explain the etiquette, like the ones forbidding bombing and petting in swimming pools.

Dark and whirling against the azure sky, the Ferris wheel is going round at a hell of a lick it seems to me and with some distinctly queasy looking customers. As a precaution, I move a little away from any possible trajectory. A woman tries to enjoin me to 'hook a duck, love' and adds something I think might be mildly suggestive from her 'nudge nudge, wink wink' delivery but I can't make it out as a large metal box on stilts next to her suddenly lurches into noisy life, like a cannibalised transit van or a monstrous *Transformers*' version of a chest freezer.

When a small and distinctly unimpressed looking young girl emerges from it, I realise that I have been in one myself. They're a sort of computer animated fairground ride that work on the principles of big screen visuals and vibrations. They have state of the art ones at the Futuroscope multimedia theme park near Poitiers, France. From my (admittedly limited) experience of the ones at British funfairs, though, most smartphone games have better graphics and most minicab rides fling you about more. But that is to miss the point. A shabby cajoling cheerfulness – and an undercurrent of crime, lasciviousness and food poisoning – is what makes our funfairs so much more, well, fun, than Walt Disney's raspberry Reich.

Beyond the mild clamour of the rides, past the gently revolving outsized teacups with their serene cargo of toddlers, a sleek wooden walkway curves out to a platform looking out over the dunes of West Beach and the town's little dock. Johnny Kidd and Connie Francis are still faintly audible on the breeze as the shrimp boats come and go between the harbour and the Solway. At a pub quiz in Wigan once, we were asked, 'What's grey and got 40,000 muscles?' My mate Tim piped up instantly 'The Solway Firth'. The answer was actually 'an elephant's trunk' but Tim's answer was bloody quick, bloody funny and probably an underestimate. Most days, the Solway is a leaden, churning sheet of salt water. Today it's huge, blue and invigorating.

The compass on the platform reels off directions and distances: 'Isle of Man 55, Skiddaw 19, Carlisle 19, Dumfries 16'. Silloth is a very English seaside resort in a county that is proudly so. The nearest major town though, as the crow flies, is a Scottish one. But the crow flies over some deep, cold, lonely water. You'd struggle to get your big shop home without wet feet.

I come back to town via the newly refurbished Victorian pagoda, an airy belvedere overlooking the Solway where a small child sits between her numbed, drawn parents, alternately screaming and listlessly licking an ice cream. I can still hear her as I slip inside the welcoming darkness and clatter of the amusement arcade.

Again, I'm something of a sucker for these places. That vestigial big kid still finds a nugget of a thrill in the lights and noise, the metallic clunk and gush of the all too rare pay-outs, the tinny rock and roll of the pinball machine, rather than see it for what it probably is, cheap and a little seedy. Such places are essentially unchanged since I was a child, the passage of time marked only in the nods to transient movies and pop stars in the games and slot machines. Most are as timeless as the sphinx.

There's the coin waterfall where banks of two pence pieces rise up in great frozen waves, defying gravity and obscurely but surely rigged. Incredibly, this was turned into a TV show a couple of years back, suggesting that Pro Celebrity Shove Ha'Penny might get commissioned soon. There's the shotgun ranges, now updated to feature laser cannons and lurching mutants. By the Whittakers Ascot Gold Cup horse racing game a young mum in a fringed leather jacket stands fixed in steely concentration next to a sign saying 'Gambling Should Be Fun, Gamble Responsibly'. This warning is, I guess, for those who were hell-bent on losing their houses 2p at a time.

As the bank holiday enters its mature last phase and the sun drops blazing toward the firth and the horizon, I make my way along with a stream of traffic south along the coast road, along miles of dunes and bleaching light. The next village south is Blitterlees, which like

Skinburness sounds like a painful and ugly epidermal disease ('I'm afraid it's Blitterlees, Mrs Warburton'). Allonby, with its one string of pastel buildings facing the wave-tossed sea and little else, reminded me of those Cornish villages like Rock. Except Allonby has fewer rangy gorgeous floppy-fringed youths lolling in salmon pink rugby shirts with the collars turned up. It does have a clutch of intriguing buildings though: a reading room, a seawater baths, the Baywatch Hotel, Jack's Surf Bar and a chippy called The Codfather, who have pinched the famous marionette-on-strings logo from the movie. Except here a juicy plaice is dangling from it.

Those affluent Cornish villages are places of pilgrimage these days for their Rick Stein endorsed chi-chi seafood outlets. Gourmets come in their droves to Allonby too, but for less formal, more affordable fare. There was a huge queue outside one building which I took to be a pub, a gig or a cinema, but which turned out to be an ice cream parlour. Not just any ice cream parlour but one of global repute. Twentyman's is world-famous, I now know, having done some research during which I found out that one customer drove his besotted, pregnant wife from London to Allonby and back in one round trip to get a fix of Twin Cornet or Nougat Wafer.

I ended my day in the fishing town of Maryport and found it transformed since my last visit on a rainlashed day in the nineties. Then I had sat in a gloomy pub watching people lose their umbrellas into the sea, eating a giant filled Yorkshire pudding from which I later got a humdinger of a stomach bug. This bank holiday was altogether nicer, and it wasn't just the Mediterranean weather either. There was a definite hint of the Cumbrian Riviera; a yellow jet ski roared around in the dock, a young lad in a Carlisle United top piloted his shrimp boat with a wave at a girl on the harbour rail. The day and the town seemed spring-cleaned and freshly painted. The marina was crowded with nuzzling pleasure craft with names like *Dolfyn* and *Lady Friendship*, on whose deck lolled a lazy dog and two ladies in caps taking a break from swabbing for a G&T. From the harbour wall, watching the little boats knock and bob, and the cottages gleaming, you could have been in somewhere much more soft and southerly – Devon or Dorset, Portofino even at a pinch. I could live like this, I thought. I might even get one of those caps.

The musician Billy Bragg once told me that when he moved from London to the Dorset coast, his friends wondered how he'd get on living in the country. To which he always replied, 'I don't live in the country, I live by the sea … it's different.' He's right. Living in that strange, debatable margin between the human hinterland and the otherness out there, on the cusp of the long argument between the land and the sea, has its own peculiar quality. I can claim some small knowledge of this as I lived in a seaside town for two years. Well, I say it was a seaside town. As all of Lancashire knows, being beside the seaside in Southport can involve a full scale expedition to the far horizon with your bucket and spade and a couple of overnight camps.

Whereas brash Blackpool's sea buffets the prom on a windy day and soaks your chips with sea water if you're unlucky, its posher cousin Southport often doesn't let the old salty dog within a hundred yards of it. Nathaniel Hawthorne wrote, 'In all my experience of Southport, I have not yet seen the sea.' But that didn't stop it being the holiday resort or day out of choice for the self-made men and their wives of this part of the north. In my childhood, when Blackpool was too far for a bank holiday ride, or you simply couldn't face its daunting full-on hedonism, there was always lovely Southport, with its rolling dunes and its pitch and putt, the rococo iron canopies of Lord Street and its wide tree-lined boulevards. These, it's said, were the model for Napoleon III's reconstruction of Paris, after he briefly lived in Southport.

Like Napoleon, I lived here briefly too; a student in the early 1980s and I loved it, mostly. Yes, we lived in what now seems comic penury, clothed from Oxfam, boiling up bones for soup, 'fiddling the leccy' (till the landlord caught on) and breaking the ice on the inside of the windows on January mornings. But somehow there was always money for ice cream, hot dogs, the latest releases on Postcard Records of Scotland, beer and curry.

My first ever proper curry on a proper night out was here in Southport. The oddly named Oriental Grill on Lord Street was the venue, I went with a girl called Carole and I had a pathia, picked pretty much at random from a menu full of tempting mysteries and still a favourite to this day. Returning after several decades, I didn't expect a blue plaque, but I was disappointed to see that the Oriental Grill has gone, replaced by what seems to be the overflow storage room of an electrical shop. I hope, as they wheel in the tumble dryers and plasma tellies, they feel a little of the frisson I had back then taking my first footling steps into the adult world; a teenager with a girl, a flat and a chequebook just ripe for overdrawing from.

I've come back, for the first time since I moved out all those years ago, to spend a bank holiday here, and a crucial part of my mission is to visit one of Britain's oddest and most wonderful tourist attractions. I'll get on to that. For me, though, freighted with memories, things start to get Proustian round about … well, round about the roundabout – the Scarisbrick Roundabout at the bottom of Eastbank Street.

Six of us lived in a rambling old Victorian pile here on Nolan Street. When I stroll down there, to the end of the cul de sac by the garage wall where number 60 stands, my stomach begins to knot and I find myself goosepimpling and prickling with a curious mixture of affection and horror. Memories come crowding in like ghosts: good, bad, weird, intimate, funny; a splurge of buried, now resurrected feelings from when I was a different person. Number 60's up for sale. By posing as a prospective buyer, I could go in, go up the stairs to where Sue would smoke dope and make dresses, to the attic room where I danced with Parminder the Indian post-grad to Wham's 'Wake Me Up Before You Go-Go', to the big communal room where we ate greasy, unidentifiable broth and smoked roll-ups in our moth-eaten charity shop jumpers and cords and watched on a tiny snowy black and white TV, Hurricane Higgins beat Dennis Taylor and Tommy Cooper die on stage at *Live from Her Majesty's*.

There's a gleaming car dealerships at the roundabout now, and a McDonald's which I guess we'd have blown some of our grant on when we couldn't face more soup, or another portion of spag bol with packet beanfeast. Our old local The Shakespeare was never particularly throbbing or vital even on Sunday, 'entertainment night', when a drum and organ duo calling themselves Roy Rocket and Mr Personality would play bored and desultory sets to a half empty function room. Now it isn't even that lively; boarded and shuttered with no trace of the last-orders arguments about anarcho-syndicalism and Echo and the Bunnymen that once raged here over eked out halves of cider.

We drank on Eastbank Street too, and shopped and signed on in the long holiday. There was a great, poky little indie record shop, now a tanning salon of course, where I picked up some much loved vinyl artefacts: the 12 inch EP of *Into Battle with the Art Of Noise*, The Residents' *The Third Reich 'N' Roll* album, 'Blue Boy' by Orange Juice on 7 inch. The street is a short, busy thoroughfare connecting the pasty shops and forlorn boozers of the town's dull hinterland with the sudden affluence and glamour of Lord Street. This is what delighted Napoleon; lovely Lord Street with its hanging baskets, fancy ironwork, comfortable in its boulevardier elegance over rival Blackpool's windy, vinegary Golden Mile.

Before Nolan Street, I lived briefly in a flat on the seafront. It stood across the road from the old Southport Theatre where I saw many bands including Focus, Elvis Costello and, by accident, the Nolan Sisters. Now it is a Ramada Hotel. Gratifyingly though my old flat is still there. Clearly, English Heritage have shown no interest as yet as it is as tired looking and grubbily whitewashed as it ever was. For old times' sake, I take lunch at the legendary Sandgrounder café, happy rendezvous of many childhood day trips and a source of much sustenance back in my student day, especially out of season when they didn't mind you huddling for an hour or two by the gurgling Gaggia machine with slim volumes of poetry. In my memory, Southport in the eighties was invariably chill or foggy, wind fanning the sand over the dunes and whipping along the front. But maybe that was just all The Smiths records we were listening to. I never remember scorchers like this bank holiday, with its parade of Ray-Bans and reddening forearms.

I stretch back on a plastic chair in the warm sun outside the Sandgrounder and order a latte and a hot dog, flush and worldly in a way I never was back then. I'm served by a very smart, articulate young Italian man. I can't say the same for the kid opposite me who sits sullenly grunting and throwing caps at the floor, causing a constant cracking like a small scale gunfire exchange and thus annoying some small dogs nearby, and me. His T-shirt reads 'Is it me you're looking for?' and I think, yes, but only in order to hunt you down and kill you. Slogans on clothes rarely conjure the gaiety or mirth intended, I think. Like a tie featuring the 'Mona Lisa' or a pair of plastic breasts, they are what 'characters' have instead of a personality.

The café attracts a varied clientele; Southport in miniature. Two bearded adult males arrive on chopper bikes – hipsters one imagines – and wonder aloud whether to have the peri peri chicken. At another table is an elderly couple in M&S casuals. She talks loudly ('tek care, luv') into a mobile phone she cradles gently like a bomb or a piece of fine crystal, just like my mum does. He smiles thoughtfully at his copy of *Private Eye*. A proud indulgent Scouse dad buys his charming little girl a big fluffy lion from a nearby gift shop. Liverpudlians have long had an affinity with Southport; it's always been their seaside 'day out' of choice. This can make for a nice upbeat vibe in the summer, though less so when the Orange lodges parade through the town on the anniversary of Battle of the Boyne. These bodies have a strong presence in Liverpool, institutions grounded in a fearful nineteenth-century English response to the influx of the city's large Irish Catholic population. The Liverpool lodges come to Southport to do their parading, a tradition which has always divided opinion in the town.

I'm back in my old haunt to generally soak up the mood of a balmy bank holiday but, as said, also for a very specific reason. Over the last decade or so, it's been nice to see the quirkier British tourist attraction going from object of derision to guilty pleasure to genuinely loved, thanks in no small part to a lovely book called *Bollocks to Alton Towers* by Robin Halstead, Jason Hazeley and Alex and Joel Morris, the team behind the wonderful Framley Examiner website. In this age of sterile mass entertainment, the soporific blandness of the multiplex and the chain pub, we've begun to cherish our proper one-offs. I'm thinking of places like Blackgang Chine, the queer, quirky theme park on the Isle of Wight; the quaint strangeness of the Branxton Cement Menagerie, just off the A697 near Coldstream and built by a local handyman to amuse his son; or the gripping and upsetting, family-run Kelvedon Hatch Secret Nuclear Bunker, six underground floors of chilling Cold War fun under dreary Middlesex farmland. But one of the very finest and oddest of such attractions is tucked away in a back street in residential Southport and, dripping in sweat and squinting at Google Maps, I was pounding the hot pavements of the old town in search of it.

I've walked so often down these streets. Head down against the drizzle, I'd bustle over this railway bridge in my long overcoat courtesy of Sue Ryder. Today, though, Southport is sweltering and so am I and I'm looking for something else, something that only arrived soon after I left town, unemployed and adrift in the north, with my Smiths records in a cardboard box. 'Please, please, please, let me get what I want,' I thought then and I think now, except then it was a job and a life, and now it is the British Lawnmower Museum.

Long after common sense has told me to give up, with those words of the Lovin' Spoonful about being 'half dead' on 'sidewalks hotter than a match-head', I'm circling and backtracking, sweat pooling down my spine when suddenly I see it. At the top of a street where I actually used to live with a trio of girls from West Yorkshire, in this 'seaside town that they forgot to bomb', as Moz once sang reputedly of Southport. (Actually they didn't forget; the Germans bombed what locals called the 'Blind Babies Home' in 1941.)

The Lawnmower Museum is the baby of Brian Radam, a two times UK Lawnmower racing champion and devotee of British engineering who opened the museum as an upstairs adjunct to dad Stanley's discount gardening store on Shakespeare Street. You still go in via the shop, which on a day like today has that deliciously cool, richly smelly interior of all hardware shops. Even if you regard all DIY as a form of blacklegging that deprives skilled tradesman of work (this is my excuse anyway), there is something about a hardware store, its potent brew of odours, its rows of mysterious, knobbly, gleaming, coiled, brassy, rubbery artefacts, that cannot fail to hypnotise, to make you feel (wrongly) that even you could fit a tap, or put up an architrave.

In fact, like the shops in M R James and Robert Aickman stories, the shop is ramshackle and delightfully odd in a way that borders on the sinister, but in a good way. I am approached by a youngish, biggish lad, mildly dishevelled, wearing a pair of frayed boot cut jeans and muddy black boots beneath an outsized purple blazer, white shirt and skew-wiff black tie. The effect is part golf club barman who got dressed in the dark on a farm, part Stone Roses roadie.

He tells me that, yes, the museum will be open for a while yet and I am welcome to take the tour. Firstly though, for research purposes, I pick up a souvenir DVD for £10, though if you don't want to stretch to this kind of outlay, there is a terrifically unfunny YouTube segment you can watch culled from Australian TV, where some bloody ocker smirks along in the 'Strewth, look at the quirky poms!' fashion. My young guide apologises for the refurbishment work and 'the exposed wood in places' and points out a few stray (and presumably historic) lawnmowers that have had to be placed downstairs. Radio 2 plays loudly. He takes my two quid entrance money and smiles, 'And now if you'd like to go upstairs into the museum, I'll begin the audio tour.' By the time I get to the top of the flight, that tour is crackling into life.

'Welcome to the British Lawnmower Museum, the nation's fore-most museum of garden machinery history. Lawnmowers are a very British obsession; we manufacture the best lawnmowers in the world, but sadly we have lost virtually all our British lawnmower companies. Nowadays when people are replacing their old lawnmowers, they purchase a grasscutter without knowing it, and consequently we are losing all our lawns as well …'

Well, there is much to ponder here. Firstly, let us mull what the difference is between a grasscutter and a lawnmower. I didn't know then, and I don't know now, even after many an hour (OK, minutes) of assiduous googling. But I did appreciate that the narrator – Brian himself possibly – did not feel the need to slow down the pace of the thrusting narrative by explaining but simply assumed I, surely a lawnmower kind of guy, would know. I liked that. So much of our modern media treats us like bovine simpletons. Here that trend was proudly bucked. The British Lawnmower Museum assumes that you're serious about gardening technology, not just some vapid dilettante in search of cheap thrills. Good man, Brian.

The other thing to ponder is the really loud 'phut phut phut' on the audio tour soundtrack. For a while, I take this to be an illustrative sound effect, a slightly too loud one, yes, but an intentional bit of colour, an early steam lawnmower perhaps. It's only later when the soundtrack features an actual lawnmower sound effect that I realise that the other constant phutting and rumbling, is, in fact, a massive, distracting glitch on the soundtrack.

Despite this the next hour is, in a very real sense, an education. The lawnmower was invented in 1830 by Edwin Beard Budding. He was working in a textile mill in Stroud, Gloucestershire, when he designed a machine to trim the nap off the cloth used for guardsmen's uniforms. In a moment of inspiration, he had the revolutionary, not to say obtuse, idea to use it to cut grass.

Now here the thought did occur to me, how had we cut the grass on lawns before? With scissors? Why weren't the stately homes of

England all obscured by chin-high thistles? But let it pass. Everyone thought Budding was nuts anyway and he was forced to test drive his new contraption at night under cover of darkness for fear of mockery. Soon, though, all of Britain was gripped by lawnmower fever and the new invention was the iPhone of its day, a cool must-have accessory for scenesters.

In the twentieth century the top brands of British engineering, marques more associated with sports cars and aircraft, produced their own elegant and desirable models: Rolls-Royce, Royal Enfield, Vincent, Dennis, Hawker Siddeley, Perkins Diesel, British Leyland and more. Packed into a handful of small upstairs rooms (with reinforced floors, presumably) is the full story of the lawnmower from vicious looking whirling scythes to the sleek Jags and Rovers of the breed, through to the minimal, plastic, retro-chic Flymos of the 1980s, made by Swedish power tool giants Husqvarna, a name more usually associated with bearded lumberjacks wielding chainsaws in petrified forests. Based on the hovercraft, the Flymo was sold door to door, like encyclopedias or clothes pegs, and was coloured orange as this was the colour preferred by potential female purchasers in a survey.

For the casual visitor though in our shallow, fame-obsessed age, the celebrity lawnmower's section will be the big draw. Over the years, Brian and his team have put together an impressive collection of gardening equipment of the stars that adds a whole new dimension to the word 'random'. Dangling from the ceiling, appropriately, is a lawnmower that once belonged to Britain's most notorious hangman Albert Pierrepoint. Behind a rope stands the ride-on model given to Charles and Diana on their wedding day and now, rather poignantly, an exhibit in a dusty loft in Southport. After that things get really strange.

There are dibbers donated by Vanessa Feltz and Lee Mack, Roger McGough's clippers, Nicholas Parsons' old secateurs, the Qualcast Panther once owned by Jean Alexander, *Coronation Street*'s Hilda Ogden. One can't be sure just how much irony is at work here, which makes it all the funnier and more eccentric, disturbing even. Certainly

I felt a little strange that on the hottest day of the year, while thousands were at the beach or sipping cooling lagers, I was standing in an attic room surrounded by ancient lawnmowers once owned by poets and executioners, staring over the rooftops at the bedroom window of that house I once shared with three girls from Dewsbury.

It's still as balmy as summer in Cap D'Antibes as afternoon gives way to evening, and I head back to the front and the welcoming and familiar sight of Silcock's Pleasureland. As a child I would get giddy at just the very sight of this place, with its implicit promise of any number of mad and pointless ways to lose my pocket money while making myself sick. I would tremble at the thought of the funhouse with its scary, funny, rickety rides and shows; the joywheel, a polished wooden centrifuge that flung you to the floor in a giggling heap and where someone was guaranteed to wet themselves from fear or laughter. Then there was the cakewalk, the 'social mixer', and what I have always thought of as 'that gigantic rotating barrel thing'.

Later, as a student, we would come here after the pubs had shut, eat greasy burgers on the beach, hang out under the pier, play Asteroids in the bright, jangling cacophony of the midnight arcade. We were carrying on one of the great traditions of our people; Pleasureland has been amiably parting the working folk of West Lancashire from their wages since 1912.

On 14 September 2006, when pictures were posted on the web of beloved ride the Cyclone being dismantled, the outcry was such that two protesters climbed to the top of it (which is bloody high) and stayed there for three hours in a doomed effort to save the famous roller coaster. They came down eventually and so did the Cyclone.

But Silcock's Pleasureland was just the upstart little brother of a far more famous and bigger institution, Blackpool's Pleasure Beach, at the heart of a town that's a byword for excess, for freedom from work, a behemoth of northern fun. People go to Blackpool all year round, the elderly returning tourists strolling down the prom, the gay clientele at the spectacular Funny Girls cabaret, the hen and stag dos coming in like an inebriate Luftwaffe on a Jägerbombing mission along the Golden Mile.

But just as you think the summer's over, Blackpool saves a little fun for the end of the season. It still has a late burst of autumnal oohing and ahhing for you as the nights get cooler and the clocks go back. Like many a Lancastrian before us, we were off to 'th'Illuminations'.

Whichever direction you come from and however you come, everyone north of Oxford knows the trip. They know that final endless stretch well across the flat acres of the Fylde plain, the narrowing arterial roads and the sparse dunes. They know the special pride in being 'first one to see the tower', because as far as the north goes, there's really only one tower. It doesn't matter if you make your journey by car, or by train or even by air; I've often peered through my little porthole over the wing to spot gleefully that black exclamation mark on the graceful sandy curve of Morecambe Bay since seeing Blackpool Tower, 'the tower', brings a skittish thrill that never entirely fades. It is the promise of good times just up ahead, of life off the leash. Here is a building erected just for fun, and for the profit that comes from fun: a monument to leisure. In centuries gone by, humans built towers like Istanbul's Hagia Sophia or the Hassan II minaret in Morocco to be nearer to God. In Blackpool, they built a tower to put you further away from your wages, and to be further away from the ground and the everyday, to leave behind the mill and the mine and the factory hooter.

As the earth has its seasons, so did Blackpool. During the Industrial Revolution, the tradition of the wakes week (originally a festival encouraged among the unruly Britons by Pope Gregory) became a fixed and regular summer holiday in the north of England. Each locality would have its own nominated 'wakes week', when the factories, mills and mines would close for seven days, maybe fourteen. All through the summer, one town after another would be on holiday in succession and the great rattle of industry would fall silent in Bolton, then Oldham, then Wigan, then Preston, and on and on. Sea bathing and sea air were thought good for the lungs and constitutions dulled by long shifts underground or in cramped, dirty factories. So seaside resorts boomed and none more so than Blackpool.

As noted, Liverpudlians and the more genteel took their holidays in Southport. Morecambe was a destination for the mill workers of the West Riding, giving it the name Bradford by the Sea. But the Lancashire working classes only had eyes for Blackpool. At its height in 1860, 23,000 people came from Oldham to Blackpool in one wakes week alone.

Then in 1879, in a smart attempt to extend the season and prolong the fading summer, Blackpool staged what it called a display of 'artificial sunshine'. Eight big arc lamps bathed the promenade in golden light during the evening. As this was a year before Edison patented electric light, it was fabulously new and futuristic. In 1912, 10,000 lights were strung in 'festoons of garland lamps' in what really was the first incarnation of the modern lights. With the odd dark interludes at times of world war, the Blackpool Illuminations, or 'the lights' as they are known, has grown into a late summer, early autumn institution, a last hurrah for fun and freedom before the coming of winter and darkness.

Every year, the honour of switching on 'the lights' is bestowed on a different luminary, which is absolutely the right word here. It is an eclectic list, and one which provides a marvellous commentary on the shifting nature of celebrity. It includes Ken Dodd, Jayne Mansfield, the cast of *Dad's Army*, Sir Josiah Stamp (a former director of the Bank Of England), The Bee Gees, Stanley Matthews, Soviet ambassador Yakov Malik, Red Rum (a horse), Status Quo and the prime minister of Westphalia. You will not be surprised to see that the current Blackpool tourist website describes the Illuminations as 'iconic', an adjective so widely and nonsensically applied (footballers, pieces of chamber music, volcanoes, fish) as to be now almost meaningless.

Alongside the dazzle of 'The Lights', Blackpool has a darker side too. A sobering *New Statesman* piece in 2014 described how:

> Every year on 10 November, Blackpool's nightly illuminations are switched off, marking the end of the holiday season, and around 2,500 people become unemployed overnight. Cheap air travel has been slowly killing the local tourism trade for decades but no one has come up with an alternative to halt the town's decline.
>
> Two hundred metres inland from the promenade, pebble-dash terraces that were once guest houses and B&Bs have been converted into bedsits renting for around £65 a week and attracting a new kind of visitor. Blackpool has become a town where 'you can turn up with a bin bag and £150 and get a flat,' says Simon Blackburn, leader of Blackpool Council.

It went on to describe in harrowing detail how, according to the Centre for Social Justice, British seaside towns such as Blackpool had become 'dumping grounds for people facing problems such as unemployment, social exclusion and substance abuse'. The transience and anonymity of seaside towns like Blackpool mean they're a magnet to those who are running away from something. If you want a sobering afternoon, especially if you're writing a book celebrating the north, wander around Morecambe. The butt of jokes since the seventies, its decline seems permanent and impossible to arrest, the glorious refurbished art deco Midland Hotel gazing with a sigh over streets filled with cheap nail bars, hair salons, decrepit B&Bs and scrub.

But for decades, all that the bulk of Blackpool's visitors were running away from was the daily grind. They came from the crowded streets of urban Lancashire, as I came to Blackpool as the dark nights began to draw in. The first sight of Blackpool tower twinkling in the dusk may still be faintly magical; the KFC and Poundland at its feet less so. Heading north along the front, Blackpool shows its cheerful hand early. There's an enormous rotating disco ball near the Headlands Hotel of which one TripAdvisor review states 'clean and friendly staff', praise which I think needs a comma. It's getting on for eight o'clock but everything is open. Madame Tussauds is ablaze with light and boasts a prominent effigy of shrill, camp TV personality Alan Carr. This prompts one passer-by to remark, 'Why would you pay to see a waxworks of Alan Carr; the bloody real one's never off the telly?'

Like Richard and Linda Thompson, I wanted to see the bright lights tonight, and just after the North Pier, the Illuminations come into their own. Traditionally, the Illuminations consisted of coloured bulbs, lighted objects and figurines hanging from the lampposts on the promenade. You could probably piece together a pretty accurate cultural history of Britain from what these have featured down the years – I'm guessing Stanley Matthews, Brains from Thunderbirds, the Bay City Rollers, Magnus Pyke, the Teletubbies, that sort of thing. These days though the affair is more high tech if still disarmingly low rent at times. There are now a variety of tableaux and series of large plasma screen TV-style panels called, with admirable concision, The Panels, which project many and varied delights into the misty autumn air. One is called Haunted Blackpool and is really, tremendously creepy; ghostly faces projected on to storeroom mannequins in Edwardian garb. Next – the randomness is all part of the considerable charm – is a section on the pharaohs of Ancient Egypt followed by a massive, glowering Noddy and Big Ears who terrified me so god help any passing toddlers. There are some vampires, then a section on Hindu weddings (obviously) and then one based on the work of the late rock cartoonist Ray Lowry and featuring drawings of The Clash. That's some line-up, I think you'll agree.

I pause for a while by the giant screens playing vintage episodes of *Sooty* and *Thomas the Tank Engine* and watch my fellow tourists pass by, as varied and lively as the panels themselves. There's a pack of teenage girls with a poodle, a Down's syndrome man, a laughing Polish family. We all stroll along amiably past, you've guessed it, more panels. Some are self-consciously classy, like the Boodle's jewellers sponsored ones in Narnia-style white jewellery. Some are predictable, like the *Doctor Who* display, and some are plain weird, as in the giant Damien Hirst style illuminated and eviscerated cow.

At Gynn Square, hunger strikes, and with a recommendation in mind and noted in my smartphone, I jump on a tram. Anyone who was sentient and had a television in the late 1980s can never board a Blackpool tram without feeling a frisson of fear and excitement. For they will surely recall the famous *Coronation Street* scene in which abusive nutter Alan Bradley tracked down estranged lover Rita from the Cabin to Blackpool Prom, specifically just outside the Ambassador Hotel, and, in the ensuing chase, got run down and 'offed' by the number three to Bispham. By the standards of today's gory and ludicrous soaps, Bradley's demise is tame stuff, but back then it was Hitchcockian in its tension and drama. '*Corry*' staged another tram accident in 2010 which by comparison looked like the *Titanic* disaster. But it was rubbish and no one remembers it, Bradley's end being far more … yes, I'm going to say it … iconic.

Tonight the trams are packed and cruising stately along the promenades, lit up like neon battleships. Like Bradley's fatal tram I am bound for Bispham, the north shore bit of Blackpool. As I disembark and stroll along jauntily, for who wouldn't here, I observe that nearly every hotel bar is thronged and lively. I gaze up and see a man seated in an armchair in the large landing window of one of the hotels. He is quietly reading a novel and I think how cultured an evening he is having, until I realise that he is completely naked. Later, on my return walk, I see the same man, this time spruce in his short-sleeved shirt worn outside the trousers, at the bar watching a football match with a pint of lager. He catches my eye and smiles. Under the circumstances, it disconcerted me somewhat.

My destination is Bispham Kitchen, a chip shop of some repute, indeed, one of the north's premier chippies. I had come across several glowing mentions online of this establishment. One man even claimed to take his annual holidays in Bispham itself just to be near it. Clearly, this was to be the venue for my tea at 'the Lights'.

By way of testament to the chippie's quality, there are four mini-buses parked outside. It's absolutely rammed to the gunnels; mainly with Scottish people. I'm used to this. Wigan had the same wakes week as Glasgow, so whenever I came here as a kid the guesthouses, pubs and cafés were always full of 'weegees', loud, good-natured and completely incomprehensible. I find a table right at the back of the large dining room, pushing and picking my apologetic way through buggies and backpacks. The Bispham Kitchen boasts a large and varied clientele: smart elderly ladies, a young family with a kid still in her school uniform, a posh woman in a plaster cast, two trendy young hipsters with vinyl albums.

The queue is long but moving swiftly thanks to a crack team of staff, handpicked it seems like a Premier League football tea from every nation in the world on the basis of their brisk and friendly expert chip retail skills. I order haddock and chips, white bread and butter, curry sauce; traditional but sound. As it is that most rare and marvellous of things, a licensed chip shop, I go nuts and order some wine. The menu sports a carafe for a few quid, so I assume it'll hold a couple of glasses tops. The Chinese girl at the till laughs, 'Are you thinking of getting drunk?' I laugh too, though the significance of this is lost on me for now.

Despite the crush, the food arrives quickly. It comes on a tray – the curry sauce in a china gravy boat, which is classy I think, a plate that can barely contain the enormous denizen of the deep that lays battered upon it, and a carafe of red wine that I would guess holds a normal bottle and a half. Now I understand.

The food is delicious. For dessert I have a vanilla slice, obviously. Like Grandma Pollards eastwards over Todmorden way, this chip shop does sensational home-made cakes. The menu contains a history of the place and my favourite section tells of its origins as an amusement arcade with the 'kitchen only separated from the rifle range by a net curtain'. Having drunk about a fifth of the wine, I decide that it's a waste to just leave it and offer it to the nice women at the next table. They seem a little unsure, and on reflection it was a little odd of me, but the sole man at the table agrees with gusto and pours himself a large one. It turns out he is their minibus driver.

I walk back down the promenade past the endless hotels. Every one of the bars is still full, and outside every one is a little knot of smokers. One such group I pass contains a Scottish man in a tinsel wig talking quite knowledgably about archaeology. I pop into a large hotel to use the loo and there's not a single table to spare. In the huge back function room, a floorful of cross-legged kids are being entertained by a magician. They look enthralled, entranced, delighted to be here.

But then why would they not be? Why would this not be fun? If I were a child, I would far rather come here for my holidays than the Dordogne, or Florence, or any of the other wonderful places that the adult me might love. Childhood is, to a degree, classless. Kids belong to a secret group whose membership cuts across class strata. What kid wouldn't feel the magic in Blackpool at night? The drama and glamour of fairgrounds in the dark, the romance of the distant sea and the lights offshore, and, let's not forget, the opportunity to eat your own body weight in batter and fried onions. What little kid wouldn't love that? This big kid certainly did.

It's easy when passing something like the tiny, unassuming Bona Vista Hotel to think it small or sad, a melancholy kind of place to spend a holiday. Then you read what people say about it on the forums and such and you realise that people come here, have fun, are well treated, enjoy themselves and come back again and again. It would be a dull world if we all liked the same things, and not everyone wants to go wine tasting in Provence for their holidays. I know I don't. I would rather go wine tasting in Blackpool since you can have haddock and chips, and not the most over-rated cuisine on earth, and then go on the amusements afterwards.

*

Fashions in fun change, just like fashions in trousers. When turn-ups and flannels held sway, Blackpool was the leisure destination of choice of the working class northern family, something it remained through the era of flares and hotpants. Nowadays you are quite likely to encounter someone sans trousers entirely on the Golden Mile, as it has become the prime venue for downmarket (or ironic) hen and stag do's, something the resort is awkwardly ambivalent about, since it provides much needed revenue but isn't great for the brand. Through all this though, Blackpool remains impervious, its smile as fixed as the Funhouse mannequins, its eyes forever on the glittering horizon. And whatever we think of the things people get up to after dark here, perhaps until the whole of a person's life is known, we should be slow to critcise their choice of fun.

Consider a relevant and wise quote from 1969, and an unlikely source, the sporadically dim Rodney Marsh, late of Queens Park Rangers and Sky Sports:

> Most people are in a factory from nine till five. Their job may be to turn out 263 little circles. At the end of the week they're three short and somebody has a go at them. On Saturday afternoons they deserve something to go and shout about.

I couldn't put it off any longer. The Bovril and rattles and floodlights were calling, in as much as inanimate objects can. It was all about to kick off.

CHAPTER 7

KICKING A BALL ABOUT

One night in Rochdale and a tale of two Uniteds

The names, the fixtures, the opponents, are so evocative of place and time that they verge on parody. Goole Town, Gainsborough Trinity, Hyde United and Worksop Town, Matlock, Chorley and Great Harwood. No 'Classicos' here, no Beautiful Games or Theatres of Dreams. The Northern Premier League of the early 1970s was about as far removed from the vainglorious, bloated, rapacious, money-sloshing global juggernaut that is modern football as you can imagine.

Look back at games of that era, even the very top flight ones, and what you see is a different world; a grim prehistoric epoch of sheepskin and mud, sleet and violence, malevolent toothless grins, Stone Age sideboards and pale, skinny wraiths from the back streets of the arse ends of the land. Compare this to the sleek, airbrushed glamour, the toned pulchritude of modern footballers and it is like looking at the early footage we have of miners or ragged children in back alleys, or the wounded coming home from war. It looks primitive, it looks poor, it looks wretched, and it was all these things.

But that didn't stop me spending silly amounts of my free time at Northern Premier Football League football between 1970 and 1974. But then I was a child and knew no better: some of the men who stood alongside me on 'the cowshed', Wigan Athletic's decrepit stand built of turf and corrugated metal and salvaged rubbish, well, some of them were grown men with wives and families. People who really should have known better. People like my dad, come to think of it.

But in among the dour and drenching nights, there were moments emblazoned on the mind like salvos of forked lightning. Like the game against the aforementioned Goole when Jimmy Savage scored with a volley from the halfway line. All 200 or so of us danced for joy as 'Latics' went on to hand out a six-nil drubbing to the Yorkshire team. 'Drubbing', by the way, like 'adjudged' and 'equalised' is one of those words that's only ever used in conjunction with football.

Jimmy Savage's goal came back to me suddenly and vividly on two occasions when I watched the Latics, as we abbreviate them, in later life. I remembered it as I sat in the stand of their new home, the JJB (now DW) stadium for the opening game of the 2005–06 season and watched Frank Lampard, Joe Cole, Hernán Crespo and Shaun Wright-Phillips, aristocrats of the mid-noughties game, warming up in front of me, as newly promoted Wigan Athletic played Premier League champions Chelsea in their first game in the top flight of the world's richest, most glamorous football league.

Grander still, I thought about it as I leapt from my seat in the Royal Box at Wembley Stadium when the final whistle went at the FA Cup Final of 2013. Forty years earlier, I'd gone to Maine Road to watch little non-league Wigan Athletic almost pull off an upset against mighty Manchester City of the First Division in the Third Round of the FA Cup. Now we met again, but this time we won, at Wembley, in the final of that fabled tournament. Wigan Athletic had won the FA Cup, something that would have seemed unthinkable when I stood dwarfed and deafened by the swaying, jostling crowd behind the goal on that terrace in Moss Side half a life before.

Those were our glory days and they didn't last. We will begin the 2015/16 season in League One, the third tier of English football, having dropped through the league above like a stone. The fairy-tale of Wigan Athletic's evanescent spell at the top table of British football is over, and the only noteworthy elements of the season gone have been embarrassing ones; chairman and manager (now both ex) were both investigated and castigated for making grubby, racist and/or sexist remarks that I won't glorify with repetition.

This might make me despair of football and the people involved with it, had I not seen a different, better, more joyous side to the game. On my travels for this book I fell a little in love with a football team called FC United and I'll tell you all about that in a while. First I have some explaining to do to the readers who are, even now, thinking of hurling this book across the room, shouting 'bloody football', or even bitterer, angrier words to that effect.

There are things you can, reasonably, leave out of a book about the leisure habits of the northern English. Reasons of space have meant that we have found no time for orienteering, amateur dramatics, go-karting, the growing of prize leeks, raffia work, home brewing, civil war re-enactments or the tango, and I hope readers will show some leniency here. But like it or not, and lots of you won't, you can't do the same with football and not have a pretty big elephant in the room, or to be more accurate, not in the room. We need to talk about football, for a while at least.

Of the 12 founding teams when the Football League was established in 1888, six were from Lancashire and six from the Midlands. No sides from the south of England or London were involved, proof if it were needed that football as we know it, the world's most popular sport, is a product of the urban English working classes. Whether it still belongs to them and why it doesn't (since the answer is a resounding no) is a subject that dominates discourse in the groves of academe, the pages of newspapers and the saloon bars of pubs across the land. But as an entity, as a cultural force, as a national obsession, its roots are indisputably in the factory towns of industrial England and their workers.

Open up a copy of J B Priestley's *The Good Companions* – and if you haven't yet, what a treat you have in store – and you will find in the first few dazzling pages not just the most wonderful evocation of the topography and soul of the north of England but perhaps the best piece of writing about football and the north anywhere in English letters. Firstly he describes the thousands of men and boys as 'a grey

green tide ... of cloth caps' flowing towards the match between
Bolton Wanderers and 'United' from his invented West Riding town
of Bruddersford. Then, having wondered aloud how these working
men on their meagre wages can afford such an outing, he immediately
answers his own question in what is a sustained poetic paean to the
sport and its joys:

> To say that these men paid their shillings to watch twenty-
> two hirelings kick a ball is merely to say that a violin is wood
> and catgut, that Hamlet is so much paper and ink. For a
> shilling the Bruddersford United AFC offered you Conflict
> and Art; it turned you into a critic, happy in your judgement
> of fine points, ready in a second to estimate the worth of a
> well-judged pass, a run down the touch line, a lightning shot,
> a clearance kick by back or goalkeeper; it turned you into
> a partisan, holding your breath when the ball came sailing
> into your own goalmouth, ecstatic when your forwards raced
> away towards the opposite goal, elated, downcast, bitter,
> triumphant by turn at the fortunes of your side, watching a
> ball shape Iliads and Odysseys for you; and what is more, it
> turned you into a member of a new community, all brothers
> together for an hour and a half, for not only had you escaped
> from the clanking machinery of this lesser life, from work,
> wages, rent, doles, sick pay, insurance cards, nagging wives,
> ailing children, bad bosses, idle workmen, but you had
> escaped with most of your neighbours, with half the town,
> and there you were cheering together, thumping one another
> on the shoulders, swopping judgements like lords of the earth,
> having pushed your way through a turnstile into another and
> altogether more splendid kind of life, hurtling with Conflict
> and yet passionate and beautiful in its Art. Moreover it
> offered you more than a shilling's worth of material for talk
> during the rest of the week. A man who had missed the last

home match of 't'United' had to enter social life on a tiptoe
in Bruddersford.

Of course, after such a passage, the keen temptation for a lesser writer
is simply to give up on the idea of writing about football. One is
never going to improve upon that. What Priestley has got right to the
heart of, and it's a truth as immutable now as it was back then, is that
football provides a narrative that both mirrors working-class life and
offers a joyous escape from it.

'Narrative', the intellectual's version of the 'journey' of the TV
reality show, is a vague, slippery notion that seems to have leaked
into every part of modern discourse, but here maybe it earns its keep.
Football matches have a narrative, a plot, set over a circumscribed
place and time, just like a ballet or a night at the theatre. The play you
get may be as dramatic and bloody as *Macbeth*, or as tense and static
as Pinter; it may be a farce, a fairy-tale, even a whodunit, but it will
always offer some kind of conclusion and resolution, even if that turns
out to be as opaque as Godot, and to some just as unsatisfying.

Your time at the football may offer you a joyous release from the
indignities and defeats of work. The third round of the FA Cup may
show you that the weak can overcome the rich and powerful. Or it
may just confirm that the world is unfair. But for 90 minutes, football,
in its riotous absurdity, offers unpredictability, justice and heartbreak
for the price of a ticket or, increasingly, a TV subscription.

That match in *The Good Companions* takes place at the end of
Manchester Road, Bruddersford, which as he says 'actually leads
you to that great city, though in order to get there you will have to
climb to the windy roof of England and spend an hour or two with
the curlews' (yes, Priestley was congenitally incapable of writing a
dull sentence). He means of course that we shall have to cross the
Pennines, and if we did just that, once we have crested the knobbly
ridge of the backbone of England and dropped into the folded
foothills, with their necklace of reservoirs, we shall find ourselves in

Rochdale, where the football folk know better than most the cruel vagaries of the Beautiful Game.

As an hors d'oeuvres for my football feast, I chose to go and see Rochdale AFC almost, but not quite, at random. Accepted to the Football League in 1921, they have never risen out of the lowest two divisions and have won nothing in their 107-year history, the only team in British football never to have done so. They have spent more seasons in the bottom flight of English football than any other team, including a 36-year unbroken residence in football's basement from 1974–2010. They also have the lowest average league placing of any team in the Football League – seventy-sixth. In 2014, the English National Football Archive (ENFA) compiled a 'Long-Suffering Fan Index' using data from the 220,000 results since the first Football League season in 1888–9. They ranked the current 92 Football League clubs by their lack of success, weighted by extra factors, like the size of their average home crowds, in order to find the least successful club and thus, their reasoning went, the most hard done to fans.

Rochdale came out bottom… or top, if you're a 'Dale supporter clutching for any kind of trophy. Yet the club's support remains proud and passionate, if a little weary. 'When people ask me who I support, I am always proud to say Rochdale,' said one Adam Fleming interviewed by the Mancunian Matters website:

We are a well-run club with the same regular fan base and a club going somewhere. I don't feel I have suffered at all being a Dale fan … We are a club that other football clubs respect – when clubs play Rochdale they say we play football the right way. Yes, it would be nice to win trophies but I would not trade any amount of trophies for what Rochdale have and what we represent. At least we're not skint, part-time or immoral.

Another fan, barman Eden Bearshaw agreed adding, 'Financial security is a reason we've had it good as 'Daleys' … Look at Pompey

[Portsmouth]. Have they really had a better time than us?' This last was a reference to the disastrous collapse of the once proud old south coast club who, thanks to financial mismanagement, plummeted from the Premier League and winning the FA Cup final to the foot of League Two (the lowest tier) in just five years, accumulating £145 million worth of debt as they did. So when I looked at the fixture list in the depths of a northern winter and saw that Portsmouth were coming to play Rochdale, I put it in the diary.

Rochdale is steeped in organised labour and its history. As well as the pioneers of the international Co-opertative movement that started here in 1844, Rochdale was also home to the great radical orator and campaigner John Bright. Today Rochdale's Labour MP Simon Danczuk is a high profile voice on the left of the party and Rochdale born business secretary Sajid Javid is one of the Conservatives' rising stars, regularly spoken of as a future prime minster. Rochdale has nurtured many a famed female voice from Gracie Fields to Lisa Stansfield to the chic *chansonnière* Barb Jungr, all of them born in the town. Rochdale Hornets were founding members of the rugby league and one of the oldest and proudest names in the sport. Rochdale is justly famous for many things, but football is not one of them.

Everyone's heard of the ground though. Spotland is one of the fine evocative old names of the game, reeking of Saturday teatimes and football pinks and the teleprinter. The sleek Metrolink trams carry you now from Manchester to Rochdale on the old Loop Line whose stations exuded a raw northerness: Failsworth, Miles Platting, Derker and Oldham Mumps. But I went the old and still quick way, from Victoria station, through a landscape that could have come straight from a Lowry – stark chimneys and little houses clinging limpet-like to indifferent hills, reservoirs behind bleak dams, the old mills lit against the darkening sky. Then into Rochdale itself, a tough looking town, its pubs like jutting jaws, bristling with charity shops and takeaways, Asian stores, cash and carrys and dark terraces spearing straight for the horizon.

Entering the ground a steward, recognising me, jokes, 'Why aren't you in the VIP end?' He searches my overnight bag and finds a can of deodorant. 'You aren't really supposed to take in aerosols … keep it hidden.' I suppose this is in case you try and give an opposition fan a nice makeover.

I head for The Ratcliffe Bars & Function Suite which is billed as:

> the official venue of Rochdale AFA … unrivalled facilities and comfort and with over 100 free car parking spaces … it's the perfect spot for a drink with friends and fellow supporters and for any special occasion. All away supporters.. you'll get a warm welcome from us at Ratcliffe Bars. Ice cold draught/bottled beers will be available along with a selection of hot pies.

I'm not arguing with that. It's full, which is heartening, and the Pompey fans have indeed been made welcome. They're composed of all sorts, hard-looking middle-aged blokes with weathered faces; two big blonde girls in skimpy tops; a clutch of student types; and a large, densely tattooed, outlandishly dressed man with blue and white dreadlocks, yellow work trousers, heavy boots and a massive stovepipe hat. This is Pompey John or to give him his full name, changed by deed poll, John Anthony Portsmouth Football Club Westwood, perhaps the most recognisable football fan in Britain. He stands at the bar, unmissable, demolishing pints of lager and clutching a large bell and a bugle that will be much in evidence as the game goes on. (One of my spies and confidantes is a Pompey supporter and she tells me that, implausible though it may seem, by day he's a rare and antiquarian bookseller.)

One of the great pleasures of the smaller football grounds, as opposed to the vast stadia of the world elite, is that you are right on top of the action. Thus it was that watching Wigan Athletic play Chelsea at our compact DW ground soon after my book *Pies and Prejudice* came out, about the same time as Ashley Cole's dreadful, self-pitying memoir, I was able to shout, 'My book's sold more than yours,' pretty much into the Chelsea and England defender's ear. Here at Spotland in the unreserved seating, I could probably have given anyone taking a throw in a quick freshen up with my contraband deodorant.

It's a freezing night but across the ground Pompey John – clearly visible at the heart of the Portsmouth faithful – is naked from the waist up, swaying and leading the team's venerable rallying cry, 'Play Up Pompey, Pompey Play Up'. You cannot help but marvel at the commitment of these 300 or so travelling fans. They have come almost the length of the country on a cold midweek winter night, probably leaving at lunchtime, losing an afternoon's pay maybe, to watch a team who have been laid low, humbled, humiliated even, through no fault of theirs but because of the stupidity, greed and incompetence of those to whom the football club means nothing. I am reminded of some more words of J B Priestley's from his fine book *English Journey*, a salutary reminder that it may have been ever thus: 'Nearly everything possible has been done to spoil this game: the heavy financial interests; … the absurd publicity given to every feature of it by the Press; … but the fact remains that it is not yet spoilt, and it has gone out and conquered the world.'

In our end, 'Come on, Day-ul' is the Rochdale chant sung to that refrain of 'If I Had A Hammer'. I can't help but think they're missing a trick here in not adopting and adapting the 'Banana Boat Song' to their own ends like so: 'Day-ul! Daaay-ul, Day-ull win and I want to go up'.

It's quite cosy in our stand. The woman in front of me practically has her head in my lap when she leans back to sip her Thermos coffee. But she may well have been sitting here for 40 years, so this is her patch. This close, the game is a different experience than observed via the multitude of camera angles, close-ups and replays on TV. Not necessarily better but certainly more intense, more inhaled than observed and of course you are spared all that wearisome nineteenth-hole banter of the ex-pros who still inexplicably dominate football discourse on telly. This close too, we get a good excuse to have a look at the player's abilities and their facial hair. Neatly, one of the Dale favourites is called Dole and he looks quick and incisive. He is also luxuriantly bearded, as they all are these days. Footballers used to look like rappers or gang members or supporting members of boy bands; now they all look like the Unabomber or the elder of an Amish village.

Rochdale run out three–nil winners and what is proving to be a fine season for them continues. Back in the bar, I talk to some Pompey lads, the indie studenty ones, who seem not unduly put out by having come all this way for what some would see as nothing, except that that is to misunderstand the complex nexus of pleasures that football brings. A rueful, gallows demeanour has become a default position for many football fans, encouraged by funny, clever, non-partisan magazines like *When Saturday Comes*. Pompey John gives a few last valedictory blasts on his bugle and they are gone into the Pennine night – back down the length of England to beds that they won't see till the small hours, in that old naval town on the Solent, haunt of one Horatio Nelson. He told us that England expected every man to do their duty, but the Pompey faithful have exceeded theirs tonight I reckon.

When did football change? Because change it has. Look at those seventies games now and it's almost unrecognisable, and despite what sourpusses and grumpy old men say, those changes have been largely for the better. The play is vastly superior, faster, hugely more skilful. The grounds are safer, more comfortable and with a seasoning of women and kids and different ethnicities to leaven the homogenised brutishness that lurked there. Some point to Nick Hornby's *Fever Pitch* and shows like *Fantasy Football League*, or records like New Order's 'World in Motion' as the ushers of a new era and the gentrification of football. Whether they caused or just reflected that change is hard to say.

Perhaps once football had reached its nadir in Britain in the mid and late eighties, with the Heysel riot, the Bradford fire and the Hillsborough tragedy, it could only go one way. Perhaps, seared and purged in some way by these ordeals, it found a new sense of purpose and humanity from such dark events. They were certainly dark times. Mr Justice Popplewell's report into hooliganism in the late eighties suggested that 'football may not be able to continue in its present form much longer'.

Whatever the reason, things did change and football didn't just continue but flourish, rising Phoenix-like not as 'the English disease' but a national religion. At some point around the Italia 90 World Cup tournament, football became hip in a way it had never been in the cloth cap era. It has stayed that way ever since, given a huge fillip in 1992 with the dawn of the Premier League borne on a tidal wave of loot from Rupert Murdoch and Sky.

Not everyone welcomed this. Take Roy Keane. Former Manchester United captain Roy is a hard man to like if you're a neutral. His violent playing style, graceless and belligerent demeanour and, latterly, dour punditry on our TV screens, have ruined many a day for football fans not of the Man United persuasion. But those fans do love him and even those who don't must credit him for one of the defining sayings of modern football culture. Commenting on the docility and silence of the home fans after a Manchester United Champions League game at Old Trafford against Dynamo Kyiv, Keane remarked 'Away from home our fans are fantastic, I'd call them the hardcore fans. But at home they have a few drinks and probably the prawn sandwiches, and they don't realise what's going on out on the pitch.'

The Prawn Sandwich Brigade quickly became part of football's mythology. These were the bourgeois arrivistes who knew nothing of Roker Park or the Inter City Fairs Cup, boot boys or stopper centre halves. These were the 'fans' for whom a competition like the Champions League was made, an expensive catwalk of millionaires and ludicrously named since not all the participants were champions and it wasn't a league.

I decided a visit to football on such a night was obligatory. I would see whether prawn sandwiches, or possibly moussaka, were on the menu when Manchester United met Olympiacos of Greece in the most glamorous and expensive club football competition in the world.

At the other end of that ENFA table of long suffering fans than Rochdale, the most cosseted, success-addled and spoiled of all English football fans are the Red Army of Manchester United. This is not just a swipe, a blast of hostile opinion, of which there is much, but statistically proven according to ENFA's research based on trophies won and league placings. United fans have had it good for as long as most can remember.

The Olympiacos game though came at a curious moment in the club's fortunes. In May 2013, Alex Ferguson, their longest serving manager and one of the most successful in the history of British football, retired and was instrumental in choosing his successor, 'the chosen one' David Moyes, then manager of Everton. Like Ferguson, Moyes was a tough Scot with a reputation as a stern disciplinarian and with a blunt style; the two men were born at opposite ends of the Clyde tunnel in Glasgow. Maybe out of vanity, Ferguson had chosen a manager exactly like himself – but in this case one who'd never won a major trophy – when the richest club in the world could have had its pick of the finest coaches anywhere on the planet. It proved a bad mistake.

Rumblings from the fans were turning into open dissent as United stumbled and fell by the wayside in almost every competition. A group of disgruntled fans even hired a light aircraft over Old Trafford trailing a banner that read 'Wrong One — Moyes Out'. The Olympiacos game, with the chance to progress in Europe and salvage something from the season, was seen as a make or break moment for Moyes and United.

Old Trafford, the 'Theatre of Dreams' as it is rather fancifully known (football fans are nothing if not sentimental), lies a few hundred yards from the Salford dockyards from which it once drew much of its core support. Bobby Charlton said that Matt Busby would often point to the docks and the stevedores sweating there, and tell his Busby Babes that they were playing for those men; men who worked at hard physical labour all week and who lived for the weekend and United.

When the Premier League began the age of the average fan was 22 and almost a quarter of them were aged between 16 and 20. Now the average age is 41, reflecting the change in cost. Like the Salford docks themselves, now home to the BBC's MediaCity, *Coronation Street* and the University of Salford, football has become a more expensive and upmarket proposition.

Tickets for tonight's game were forty quid, which seems a lot, especially if you're a dad taking his sons (or daughters), but there is, of course, another way of seeing this. Yes (as critics constantly point out), for this kind of money you could go to the opera, or see Shakespeare performed in Stratford. But logically, why shouldn't it cost as much as attendance at those events? Even if you loathe Manchester United (and if you do, then substitute Manchester City, Liverpool, Arsenal, Barcelona or whoever), you have to acknowledge that these are some of the finest practitioners of their art in the world, playing at the very highest level. Why shouldn't it cost as much as a night at La Scala or seeing Yo-Yo Ma conducted by Simon Rattle? This is a contentious position, and I'm not even sure it's mine, but it's worth a thought.

Tonight I got my ticket thanks to my companion at the game, Luke, a friend of mine who's a writer and Man United fan. He's currently working on a book about the giant global brand that is Manchester United. Research suggests they have 659 million supporters around the world, 80 million in the lucrative Asian markets, in places a long way from the Stretford End; places like Riyadh, Phnom Penh, Seoul and Djakarta. Here they will turn out in their thousands for United's pre-season tours. Last year this tour took 73 staff and the marketing team outnumbered, and were probably as vital as, the players. The club have 29 international commercial partners, from Mamee Noodles, Aeroflot and Casillero del Diablo wine to Kansai Paints, DHL and Mister Potato, 'Official Savoury Snack Partner of Manchester United'.

Luke tells me that the Russian supporters club (called satisfyingly the Moscow Reds) get two tickets each for every away game. Perks like this rankle with some hardcore British supporters, who Luke suspects secretly don't mind the team's current poor form. A few fallow years might see off the johnny-come-lately's and the glory hunters and make a little more room for the long term fans being elbowed (and priced) out of the ground. This isn't the mood in the boardroom, of course, where the financial indices and stock exchanges are being viewed as closely as the League tables.

If United's support is on the wane, you wouldn't guess it from the mood in Stretford tonight. The square mile or so around Chester Road and between Old Trafford and its sister cricket ground is the heart of United Country. Even the chip shop is called Lou Macari and is owned by, unsurprisingly, Lou Macari, United stalwart of the 1970s, a decade of even more wildly variable fortune for the team.

The atmosphere is extraordinary even for someone who's been to a lot of football matches. You're used to seeing street scenes like this on news programmes, funerals for assassinated leaders in Tehran or Mombasa, demonstrations in Cairo or Grozny, but less so Tuesday nights in Lancashire. Every street is packed with surging tides of chanting people, chaotic and feverish, a vibrant mix of classes, accents, ages, sexes, ethnicities. It is wildly exciting and even a little intimidating, although there's no hint of acual trouble.

Those theorists and writers who bemoan the erosion of football's traditional working-class support would find much to back up their theory here. I chat to two Brazilian girls, a Chinese student and a middle-aged couple from Holland. But really, is that so bad? There is still a thick enough testosterone fug around for those who want that kind of thing, and enough white, male faces to keep any UKIP member happy, I'd have thought. Me? Well, at the risk of sounding crass, I'd sooner drink my weak fizzy lager in a plastic glass with two sweet girls from São Paulo than have a potato-headed bloke in a bad anorak off the market tell me to fuck off.

We are standing drinking outside the Bishop's Blaize. There's been a pub of that name here since the mid-fifteenth century, named after the patron saint of Woolcombers. It's just a regular chain pub, a

Wetherspoon's, but there is a queue at the door, security guards and a £1 admission charge enforced by strict and elaborate ticketing policy. That's because on match days, the Bishop's Blaize becomes a sort of informal rally-cum-concert; a pulsing, raucous, jostling cauldron of primal energy and noise.

That noise is unbelievable. Everyone, bar me and a couple of frankly bemused looking Japanese guys, is singing lustily, aggressively even, conducted by a man standing on a table in the centre of the room. This man, Luke tells me, is Pete Boyle. He is Manchester United's guerrilla musical director. He invents most of these songs and chants. Boyle can actually sell out concerts in United-mad Northern Ireland and you can buy albums' worth of them from his website.

Boyle is a smart and discerning chap. He bridles at the suggestion he is United's Oasis, preferring to be known as the club's Morrissey and Marr of The Smiths, and his compositions are often funny and sharp. Some classics are 'Giggs Will Tear You Apart Again' to the tune of Joy Division's 'Love Will Tear Us Apart' and 'We'll Drink A Drink To Eric The King' (an Eric Cantona tribute to the tune of Scaffold's 'Lily the Pink'). One of his most ambitious and sadly stymied by the player's move to Aston Villa, was 'You'll Never Stop The Cleverley', a song about midfielder Tom Cleverley adapted from Jona Lewie's Christmas novelty 'Stop the Cavalry'. My particular favourite concerns United's former Korean striker Park Ji-Sung which borrows the tune of 'Lord of the Dance' and manages to maintain an air of hymnal innocence while casually slurring the people of both Seoul and Liverpool. You will have to investigate yourself I'm afraid as it is slightly indelicate.

While many of Boyle and the Stretford End's songs are witty and clever, some rely for their force on good old-fashioned spite and vulgarity. The song I heard most tonight was aimed at their local rivals and is sung to the tune of 'This Old Man', culminating in the pleasant refrain 'With a nick nack paddy wack, give a dog a bone, why don't City fuck off home'.

This, along with the simple but effective 'Twenty Times', a refer-ence to their number of league titles and aimed squarely at the loathed Liverpool, rings out around the swelling ground before kick off. So does the 'United Calypso', recorded in 1957 by the Caribbean singer Eric Robinson and a tribute to the Busby Babes, recorded and thus given all the more poignancy by the fact that just a year later many of that magnificent young team were killed in the Munich air disaster.

We're in the corner of the East Stand, to the right of the Sir Alex Ferguson Stand and opposite the famous Stretford End, home of United's most fanatical support. Over my left shoulder, high up in the gods (appropriately), are the several hundred supporters from opponents Olympiacos, champions of Greece and based in Piraeus, the port district of Athens.

They are the most successful Greek club side ever, much to the chagrin of their deadly Athenian rivals Panathinaikos (with whom they contest the wonderfully named 'Derby Of The Eternal Adversaries'), but they have never won a game in their previous 11 visits to England and along the way they've conceded 37 goals.

Bearing all this in mind, and the fact that at this point the Greek economy was trembling on the verge of complete collapse, you have to applaud these fans' commitment and the proud way they belt out the club song. This seems to be Boney M's 'Rasputin' with new and to me unintelligible lyrics, while from all corners of the ground, United fans respond with the internationally recognised gesture for onanist.

The mood in our stand is different from what it would have been 30 years ago, I think, less chaotic and febrile maybe, but still with nothing of the concert hall or gallery. A current of cold aggression and suppressed rage runs thinly but perceptibly through.

A young steward with a bird-like visage, a tie beneath his tabard and a nervous laugh comes to tell the blokes around me who are standing up (in contravention of current stadium regulations) to, 'Sit down boys!' 'Why? ask these older, hard faced men with grimaces of menace. Having no answer, the kid retreats. The man beside me has a face that has never seen a moisturiser, I fancy, and he chants along under his breath, undemonstratively but threateningly, turning occasionally to give the travelling Greeks an obscene gesture. He conforms to my gut feeling that hard-looking blokes are scarier when they speak quietly, which is why current Leicester manager Nigel Pearson is so unsettling.

If you've never been to Old Trafford, and you are unburdened by a partisan hatred for United, then you will be impressed. Huge and imposing, it is the largest football ground in England after Wembley and far more atmospheric. Oddly though, its record attendance is for a match when United weren't actually playing; the FA Cup Semi-Final of 1939, when 76,962 spectators watched Wolverhampton Wanderers take on Grimsby Town.

Due to its proximity to Trafford's industrial estates and the Manchester Ship Canal's Salford docks, Old Trafford took a pounding from air raids during the Second World War and it took eight years to rebuild. During this time they had to play at rivals Manchester City's Maine Road ground, itself now demolished. Manchester had its belated revenge on Germany in 1999, when they beat Bayern Munich with the last kick of the game in the Champions League final.

That was the year that veteran Scottish striker Brian McClair left the club. Interviewing him was the reason I first came here as an *NME* reporter in 1989 as, along with Pat Nevin, he was one of the few footballers regarded as remotely cool. He told me that he had bought Win's *Freaky Trigger* album on the strength of a gushing (and entirely deserved) ten out of ten review I'd given it in the paper. I recall being desperately chuffed with this. For the pictures, we went out into the centre circle and I recall looking around and imagining what it must be like to play here in a big game when those enormous stands were full. It was an awesome experience, in the original sense of the word, the only dampener being photographer and Manchester City nut Kevin Cummins who grizzled and moaned the whole day about having to be there. (I seem to recall once missing a flight in Chicago because Cummins wouldn't fly United Airlines but he insists I have made this up.)

The game itself is pretty average fare. The Greeks look unimpressive, particularly in defence, and they come bearing several gifts for United's strikers. Robin Van Persie ('RVP') scores a hat trick and receives several choruses of his name song sung to the tune of White Stripes' 'Seven Nation Army'. In an early clash of heads, United's Valencia gets a whopper of a black eye that swells to the size of a grapefruit that would have definitely got a boxing match stopped. However unremarkable the game, a big sporting event at night is still utterly thrilling, the emerald greens and halogen whites, the noise, the crackle of expectation, the sense of collective theatre.

United win and the relief is tangible; it's plainly visible in the elated faces and fist-pumping of the players. Moyes is granted a brief stay of execution and Wayne Rooney, via that most modern of media Twitter posts (presumably from the communal bath if they still have them) says: 'Great performance from the lads and another brilliant atmosphere at Old Trafford. That one was for the fans!'

Those fans are now swarming out into the dark Salford night, carrying Luke and I along with them, down floodlit thoroughfares of food stalls, avenues formed from crash barriers and chain link fences, burger vans and queues for the bars. All of this – the bouncers, the lines, the beer in plastic glasses – give the sense of a tough, working-class Glastonbury. From one of the vans, a tattooed girl with a mass of piled blonde hair gives me the best cheeseburger I've ever had. At £4.50, this would be still cheap at Glastonbury prices but it's pricey by 'outdoor van in the north' prices. But then returning to my thoughts on the ticket price, we are in one of the most famous and prestigious temples of sport on Earth, one of a handful of places that are globally known and places of pilgrimage even, a Glyndebourne or Bayreuth or Stratford for the proletariat.

There'd been rumours before the game that angry disillusioned fans intended to tear down the 'Chosen One' banner. This hubristic giant pennant was originally unveiled at Old Trafford in support of David Moyes, and bears his determined face. That doesn't happen, at least not for another month or so, but the Olympiacos victory turned out the last hurrah of a dismal tenure for the Scot, and he was sacked at the end of April 2014. The banner went too and the optimistic fans who originally commissioned it for 450 quid said they intended to auction it for charity. Maybe it's now on a wall in Stockport or Seoul or perhaps it's still folded up and gathering dust on top of a cupboard in a stockroom somewhere in the bowels of the Theatre of (in this case Broken) Dreams.

I don't go to many United matches. In fact, I've been to about four in my life. In that regard, I have much in common with an American family that, unusually for them, flew in from the States to watch that Olympiacos game. My excuse is that I'm not a Manchester United supporter. They have rather less justification for staying away since they own the club. All the more astonishing is the fact that the head of that family, who bought Manchester United, never set foot inside Old Trafford. Astonishing, or as others may put it, disgraceful.

Malcolm Glazer's story is the American dream writ large. The fifth of seven children of a Jewish Lithuanian immigrant to Rochester, New York, he inherited his dad's watch repair business and dropped out of college to run it. He got the watch repair concession at a local air base (who knew air bases had watch repair franchises?) and from these modest beginnings became a wealthy man investing wisely in real estate, then nursing homes, then TV stations and eventually the Tampa Bay Buccaneers football team. Under Glazer, the Buccaneers prospered. Attendances rose and they reached their first ever Superbowl in 2003. Glazer was poised for his biggest acquisition yet, the purchase of the most famous football club in the world. This he did in 2005 from under the noses of several other oligarchs and billionaires, among others, Rupert Murdoch.

It was how he did it though that rankled with some of the United faithful and football fans around the world. The Man Utd purchase was funded with money Glazer didn't have; borrowed from here, there and everywhere at dizzying interest against future profits ('leveraged' is how financiers describe this kind of deal). Previously debt free, in fact supremely wealthy, overnight United were in hock for millions. By the end of the brief Moyes era, United had paid out over £680 million in interest fees, bank charges and debt repayment, twice as much as they invested on players.

Football fans often talk a good fight but, disappointingly in view of the game's roots in the industrial heart of Britain, they are by and large quiescent and even depoliticised. Compared to Germany, where fans control the clubs and ticket prices are correspondingly low, or even Italy where, for good or ill, teams like Roma and Lazio have deeply entrenched political allegiances on the left and the right, British fans have been a pretty docile lot, saving their anger for other supporters rather than the game's establishment. When Glazer bought Manchester United with borrowed money and plunged them into debt there was some outcry, but most fans simply rolled their eyes, shrugged and carried on handing him their money. Some fans organised a protest by which they sported yellow and green scarves, the club's original colours back when they were called Newton Heath. The Supporters Trust chairman explained it thus, 'We need to embrace 21st Century campaigning techniques and while there is still a place for traditional protests the way to get really large numbers involved is to use the available technology and create a viral campaign which once unleashed becomes unstoppable.'

All very nice, but none of this affected the Glazers' bank balance of course. The scarf wearers still handed over their 40 quids, still cheered on the team, however little it belonged to them. High profile but almost entirely ineffectual, it was in some ways the quintessential modern gesture.

All football fans have at their disposal of course a highly and instantly effective tool with which they could get their own way on just about any matter. They could stay away. A weekend of empty stadiums, seen on TV around the world, slashing profits for owners and ruining the lucrative product for TV companies, could effect any change the fans wanted. This however is seemingly unthinkable in our indulged age. When one brave soul suggested it on a football phone in, Robbie Savage, journeyman player turned abysmal pundit, spluttered, 'You can't do that, you can't do that, it ... it's not fair on the players.' Au contraire, Robbie. In a free country, you can do what you like and withdrawal of support, like withdrawal of labour, is one of the few weapons working people have against the might of capital. One would have thought even Robbie Savage knew.

But some United fans were made of sterner, better stuff and they did just that. They went away and stayed away. But they didn't just turn their back on the club they loved and had had stolen from them. They did something much more positive and idealistic. They built their own club from the bottom up, and in the teeth of ridicule and derision from fans and pundits who lacked their courage and idealism. They are called FC United of Manchester and they are my favourite football team, and, wherever you're from, whoever you support, they should be one of yours too.

That probably doesn't include Sir Alex Ferguson. He dismissed the people behind FC United of Manchester as 'attention seekers' when they decided to start their own football club in 2005. Quite what the ennobled, supposedly socialist Scot, thinks of them now is not known. Perhaps he's too busy with his ambassadorial role at Old Trafford, for which he is said to be paid a hundred thousand pounds a day, a sum that would keep FC United, all its outgoings, all its players and staff, in business for a year. At an away game in the rarefied surrounding of a grassy embankment at Halesowen Town FC an FC United fan told me that they do not by and large hate Manchester United. They don't hate Sir Alex. In fact they acknowledge the great debt of gratitude they owe him. It's just that they find disparaging remarks like his a bit rich, which in his case is le mot juste.

FC United were born of frustration, as Manchester band James once sang, over a bhuna and a tarka dhal in a restaurant on Rusholme's

Curry Mile. In what the *Guardian*'s Julian Coman described as FC United's "Granita' moment', a bunch of vocal and aggrieved United fans and fanzine writers, led by Andy Walsh of *Red Issue* magazine, decided to take what they called 'the nuclear option' of starting their own club. At an initial meeting, a breathtaking £100,000 was pledged, and the founders chose the name FC United, later rejected by the FA as 'too generic'. A later postal and net vote chose Football Club United of Manchester over AFC Manchester 1878, Manchester Central and Newton Heath United.

Open trials produced a squad of 30 with applicants coming from all over the world. The first game, a friendly held at Leigh, drew a crowd of 3,000 and, as one of the founders, journalist Tony Howard, wrote 'for the first time in football history, a celebratory pitch invasion greeted a 0-0 draw in a friendly.' Writing about the club's early matches, like their first ever league game at Leek, he wrote of the novelty too of being 'greeted with open arms by pub landlords and locals alike – a new experience for those of us used to keeping our heads down on visits to opposition towns because of the hatred the country feels for MUFC.'

In the beginning, they met with opposition from within the ranks of 'Big United's' support. They were called worse than 'attention seekers'. They were called 'traitors' and 'splitters'. People squared up to them in Manchester boozers. When they first announced that they were going to start their own team and play matches at Bury's Gigg Lane, 30 minutes by tram from Old Trafford, there was some hostility. Some said they would stop them. They didn't succeed. Now I was headed there too.

I am not the first visitor from Wigan to Gigg Lane, Bury. There was the team from Wigan who came to play Bury FC in the first ever match at the ground in September 1885. We lost. These days the Gigg Lane is actually technically called the JD Stadium after the sportswear firm who sponsor it. Nobody does though, at least none

of the people I encounter as I make arrangements for my first trip to
see FC United.

For the first decade of their existence, FC United borrowed or
rather rented grounds, primarily this one, Bury's Gigg Lane for which
they pay £5,000 a match. It is a neat little ground with a long history
and, like Spotland, one of those grounds whose very name can make
football romantics dewy-eyed with nostalgia. One of the very first
games ever played under floodlights happened here on Bonfire Night
1889 – when a crowd of 7,000 watched Bury lose 5–4 to Heywood
Central under 'Wells Patent Lights'. This was several years before the
FA actually allowed floodlit matches so the ground has a good track
record of sticking it to 'the man'. There is a Manchester Road Stand,
a South Stand and, best of all, a Cemetery End.

The Gigg Lane car park charges three quid to park ten seconds
from your seat. My ticket costs £8 and the lady with the metal
moneybox has no change for my tenner. I say keep the change because
a) it's a good cause and b) I will never, ever say 'keep the change'
again at a football turnstile. On research trips for my books, I tend to
just turn up at places unannounced and incognito, if not always alone
(there's a word about this at the end of this book). But sometimes it
seems right or practical to say I'm coming, thus I'd been put in touch
with the people at FC United via Luke, who'd sorted out my trip to
the Olympiacos game.

To my mild embarrassment this means when I arrive at the ground
I have been put on some kind of list that I hesitate to call VIP but
which has apparently singled me out for some special treatment. I ask
if there's anywhere to get some food and am told there is a burger
van outside 'but' the nice lady adds with a conspiratorial nod as if to
acknowledge my special status 'you can bring it in and eat it in the
lounge where it's warm'.

The lounge at Gigg Lane is light and airy, and sits at low touchline
level with large windows overlooking the pitch. It's nicely busy half
an hour before kick off, but I find a table and mull the programme

over my burger, chips and pint of Lager. FC United have had a busy and successful first ten years. They entered the North West Counties Division Two in 2005, winning the league in their inaugural season. In their second season, they walked off with the Division One title which saw them promoted to the Northern Premier League North. 2007–08 saw them promoted again, and since then they have played in the Northern Premier League (sponsored by Evo-Stik). Tonight's opponents are Chorley, who I would regularly see against Wigan when we were in this league in the mid-1970s. Chorley are still there but doing well, and tonight is a top of the table clash that will have a definite bearing on the title and promotion races. A 'six pointer' as the modern football cliché has it.

The game gets under way. The pitch is muddy and threadbare which doesn't help the overall standard of play early on. There are lots of hopeful balls that plop pointlessly in no man's land, much one-footedness and many speculative passes hit high into the air. Slowly though it becomes more coherent. Chorley look tough and well-organised and FC United are far from having it their own way, even though they are, theoretically at least, at home. After 12 minutes Chorley go ahead to a very dubious penalty while United are denied what seems a clear cut one.

The real revelation though is the support. FC United's fans start singing before kick off and quite literally do not stop for the duration of the match. It becomes quickly apparent that this is more than just the usual ingrained tribal support for one's club. There is a zeal about this that's almost evangelical. This is a mission. There's much talk around FC United of this being Punk Football, a DIY alternative to the slick, expensive mainstream stuff. So it's apt that one of FC's top songs is a reworking of 'Anarchy in the UK' as manifesto: 'I am an FC fan/I am Mancunian/I know what I want/ And I know how to get it/I want to destroy Glazer and Sky/Cos I wanna be at FC'. Other big numbers in the repertoire are a version of Cornershop's 'Brimful of Asha' adapted as a paean to former skipper David Chadwick:

He's big, and he's Chaddy, and he's 31,
He's big, and he's Chaddy, and he's 31,
Everyone needs a nutter in the middle,
Everyone needs a nutter.

There is also a fairly straight love song rendition of The Carpenters' 'Top of the World', born of a night high up in a deserted Hamburg stadium where the club had gone to play a friendly with kindred German spirits, the fan owned, cult club St Pauli. This team, maverick, leftist and defiantly 'other' are seen as a kind of template for FC United, and the teams that will hopefully come in their wake.

Most of the chants though are derogatory to one degree or another to either Sky or the Glazer family, though not to 'Big United' itself. Andy Walsh, now general manager of FC United has said:

I was born a Manchester United fan and I'll die a Manchester United fan ... My father took me to my first game when I was five and I took my own children at the same age. Deciding to withdraw my season ticket application was one of the most painful decisions of my life, but I just couldn't afford to take my family to matches. The Glazers have shown they're not interested in fans like us. All they're interested in is people with big wallets.

I'm seated next to three guys with varying degrees of visual impairment excitedly following the game through miniature telescopes and relaying the action to each other fluently and at speed. When a controversial sending off occurs they see the incident far better than me, and describe it to me in detail and, it later turns out, absolutely accurately. It would be naive to say that FC United are anything as anodyne as politically correct; the language used about Glazer, Sky and Manchester City is salty and robust enough to disabuse anyone of this notion. But there's certainly an ethos at work here – egalitarian, socialistic, progressive, call it what you will – that you don't feel at other clubs big or small.

It's one–nil to Chorley at half time and I pop back into the bar where a friendly chatty guy called Mike brings round the raffle tickets. I buy a tenners' worth and he seems genuinely chuffed and grateful for the support from a neutral. He shares my love of northern soul and he tells me of his youth when the mere rumour that someone had a copy of Frank Wilson's 'Do I Love You' would send you driving for miles, in those pre-CD, pre-internet days before everything was available instantly. Over a pint, Mike explains the real appeal of FC United and what underpins his support for the club:

> I don't care if we go up or not really. I just want the thrill of owning my club, of paying twenty quid to go on the coach to the north-east with like minded people to play Blyth Spartans. We don't have a fat cat owner. We have a board and they make the day-to-day decisions. They're not always the right decisions and they can take forever but you are bound to get dissent and argument in a democracy. Three thousand people own this club and they are all fairly left wing. That can make things quite lively …

Via Mike I'm introduced to FC's press officer Adrian. (The 'press room' at Gigg Lane seemed rammed with blokes drinking and shouting so I doubt any one was filing elegant profiles for the *New Yorker* from there.) Adrian's from Middlesbrough but his wife is a lifelong 'Big United' fan so he has never had any real antipathy or resentment for the larger club. He reckons that support for FC United is fairly evenly split between old United fans who still watch both, real refuseniks who will never set foot in Old Trafford again, and people who simply think this is how a football club should be run and that FC are a good, even romantic, cause worth supporting. The category I seem to have fallen into in fact.

The second half is much more eventful. As well as my burgeoning affection for United, I also nurture a petty local grievance against Chorley since the small borough is a near neighbour of Wigan, and I become more partisan as the game wears on. In fairness to Chorley, though, their support too is extraordinary. They've brought about a thousand fans and they sing their hearts out throughout. Against this comes the constant barrage of noise and movement from the FC United 'Ultras' behind the goal, who sporadically set off crimson and scarlet flares. It looks fun.

When I was a Wigan Athletic season ticket holder, I would sit in the fairly demure West Stand at home games, but I would sometimes feel a pang of desire to be with the 200 or so nutcases who would butt right up against the huge blocks of support that the big teams would bring with them and taunt them, good naturedly and sometimes not. It was nothing to do with hooliganism, just an acknowledgment of what I think is a fundamental truth and allure of football, maybe the one Rodney Marsh was hinting at; the desire to support a cause wholly and a little irrationally in the face of all odds and as an escape from the tame logic and order of the everyday.

Those FC Ultras go berserk when United player Charlie Raglan hits a sweet volley home from the edge of the box and it is mayhem when, in the last two minutes, they equalise and then have another player sent off. It's a ludicrously exciting end to the game and an FC banner reading 'Children of the Revolution' swirls through clouds of smoke and light. Most FC United songs are lusty and galvanising, but one is poignancy itself; their version of Ewan MacColl's 'Dirty Old Town'. It's a song about Salford that becomes a melancholy but defiant pledge about home and hope:

This is our club, belongs to you and me
We're United, United FC
We may never go home
But we'll never feel down
When we build our own ground

And now they have. In late May 2015, I went to my first match at Broadhurst Park, a 5,000 capacity stadium in Moston, a beautiful edifice in steel, concrete and wood in the style of railway sleepers, a tribute to the railway men of Newton Heath which begat Manchester United. That first match was against Portuguese champions Benfica. This too was a nod to Manchester United's past, as they beat Benfica in the 1968 European Cup final; a totemic game from the era of Best, Law and Charlton. Tonight FC United lose by a single goal scored by Diogo Gonzales, 'who clearly hasn't read the script' as the announcer hilariously put it.

Broadhurst Park stands on the site of the old Ronald Johnson Playing Fields, Moston, and paid for (with a little help from the council) by the dreamers of FC United at a cost of some £6 million. The name was voted for by FC's fans. One of the narrowly rejected proposed names, using an acronymic of FC United of Manchester, but with a cheeky twinkle, was FCUM Hall.

I was told this by Dave, project manager for the new stadium, at the Halesowen Town away game. Yes, soon after my first time, I went back to see FC play, in Halesowen on a tiny patch of grass in the middle of a housing estate in the West Midlands. I soon became addicted to what some wags call 'the crystal meth of football'. Since that first game and before the opening of Broadhurst Park, I travelled to see FC play at their borrowed homes, Gigg Lane of course, the Tameside Stadium in Ashton-under-Lyne and, most evocatively, Bower Fold, Stalybridge (Stalyvegas), for a night game in the hills. That night, seven balls were lost by being kicked out of the ground into the depths of the adjoining woodlands, and a horse and rider made their way across a ridge in the hills behind the stand, in the moonlight, as if King Arthur were an FC fan who'd popped down for the second half. By the time I was getting a cab across the Midlands on a bitter, bleak Saturday to watch them play in Halesowen, I had to acknowledge that I had a problem. But I can handle it.

What gets in the blood about FC if you love football is the sense that there is an alternative. An alternative to what football has become and how it has been wrested away from the people who made it and who loved it, taken out of their towns and control, and handed to a self-serving elite of plutocrats. Tony Howard, who still does the excellent match day programme, sees much about FC United's raison d'être as explicitly political. He is a committed trade unionist and, for him, these values underpin the club, enshrined in ideas like a 'pay what you can afford' season ticket, for which some chose to still fork out the 600 quid they had at Big United.

Not every old school supporter took naturally to new and very different ideas, like FC United LGBTQ, the team's lesbian, gay, bisexual, transgender, queer and other minority sexuality supporters. But the 'narrative' (sorry) is one of progress and success. They have found kindred spirits with Rob Lees and the MaD Theatre Group, who have similar aims for the accessibility of theatre for working-class people. Their relationship began when FC asked some of our youth members to run workshops before games with their fans. A play called *She's Just Nipped Out For Fags* at Bury Met in 2008 was staged as a joint venture with MaD and FC. Fans filled the theatre with flags and scarves creating a football crowd in a theatre and special FC/MaD half and half scarves were produced for the event, which supporters still wear to matches.

Perhaps the main thing I like about FC United is the refreshing lack of mardiness and cant that characterises modern football: Robbie Savage bleating that 'you can't do that' about a fans' boycott; grown men spectators, who spend all match viciously abusing players and then become delicate flowers who complain to the police if one of them answers back; players not celebrating goals against their old clubs out of 'respect'. FC United, a club forged in adversity and with a political will, don't seem to have any of this feeble baggage around them and I like them for that. These are ordinary men and women taking charge of their own destinies and communities. FC may have a lesson for all of us in spheres of life far away from Gigg Lane.

In their refusal to knuckle under and bow down to vested interest, money and power, they have less in common with most football fans than they do with, say, the people who defied landowners to reclaim the high hills of the north during the Kinder Scout trespass of 1932. Like football, taking to the hills has always been a powerful diversion and recreation of the northern worker. As well as his ambivalent love letter to Salford, 'Dirty Old Town', now taken up by FC United, Ewan MacColl commemorated the trespassers in a song called the 'Manchester Rambler' whose narrator has 'been over Snowdon … slept upon Crowdon … camped by the Waynestones as well':

> *I've sunbathed on Kinder, been burned to a cinder*
> *And many more things I can tell …*
> *I may be a wage slave on Monday*
> *But I am a free man on Sunday*

A L Sidgwick summed all this up brilliantly in a piece of 1912 that never fails to stir. 'And in the darkest hours of urban depression I will sometimes take out that dog's-eared map and dream a while of more spacious days; and perhaps a dried blade of grass will fall out of it to remind me that I was once a free man on the hills…'

Dog-eared map, pork pie and Thermos in hand, I was off to join the free men and women. In the words of Walt Whitman the great American poet and egalitarian:

> *Afoot and light-hearted I take to the open road.*
> *Healthy, free, the world before me,*
> *the long brown path before me leading wherever I choose.*

And I chose to go to one of Walt Whitman's favourite places; Bolton of course.

CHAPTER 8

GETTING A BIT OF FRESH AIR

To Catbells, Anglezarke and Werneth Low,
and a drop of wine with Walt Whitman

As clockwork as the first cuckoo, and as seasonal as the snowdrop, it comes around. Regular as the backward and forward motion of the clocks, the springing forward and falling back that no one ever remembers with complete confidence, whether it is backward or forward or darker or lighter in the morning or evenings or both. With every public holiday comes the refrain from officialdom on high: 'Don't travel unless it's absolutely necessary'.

This official advice is routinely and irritatingly given during spells of bad or, as I like to think of it, completely normal winter weather, or over Easter or bank holiday, when trains are needed most, to remind us that said trains won't be running and there will be, in the three most chilling words in the English language, a 'replacement bus service'. But the unnecessary travel admonishment annoys for two distinct and separate reasons. Firstly, exactly who is making all these unnecessary journeys? What are we, a nation of flâneurs and idle boulevardiers? If I can get away without going to work when there's three feet of snow and the trains aren't running, believe me, I try.

But secondly, much of the gaiety of life is gained from doing things that aren't absolutely necessary. Things that are pointless, ad hoc, speculative, silly, and therefore good for the soul. In that category

I would put the unnecessary travel that compels you to follow that path as it rises, to wonder what's over that next hill, that leads you to the tops of those hills, through forest tracks, over rolling ridges and along rivers to the sea. There's a Thom Gunn poem called 'On the Move' that for me gets right to the core of this impulse:

> *At worst, one is in motion; and at best,*
> *Reaching no absolute, in which to rest,*
> *One is always nearer by not keeping still.*

Stirring words for me, speaking of urgency and momentum, vigour and action, all the stuff that the Romantics like Wordsworth and Rousseau believed that striding out into the world should be about. It is the spirit of the famed painting by Casper David Friedrich, 'Wanderer above the Sea of Fog'. You know the one; a young chap in an overcoat stands on a crag with his back to you. He gazes out on a landscape covered in the aforesaid sea of fog, which partly obscures nearby ridges, shrouds the mountains, forests and plains, all the way to the far horizon. Quite what he is doing I don't know. Many a critic and commentator have argued over this. Is he surveying the landscape he has mastered, conquered by an act of physical will? Or is he contemplating his own insignificance in the face of nature's majesty and power. Who can say? I know what he isn't doing though. Rambling.

In the same way that birdwatchers don't actually like being called 'twitchers' (they prefer 'birder'), if you're a walker, I bet you don't like being called a rambler. I don't like it either. I know it's the name of a fine organisation that campaigns tirelessly for our rights to roam and such, but it conjures a drippy Fotherington-Thomas type in a woolly hat and a little knapsack skipping down a path saying 'hello clouds, hello sky'. That, or someone who's going a little senile. I don't want to come over as some 'macho' walking bore here. I have little time for the 'heads down', 'route marcher' walker, the one who measures his day in miles and peaks rather than views and conversations and experiences. The type of SAS wannabe who's been up Scafell 42 times but not lovely litte Loughrigg Fell because he doesn't bother with 'the small stuff'. The one who never stops for a flask or a butty but stomps out ahead of his long suffering wife and kids, who secretly hate him and are hoping he falls into a ravine.

No, begone with that. But we deserve a name that implies purpose and dynamism rather than losing one's thread in the middle of a dull anecdote. When the Ramblers Association rebranded some years ago in an attempt to sound more youthful and inclusive, they dropped the Association and became 'Ramblers'. Personally I don't think that 'association' was the problem. One contributor to WalkingForum. co.uk who styled himself 'Angry Climber' was, as you might have guessed, really tetchy about it all. So tetchy he didn't bother with full stops: 'I know the ramblers association have tried to relaunch themselves but the biggest dislike I have of them is purely the word Ramblers I think it just is an old fashioned word used by old fashioned people and that is the main reason it is particularly the older generation that go on these walks'.

Tricky one. Even if you don't like being called a rambler, there's the weight of tradition and a grand old reputation to contend with. Ramblers have been called Ramblers since the days of the Kinder Trespass. The association grew out of the Communist British Workers Sport Federation, which has something of a ring to it, I think. Anyway, I have on my desk before me two slim volumes, which show their age by the innocent pleasure they take in the word 'ramble'.

One is a reproduction of E Mansell's *The Rambler's Companion* of 1937, reprinted later as *The Wayfarers Book*. You can now pick it up in a facsimile edition to feed our nostalgic ache for a different England, that gentle ache evident in our longing for Keep Calm and Carry On mugs, *Downton Abbey* and Michael Portillo pootling about on rickety trains in a canary yellow sports coat.

Mansell calls this sweet little book 'a collection of scraps and oddments' and these are his random jottings and musings about the things one might encounter as you 'rambled' through our green and pleasant land before the Second World War. He describes and explains the miscellaneous delights encountered – windmills, dolmens, the Parsons Posts of Yorkshire, men on stilts picking hops in Kent, tithe barns, dove cotes, dew ponds – in the manner of those kindly teachers or favourite uncles that have probably never existed, his briar pipe in hand as he leans thoughtfully on a five-bar gate. Rich in detail, it sings of a vanished England before the coming of the agri-barons and the polytunnels, a land of churches and farms, sleepy villages and quaint traditions like the Biddenden Dole, where bread and cheese are given to passing strangers. It's only when you come to the chapter on those delightful old artefacts the ducking stool, the whipping post and the pillory that a different, darker side of pre-industrial England emerges.

The other book on my desk is a few decades earlier and from a different England still, from the last days of that prelapsarian Avalon before the shadow of mass industrialisation and war darkened the land. It was also before recreational walking in the country had gained its political edge. The book, which I must have found in some now forgotten dusty second-hand bookshop, is John T Hilton's *Wigan Town and Country Rambles: With Views and Interesting Historical Incidents*. It was published in 1914, just weeks before the Great War changed the country and the world forever, and put paid to the long summer evenings of country walking for a generation. It has become a cliché to talk gravely of the lost idyll of England before the First World War. But there is truth in it. Some of the sentences in Hilton's modest book have the same elegiac sense of that faded world as the music of George Butterworth or the poems of Housman.

> To be in the lanes and meadows in the warm days of summer, within hearing of the swish of the scythe or the whir of the reaping machine, to see the work of tossing and the binding of sheaves, and to hear the voices of the harvesters, gives zest

to life … the trilling notes of the thrush, the humming of the bees, the silvery ripping of the brook and the loud rushing of the waterfall.

At this point, I had to turn back to the cover to make sure that this was the Wigan I knew, and not a village in Laurie Lee's Gloucestershire with the same name. But it was. Advertised at the rear were the pubs and shops I remembered from my childhood; ancient and fusty old institutions by then but in John T Hilton's day they were brash new enterprises and upscale attractions: 'The Minorca Hotel And Grill Room; Private Rooms For Select Parties', which by the time I was in my teens held a cool midweek northern soul night, or Pendlebury's Furniture Store offering 'Gunn's Sectional Bookcases, the most satis-factory way of keeping your books commodious and adaptable', or the Royal Hotel where I would skulk in the back bar as an underage drinker. In 1914, it was a 'Commercial, Family And Motorists Hotel convenient for all places of public interest and electrically lighted throughout'.

The subtext of Hilton's book, actually the explicit thrust, is the old notion of *mens sana in corpore sano*; a healthy mind in a healthy body, and thus a workforce fit for the demands of industry thanks to time spent in the great outdoors. 'The highest medical authorities have pronounced in no uncertain voice the great need for the workers of this country to avail themselves of more active recreation. The needs of the times demand it.' To this end, Hilton comes up with, in best Edwardian style befitting the frock coated and collar studded pillar of society on the frontispiece, 'a tribute of praise to his native town whose scenery for miles around cannot be surpassed for its pleasing variety and rural beauty'.

This is admirably loyal of Hilton, but manifestly crackers. Wigan's rural beauty cannot be surpassed? Had he not seen any watercolours of the Alps? Had he never been to the Lake District? Had he even wandered about in his tailcoat on the dunes at Ainsdale? Had he, in fact, been anywhere at all except Wigan? My home town in 1914 was not the smudge of post-industrial sprawl it is now. But even then it was no Buttermere.

Still, well played for the team John T Hilton, who goes on to describe the various bucolic excursions available from the town – Haigh Hall, Fairy Glen, Parbold Hill, Ashurst Beacon, all of them known to me from healthy and not so healthy teenage days, sometimes with fizzy pop and grazed knees, other times with Lambert & Butler and Merrydown cider. Best of all these itineraries lies just outside the town, where the ground rises high beyond these days the white metallic spider of the once Reebok, now Macron Stadium. The West Pennine Moors; playground of Wiganer and Boltoner for centuries, and the place where every 31 May Walt Whitman gets a most unlikely birthday party.

Walt Whitman never came to Bolton. But the town regard the great, revolutionary American poet as a favourite adopted son to rank with Peter Kay, Ian McKellen or Big Sam Allardyce. The Whitmanites of Bolton have been singing Walt's praises, often literally, since J W Wallace of the town, chum of Keir Hardie, fell under Whitman's spell. Wallace was smitten with Whitman's progressive philosophies and inspirational verse concerning comradeship and the open air, and instigated a correspondence with him starting – ahh bless – with a birthday card in 1887.

He was not alone in his admiration. Many of the early English socialists were fervent Whitman fans, and their magazines regularly carried adverts for his verse manifesto *Leaves of Grass*. Whitman, with his rakish bohemian cap and dress, his shock of snowy hair and beard, was a rock star Gandalf for the burgeoning Labour movement in Lancashire. One of their number, Boltonian Allen Clarke, wrote that 'it is fitting that Bolton should be distinguished above all towns in England by having a group of Whitman enthusiasts, for many years in close touch, by letter and visit, with 'the Master', for I am sure Walt Whitman, the singer of out-door life, would have loved to ramble our Lancashire moorlands.'

He never did get around to that. But the Whitmanites of Bolton soon began to do it for him, roaming the moors of Rivington and Anglezarke, and celebrating Walt in these walks and recitations. In 1885, in a terraced house in town, they set up the Eagle Street College, a gathering of kindred spirits inspired by Whitman's verse and teachings. Walt was touched by all this fervid fandom and reciprocated with letters, poems, papers and even a stuffed canary that form the basis of Bolton Archives' Walt Whitman Collection, the finest repository of Whitman related material outside of America. I myself have donned the latex gloves and leafed through these valuable papers and such, when I made a radio programme about the Whitmanites of Bolton and went walking with them over the moors.

Yes. The Whitman Walk is still going strong. I made my way up to Barrow Bridge a few years back to join the celebration that still takes place each year on the Saturday nearest to Whitman's birthday. And what a day it was, egg-yolk yellow and egg-shell blue; a watery heat rippling over Adlington and Horwich, with the larks and song thrushes putting on a fine al fresco concert. But pleasant though it is, there's more to the original and the revived Whitman Walk than birdsong and pretty views. Many of the Whitmanites today are part of the town's Bolton Socialist Club, an organisation that brings together under its (reddish) rainbow coalition trade unionists, vegan punks, Trotskyists, CND-types and generally anyone whose thinking runs a little leftward or outside of the mainstream. If you set out to design an organisation with the express purpose of making the throbbing artery in Sir Bernard Ingham's temple explode, it would be the Bolton Socialist Club.

The original celebrations of Whitman's birthday went on long after the deaths of most of the original participants (and Whitman himself), but petered out in the 1950s. In the early 1980s, though, Paul Salveson, researching a doctorate on Lancashire history, came across the records of the Eagle Street College in Bolton Library. Fascinated and inspired, he enlisted his mates from Bolton Socialist

Club. These new Whitmanites revived the tradition of the Whitman Walk in 1985, at the high water mark of Thatcherism, as a celebration of other, more human values. There are now seven plaques devoted to Whitman and his Boltonian brethren dotted about the town and the surrounding moorlands. The walk, which takes many of them in, is open to all and has become popular with liberals of every hue and allegiance, old school Marxists and the gay community, as it seems pretty clear now that Whitman and many of the Whitmanites were probably gay, though not always 'out' in today's sense.

The early Whitmanites would take a brisk walk up Rivington and then across the moor, sporting sprigs of lilac and reading from their hero. Once on the tops they'd commune with nature, sing a few songs, read a little more Whitman and refresh themselves with the passing round of a three-handled 'loving cup' containing spiced claret, before taking the long route back to Adlington. This remains the pattern today though the loving cup, as I can vouch, now holds a decently robust supermarket red rather than spiced claret.

Obviously, desiccated cynics will find all this 'weird'. But most good things have a little of the weird about them, or at least the unusual. In these terrified times, when the slightest deviation from the norm, the regular and the party line, the uttering of anything that might offend or perplex or go off script must be avoided and apologised for, we need more of us unafraid to go against the grain, to change the narrative, to think the unthinkable, to propose a different way. Humanity moves on not by acquiescence but dissent, and there's a modest reminder of that up on the moors along the Whitman Walk.

We started at the old mill hamlet of Barrow Bridge and finished with very welcome ice creams at the Bryan Hey Farm tea room. But we stopped for a Thermos, a handful of wine gums and a moment's reflection at a low stone plaque embedded in the grass bank by the moorland path. It's a commemoration of an act of mass trespass that's less well known than the one on Kinder Scout. But it speaks of the same impulse. Freedom.

In September 1896, members of the Bolton Socialist Club were involved in a huge trespass march over Winter Hill. A local landowner called Colonel Richard Ainsworth had effectively annexed the hillside by closing and barricading the path claiming he'd bought it as a private grouse moor. Ainsworth tried to prevent Bolton people from using public rights of way and in this abuse of their rights he was assisted by the local police. But they were no match for the 10,000 walkers who confronted them that day, singing a special song composed for the event by Bolton socialist poet Allen Clarke, titled 'Will you come o' Sunday mornin'?'

Ten thousand people gathered to be confronted by gamekeepers, police and their barriers. But the crowd simply hurled the coppers over the fence and climbed the hill via Smithills Moor before descending to Belmont. Belmont is the village where my old band The Young Mark Twains made several excellent demo recordings, in a studio there in the hills, and where I once went swimming in the reservoir at dawn. Unlike the trespass, however, there's sadly no plaque or memorial to these memorable events.

The tourist leaflets and the brown signage calls them the West Pennine Moors. We in Wigan never thought of them as that till recently, but they have always formed a kind of backcloth to the dramas of life, in a minor way, rather like Skiddaw does with Keswick. They loomed large in my youth. You could see them from the bottom of my street and measure the passing seasons from their changing raiment, from heavy shawls of snow to necklaces of rain, to thin scarves of mist across their broad shoulders. Sometimes they would not be there for weeks on end, hidden behind clag and shadow, and then the curtains would part and the sun would ebb and flow across them as the summer came and went.

More prosaically it's where we got our TV pictures from, from the slender mast that flickered scarlet through the dusk, there high at the heart of 'Granadaland'. During the sixties, seventies and eighties, people around here identified themselves strongly with our

Independent Television franchise Granada, more so than the BBC, I would concede. Created by Sidney Bernstein and run by visionaries like David Plowright, it established itself as a powerhouse of freethinking, risk-taking, exciting TV from *World in Action* to *Coronation Street*, Tony Wilson's pop shows to Olivier's definitive TV *Lear*.

When, in the early nineties, Plowright was ousted as chairman by Gerry Robinson, ex-head of Compass Caterers, who wanted to cut budgets and extract more profit, there was outrage in the media. Granada executives signed a letter of protest which said that the removal of 'this efficient and universally respected programme maker has undermined the morale and intentions of the Granada Group ethic … we await to see whether they [the new owners] will reassert the Granada ethic of quality and diversity.' John Cleese was more direct. He sent Robinson a fax which read 'F*** off out of it, you ignorant upstart caterer'. Normally this kind of snobbery would annoy. But I took his point. When we looked to those masts or the old Granada building in Manchester, north-westerners were proud of their channel and the fact that its programmes were the envy of the world, all from that needle of metal on Winter Hill.

My favourite of all those moors now, though the one I knew and had visited the least till last summer, is Anglezarke. You have to be dull of spirit not to be seduced by just the name I think. It has a high, wild northern echo, taken from the Old Norse name 'Anlaf' and the Viking word 'erg' for a hill pasture or shieling. It has a lonely ring to it, and these days it is. At the 2001 census its population was just 22. On the surrounding heights lie the remains of 48 lost farms and there was a thriving little hamlet at White Coppice where now all that remains is a cricket ground and its team.

About a century-and-a-half ago, this patchwork landscape of farm, field and river was transformed when first the Chorley Waterworks Company and then the civic might of Liverpool Council built the reservoir system. The building of these brought a massive influx of workmen stationed in shanty towns and huts on the moor. Hard-labouring navvies in the main, as well as engineers, surveyors and stone masons, and all had a thirst on when the day's work was done.

The old Clog Inn at Anglezarke didn't know what had hit it, perhaps literally. Its two small beer parlours were crowded every night and the 'Clog' simply could not keep up with demand. Enterprising locals set up as unlicensed beer vendors, brewing their own ale and selling it from their back doors, raking in big profits. There were illicit stills secreted away in the hills where a rough, potent 'poteen' whisky was distilled, for those who preferred spirits and weren't overburdened by an excessively refined palette.

The men have gone but that era of rampant industry gives the area its flavour and geography now, though much quieter of course. Anglezarke now is a place of secretive sylvan glades and small hills folded together over several high glittering sheets of water; Yarrow, Healey Nab, High Bullough, Lower Rivington, Anglezarke itself and more, some bold and wide, some shy and hidden. The 'Little Lake District', some locals have called it; a trifle imaginatively maybe, but it is a magical place, especially tonight.

I arrive at the first settling of dusk, that lambent phase of a golden summer midweek evening, between the demands of work and the routines of home. This is when the discerning local people come up to Anglezarke.

A bloke in his thirties in dusty overall and work boots gets out of a battered estate car, lifting his tired face to the last of the sun before then pulling a hefty, expensive looking camera out of its case and stomping off up the slope into the tree canopy. He's been thinking of this all day, while he's been smoothing plaster or grouting a bathroom or driving a forklift round an echoing warehouse stacked with pallets; his time, an hour in the open air, him and the camera and whatever it is that he comes to capture – birds, sunsets, who knows – and then a couple of pints at the bar to reflect. Of course, this could be just me seeing the scene through a gauzy filter of urban romanticism.

He could be a Pulitzer Prize-winning photographer on assignment from *Time* magazine who fell in a pile of flour on the way here. We shouldn't jump to conclusions.

Anglezarke is never as busy as its neighbour Rivington, where Lord Lever built a series of summerhouses and terraces and which on an Easter Monday can seem like the Golden Mile at Blackpool. Anglezarke is more of a connoisseur's hideout, perhaps for the simple reason that it's more awkward to get to; asking directions from a kindly soul en route involved him grimacing and sucking in his breath and indicating wide arcs with waves of his arms.

I got here in the end though, and on the winding hidden track that leads from the car park down to the reservoir, I bump into a woman bringing a sodden, delirious dog back from his evening dip. She's no stranger to the outdoors evidently; shorthaired, skinny and freckly in tight black Lycra. The dog is daft and boisterous.

'He's a Rhodie without a ridge,' she tells me. 'Got him off a friend. Couldn't handle him. He tore up the kennel. I've had him a couple of years though and he's alright now, aren't you?' She lifts a hand and, besotted, he bounds towards her, giving us a refreshing little shower as she does. She's rescued 60 dogs over the years, she reckons. Doesn't know what magic she works on them but 'it must be something right I guess. He's too skinny though,' she adds, narrowing her eyes in concern, 'you can see that when he's in the water.'

That's the water I'm headed towards now, and as I go I mentally tick off the music I can call to mind inspired by Anglezarke. A musician and artist called Richard Skelton has made a serious of sombre and affecting word-and-music pieces based around how this landscape and his immersion in it gave him solace at a time of bereavement and grief. Then Thickens have an album cheerily entitled *Death Cap At Anglezarke*. It's a morbid ode to the poisonous mushroom growing hereabouts, whose toxicity is not lessened by cooking, drying, freezing or curing, and that will kill you in the most horrible and lingering way should you mistake it for something else. Several people do just that every year, making it the fungus most responsible for human deaths. Even Doves' 'Winter Hill', a 'chartbound sound' and hit single no less in 2009, has a chill about it.

Nothing of that tonight though. The hills are bathed in light and the sun glows warm on my grateful skin, falling huge and blazing across Anglezarke Reservoir. If this is the Little Lake District, Anglezarke 'Rezzy' is its Windermere, expansive and serene, blinding in the sunset, and surrounded by bosky twilit hills, too inviting not to venture into and linger for a while as the day and the world slipped away. It is an unforgettable, blissful end to the day.

After a while, and after all this rapture, as I return reluctantly to the tarmac road that winds along the shore, I realise that I'm starving. There's a gastropub called The Yew Tree over the brow of the hill but they seem to lack the enterprising nature of the old Anglezarkians with their homebrew and moonshine. On a gorgeous evening, as thirsty and hungry folk are tramping, cycling and driving back down the hill from Rivington, the pub naturally isn't doing food. The north of England has undergone a dining revolution over the last couple of decades, as discussed a few chapters back. But there are still lingering hints of the bad old days. I'm reminded of a couple of occasions when I'd 'dined out' in my home town and found them caught uneasily between the old worlds and the new.

Ordering a single espresso in a Standish restaurant, I was brought it in a mug full to the brim. 'You're in luck,' I was told. 'We're all out of those stupid little cups so you've got a decent drink.' It was a thick black drink of a volume that would have kept me awake, saucer-eyed and twitching, for a month. Then there was the time I took my folks for lunch in Wigan having been assured by some friends that a certain place in town was terrific. On arrival, I gathered from the menu that the lunch deal promised three courses with choices at each stage. But I could only see soup offered as a starter. Do you have an option for every course, I asked the friendly local waitress. 'Oh yes,' she replied. Thought so, I replied, but you don't seem have anything except soup as a starter. What's the option there? 'Well, you don't have to have it,' she said, brightly. After a moment's reflection, I had it.

'Little Lake District' is a charming nickname, but it doesn't really make sense. Before the boundary changes that created Cumbria, much of the South Lakes, from the brooding massif of Black Combe on the Furness peninsula to the airy promenades of the Coniston Fells and the Old Man himself, were actually in Lancashire. (Rooted in the reality of an ancient kingdom called Rheged, Cumbria has been much more successful a creation than some of the other invented counties. Cumbrian folk call themselves just that, and they talk of Cumbria in a way that the people of Hartlepool never spoke of Cleveland, and Wiganers never declare an allegiance to Greater Manchester.)

I once threatened that, though the shelves of bookshops are already groaning with Lake District literature, I was sure I'd add to that before too long with my own book on the place that I love. That day still hasn't come yet, but I couldn't in all seriousness write a chapter about outdoor recreation and northern folk without mentioning the Lake District.

In my part of the world, if we fancied stretching our legs a little further than the West Pennine moors and seeing some real mountains, or just fancied a boat trip, an ice cream and a bit of Peter Rabbit, we would throw the travel blanket in the back and head north up the M6 for the Lake District, shielding our eyes as we passed the siren call of the Blackpool turn-off.

Lancashire lads and lasses have been coming to 'The Lakes' for generations though Lakes laureate William Wordsworth wasn't keen on this at all. Snob and establishment lickspittle that he was in his old age, he fought hard against the coming of the railways to Cumbria, which he thought would bring the wrong sort of people here. By this, he meant the workers of industrial Lancashire of course. He failed, as all of his kind who set their face against the people are doomed to fail, and we bloody well came, first in our bonnets and hobnails, and then in our clinkered boots and our flip flops, to a clatter of walking poles and car radio; the great, unstoppable caravanserai of the north on the move in search of a good time and healthy diversion. Sorry William.

To a degree, of course, this was all William's fault, for writing such celebrated paeans to the landscape and, furthermore, a travel guide. By 1835, when his guide was in its fifth printing (and no longer anonymous, his poetry and fame by now firmly established), guesthouses had sprung up. 'The lakes,' he wrote, 'had now become celebrated; visitors flocked hither from all parts of England… and [the lakes] were instantly defaced by the intrusion.' It wasn't long before charabancs and trains and then eventually the private motorcar, plus of course cheap B&B's and Youth Hostels, meant that the average person rather than the aristocrat could visit the Lakes in vast numbers and, inevitably, change the nature of the place.

It's a dilemma that was wrestled with constantly by the greatest of all Lakes guide book writers Alfred Wainwright. A Blackburn lad, he first came in 1930 when he was 23. He walked up a small height called Orrest Head and was instantly smitten, like many of us since. His seven volume *Pictorial Guides* have become the definitive work of Lake District and fell walking literature, precise and useful as field guides but, more than this, a beguiling blend of lyricism and bluffness that made him an institution and a millionaire. He gave all the considerable money he made away and set up an animal charity, asking 'what kind of man would want payment for a love letter'?

When this Lancashire lad came as a teenager, I came for the fishing, beer and camaraderie, and the distant, largely unrealised prospect of girls. We came in Joe Mather's van and poached eels from Esthwaite Water through the night, and boiled them, grilled them, sautéed, fricasseed and fried them every which way in the campsite in the morning until I was heartily sick of them. These tales I have told elsewhere and I mention them again now just to make the point; Lancashire people feel the 'Lakes' is their playground and their birth right, and we come in Gore-Tex and Armani to enjoy it how we will.

They come in their droves to the fleshpots of Bowness, Windermere and Ambleside, which can seem as brash as Blackpool if you
came to wander lonely as a cloud in your frock coat. But push on
further north, over Dunmail Raise – named after an ancient king who
lobbed his crown in Grisedale Tarn, they say – and you meet up with
the Geordies and West Cumbrians and Scots. In fact you'll meet up
with everyone, in Keswick.

Keswick is all the fabulous contradictions of the Lake District in
one. It's unmistakably a working town, though now that work tends
to be feeding and clothing rather than wool and mining. But then
it's also got a holistic, Hebden Bridge/Haight-Ashbury feel too. You
could definitely get your chakra realigned here, as well as your boots
re-soled. But you will struggle to find peace. There's just too many of
those walking poles clattering along its streets 365 days of the year.

Pretty and busy and almost alpine, sheltering under Skiddaw,
Keswick's streets are packed with mountain equipment shops and its
pavements crowded with people kitted out for Annapurna in winter
but going no further than Bryson's cake shop for a Cumberland rum-
butter tea. Uncharitably, you may be reminded of the phrase 'all the
gear, no idea' but that would be mean-spirited of you. At some point,
surely these good folk will take to the hills, and the hill they take to
will probably be Catbells.

Compared to the hairy, macho mountains roundabout, Catbells
is a squirt. But, like Anglezarke, the name will surely cast a spell on
you, and once you'd seen its fine summit outlined against the sky
across Derwentwater you'd be eulogising like Wainwright himself: 'It
is one of the great favourites, a family fell where grandmothers and
infants can climb the heights together, a place beloved. Its popularity
is well deserved, its shapely topknott attracts the eye offering a steep
but obviously simple scramble.'

On this bright bank holiday morning, the Keswick Launch would
have groaned under the weight of its human cargo across the lake –
the young, the old, crying babies and yapping dogs – if this elegant

old craft could ever do something so uncouth. The aristocratic *Annie Mellor*, *Princess Margaret Rose*, *Lady Derwentwater* and *Iris* criss-cross the lake all day long, Derwentwater being one of three of the lakes that have regular powered services for the public, along with the Ullswater Steamers and the Coniston Gondola. Each of them has their leaflets, encouraging you to use the boats as the basis of walks in the surrounding hills, and in the Keswick Launch's case you will find 'Hawse End to Brandlehow via Catbells. Strenuous walk to top of Catbells but you are met with some of the most beautiful views in the Lakes. Time: 3 – 4 hours. Grading: Difficult.'

This would bring a snort of derision from those bearded types who are even now negotiating crablike the rocky razor fin of Sharp Edge on Blencathra, or gingerly creeping up the exposed flank of Jack's Rake. But the Keswick Launch is popular with all, and the writers of this little leaflet don't want to be accused of underestimating the effort. Catbells is a proper mountain and will be the highest thing most of the folk setting off for it today have ever scaled under their own power. The Mountain Rescue reports are full of casualties who took the hills for granted. Do that, and they will bite you.

I once stood by amused and appalled in the climbers shop at the head of Wasdale while the young staff member tried to gently dissuade a balding granddad in a cardigan and pipe from setting off to the summit of Scafell Pike with his wife and tiny granddaughter. 'But it's only three and a half miles. We can walk that!' blustered Granddad, as the lad tried to explain that it was not so much the distance, which would be nothing along a towpath or pavement, but the 3,500 feet of elevation and constant climbing in some of the most inhospitable terrain in Britain. I think he succeeded in putting them off. I didn't notice Granddad in the deaths section of the 'Lake District Mountain Rescue Incidents Annual Report' anyway, my favourite yearly reading.

Even sans leaflet, and if I hadn't known the way from Hawse End jetty to Catbells, navigation wouldn't have been a problem any more than it would finding your route up Wembley Way on Cup Final day;

it was simply a case of following the crowds. Like the passengers on the *Princess Margaret Rose*, the hardy adventurers came in all shapes and sizes. There were elegant Italians with chic leather handbags, large noisy Asian families with recalcitrant toddlers, lads in replica Newcastle tops, sweet elderly couples, crocodiles of children. Faced with his first glimpse of Catbells' rugged south face, a young Yorkshire lad in a Superdry T-shirt turns to his dad aghast, 'If ah falls off to my death, it's tha fault.'

You'd have to be supremely unlucky or daft to fall to your death this way, but nevertheless you shouldn't underestimate the ascent. This is the way everyone comes, the winding path that lures you as you sit sipping your latte in a Keswick café. But it's no 'hands in pockets' stroll. The path winds up Skelgill Bank, in and out of rocky excrescences and tumbled stones with the views across the lake and into Newlands Valley unfolding as you climb. In Hugh Walpole's hugely popular Lakes potboiler *Rogue Herries*, they were always going backwards and forwards over Catbells, as you and I would go in and out of the kitchen, but they were clearly made of sterner stuff back then. Dip into Dorothy Wordsworth's journals and marvel at how they would think nothing of walking a tipsy Coleridge the 13 miles back to Keswick over Dunmail Raise after an evening's declaiming and chatting.

Even with stops for the flask and the views, getting your breath back over a quick and unnecessary look at the map and the best sausage rolls on the planet (which you will have bought from Cranstons of Penrith in advance if you are wise), you will still be at the top in an hour or so. At the summit on this day, we all commented on the sheer brutal force of the wind and the magnificence of the view. Small dogs abounded, displaying as all dogs do, that infectious boundless zest for life that make them such great company. (Is there any more joyous expression than that on the face of a dog with its head out of a moving car window?) At the top, I offered to take a group shot of a man and two ladies from Liverpool. They wanted one on each of their phones, and as I put one into my pocket briefly to use the other, one lady remarked, 'Eh, I bet you get a fair few mobile phones like that.'

And it was lovely. All of the books and guides will bang on about the crowds and suggest all manner of detours and circumnavigations to avoid the day trippers and I love a spot of high mountain solitude myself. But really is it so bad to spend some time shoulder to shoulder with one's fellow folk? After all, diverse as they are, these are the best of people. On a day of freedom, they've chosen not to slump before a screen or plod around a shopping centre, but to take England's free air on the top of a mountain. They are good company to be in.

It's different kind of pleasure from that of having the viewable world to oneself, to stand upon a lonely summit in splendid isolation. But it's grand to see so many people of so many different races and types enjoying the open air and the joys of the British countryside. William Blake once wrote, 'Great things are done when men and mountains meet; this is not done by jostling in the street.' Here on proud little Catbells, work, mortgages and jostling in the street are forgotten for one day, and somewhere here a lifelong love affair was being kindled. A love of the outdoors, of putting one foot in front of the other, and the landscape of the north.

Of course, to some people, I'm a Midlander. A son of the soft south even. Penrith and The Border MP Rory Stewart has made TV programmes about Cumbria and Northumbria describing them as The Middle Lands, which technically they are I suppose. Meriden in Warwickshire is the centre of England, but the centre of Britain is, as the board proudly reads as you enter the town, Haltwhistle. But, this is surely only if you are working merely from map latitudes rather than casts of mind and outlooks on life. This is the danger in trusting too much to facts, figures and statistics for me. It's said a statistician is someone who, if you put his head in the freezer and his feet in the oven will say that, on average, he feels fine. I'd add that a statistician is someone who will tell you that Haltwhistle, Northumbria and County Durham are in the Midlands.

Picture me this then. Picture me 'a northerner'. Hold that thought. What do you see? A sooty-faced man emerging from a cage at the pithead? Elsie Tanner? Eric Bloodaxe doing a spot of light berserking? Geoffrey Boycott speaking as he finds and not suffering fools gladly? Someone with a whippet, a flat cap and rickets? Liam Gallagher perhaps?

The image that probably hasn't formed in your mind is a flamboyantly gay, privately educated, communist poet called Wystan wearing a floppy hat and possibly a cravat. And yet W H Auden was perhaps the quintessential northerner. He called the north his 'Mutterland' and memorably said of it 'my great good place is the part of the Pennines bounded on the South by Swaledale, on the North by the Roman Wall and on the West by the Eden Valley.' Even in the American exile of his later years, a battered Ordnance Survey map of Alston Moor hung on his wall in New York.

Auden was born in the original York. As an 11-year-old, when his peers might have pored over stamps or strikers or steam engines, he was obsessed by County Durham's lead mining industry and wrote in his diary of the magical places he hoped to visit one day, not Disneyland or Narnia, not even Blackpool Pleasure Beach but Rookhope, Allenheads and Killhope.

> *And from my sixth until my sixteenth year*
> *I thought myself a mining engineer.*

He first came to County Durham in 1919, and the love affair was consummated swiftly and passionately and affirmed for life. He was 21 then, and when he was 60 and remarkably well travelled, he still called himself a 'son of the north'. His friend Christopher Isherwood said of him that 'his romantic travel-wish was always towards the north. He could never understand how anyone could long for the sun, the blue sky, the palm-trees of the south. His favourite weather was autumnal, high wind and driving rain.'

No wonder then that he loved the lonely, north-eastern corner of England; the North Pennines, Weardale, County Durham and its Dales. He even tried to lure American tourists up here, away from the soft, easy, moneyed pleasures of the Cotswolds and Piccadilly Circus, in an article about the North Pennines he wrote for *Vogue* in 1954 called 'Six Unexpected Days'. Sixty years later, I had a few days of my own there, as I wanted to see some of the region's mining country, the places that so obsessed Auden and had now, strangely, become tourist destinations in themselves.

I say strangely since it would have appeared that way to the Pitmen Painters. They were from this area, Ashington in County Durham, though largely they worked the huge Durham fields for coal, rather than lead in Weardale. The group, whose latterly famous members included men like Oliver Kilbourn, George Blessed, Jimmy Floyd and Harry Wilson, came together in 1934 through the Workers Education Association to study art appreciation. However, their tutor Robert Lyon encouraged them to learn by painting themselves and this they did with great skill and success, being critically feted by the London art world and artists like Henry Moore.

If the genesis of the group was artistic, other forces were at work too. Most of the group were members of the Independent Labour Party and drew up an extensive list of regulations by which all members had to abide, and they always preferred the name Ashington Group to Pitmen Painters. Also of course their art, which covered everything from life underground to domestic scenes to evocations of the north-eastern landscape, was an escape. These were men whose working lives were spent in conditions we can barely imagine. To sit and paint in the fresh, lonely air of Weardale and Country Durham must have been bliss after the filthy and dangerous world of the mines.

The group lasted until the early 1980s, still meeting weekly, producing new art and taking on new members. In the 1980s, the group's 'Permanent Collection' became the first Western exhibition in China after the Cultural Revolution. Though their meeting hut was demolished in 1983, you can still see the paintings free in Woodhorn Museum and a book about the group has been adapted into a hit play by Lee Hall of *Billy Elliot* fame.

Headed for those harsh uplands, I arrived via Teesdale, one of those places that guidebook writers are so fond of calling hidden gems that they can soon become neither. Not so Romaldkirk on a Sunday evening in August. The timing is nicely appropriate as I find myself in the midst of a scene straight from ITV's summer Sunday evening TV schedules of comfort viewing re-runs and cosy old favourites. Except that if the writers of *Miss Marple*, *Downton*, *Midsomer Murders* or anything of that ilk had produced this, it would have been dismissed as fanciful, *de trop*, cheesy even.

The sun is dipping behind the ash and beech trees that nestle the village green. There is a dreamy late-summer mood to the air and in it the first hint of sweet, warm rain to come. Across the green, from a high and handsome church, comes a bright peal of bells suddenly augmented by, from the village hall, a lustily sung, stirringly harmonised version of 'Land of Hope and Glory' by – it would seem – everyone in the village. One of them, the doctor, tells me that 'the footpaths hereabouts are all kept open thanks to the efforts of the village people.' Sipping my single malt, I smile at this. I'd have thought they'd have been too busy perfecting their act and trying out those construction worker and motorcycle cop outfits.

The next morning is squally, bright and wet, and I arrive at breakfast with my maps and books just as a lady is leaving with a partly consumed breakfast in a doggie bag. 'For the dog,' she explains, lest I think she is taking it back to her room for a furtive slice of black pudding and congealed egg at midnight. Romaldkirk is one of a series of villages that are strung along the dark rope of the slanting River Tees like pearls along a necklace, Romaldkirk, Mickleton, Cotherstone. I plan to get a little of the lie of the land with a 'leg stretcher' along the old railway path towards Middleton-in-Teesdale.

In 1963, between the end of the Chatterley ban and the Beatles first LP, sexual intercourse was invented according to Philip Larkin but in a less welcome development, a bristling moustachioed chap called Beeching made himself the most hated civil servant in British history by closing a third of the nation's railways. The good doctor thought that trains were there simply to make money. He understood or cared nothing for railways as a resource for the community, or had any feeling for the unique place railways have in our national psyche, from *Brief Encounter* to Conan Doyle, *Thomas the Tank Engine* to *The Railway Children*. But the one good thing to come from Beeching's miserable and short-sighted plan was that now these long-dormant lines make perfect flat and navigable walks along old lines, passing though gentle countryside, each echoing in one's imagination with ghostly rattles and whistles, the waving of little flags and the slamming of carriage doors.

Middleton-in-Teesdale is, so say those guidebook writers quoted above, a hidden gem of a village, well a town actually. It has the gentle, pastoral feel of village life to a degree but also a briskness and sense of purpose. People are coming and going, tourists and dawdlers, yes, but also men with paint brushes and buckets, and women with books and bags of shopping.

'Hello stranger,' says one to another in one of Middleton's many real shops, selling fruit and kettles and dressing gowns as well as postcards and scented candles. 'I did wave t'other day,' comes the reply. The feeling that these are living places of home, school and work, as well as leisure, is what sets the Teesdale villages apart from those somnolent picture-book hamlets of Oxfordshire and the West Country, where hedge fund managers from the square mile pretend to be country squires for the weekend. Of course, there's a deal of that up here too of course. The moors around here are ideal for the slaughter of tiny birds, should that be your thing, and they come in their tweeds and their SUVs from Clerkenwell and Canary Wharf to do just that.

From Bowlees you can walk along the river to High Force, the big scenic draw around here, and take in some public art along the way. Or, if you have been rendered inert by the Teesdale Farmer's Lunch at the visitors' centre, you can try something smaller and pay a little toll to descend the accessible path, remade after the bank was all but destroyed in a storm in 1992. This new path winds slowly down, with views improving all the time on the left across the yawning ravine. Below the clear cold Tees moves along the valley floor with the an easy serpentine muscularity, swirling and eddying through a jungle of dense mixed woodland and bouldered shores that, it strikes me, must have looked exactly like this millennia ago, maybe even during the Carboniferous era when we were on the equator. While trying to get my head around this geological titbit, I turn the corner and something else strikes me.

High Force is England's 'largest' waterfall. Not highest – that is Cautley Spout, on the other side of the Pennines, but High Force trounces it in terms of the size and length of the downfall. Essentially, all of the River Tees plunges here over the huge precipice of the Whin Sill, a grand high and bony shoulder of igneous rock that is one of the North Pennines' most dramatic features. If you wanted to be deliberately, deflatingly prosaic you might say that it looks initially, as you turn the bend, as if an enormous bowl of used washing-up water were being tipped out by some slovenly giant in a huge primeval kitchen; a frothy, dirty torrent crashing down with a manic roar of rage.

I get nearer and leave the path to descend over the rocks. You need to watch your step here; the boulders are always slick and in winter positively treacherous. But I want that jolt of the visceral, to feel the spray and the churn, the amoral but not immoral power and force that courses through nature and that draws some of us to precarious, wild and lonely places.

High Force does not care what you earn or how new your car is. It doesn't give a damn about the price of your house. The granddad on the riverbank path ahead of me knows this as, seeing his grandchild beginning to clamber unsteadily over the wet, black rocks, he sweeps up his little charge into his arms. 'I don't think so, littl'un,' he says with a smile, and we all look back at the Force. To the left and right of the great downfall of water, there are thin-webbed fingers of tiny cataracts sneaking down the rock face. Driven remorselessly by current and gravity, unless we interfere of course, in another few thousand years, maybe a few million, these will be as mighty as High Force, and I wonder who will see them.

The hills of the North Pennines, of County Durham, Teesdale and Weardale, are lovely but harsh, compelling but unforgiving. In the 1970s, an ITV documentary made an unlikely star of an unassuming Daleswoman called Hannah Hauxwell. Hannah was living a solitary, frugal, isolated life at remote Low Birk Hatt Farm when firstly a *Yorkshire Post* article and then a TV programme in 1973 made her famous. Viewers all over the world were moved and gripped by her story and her gentle, gracious stoicism in the face of the barely endurable winters of the High Pennines.

I'm looking at Hannah's old farm now from the high ridge across the valley, and wondering what life for that kindly, middle-aged spinster must have been like for all those winters before the world knew of her. Eventually those winters grew too much, and Hannah went down to live in a little house in Cotherstone, a neat village down in the dale where she still lives. I've been to Cotherstone once before and remember it chiefly for two reasons, a tasty, chalky local cheese, and a pub landlord who came out to supervise somewhat hawkishly our parking. So today I'm staying high, perched with the lapwings on the moors that Hannah would have known, loved and maybe feared. I can see Low Birk Hatt Farm across the reservoirs, which today are as black and choppy as the North Sea, and with names that when traced with a finger on the map sound as incantatory as a poem: Grassholme,

Selset, Hury, Blackton; echoing across the page like something from *Beowulf* or the Icelandic Eddas.

I'm on the flat, rocky top of Goldsborough Rigg, a gritty out-cropping riven by freeze-thaw action high in a vast squelching morass of boggy moorland. The stony, shattered summit looks uninviting but must be a welcome waymarker on this stretch of the Pennine Way which picks a shrivelled thread across Cotherstone Moor. The rain scuds in over Clove Lodge Farm and the forbidding sounding Hagworm Hall, and even in August the going is spongy and, should you be walking the Way, will surely give you calves of iron and a sense of wild exhilaration tempered by deep bottom notes of discomfort and despair. Just as at High Force, the thought occurs that most of this landscape won't have changed since William the Conqueror harried the north.

Later, back in the lowland dales, like the Normans might have done, I go harrying the north in search of a charger. But whereas with William it would have been a war horse, in my case it's for my iPhone.

I'm in Barnard Castle now, one of the jewels of a county that's described on some of the brown signs hereabouts as 'the land of the Prince Bishops'. The Prince Bishops always sound to me like a northern club circuit comedy pop troupe of the seventies, rather like The Grumbleweeds or The Black Abbots, but they were in fact the ecclesiastical rulers of County Durham in the wake of the Norman Conquest. The town sits imperiously on a high perch of rock overlooking the Tees and is named after the fortification that Bernard De Balliol built here when he owned the gaff and before it fell into the hands of Richard III, or Dickie III as he is known among the luvvies of Stratford Upon Avon.

On the trip where I first encountered the fine cheeses and limited parking of Cotherstone, I visited Barnard Castle, too, and was very taken by it: by its wide and bustling high street called the Galgate, that curious circular octangular bandstand thing which is actually the old Butter Mart and by its general air of brisk attractiveness; again a purposeful town and a pretty one, but one that doesn't spend a great deal of time preening itself in the mirror. Charles Dickens stayed at the King's Head on one of his 'rock star' style tours, and popped into the local clockmakers to ask who made a particularly fine clock in the window. He was told by the clockmaker that it was the handiwork of his boy Humphrey and Chas is said to have been inspired to call his new periodical *Master Humphrey's Clock* in which Barnaby Rudge and The Old Curiosity Shop first appeared.

My old curiosity for the shops (sorry) takes me down the Galgate. One thing's for sure, you certainly wouldn't starve in Barney. Muffins and panini lounge alluringly in every window and alley. You wouldn't perish for lack of art either. There are Goyas and El Grecos in the Bowes Museum, just a stroll out of town. You needn't even go short of vintage clothes. There's a vintage emporium on the High Street and I ask the young woman owner where I might get an iPhone charger. 'You won't find one in Barney. You might in Darlo or Bishop,' which, with my almost Sherlockian razor-sharp deductive faculties I spot to be Darlington or Bishop Auckland. How far are they, I ask. 'Sixteen miles and fourteen miles respectively,' she replies instantly, adding intriguingly, 'Don't ask me how I know that.'

I'm headed for the lonely lead mines of Weardale, and for a rendezvous with a reclusive rock star in the beautiful and faintly mysterious village of Blanchland, and so I bid Barney goodbye, thankful that, though the Scots tried, Simon de Montfort tried, King John tried and the Nazis tried, none have yet managed to reduce Barney to rubble. Thank you. I'm here all week.

I break my journey in Durham, to get that charger and simply because you always should. You will not be alone in this. The late Jon Lord, organist with Deep Purple, wrote a fine, elegiac Durham Concerto, whose first movement 'The Cathedral at Dawn' is grave and beautiful, full of echoes and hints of the day to come. Leave it much later than dawn, though, and you will be sharing the green between the cloister and the castle with tourists of every nation, ice cream vans, joggers, buskers and choristers. But, even so, this is part of Durham's charm. Again, it has none of the prissiness of Oxford. You will struggle to see canary yellow trousers here, or a straw fedora, or a crumpled white linen jacket. You are actually more likely to see a replica Newcastle or Sunderland top, and I enjoy this contradiction in its character. It's an old and very lovely city, a beautiful place of charm and antiquity, and yet one that is known around the world for its miners' gala rather than its May ball. I like that.

The students bring life and youth and diversity to the town though which is a joyous thing. Durham University is prestigious and world-renowned and rightly so. And who wouldn't want to be a student here, in this ravishing, fabulous, lively, lovely city on a grand river. The castle is a hall of residence as well, home to about 100 lucky students, and I'm told that they are so desperate for this very desirable accommodation that they will share rooms. If my hazy memories of college are to be trusted, this would seem to be a very major hindrance to the full enjoyment of student life and a testament to just how gorgeous the place is.

It's a flying visit for me. But I enjoy my night in the castle's Chaplains Suite, with its ivy-shrouded windows and its arrow slits (which I don't make full use of, to be honest). I am told that the Queen stayed in this room on her Golden Jubilee tour, and as I pour the bath foam under the steaming, rushing tap I realise that the Queen has probably been in this bath, which even for a mild republican is a proud moment in my bathing history.

To Blanchland. When I'm ever in roughly this part of the world, I try and look up and drag out my old friend Paddy McAloon, whom some of you may know. Paddy comes from Witton Gilbert, lives now in Leadgate and is one of the greatest British pop songwriters of recent decades. His band Prefab Sprout are loved by millions around the world, even though they never play live and release records gallingly infrequently.

I ring Paddy and tell him that I'm headed for Blanchland. He is a little shocked. 'Blanchland? Have you been there? It's like Brigadoon.' Paddy wonders if I have read Jesse L Weston's classic study of myth *From Ritual to Romance*, used as a source by T S Eliot when writing 'The Waste Land'. (Incidentally, these are not the kinds of conversation you have with Liam Gallagher.) Apparently, in that work, Weston quoted a reference to Arthurian Grail mythology and a possible location for the Grail 'in the tract known as the Blaunche Launde'. Early scholars assumed wrongly that this was in Shropshire. But Weston spotted that:

> ... further north, in Northumberland, there was also a Blanchland, connected with the memory of King Arthur, numerous dedications to Saint Austin, and a tradition of that Saint driving out the local demons ... I therefore suggested that ... the Northern Blanchland, which possessed a Chapel of Saint Austin, and lay within easy reach, was probably the original site ...

He went on to suggest that the Arthurian court of Camelot may well have been situated in Cardoil, modern Carlisle, which will come as a shock to anyone who has found themselves outside the kebab shops of Botchergate on a Friday after the pubs turn out.

How exciting then. I was on the trail of what could only be described as the Holy Grail of all romantic historians: the Holy Grail.

I arrange to meet Paddy at my hotel in Blanchland, indeed the only watering hole in Blanchland. The Lord Crewe Arms has an enormous fireplace with a wonderful, crackling reeking conflagration, delicious food and rooms, and a Consett postcode but, and this is meant as no slur on that great old steel town, Blanchland is somewhat different to Consett. The Brigadoon comparison is perfect. As you crest the rise and drop down into the upper Derwent Valley, the sight that greets you is magical, but a little unreal, a touch disturbing even.

A film set of a village in the middle of empty moors; all honey stone and pretty red-doored cottages, an ancient church, a welcoming inn, a slender river with a charming bridge, crenellations and crannies and architectural features I lack the knowledge to name. It seems too good to be true. Perhaps it is.

The village was built in the twelfth century from the stones of a ruined abbey and has a population of 140. But today, 13 August 2014, they are nowhere to be seen. Perhaps they are all behind their pretty red doors, watching me. The Post Office is shut for lunch but the noticeboard bears robust traces of life. There is bingo every fourth Saturday and Leadgate Working Man's Club's Leek Club now hold an Open Pot Leek Show (the Pot Leek is a north-eastern horticultural speciality) with a tempting 150 quid first prize. 'Benching from 1–3.30' if you're interested.

The promotional website talks of the village's 'special atmosphere' and this is no PR puffery. Blanchland feels, in every sense of the word, enchanted. Lovely, enigmatic and a little eerie. Paddy and I put away a few in the bar of the hotel. In view of my earlier obdervations on County Durham fashions, I smile when I see that he is wearing canary yellow trousers, a straw fedora and a crumpled white linen jacket. He might have come straight from Oxford, which is rather splendid, as is the evening, full of drink and gossip and tales about figures as disparate as Eric Morecambe, Charlie Chaplin, David Bowie and Neil Tennant of the Pet Shop Boys.

As we chat in the garden's lengthening shadows, I tell Paddy that tomorrow I'm headed for Weardale, lured by those high lonely moors we can see all around, sombre grey purple in the late summer twilight, and more alluring to me than even the prettiest village. He tells me that over the hill lies Stanhope, a no-nonsense place where local boy Neil Tennant – he still has a house nearby – used to buy his records. It's a picture of incongruity I find hard to shake, little Neil on the front seat by the driver – he is in short trousers in my mental version for some reason – excitedly clutching a 12-inch disco remix of

Sylvester's 'Born To Be Alive', as the bus rattles past a spoilheap and some rusting old winching equipment.

This is, or was, lead mining country and the stuff runs through these villages, towns and hills both literally and metaphorically: a vein of blue-black blood that once pulsed life into Blanchland and Leadgate. For six centuries, lead lined the pockets of the bishops of Durham, the rectors of Stanhope and the moor masters. The miners themselves barely scratched a living from the rock and were often seasonal farmers too, working on the little farms that, seen from afar, dot the hills like sheep droppings. More accurately, many of these were 'shielings'; temporary summer dwellings only used before the white, swirling hostility of winter set in.

Now the miners have gone completely and left the moors to those few secretive farms, the lapwings and me. High Aukside, Edge End, High Skears, even the farms' names sound harsh and forlorn like the clang of a pick or the caw of carrion birds, and many of them – open to the sky, abandoned, ruined – make Hannah Hauxwell's place look cosy.

The fell road out of Eggleston Burn, like the one out of Stanhope, like all the roads around here, will sooner or later curl and loop into a high and keening bleakness that is breathtaking – if, like me, and Auden, your breath is taken not by Beatrix Potterish gardens but by wildness and solitude and mystery. I wander a lot that afternoon. To Coldberry Mine, abandoned and ghostly but still remarkably intact – the forbidding looking main building, the dormitories where the miners slept – marooned by the tides of industry in high hills like Outberry and Harnisha. To Pawlaw Pike and Monk Moor. Over those hills, in Killhope, they have recreated the mines and the miners' lives in a justly popular attraction, a fully restored Victorian lead mine with a huge water wheel, a jigger house, and an underground tour which would have thrilled the young Auden. But there is something just as evocative about being up here in the wind and the last of the light; up here now on the moors above Blanchland, walking across the sparse,

lingy moor towards Bolt's Law, picking a way between the ragged
sheets of water, the ruined chimneys, the haunted levels.

My travels in Weardale and County Durham took place in the summer
of 2014, a summer of national remembrance, when thoughts often
turned to the summer a century before. As when leafing through that
1914 book of Wigan country rambles, it's taken on the nature of
a truism to see that summer of 1914 as a rupture in our national
psyche. It was the summer when the blithely patriotic adventurism
of British manhood was choked in the mud of Passchendaele and on
the bullets of the Somme. 'Never glad confident morning again' after
those horrors.

Britain's notions of national purpose and a sense of youthful
innocence perished then. Often, as I walked through northern hills
and dales, I wondered how many lads from the mills and the factories
and the farms dotted across this landscape had left these happy
stamping grounds in 1914 and never seen them again, deserted them
willingly for the barbed wire and carnage of the Western Front.

Googling for 'most beautiful war memorial' in Britain, I found
Colchester making a bold claim along these lines. It's certainly striking.
But it is in a public park in Colchester which, with all due respect,
cannot be as wonderful a setting as the one on Great Gable. In 1924,
the *Manchester Guardian* said:

> On Great Gable, perhaps the most wholly beautiful of English
> mountains, there was dedicated yesterday one of the grandest
> and most appropriate of all war memorials. A tablet there
> will now record the names of those Lakeland mountaineers,
> members of the Fell & Rock Climbing Club of the English
> Lake District, who were killed in the war … The instinct of
> comrades has put this tablet far out of the way of indolent
> crowds, in the midst of the crags where life used to run
> highest in those whom it commemorates, and where it will

bring them back to our minds in some of our moments of happiest effort and most radiant health.

It is a simple tablet, but its solitude and the effort required to find it imbues it with a profound presence.

But the finest I think stands sentinel on Werneth Low, a hill on the fringes of Stockport, silently watching over the little town of Hyde. Leave your car down in the country park and, before you know it almost, just a few yards up a good path, suddenly, thrillingly, something you did not expect, a view takes the breath away; especially on one of those sudden, unexpectedly fine nights in April or October, when the north seems rinsed clean, powder blue and laundry fresh after an afternoon rain storm; cool, clear, limpid.

Werneth Low isn't actually. Low that is, though its name has nothing to do with height but comes from the old Northern English 'hlaw' meaning hill or mound, a sense now obsolete except in places like this. But if it were a hundred feet higher, it would break that significant 1,000 foot barrier and some reckless types might even call it a mountain. It feels nothing like one though; just a proud arm of the rolling Pennines and a spot much loved by the folk of Hyde, Mottram and Romiley and the towns of the Cheshire/Lancashire border. It's an airy platform and good for taking in the range and the richness of this corner of the north.

Left and north is the compact knuckle of energy of Manchester, a glittering urban sprawl with the weird tuning fork of the Beetham Tower, bristling with self-importance, jutting towards the sky. Nearer is the black sheet of Audenshaw Reservoir, and behind it the whaleback of our old friend Winter Hill and its radio mast. Next Oldham and the bulk of Chadderton Power Station, then the Pennines start to bunch and get going, a backdrop to Mottram, a lovely village I'm told. In the foreground, near enough to touch, a Lego of redbrick that is Hattersley shelters under gaunt moors. Or look east into the shallow, inviting valley of Longdendale, the kind of high carved landscape you get used to on the fells but here it catches the eye, low and shallow, scooped between the rocky uplands.

Turn back to Werneth Low, though, and its cenotaph on Hacking Knife, the bloodily named highest point of the hill, proud and solemn on the summit, guarded by a little railing in its own reverent patch. It's made of Cornish granite, like its grander, Whitehall cousin, and on one face an inscription in black oxide reads: 'They willingly left the unachieved purpose of their lives in order that all life should not be wrenched from the purpose'.

When it was unveiled on the Saturday afternoon, 24 June 1921, 12,000 people assembled here. They still come. There are fresh wreaths here, tonight passed by dog walkers, a balding jogger, a young woman with an inquisitive daft spaniel. The scene is one of birdsong and peace and the quiet north below. This is the peace they fought for, the one they gave up, the towns and hills they loved, the lads from these factories. And the pride of place is entirely right. They didn't have estates and titles, but this was their north, and it's right they should be remembered here above it.

The summer evening suddenly changes. When you're down on the street, penned in by buildings and cars and the smallness of the streets, weather is an inconvenience, felt from the inside of a goldfish bowl. To know weather, you have to get up and see it coming, watch its theatrical movements, hear it, feel it. There's another storm coming over Manchester, angry, bruised and bloody, a shroud of dark, a curtain of rain against a bloodshot sky and then, leaping down to flicker among the skyscrapers, white crackles of lightning. If you want to see the north arrayed like this, you usually have to buy an overpriced cocktail in a bar filled with braying property developers or footballers and their paramours. But here it will cost you nothing, and you can share it with spaniels, pensioners, cheery golfers.

But the natural landscape is the star of the show, the Pennines in all their quiet, lonely unshowy glory; in the distance Ingleborough and the blue smudge of the Welsh mountains, the bowls of the hills that cradle the little towns.

It was from these little towns that the lads who this simple obelisk commemorates came to stomp, act daft, fly kites and court girls. It was from these little towns that they marched in blissful ignorance and patriotic fervour, never to return. It was for the freedom of the hills, the joy in the simple physical act of walking, the pleasure of the fresh summer air on nights like this, the comforts of those little towns, that they sacrificed their lives. This is a perfect quiet spot to remember them.

One such little town was Dobcross, a village really. You might even see it from here, on tiptoe maybe, 12 miles away over Stalybridge and Hollingworth Lake. Dobcross lost sons too in the First World War and it too will be remembering them over the conflict's centenary. Dobcross is doing it the way it knows best, sending its world-famous Silver Band in their scarlet finery, with their cornets, 'euphs' and tubas, to play the last post at the Menin Gate, the memorial to the fallen at Ypres.

This is brass band country, and on Whit Friday these hills are alive with the sound of music, as well as laughter, the opening of bottles, the clink of glasses and other rhapsodies of fun. The north likes a good tune, be it the Halle or the Happy Mondays, northern soul or Musique Concrète, Grimethorpe Colliery or Arctic Monkeys. The north revels in the communality of music, either on the stage or in the audience, in the conservatoire or in the nightclub. The north has never been bashful about singing its own musical praises in its own lovely singing voice; nor shouting from the rooftops about its subcultural clout; its pre-eminent role in the nation's musical life; its tacit, taken for granted status as the musical capital of Britain.

Dobcross was on my list of places to visit as I went in search of the musical north, determined to make a song and dance about it.

CHAPTER 9

STRIKING UP THE BAND

Prog rock in Huddersfield, opera in
Leeds and brass bands in Dobross

In the same way that no one boasts of having no sense of humour, I've never met anyone who claims to no taste in music. Someone who cheerily claimed they can't stand the stuff and wouldn't care if they never heard a note of it again. Your friends and kin and co-workers might admit that they have no taste buds, no appreciation of art, no enjoyment of the countryside, no ear for poetry (though that often doesn't stop them writing it) and no great love of literature. But accuse them of having a tin ear for melody and they will bridle. You're effectively saying that they're a dolt, a dullard, a philistine. You're accusing them of having no soul, no sexuality, no style. Everyone loves music and everyone thinks they know a good tune when they hear it. This would explain the otherwise unaccountable popularity of the dreadful … ah, you can fill in your own examples here. I know you will have them.

A radio programme called *Desert Island Sonnets* wouldn't run for eight weeks, let alone eight decades. They give you three books on that island, one luxury and no way of catching or cooking your food. But they let you have eight gramophone records. Significantly, they don't think of these as luxuries. Those records are a necessity of civilised life even when you're running around in a grass thong eating grub larvae and seaweed. You can see where our priorities lie.

People will happily boast though that they have their individual taste in music and which chimes with or runs contrary to what's going on in the wider world, especially with popular music. When the hipster or hairy sneers at One Direction, they are marking their patch and declaring their allegiance to their own particular herd as much as any besotted Harry Styles fan. Most people don't have a favourite late Beethoven String Quartet, but if you're over the age of 20 not having a favourite Beatles song or at least being able to name one you like, would be a little weird. When PMs Gordon Brown and David Cameron claimed that the Arctic Monkeys and The Smiths were their respective favourite bands, we knew that they were trying to show us their 'men of the people' credentials. Of course it backfired. When quizzed Brown couldn't name a single Arctic Monkeys' song and Johnny Marr of The Smiths was so annoyed by Cameron's (disturbingly sincere) declaration that he gave a statement saying 'I forbid you to like The Smiths'.

Noël Coward called popular music 'cheap music' and he meant it as a kind of compliment I think. In the same way, in a famous essay of 1972, the great E P Thompson talked of '"Rough Music": Le Charivari Anglais'. Bashed out and blown on pots, pans, percussion, bells, brass and all kinds of primitive instrumentation, rough music was a form of social control exercised by the community on all kinds of miscreants; wife-beaters, adulterers, scolds and the like, and was designed to embarrass them and hold them up to ridicule. Thompson contrasted the 'conscious antiphony' of rough music with the self-conscious delicacy and grace of the classical symphony. Though both were products of the eighteenth and nineteenth centuries, rough music and the classical symphony were very different from each other. Rough music was more like free jazz, or African tribal music, or even rock and roll. It carried the latest news and gossip, songs of sex and scandal and politics, improvised collectively. Anarchic and vital, the point of rough music was only partly to entertain, but it seems to have been entertaining enough, if you weren't the one being mocked. Most intriguing of all of this, the chief purveyors of and participants in rough music seem to have been loose bands of young men of uncertain musical ability but great charisma and verve, taken very seriously by the community at large. Sound familiar?

Rough music, cheap music, folk music, popular music; all are part of a strain of music making and enjoyment that has always been alive in the north. To generalise, we might call it the music of the street not the salon. That's not to say that it isn't high quality, respectable or worthy of appreciation. But that it seems to have a rich vein of collectivism and communality running through it – subscription concerts, brass bands, dance halls, pop festivals, indie music collectives and labels, night clubs – rather than the cliché of the tortured genius in his room, composing in anguish, alone against an uncaring world, however much this might remind us of Morrissey. Northern musical culture takes the rough with the smooth. It encompasses Peter Maxwell Davies and Harrison Birtwistle, the angry young men of 1950s Salford, shaking up the classical world from the tumult of the Royal Northern College of Music down Oxford Road, Manchester, and the Happy Mondays and the Stone Roses doing the same thing for pop music from the Haçienda Club, a few hundred yards away and three decades later. It's the massive contradiction inherent in, say, the Houghton Weavers singing 'Poverty Knock', a chilling, despairing song about the grim life of the textile worker, for the enjoyment of just those textile workers, like my mum. (The loom would knock when it was empty, meaning there was no work, and echoing the empty bellies of the child workers.)

Like some of its mouthy, voluble practitioners, pop music tends to boss any room and dominate any discussion that you let it loose in. Rich and powerful and super-served by books, radio and TV as it is, pop can stick up for itself – so we're going to shortly head further afield in search of what the north gets up to on its musical evenings. But before we do, a quick dip again into *The Uses of Literacy*. Have you your copy to hand?

In it, Richard Hoggart declares that 'the finest period in English popular song seems to have been between 1890 and 1910'. Great man though he was, he was dead wrong here, or at least premature.

Hoggart believed this was the era when working-class performers and audiences held greatest sway, dominating the musical culture. In fact, though he couldn't have known, that golden age was just about to come.

As he wrote his venerable text in the Hull of the mid-fifties, not far down the road in another northern port, a bunch of Scouse teenagers were strumming the overture to an entertainment revolution (albeit one with music hall roots) that would eclipse the reign of Marie Lloyd and Dan Leno. From little houses on mundane streets and estates, like Paul McCartney's childhood council-house home at 20 Forthlin Road, Allerton, drab streets, from mill towns and ports, factories and coal fields, were to come working-class kids who would shake the world with every shake of their heads.

In his own classic cultural summary of a decade later, *Revolt into Style*, George Melly implied that rock and roll immediately made Hoggart's observations irrelevant and out of date, and that the Beatles and Bob Dylan ushered in a new classless intellectualism in pop. There was some truth in this, but what neither grasped was that the best pop music was made by working-class kids for working-class audiences, and it wasn't just about romance or going on with life with a cheery whistle as Hoggart claimed, or the personal philosophising of Melly's era. It could be about life as it is lived in the real world. Twenty years apart, in very different Britains, two songs by Liverpudlian pop groups about their home city captured the north of the day better than any academic treatise could ever manage.

In 1967, the Beatles released 'Penny Lane' in a double 'A' side with 'Strawberry Fields Forever', often cited as the greatest seven-inch vinyl single ever released. Both songs, the former by McCartney, the latter by Lennon, are named after areas of Liverpool, but it's 'Penny Lane' that says most about place and city itself.

McCartney's song is a strangely childlike nostalgic evocation of Liverpool on a psychedelic suburban afternoon, a never-never land that is both cute and spooky and peopled with figures who are at once

recognisably real but hauntingly surreal. The fireman, the barber, the
banker sitting waiting for a trim, the pretty nurse selling poppies from
a tray who 'feels as if she's in a play' and 'is anyway'. Playful, radiant
and mining the mysterious and luminous in the everyday, it is typical
of McCartney's genius and typically underrated by those whose tastes
run to songs more plodding and sententious. (Against the stinging
barbs of these critics, McCartney has only his immense wealth, full,
rich life and place in history to console himself with.)

'Up Here In The North Of England' is a song by Liverpool rock
band The Icicle Works written and released as a single in 1987. It was
composed by leader Ian McNabb as a response to a time of ferment
and unrest in what felt like every corner of British life, but specifically
about how life was in the north of England, in the bitter, fissile imperial
phase of Thatcherism. It has none of Penny Lane's balletic joy; it is
baleful and remorseless – if sweeping – in its arrangement and its tone
is dark and savage. But it is as deft and brilliant and as evocative of
its time as 'Penny Lane'. The sunny optimism of the summer of love
has gone, to be replaced by an anthem for doomed youth, doomed
everyone really; unemployment, drugs, football violence, urban decay.
But this is not delivered with the wringing of hands but with a kind of
unfazed shrug, a wry laugh and a flinty, funny jab of defiance.

> *Right now, we're in a jam*
> *We'll call you back when we get straight …*
> *There's lots of food for thought*
> *But not a great deal on our plate*
> *The Southerners don't like us*
> *Who can blame 'em seems we're always in the spotlight.*

The north relishes that position in the spotlight. The music business
may be based in London but the business of making music happens
elsewhere, many latitudes north. We take this as a truism; the notion
of the Soho entrepreneur, the A&R man, the starmaker coming north

in his Roller or Jag to exploit the raw talent of the northern pub, club or cabaret bar, and one that is as old as popular music itself. We sing as we go, Gracie Fields claimed, slushily but with some justification, even if the song differs from place to place.

If we think of the north starting at the Watford Gap, or even Watford, as some hardened Hampsteaders do, then in the Black Country we find the foundries and the bands making metal. From the iron triangle of Wolverhampton, West Bromwich and Brum came Led Zeppelin, Judas Priest, Slade, Black Sabbath and more, while from Birmingham itself there has always been a maverick strain of psychedelia, blues and electronica. They love their psychedelia in Liverpool too, nurtured by woozy days on the dole with older brothers' Zappa and Floyd albums. Manchester is just Manchester, of course, claiming to have invented everything, with big contradictory seams of high-rise gloom like Joy Division and high-grade hedonism at clubs like the Haçienda.

Sheffield has two sides to its character, too, what local hero Jarvis Cocker calls 'a sci-fi element, a fascination with the future', heard in bands like the Human League and Cabaret Voltaire, and the gritty romanticism that runs through Jarvis's own work with Pulp, the Arctic Monkeys and Richard Hawley. Neighbouring Leeds has become the modern jazz capital of Britain, thanks to its college courses and vibrant gig scene, where you can hear punkish young men and women in black play 'muscle jazz', a wild, anarchic take on the legacy of John Coltrane and Ornette Coleman.

However, even that can seem middle of the road compared to what they get up to in Huddersfield when the Yorkshire town hosts the UK's largest, and one of the world's foremost, festivals of contemporary music. Even after almost forty 40 years, and a roster of guest composers and artists in residence that's included Karlheinz Stockhausen, Terry Riley, John Cage, Steve Reich, Brian Eno, Pierre Boulez, Brian Eno and Sir Harrison Birtwistle, that still sits a little awkwardly with even the most well meaning.

*

I love Radio 3. I would say that even if they didn't let me broadcast there from time to time. When I was an impecunious teenager and later a flat broke student, I was lucky enough to receive an unorthodox but enviable state education in modern classical music via the good offices of Wigan Library, the music library of Edge Hill College (as it was then) and Radio 3. From Wigan Library, I lugged home various much-used and collapsing cardboard boxed sets on crackling vinyl – Bartók's Six String Quartets, the complete Debussy Piano Preludes, Shostakovich Cello Concertos – held together with Sellotape and staples. These provided the best borrowing value, counting as one item each, and these things mattered when you are consuming music, voraciously, like a shark drifting though elvers. From the music room at Edge Hill, when I should have been parsing Chaucer, I sat dreamily with headphones on by the Grundig music centre and watched the term and the girls of John Dalton Hall drift by while discovering Vaughan Williams, Poulenc and William Walton.

And I filled tape after tape from Radio 3; furtively, illegally, fingers poised over play, pause and 'rec'. I assembled a collection of cassettes that I must still have somewhere; felt-tipped scrawled index cards reading 'Proms Premiere' or 'Composer Of The Week', cradling tapes that accrued with every pass a crust of audio barnacles, oxidation and hiss. But through it, I could hear the rare, special music I played again and again and could never have afforded to buy; Panufnik, Petr Eben, Rautavaara. It was the best musical education money could buy, but I didn't have to buy it. It had been paid for by generations of British people before me, proudly and cheerfully, from taxes not begrudged, and licences fees not carped at, at least not when they could see the kind of country it built for them and their sons and daughters.

So believe me, it was with affection as well as exasperation that I listened to Radio 3's trail for their coverage of the Huddersfield Contemporary Music Festival 2014. The tone was pleasant, genial even, but it sounded like the Blue Peter team about to blast off for the barren wastes of one of Neptune's outer moons: 'Once a year, we put on our warmest coats and biggest boots and head up to the hills and the chilly, windy northern town of Huddersfield ...' I think they even have gone, 'Brrrr ...' Well-intentioned, intended indeed to be engaging and chatty, it came out hopelessly patronising and metropolitan, as if the Arts Council were off to meet the Moomins.

Being made of hardy northern stuff, I had prepared myself for Huddersfield not by goose greasing myself or packing snowshoes but by announcing my itinerary on Twitter like the metrosexual I am. One tweeter assured me I would enjoy myself in what they described as 'the most chilled out town in the North'. I should point out that they meant in the sense of 'easy in its own skin' not 'you'll need your thermals'. Huddersfield, in fact, has a temperate oceanic climate, comparatively mild for its northerly latitude and moderated and warmed by the Gulf Stream. Concerns that it shouldn't get any warmer though clearly exercise the townsfolk; Huddersfield elected Britain's first ever Green Party councillor. It has also produced two prime ministers, Herbert Asquith and Harold Wilson, the latter commemorated in a statue at the railway station.

That station was described by no less an authority than John Betjeman as having 'the most splendid station facade in England'. It is a Grade 1 listed building and looks more like a stately home than a railway station, except of course more useful than any stately home and therefore more splendid by far. Huddersfield is a grand looking town, an architectural enthusiast's dream. Friedrich Engels called it 'the handsomest by far of all the factory towns of Yorkshire and Lancashire by reason of its charming situation and modern architecture.' By modern, he meant Victorian of course, and its buildings have all the thrusting civic virility and bullishness of that era. If you'd prefer a compliment more even-handed, back-handed even, then how about Derek Lindstrum's assessment: 'The post-war rebuilding of the larger towns in the West Riding is a dismal story... relieved only by the example of Huddersfield.' But you can't argue with the stats. At one point, Huddersfield had more listed buildings than Bath and with 1,660 still boasts the third highest number in Britain.

All of this speaks of a town that confounds expectations, especially southern ones. I say that not to be parochial or insulting. Huddersfield – 'Odersfelt', as those distinctly non-jessie southerners, the Normans, knew it in the Domesday Book – sounds thickly, resolutely northern, even to northerners. It sounds both bovine and bruising, flecked with rain and spittle, ruminative and slow. But culturally, it's a powerhouse, one that can show Bath a clean pair of heels I reckon. It's a hotbed of poetic talent to the degree that one can talk straight-faced of the Huddersfield Poets. It still has a thriving reggae soundsystem scene, a survivor of its seventies heyday when the town's West Indian mill workers made it a rival to London. Sadly, there is no West Yorskshire equivalent to the Clash's White Man In Hammersmith Palais, a tribute to the soundsystems called 'White Man In Huddersfield Town Hall'.

TV presenter Nicholas Crane, he of the coastal adventures with an umbrella in his backpack (sorry, I'm sure he's a lovely man but that wacky affectation brings out the Maoist in me) said of it that 'it was a town no one seems to want to leave'. It is very definitely a town, by the way, and proud of it. The football team are called Town and, furthermore, nicknamed 'Town'. Unlike some lickspittle, greasy-pole climbing boroughs, they have never applied for city status. They've got better things to do.

Even if you have no interest in Victorian architecture or Labour history statuary, you must visit the railway station simply because it has a cracking pub. In the East Wing, on George Square, there's the King's Head currently undergoing renovation, which will bring, as the *Huddersfield Daily Examiner* puts it 'the serving of meals for the first time and a longed for rehabilitation of the toilets since the year Margaret Thatcher came to power in 1979.'

I take refreshment in the Head of Steam though; four big rooms and an absorbing stash of railway memorabilia. Speaking as a Lancastrian, the barmaid strikes me as a very particular Yorkshire type.

At first she seems as hard as nails, hostile festooned with lurid home-made tattoos featuring the names of former boyfriends that she has presumably killed; the sort of person who regards smiling and such pleasantries as the mark of the degenerate and soft headed fop. But get her talking, make a few complimentary remarks about the beer or the menu, and she opens up, showing her kindly nature almost against her will. It's as if some folks from round these parts have taken their own publicity too much to heart, all that weary guff about 'speaking as they find', and they don't want to let on that they really are good people, generous and funny, and not at all like Geoffrey Boycott. They have been up to this game for some time though. In 1757, John Wesley wrote, 'I rode over the mountains to Huddersfield. A wilder people I never saw in England... [they] seemed just ready to devour us.' Maybe that's what happened to the lads whose names are memorialised on the barmaid's arms.

There is time before the evening's concert to take in some of the sights of the town. If you come by car, be advised that there is a spectacular view from the south-east corner of the top floor of the multistorey car park. From here you can see Castle Hill, the town's most prominent landmark and a cool place for Kirklees folk to hang out, have political meetings, barter, wrestle, etc., from the Mesolithic period to the Chartists. The town itself is busy, and everywhere there are signs of that most quintessential of Yorkshire qualities: pride. A Rotherham friend of mine claims he once heard a Rotherham man vox popped on local TV eulogising his county. 'Yorkshire people are proud of where they come from.' And what exactly was he proud of? He thought for a moment, then replied, 'The pride.'

Sometimes, the signs of this deep-seated pride are literally signs. The Merrie England café proclaims our 'famous roast beef is now available to take home' with the proud but understated assumption that only a lunatic would not want to do just that. Outside the Grove Inn, a blackboard proclaims 'Lovely Yorkshire pub food'. This again is typically Yorkshire. I have never seen a pub in my own county boast 'Lovely Lancashire pub food'. Yorkshire has a shared mentality other counties lack. Wigan is different from Lancaster, Blackburn is different from Southport, and Manchester is very, very different from Liverpool. But sporting rivalries aside, scratch a bloke from Helmsley and a bloke from Pontefract, or Barnsley or Sheffield and you will find the same underlying bedrock. The pride.

The art gallery is superb, and gives one an object lesson in the place of art in the community instantly, in that there is an elderly Asian man in the first room eating a giant pasty and gazing at a Lowry pencil sketch of the town. In this wonderful gallery I make some new discoveries that I'm keen to find out more about, like the reclusive Harold Blackburn and his bright urban pastoral 'Daisies on the Piazza', or Mary Lord whose 'Winter Morning Over Highburton to Holmfirth', an austere rhapsody of sky and space, will fill any northerner with an ache that is laced with dread.

Most of all, though, I am taken by the work of Peter Brook. In this I am not alone I find when I do a little research, since he was apparently a friend of the actors James Mason, Rodney Bewes and Tom Courtenay. But if this sounds clubbable, the work is anything but. 'Midwinter, Lonely Pennine Farm', 'Abandoned', 'Outside' are all as stark as the title, and the one on the wall here, 'West Riding', is typical; haunted figures imprisoned on a grim street, behind the roofs the cold detachment of the hills beyond. But there is a stony love of the north at the heart of them all. It's the same one that runs like cold beck water through Jake Thackray's wonderful 'The Rain on the Mountainside'. Against stiff competition, this is maybe the best song about the northern landscape ever written, and one that expresses the link between us and the hard, beautiful 'grim indifference' of the countryside we grew up in. Go and listen to it the minute you put this book down.

Outside on Chapel Street, the same one immortalised by a Lowry on the art gallery wall, the wind is so raw and bitter that I start for a moment to change my mind about that Radio 3 trail. And that of course is why I am here; for the Huddersfield Contemporary Music Festival. 'Huddersfield is a town with music coursing through it as powerfully as rugby league or poetry or Pennine winds. It has three professional choirs, which is three more than many more genteel towns of similar size. It has numerous music societies, brass bands, folk clubs and the like.

But it is the Contemporary Music Festival where Huddersfield, and by extension the north, shows a truly ruggedly individual side to its nature; a celebration of radical sounds from the furthest shores of experimentalism in jazz, classical, rock, improvised music and electro-acoustic work. It began in 1978 in a spirit of cussed DIY fervour from some of the town's passionate music fans. Fog nearly forced them to abandon the inaugural festival but it has grown into a British cultural institution with a global cast and an international reputation. The town is justly and mightily proud of it. Maybe I didn't hear anyone in a chip shop saying, 'Hey up Doreen, look sharp, tha dunt want for't miss start o't Morton Feldman. It's reyt quiet and repetitive,' but the daunting lady behind the bar of the Head of Steam knew of it. The taxi drivers and shop keepers know of it, even if they might run a mile from the music itself.

A word on that sort of music. I have a radio show called the *Freak Zone* which reflects part of my musical taste, what some people might call 'weird shit'. The older I get, the more I've come to realise that in music, I like danceable, attractive, well-crafted pop and I like weird shit. I like Abba, Tamla Motown and disco, and I like stuff that frightens horses and has people asking, 'What the hell are you listening to?' That's a simplification but it tells you a little about the music too. Abba and Chic are more deep and complex than you think, and weird music is fun too if you give it a chance.

What I don't like is the stuff in between; middle of the road rock, landfill indie, earnest singer songwriters, self-important rock stars who think they're old bluesmen or great poets, stadium rock bands, divas, legends, anyone who has got to the stage in their career when they now wear a hat thinking it makes them interesting, all the stuff that ends up in those rock critics' list of the 100 Greatest Albums. Brian Eno once said that he didn't like relaxation music and background music because it made him tense. I get that. In a lift or waiting to be put through to the gas board, I would much rather hear Penderecki's 'Threnody For The Victims of Hiroshima', George Crumb's Black Angels On The Point Of Departure or Tuvaluan throat singing than Van Morrison or Oasis. So the Huddersfield Festival of Contemporary Music is my kind of party, and Henry Cow is my kind of party band.

I once asked Richard Branson about Henry Cow and even the genial Croesus-alike blanched at the very mention of their name. It seems that even now as he reclines on a li-lo on Necker Island, glamorous companions and frozen daiquiri to hand, he still remembers the nightmare he had when he signed Europe's most prominent hard-left jazz classical prog ensemble to his label. He had a much easier time with Culture Club I bet. Then a few months after meeting Richard, I met the drummer of Henry Cow, Chris Cutler. I told him how Richard reacted and a thin smile of satisfaction played round his owlish features. 'Up The Workers', it seemed to say, in 15/8 time.

Henry Cow were in the vanguard of a movement that they called Rock In Opposition, which included bands from Britain, Italy, Sweden, Belgium and beyond. It was a kind of Revolutionary Socialist Atonal Contrapuntal Eurovision Song Contest. Musically the bands were very different but all were challenging and adventurous and espoused Marxist politics and a distrust of the banalities and corporatism of mainstream seventies rock. At one point, in an effort to get more hits and subvert the system from within, Henry Cow merged with the avant-pop group Slapp Happy who weren't averse to choruses. This didn't work out and the Cow (as no one called them) ended up kicking Slapp Happy singer Peter Blegvad out for being too 'flippant', something Blegvad will tell you with delight. Eventually, Henry Cow disbanded in the late seventies and fractured into several equally daunting and brilliant offshoots like the Art Bears and News

From Babel, none of whom got mentioned on the Chart Rundown with Mark Goodier.

When Henry Cow announced that they were going to reform for two shows in 2014 as a tribute to their late member and composer Lindsay Cooper, there was flurry of excitement among those of us who get excited about such things. Tickets sold out in a trice for both shows. The first was at the Barbican in London and attracted a fabulously diverse crowd, including comedians Stewart Lee and Vic Reeves, snooker player Steve Davis and novelist Jonathan Coe. The only other show was at the Lawrence Batley Theatre, Huddersfield and it attracted, among other people, me.

Henry Cow are about the nearest to a regular rock group that will ever play the Huddersfield Contemporary Music Festival. They have a drummer, singers, amplifiers, electric guitars, probably a rider of a few cans of average lager and some Doritos and such, but after that any resemblance to Coldplay ends. (Come to think of it Coldplay probably have something fancier than lager and Doritos; Faustino Rioja and Kettle Chips I bet.) The music is technically complex and draws as much on Schoenberg and Elliott Carter as it does on Chuck Berry and Eddie Cochran. It's also underpinned with a pretty rigorous political philosophy, a radical socialist critique that, Manic Street Preachers and Scritti Politti apart, has little in common with the hippy vagaries most bands spout. They were always more feted in Europe, where progressive rock and leftist politics sat happily together, than they were here. One Italian rock website sums them up thus: 'Virtually ignored by the press and by histories of rock music because their albums never entered the charts, they were actually one of the most significant groups of all time.'

Henry Cow were not a typical rock band then, and this is not the typical rock band crowd either. It is a truism of all public events that the ladies' loo will have a far longer queue than the gents. Not here. I have to queue up for ages with other men of a certain age and weakening bladders. In fact, I feel quite perked up by being, for the first time in ages, the youngest bloke at a gig, me having been just leaving the juniors when the Cow were in their pomp, while these guys were doing their mock O levels, I guess. That would be around 1971, a big year for Huddersfield and Henry Cow. The band were getting their first John Peel plays and the town's football team were briefly in the First Division, led by striker Alan Gowling who because he had a degree was nicknamed 'Bamber'.

And here come Henry Cow! The men in the band mirror many of the men in the audience in looking like they might teach European Literature or Film Studies at a redbrick university; linen jackets, leather blousons, severe glasses, lots of black.

Legendary guitarist Fred Frith sits barefoot and Buddha-like on a low chair, guitar in lap – no feet up on the monitor in Henry Cow – looking left wing and professorial and conducts the band from this position. The insanely complicated opening number falls apart under the sheer weight of its own complexity, like a collapsing star, but Fred turns and looks over his shoulder, and counts them back in a few beats later and they pick up the thread like a unicyclist wobbling away on his bike.

Dagmar Krause is still one of the most striking and unlikely singers ever to make 'pop' records, with a voice that can go from icy *mittel*-European operatics to girlish levity in a bar. John Greaves and Chris Cutler may be the greatest unsung rhythm section operating in what we might call rock; for all the music's density and detail, they gently swing through it, keeping even the most didactic moments light on their feet and graceful.

A row of Singaporean students lean forward as one to catch a shriekingly intense violin cadenza, as gleefully excited as teenage girls at a One Direction show. The final number has what for Henry Cow is a 'lighters in the air' moment, a 'Robbie Williams Angels' moment, except that theirs has a chorus that goes 'Let ownership devolve to all' which is just perfect. Then it is out into the Yorkshire night, with the merry, mesmerising tunes ringing in the ears. Looking back it was, for all kinds of reasons, a very special night. Who'd have thought it? Huddersfield; 'a town no one seems to want to leave'. I certainly didn't.

Those earnest Italian fans of Henry Cow will know the phrase *Il letto è opera del povero*, 'bed is the poor man's opera', by which is meant that what the upper classes get out of opera, the lower orders find via sex, by which I assume they don't mean long stretches of boredom interrupted by random bouts of yelling and the occasional stabbing. This is me letting my prejudices show, but it seems I am in good company. The great Claude Debussy said that 'in opera, there is always too much singing', and I know just what he means. American humourist Dave Randolph said *'Parsifal* is the kind of opera that starts at six o clock and after it has been going for three hours you look at your watch and it says six-twenty'. I know what he means too. Lovers of opera contend that it is the highest of all the musical arts, one of the great achievements of human civilisation. Conversely, this writer feels that opera might be the silliest of all musical forms, and I say that being fully aware of the existence of both skiffle and trad jazz, two other genres whose popularity baffles me.

I have long suspected some kind of snobbery at work, and my suspicions were not allayed when I went to Glyndebourne for the festival. I have now no recollection of what I saw except that it was sung in Italian with English surtitles that ran along the top of the stage on a red LED display, like the ones that tell you that the 11.47 to Didcot Parkway has been cancelled due to failure of lineside equipment.

What I remember chiefly is the sheer preposterousness of the evening. The first 'half' went on for about two hours and then we all shuffled out into the sunlit gardens and grounds of the theatre for an interval that lasted ONE HOUR AND 40 MINUTES. This was called, not without good reason, 'the long interval', an unarguably accurate name for an interval that lasted longer than a football match. During this time people lugged (or had lugged for them by liveried luggers) hampers onto the lawn and ate cruel exotic pâté and swan roulade and sipped champagne. There were a lot of Japanese people there and a good many blokes who looked like hedge-fund managers or arms dealers. Then we went back in and were shrieked at in Italian over fairly nondescript tunes for about 20 MINUTES before it finished, bringing the whole lopsided event to a close. Then everyone went nuts. Really nuts. People leapt to their feet as if a high voltage current had been passed through the stalls. Most of Kew Gardens was flung at the prima donna, who took about 30 curtain calls. It was a ludicrous way to pass an evening, and the music was terrible.

I keep trying. I can claim some expert acquaintance with the Immortal Bard's *Macbeth*, having played the title role in a production that is still talked of in hushed tones in the Wigan area. So I decided this would be the perfect one of Verdi's operas to begin with. What dawned on me quite quickly is that it all sounds the same. Now you could say the same for Phillip Glass, and I quite like him, but it's a real drawback if you're telling a story. Flipping through the CD tracks at random, I expected to be able to tell what kind of scene was playing, if not exactly where in the drama we were. But no. Late night smoochy chat between Mac and wife, horrific slaying of Duncan, appearance of Banquo's ghost, tender moment between Lady MacDuff and child, long drawn out conversation between MacDuff and Malcolm, eerie bit with Lady Macbeth wandering around castle at night … all sounded exactly the same, that is like people shouting at the tops of their voices in order to be heard over an orchestra that is playing a series of bombastic gestures with no discernible tune.

But I was determined not to be thought a philistine, or to be accused of being a quitter. Here was the perfect opportunity to combine my ongoing attempt to learn to love opera with a look at the north at play. I also wanted to avoid the crass line taken by both some on the left and the populist right wing press that opera was some kind of fanciful, useless amusement for poshos and didn't deserve such things as Arts Council grants or Lottery subsidies.

I knew first hand that working-class people could enjoy opera because I grew up with my mum singing the hits as she washed up or peeled potatoes. My house as a kid rang to my mum's wobbly contralto versions of various ageless arias. I knew 'Il Pagliacci', 'Catari Catari', and 'Nessun Dorma' long before it became a football theme. I knew every groove of *Peter Firmani Singing Your Requests*, an album made by a tenor who sang in the Labour and social clubs of Lancashire, belting out arias from Donizetti to packed houses of miners and mill workers. So I know I am not representative of all my countrymen. The north loves its opera, and I knew where I needed to go to see that love. The clue was in the name.

Opera North was founded in Leeds in 1977 just as punk rock also raged across the cities of the north. In its own way, it was just as revolutionary and just as ideological in thrust. Its stated aim was to bring first rate, high-quality opera to the north of England, which then had no permanent or properly established opera company and was something of an operatic wasteland. Its first production was Saint-Saëns' *Samson and Delilah*, its first director was David Lloyd Jones, and since then has gone from strength to strength through sometimes demanding financial and artistic climates. (I am embarrassed to tell you that I scrolled with real excitement to a section of the Wiki entry called Opera North: the Paul Daniel years before I realised my mistake – he is a conductor and was their music director.)

Why Opera North then? There is no Opera South, but then there doesn't need to be, in the same way that there's no need for a south of England correspondent on the BBC News. The centre of gravity, the attention, the implied and real power, the money, is in the south already. In the V&A's several pages of its online history of opera in England, 'regional' opera merits four lines. Most of those are about Opera North.

The fact that Leeds is twinned with Ulan Bator, capital of Outer Mongolia, is always going to be worth a chuckle, but in truth, as a city it's the Barcelona of the West Riding. It is steeped in art; hometown of

Henry Moore and Damien Hirst. Writerly wit abounds here, from Alan Bennett to Keith Waterhouse to Helen Fielding. Jude Kelly made the West Yorkshire Playhouse one of the county's theatrical powerhouses. But it wears all this learning and culture lightly, and it knows how to have a good time. Come to Leeds on any night, not just a weekend, and you will find its streets buzzing, thronged with people in search of thrills cheap and otherwise, shouting lustily to each other, crossing the roads erratically in implausible heels and dresses. It is a big student city, and many of them never go home. Well, to paraphrase the old song 'how you gonna keep 'em down in Sidcup after they've seen Briggate on a Saturday night'. And as well as my favourite market, my favourite Italian restaurant and some of my favourite hotels, my favourite indie club in all the world is here, down on the aforementioned Briggate, where they have got their bands and their wires wonderfully crossed. The sign above the door quotes a Smiths lyric: 'There's a club if you'd like to go, you could meet somebody who really loves you' and ending 'Welcome to …THE STONE ROSES CLUB!'

But there's also a posh Leeds, a moneyed Leeds, and it likes to go out and have its own good time. I have come to see Opera North's production of *The Marriage of Figaro*, which has been getting rave notices everywhere, even in them sniffy London papers. 'Delightfully spoofy' said the *Guardian*. 'Rich in charm, humour and vitality: beautifully sung, sensitively staged. For pure enjoyment, what more can opera offer?' Gosh! Consider it sold. What, as they say, is not to like?

The Marriage of Figaro is probably the world's favourite opera. Mozart's charming tale of clever women, daft men, class struggle as soufflé and what used to be quaintly known as 'the battle of the sexes' is smart enough for the intellectuals but light enough for everyman. In essence, it's a supremely sophisticated rom-com with great tunes, although oddly none that I could bring to mind on my journey to Leeds.

According to Thomson Smillie's *The Marriage of Figaro: Opera Explained*: 'One definition of a masterpiece could be a work that delights successive generations and gives pleasure to people of different levels of sophistication. On that basis *The Marriage of Figaro* qualifies as the supreme operatic masterpiece.' High praise indeed. There's a theory in the theatre that *Macbeth* is not regarded as unlucky because of any supernatural connotations but because of its sheer commercial appeal, and the fact that most rep companies knew it meant it was often staged as a fall-back when another production had bombed and had to be taken off. Hence if you were in a production of *Macbeth*, you may have just had a flop. If this is the case, then *The Marriage of Figaro* should be as unlucky as heck.

Even before curtain up, there's a bit of drama. A spokesperson comes on stage, provoking a 'this isn't supposed to happen' flutter in the audience, and announced that due to illness, the part of Figaro will tonight be taken by Bradley Travis. An understudy! In the title role! If there's any disappointment in the audience, I didn't pick up on it. Indeed, the two ladies behind me were propelled into full Broadway musical mode. 'An understudy! This could be his big break.'

This gets me thinking about the whole notion of the understudy, which I find fascinating. In this I am not alone. Tom Stoppard's brilliant *The Real Inspector Hound* (another of my am dram triumphs, cruelly overlooked by *The Stage*) has an extended, freewheeling riff on the nature of understudies, twelfth men, seconds in command and the like, and the secret jealousies that must lurk in the most benign and genial of companies. Sarah Estill, a chorister of Opera North, has actually written, rather wonderfully, about all this in the Opera North blog.

To the soloist, their cover is both a security blanket and that little extra incentive to keep soldiering on just in case once replaced it turns out the management prefer the alternative. To the cover, the soloist is both their inspiration and aspiration but also a perceived obstacle in the way of their true path to stardom. And whilst most covers don't go as far as laying trip wires and lacing water-bottles with laxatives, there is always that suppressed hope somewhere deep in their subconscious that wishes for a temporary, deeply debilitating but ultimately recoverable minor ailment to afflict the soloist, even if just for one night, preferably the night friends and family are coming to see the show.

By now the famous overture, which even an opera refusenik like me recognises, is playing and the curtain is up. *La Nozze di Figaro* begins with a famous song about measuring up for a bed that is ripe for parody in a Jewson's advert. Actually, this production doesn't start like that but with an interesting bit of staging which shows the back of the set and the reverse of the flats and backdrops around which members of the cast scurry giggling. It's a neat touch, designed one imagines to remind us that what we are seeing is artifice and that what is going on out of sight is crucial to the piece's farce and frivolity. Nicholas Hytner has said that you could stage *The Marriage of Figaro* on the moon as long as you put the doors in the right place. No one's tried that yet to the best of my knowledge, but you get his point. Leslie Travers' set design, all faded glamour, peeling wallpaper and leaky ceilings, speaks of a world in decay and ripe for change, pointing up the melancholy under all these larksome social gavottes.

Time and inability precludes me from describing in detail the events of the first half or offering a detailed critique beyond saying that I really liked it. It was sung in English, clear as a bell, and in a terrific translation which was modern enough to be funny and accessible, but without any cringy lapses into dated slang or clunking period references. At one point someone was described as having 'buggered off' which went down very well with a Leeds audience, naturally. Plotwise though – and this is one for Mozart rather than Opera North – I do have some very strong reservations.

If you suspect that your partner is having an affair or that your boss is going to sack you or that someone you trust is going behind your back on some important matter, you have various options open to you. You could ignore it and blithely carry on with life. You could ask around or conduct some investigations of your own. You could, if you're that kind of person, come straight out and ask about it, mildly or combatively. It's up to you.

What I would definitely not advise you to do is dress up as someone else, or send them a letter purporting to come from someone else, and then try to trap them in some weird tryst in disguise. Try being vaguely honest with them. That, or have a massive row, or anything really. Just try to avoid disguises and messengers. In my experience, it never goes well. It never goes well in Shakespeare (look at *The Comedy of Errors* and *Romeo and Juliet*). It doesn't go well in 'Escape (The Piña Colada Song)' by Rupert Holmes or 'Babooshka' by Kate Bush. And it nearly goes really badly in *The Marriage of Figaro*, except that in the manner of these things, it all gets laughed off, and sung off, pretty casually by all concerned at the end.

The end is still someway off though, and I mull the plot over my half-time G&T in the bar. The Leeds Grand is a beautiful, ornate, labyrinthine theatre, which is lovely to look at but difficult to negotiate when everyone is desperate for a sharpener. Still it gives me a good chance to earwig and eavesdrop. I hear one lady say to another, smoothly and conspiratorially, 'Well, I do know Eric Knowles a little actually ...'

The second half begins with a good deal of that old staple of comic theatre, cross-dressing. The two elderly ladies behind me find this a hoot. So does the gentleman a row in front, but it seems to set him off on some kind of mild fit which he manages to bring under control but whose legacy is a nagging, repetitive, furtive cough that lasts all through the act and leaves me torn between pitying him and wanting to kill him.

By the last act, everyone seems to be dressed up as everyone else and I have no idea who has written which secret letters to who or why. There is some baffling business with a dropped pin which I think may be like the stuff with the purloined hankie in *Othello* but I wouldn't like to say. I didn't mind because I was just floating along, buoyed by the nice tunes, wine gums and the gin; I think it all turned out OK. There was some stuff in a torchlit garden at the end that threatened to go a bit Ku-Klux-Klan meeting, but it all sorted itself out. Figaro got hitched I think and Bradley Travis's rave reception at the curtain call was a really lovely moment.

So had I enjoyed my night at the opera? My night at the Opera North, to be exact? Yes, I had very much. The production had bags of energy and brio, it was clear and funny and light and smart, everything that I remember my night at Glyndebourne wasn't. But I have to acknowledge that this may be down to the fact that they were very different pieces as well as smouldering class resentment and dislike of braying. There were nowt of that here. Just people who liked opera and fancied dressing up – no, not like that – and having a night out. It's not cheap, no. But then again, it is no more expensive than taking the lad to Old Trafford or the Etihad. Lasts longer too.

The problem is maybe one of perception. Opera conjures up cummerbunds at Covent Garden, a diversion for the idle rich to snooze though. Opera is the rich man's bed, you might say, not the lusty public entertainment that the Italians have long enjoyed. Opera North do their best to fight those fustian stereotypes while staying true to the spirit of opera. I am never going to enjoy Verdi in the same way that I enjoy The Vandellas, or Vaughan Williams, or any other alliterative example from any of the many kinds of music I enjoy. It's still too close to pantomime for me and there's too much shrieking. But if I do go again, it will be to something from Opera North.

Back out on the streets, Leeds is its usual mad, garrulous self and the Leodiensians are as loud and chaotic and terrible at crossing the road than ever. There is a downside to all this, of course, as seen by the fact that my train is late having 'struck an inebriated person at Cross Gates'. This news is being hotly discussed on the platform by gangs of blokes, each holding giant foam fingers saying Betway. But eventually it arrives and I find a seat across from a quirky hipster student girl and a 'townie' lad in his twenties who is clearly a) a little taken with her and b) a little tipsy, and is chatting her up in a rather sweet way. He's telling her about a DVD he's got in his hand, the movie *Northern Soul* by Elaine Constantine. He explains a little about the music, which he says is 'the best'. They chat and she tells him that she's training to be a barrister. As he gets up at his station he bids her farewell with a cheery 'see you in court maybe'.

I won't go into detail about northern soul here. I've banged on about it elsewhere and will do so again, and we're headed in search of another kind of northern soul music to finish here. But I should say something about that DVD in the lad's hand because it's a great film. The evocations of the scene is vivid and spine-tingling and it is the only movie or drama that has ever captured anything of the spirit of the music and the clubs and the nights. Believe me, others have tried.

Nearly all emphasise the swearing, the grittiness, the grim nature of life in the north in the early seventies, when we were all either unemployed it seems or working on production lines, Arthur Seaton style. Beyond that they get everything wrong, sometimes laughably. In one dire example called *SoulBoy*, the protagonist has gone to a northern soul night to get off with the girl of his dreams, a ludicrous notion in itself since no one went to northern soul nights to pull. (People did 'cop off' but that was a happy by-product of their shared enthusiasm for the music.) However he takes some unnamed drug before taking to the floor with her – another gaffe, dancing was both individual and collective but never paired – and starts to hallucinate. Northern soul was awash with drugs but almost exclusively these were uppers and speed, designed purely to keep you awake, not to send you on voyages into the depths of your psyche. A northern soul dancer would no more drop acid than a Buddhist monk would snort from a Benzedrine inhaler.

The film *Northern Soul* treads close to cliché in some of the 'it's grim up north' sections. But then, well, it was. There's an idea to be pursued, indeed I've pursued it often, that the obscure and overlooked soul music of the 1960s was embraced by kids in the

industrial north of the 1970s because at some level there seemed a
kinship, a brotherhood, a shared experience of life. On grounds of
taste, as well as common sense, we shouldn't push this – no one ever
got lynched in Wigan – but both groups were largely excluded from
power or the profits of the economic mainstream, seen as outsiders by
middle-class central government, and thus fell back on the dramas of
everyday life – love, sex, dancing, friendship, the need to make a buck
– and enshrined it in the music they love.

Most great northern soul came not from New York or LA but
from America's brawny, big-hearted industrial cities like Detroit or
Chicago, with their factories, mills and car plants. These were cities
and lifestyles that kids from Lancashire, Sheffield, the Black Country
could recognise and relate to. Though 'Northern' songs are often
heartbreakingly vulnerable and tremulous with emotion, they are never
maudlin, never self-indulgent. Northern soul is a tough and tender
music for tough and tender people, people unafraid to show their
loving side. You would never call the lads who danced so gracefully
and balletically at Wigan Casino 'puffs'. It was not an insult the culture
understood, because it revelled in being different, an outsider, not one
of the herd. Also, they would have kicked your head in.

Twenty years after northern soul ensnared the youth of Lancashire,
another underground music from the clubs of Industrial America did
the same. This time it was acid house and the parallels with northern
soul are many: obscure sides from anonymous artists picked up by
cool tastemaker DJs and played at all-nighters to working-class kids
taking drugs and escaping the everyday. The heart of this was the
Madchester craze, the northern soul of 1990, and centred around
The Haçienda Manchester rather than Wigan Casino (which burned
down in murky circumstances in 1986).

The artist Jeremy Deller's project *Acid Brass* made explicit the
link between two styles of music loved and embraced collectively in
the north-west. One of these was acid house and the northern variants
of it, and the other was the brass band tradition. At first it sounded

gimmicky. But nothing Deller does is ever that, however novel and quirky it may first seem. When Deller asked The Williams Fairey Brass Band of Stockport to perform arrangements of rave and house anthems like 'Voodoo Ray' and 'Strings Of Life' it was no gimmick but a brilliant, witty yet affecting merger of, as Deller put it, 'two authentic forms of folk art rooted in specific communities'.

One of those communities is Dobcross, one of those Northern places like Wingates or Grimethorpe, that many associate immediately and automatically with their brass band. Actually that should be their silver band, a term once used with a certain hauteur, as it implied your band could afford silver-plated instruments and thus were more successful, but now the terms are pretty much synonymous.

Not so in 1875, when the band formed, or not long after, when the picture I am looking at was taken. Here are the menfolk of the village, young whippersnappers and paunchy stalwarts, captured in their mutton chops and brass buttons, their bowler hats and waistcoats, proudly clutching their cornets and trumpets, looking squarely at you down the long years.

The picture is on the back of *That The Medals and the Baton Be Put On View: The Story of a Village Band 1875–1975*, produced for the band's centenary by the playwright Henry Livings. It's a charming, slim volume, beautifully written with tenderness and a roguish wit, and is as much about people and place as music, since the one flows from the other. If I thought that wandering around the north musing about work and play made me unique or pioneering, Livings soon disabuses me of this notion in the sweetest of prose.

As the goatherd's pipe, the mother's lullaby or the herald's fanfare are natural products of a useful activity, so is a brass band … our lives may be split in two by the need for wages, may be artificially split into labour and leisure in a way that a farmer or a mother hardly understands, but we heal the cut when we make music, because we belong to a place.

Dobcross is one of those places the north has been keeping to itself for years, and with good reason. One of those places that we in the north didn't know how lucky we were to have come from and to live in, until we'd been strap-hanging on the Central Line for a few years, or breathing in exhaust fumes on the M25. It is beautiful, but in an entirely different way from the soft loveliness of a Cotswolds village. There's a hardness here, a darkness to the stone, a shadow to the skyline, what Auden called 'the oceanic whisper' of ancient geologies and industries. I could live here. Who couldn't, I think, as my taxi pulls up to the village square from Uppermill in the dusk. Below me I can see the snaking lights of a traffic jam that has brought that village to a standstill, as the whole place has turned out for the funeral of the pub landlord. That tells you a lot about these kinds of places. That and the headline in the local paper: 'Dobcross Village Blocked: Traffic blocked on both sides for over an hour as the 184 bus unable to pass the wagon in Dobcross Square.'

No such drama in the square tonight as I get out of my cab and into the Swan, where there's already a pint on the bar for me thanks to a small welcoming committee. Each in their own way is something of a local legend. Mike Sweeney's distinctive Salford drawl has been heard on records and airwaves for decades, either with his punkish band Salford Jets or as a broadcaster. In the 1980s, he came here on a Piccadilly Radio charity broadcast, fell in love with it and bought a house here. David Morris is the World Whistling Champion, and former principal cornet and musical director of the Dobcross band. Peter Young is the man who invited me to Dobcross. He's a marketing man for Lancashire County Cricket, and tireless organiser and fundraiser for the village in general and the Dobcross band in particular. His son joined Dobcross Youth Band 25 years ago, progressed to the senior band, and he still plays for the famous Grimethorpe Colliery Band, who he's travelled the world with 'so I owe Dobcross Silver Band a few favours I reckon'.

Peter contacted me to ask would I play a 'gig' in the pub for their fund for the band's Menin Gate trip mentioned in the last chapter, and I readily agreed, asking as a fee an invite to a band practice in the band hall, which is where we're headed after our classic northern tea of cheese and onion pie, chips and beans – something of a specialty of the house and bloody gorgeous – and oh, go on, just a quick one then.

Sated, we wander up the lane to the band hall, a compact building on the edge of a floodlit bowling green, about which David tells me a story that is entirely unrepeatable. Inside, we have another pint, obviously, and I'm introduced to some of the other band officials, the treasurer and musical director, and of course the band, who are assembling in the big room next door.

The musical director, Tim, is a young percussionist who comes over the Pennines from Wakefield. The prestige of playing for the top bands is such that bands like Black Dyke and Grimethorpe have players who live as far away as Wales, and who make huge round trips for twice weekly practice. These are Coldplays and Beyoncés of the brass world, and they are justly famed. The second ever single released on the Beatles' own Apple Records in April 1967, was a track called 'Thingumybob' by the Black Dyke Mills Band. It was written for them by Paul McCartney, and reflects the Fab Four's love of a good brass band. Dobcross are not quite in this league, but they are well respected, resurgent even after a period of decline, and flourishing on all fronts with a youth band and a group called the Brass Monkeys comprising adult beginners who are picking up their tubas and trumpets late in life.

Of course, there's money as well as glory in it for the very best. On Whit Band Day, there are thousands of pounds of prize money to be had, and the villages here about become awash with bands and booze. The judging procedure is wonderfully quirky and arcane. Each band parades down the street and through the squares of the 35 or so villages that host the bands and is judged by an expert sitting in an upstairs room with the curtains drawn, so that they can hear the music but not see the band, and thus are scrupulously fair and purely musical.

Back at Dobcross Band Hall, the Silver band are preparing for a concert in Shaw, near Oldham, that had to be re-scheduled after bad snows last winter. 'Only half the band got there, and they came skidding down the hill and nearly crashed into the venue.' A nice lady called Phillippa – D Tenor Horn – shows me the programme she has designed for the event, for which there are eight tickets left. There's much chat and laughter as the players assemble, pulling off their coats and taking instruments out of cases. They're a mix of ages and sexes, and many will have come straight from work. As the movie *Brassed Off* showed so powerfully, collectivity is at the heart of banding. Though the band might now feature a mill director, a hairdresser, engineers, nurses and teachers, there is a fundamental commitment to what we might call working-class values and ways of life. In the old days, if a band folded, it was sometimes difficult if not impossible to know what to do with the instruments, which would moulder in storage. They had often been bought by public subscription and belonged to the village or town, not individuals. As Henry Livings asked, 'Whose are they but the property of ghosts?'

In Livings' book on the band, he also addresses the matter of booze. 'Many bands resist the idea of having a bar where they practise, and certainly a pint pot under the chair is a sign of a poor band.' There's a bar here, but the pint pots beneath the chairs are full of lime and soda and orange squash. The only people drinking are me and my hosts, which we seem to be doing at an alarming rate. (The aforementioned Whit Band Day is one of the booziest days in the social calendar, but the bands themselves take the playing very seriously, at least until the results are in.)

And then instruments are raised to lips and something wonderful happens. I am not a musical snob or a purist, and I roll my eyes when some bore starts banging on about 'manufactured music' since all music is manufactured. Also, if changing your hair, clothes, music and drummer because your manager tells you to isn't manufactured, I don't what is. Ladies and gentlemen, I give you … the Beatles. But we hear so much processed music, music of such similar character and sound, a kind of Golden Arches pop that homogenises the world and its differences, smooths out the folds and ridges, that it is thrilling to now and then hear a sound that is totally its own, be it a male voice choir or Swedish folk or dub reggae or Nashville country or Bulgarian female vocal music. A sound that instantly speaks of place and history. That is the sound of a brass band, and as it rings out in that hall in Dobcross it has an almost physical effect.

The piece is Malcolm Arnold's 'Little Suite for Brass'. As well as the versions by the great British brass bands I later quickly find versions by some Japanese teenagers from the Nanyang Academy and the Ceremonial Brass band of the United States Air Force. (Write something for brass band and you can guarantee it will get played.) I have a soft spot for the music of Arnold and you'll know him even if you think you don't, either through his famous arrangement of 'Colonel Bogey' as part of his music for the film *The Bridge Over The River Kwai* or his jaunty 'English Dance No 5', for many years the tune to a programme I loved as a kid called *What The Papers Say* (which says a lot about me). The Guitar Concerto is lovely too, and I once saw Arnold, a troubled personality who might now be classed as bipolar, swing Julian Bream's guitar around his head after a performance at the proms.

The 'Little Suite for Brass' is charming and its highlight is the lyrical second movement. Just as its opening chords begin to drift from the euphoniums and trumpets, a man in a parka dashes in, takes his seat to the left of the conductor, pulls a cornet from his case and proceeds to play the solo melody with commendable grace and poise under the circumstances. 'He's come straight from work, that lad. He's good. You'll hear the whole band get better now.' Next they launch into Kenneth J Alford's stiff-backed military march 'On the Quarterdeck', but soon director Tim is slapping his forehead in mock exasperation. 'This is my favourite march and you lot have ruined it for me in two bars.'

'Sorry,' comes a reply from the second row cornets, 'just getting the fingering sorted out,' and everyone laughs. Brass joke obviously.

In the middle of this row sit two teenage girl cornetists in Ugg boots and jeans occasionally checking their iPhones for texts as well as playing up a storm. The Dobcross brass band is a healthy mix, I'd say, compared to the very masculine enclaves of orchestral brass sections, which is perhaps why they have a reputation as being the drinkers of the orchestra, that and the fact that it's thirsty work. The orchestral 'fixer' of the City of Birmingham Symphony Orchestra told me that the brass section pride themselves of being at the bar of the pub next door in less than three minutes from taking their bows.

Next is a British light classic called 'The Arcadians', or as David introduces it to me in the compressed vernacular of the north 'Th'Arcadians'. I love these formations, especially when the word is an unusual one, as in when you hear people talking of 'having a walk up t'hill to th'obelisk'. Things seem to going be fine to me, but Tim waves them to a halt.

'Come on guys, there's a fine line between "swagger" and "slow" and we have to get it bang on. More bass, less youth, Tom. Are we OK on there? We seem to be having a bit of trouble.' A bald man throws his hands up in self-rebuke. Then there is a debate about the score, 'What do you make of that? It looks like a trill to me.'

A chap called Andy joins us after a few numbers, sitting at the back with our pints, and tells me how he got drawn in by his daughter, indicating one of the young female cornetists. 'She wanted to come and play and I started by dropping her off and then I got reeled in, I suppose. Now I'm chairman and treasurer and events organiser. It takes more time than my actual job and we're all voluntary, but it's just a nice place.'

Andy's daughter is in the trio piece which is up for rehearsal next. The three cornet players, the two girls and the late comer, take their music stands into a corner and play as a trio of soloists, with accompaniment by the band. The tempo is brisk and the arrangements are light and speedy. They fluff some bits but josh each other and giggle. It is, in every way, a lovely thing to see.

Then, the whole band go over the end of 'Arcadians' again to get that warm, major chord resolution right that will send the audience home smiling. Dave Rowntree, drummer with Blur, learned his musical chops as the drummer in a big military brass band as a teenager, and he once told me that nothing he'd experienced in a major rock band in the arenas of the world could match the musical thrill and the sheer sensory delight of sitting in the middle of that full and enveloping sound. Even as a listener, sitting with a pint in a village hall on a weekday evening, when the band mesh and 'kicks in', it's an amazing sound, full and dazzling. I think about the Sydney Smith quote about heaven being 'eating caviar to the sound of trumpets'. Caviar is, of course, horrible. But if he'd said bhuna or steak pudding or Roquefort, he might have been on to something.

When the lady flugelhorn player finishes her solo bit, everyone applauds, which is delightful. I wonder if brass bands work a bit like a football team, second desk players acting like holding midfielders or playmakers, setting up the star soloists. The lad in the check shirt and his fellow euphonists and trombonists are certainly working hard, sweating and pumping away at the heart of it. I bet the trombone takes it out of you, and you get an inkling why brass players are the bibulous, big-hearted rough diamonds of the orchestra.

There are more pints to be had down the hill in the Swan, and I ask Dave about the world champion whistling title. He travels the world in competitions and has shared stages with bands he rather splendidly refers to as 'T'Foo Fighters' and 'T'Kings of Leon'. You may well have heard him on adverts too, 'Mini, BMW … oh yes, the Golden Eagle has shit all over me, lad', a new expression on me but one I take to mean business is good.

The evening being late and the pints downed being numerous, Dave is persuaded, with not too much effort, to do a spot of whistling for us. It's not at all what I expect, not the fussy, warbling Roger Whittaker stuff at all, but more like a theremin or, well, a cornet, soft and diaphanous, bright and melodious. At the end of a lovely rendition of a selection of film soundtracks, Peter takes a sip, thoughtfully, and says 'I whistle too … in the bathroom but I don't keep bloody going on about it.' We all laugh and, if memory serves, which is far from certain, order another pint.

CHAPTER 10

TRYING SOMETHING A BIT DIFFERENT

*Zombies in the Trafford Centre, ghosts in
Clitheroe and gags in Manchester's Studentville*

As anyone who has walked along Blackpool's Golden Mile will attest, the north loves a novelty. In fact, we took the very word for 'new', for 'innovation' and 'invention' and we turned 'novelty' into a word for plastic dog poo, a rubberised David Cameron mask and a flashing illuminated cutlass. These are what northerners call 'novelties', and there is a whole warehouse full of them in Blackpool called SuperFunStuff down on Amy Johnson Way. I mention this in case you could do with a new inflatable pterodactyl.

The novel is what we do, and we've being doing it in the more respectable and scientific sense for centuries. In the scientific societies and universities of Newcastle were born the aeroplane joystick, the iPod Nano and the electric lightbulb. Derbyshire gave us the hot dog, Swarfega and Lara Croft. Liverpool was home to the railway tunnel, orthopaedic surgery and Citizens Advice Bureaux. Rutherford split the atom and Turing invented the computer in almost adjoining buildings in Manchester, and now next door they are working on a substance Manchester scientists discovered in 2004 called graphene, one atom thick (a million times thinner than a human hair) and a hundred times stronger than steel, and set to revolutionise our world. In a nice mix of science and art, the musician Sara Lowes is working on a commissioned composition to celebrate it.

Our northern zeal for technology has been entrepreneurial as well as academic, as seen at Blackpool illuminations and Belle Vue Speedway. And from the bearded lady to the ghost train, if you can make it something ghoulish as well as novel, a real shock of the new, then all the better. No one knew this better than Louis Tussaud. When his flagship Regent Street Waxworks burned down, which is surely about the grisliest fate than can befall a waxworks, he relocated to Blackpool, opening there in 1900. For a century, there was fruitful tension between Louis' company and his great-grandma's, Madame Tussauds, equally famed for its wax creations, and which eventually took over the Golden Mile wax museum in 2010. With little familial loyalty, the Madame Tussauds website explains:

> For the last 80 years Louis Tussauds, up until 2010, was situated on Central Promenade, entertaining and often frustrating holiday makers and customers with their many unrecognisable celebrity figures.
>
> Visitors often thought they were entering the world famous and original Madame Tussauds, only to be disappointed by the unrecognisable celebrities, lack of interactive fun and restricted access to their figures – a very different experience to that of the original Madame Tussauds that is now in over 12 different countries.

When I was a kid, the most popular part of the Louis Tussauds Waxworks on the Golden Mile was the Chamber of Horrors. The most popular part of that, surrounded by eager gawpers and even a few saucer-eyed little kids who'd snuck in underage and under dad's overcoat, was the car crash tableau. A bloody assemblage of metal and gore and severed limbs and dead children, it pictured the aftermath of an M6 accident. Nice, eh? We are such redoubtable folk that we will turn anything into fun, however dark, however gory, however melancholy.

I think about this on the night the zombies invaded the Trafford Centre. I don't mean this as some plonking satire on the emptiness of consumerism. No, I mean actual zombies; the undead, hollow-eyed and rapacious, moaning and lurching and pawing at you, intent on making you one of their hideous, cadaverous brood. Well, to be honest, I don't mean that because there are no such things as zombies obviously. If you think there are, I have to say to you now, pull yourself together. But I am fascinated with how they have become a 'thing' as you young people say, a trope, a meme.

You can watch films on them and play games featuring them. You can buy books on their habits and physical make-up and how to survive an attack by them. You can partake of an entertainment whereby you pay 30 quid to get chased by them around a massive warehouse in Stretford. I know this, because that is what I and several hundred apparently normal people did for fun on a frosty autumn night in late 2014. In the manner of the young women who greet you at the door of a Harvester, I feel I want to ask you, have you ever been to a Zombie Apocalypse? No. Well, there isn't a salad bar.

A few of us made our way here from another northern innovation, the BBC's MedicaCity based in Salford. Being unsure what to expect myself, I was gratified that some of my workmates were also a little dubious about it. I've always felt uncomfortable among overly gung-ho people and I don't really like being scared. One of my colleagues asked, a little weirdly, 'Will I get punched?'

Well, let's look at how the organisers bill it. Apparently it is:

> ... a new scare attraction like no other ... a live immersive, interactive experience which sees EventCity next to The Trafford Centre turned into a safe zone to keep terrifying zombies at bay ... Prepare for the biggest challenge of your life, where only the best will make it to the other side. With

four hours of terror that will send shivers down your spine at every turn, with only your wits and the might of the Military to protect you, you must be on your guard at all times. The Zombie Apocalypse has begun and there is no escape – it's too late! They are already here, you are right in the middle of the action! Manchester is being attacked and only the military stands between the Zombies and the Earth's annihilation. This is the final battle – can you face the fear and be a survivor?

Excitingly, all this came with a postscript:

WARNINGS AND DISCLAIMERS
SCREAM PARK UK reserves the right to refuse entry to anyone. You will be exposed to a variety of conditions including intense audio and lighting, low visibility, strobe lights, fog, damp or wet conditions and at a times a physically demanding environment. We advise that you should NOT participate if you are pregnant, have claustrophobia, prone to seizures, heart or respiratory problems. You will not be admitted if you appear to be intoxicated or are wearing any form of temporary cast, using crutches or a medical brace …
If you are of a weak or nervous disposition we advise you to STAY AT HOME.

Initially, though, our taxi driver is far more worrying than the undead. First he takes us a way that seems to negotiate all of the inner circles of hell, slowly, and via the scenic route. Then, when he asks where we're headed, he starts making really terrible zombie noises. They are really pretty third rate. But however poor a zombie impersonation is, it's still fairly disconcerting when your taxi driver is making them. Not getting the desired response of terror or mirth, indeed not getting a response at all other than bemused looks, he desists. Then we pass Old Trafford football ground, illuminated red against the rainy sky.

He asks, 'Do you want me to take your picture here?' Surprised to learn that we do not, thwarted, and more than a little resentful I think, he goes back to making zombie noises.

Eventually, he drops us after I've talked him down from his initial enormous piss-taking fare and we queue up in a vaporous November drizzle outside EventCity, Manchester, a huge leisure park/venue-type-thing where you can watch a golf exhibition, ski down a massive artificial piste, or, in my case, be chased by zombies. You take your pick really. I could say that EventCity is like an aircraft hangar, but I'm aware that as I've never been in an aircraft hangar I'm just using the standard unit of measurement for any large indoor space, just as Wales and football pitches serve this function for outside areas.

Once inside, there are a great many men in black paramilitary garb, intended to be some kind of future militaristic police force, barking orders and jabbing really quite fearsome looking weaponry at you as they herd you along. This gives me the same thought that always occurs on the gate at Glastonbury when an officious hairy in a hi-vis tabard is yelling orders at me, namely that if someone from a refugee camp in Darfur were here they would think, 'You people pay to be treated like this?'

OK, the premise. There seems to be some kind of mass zombie invasion taking place in a fairground, which is extraordinarily good or bad luck depending which way you view it. It would have been more containable had it happened in a bus station or, well, an aircraft hangar, but less fun to watch. There are hundreds of the aforesaid zombies, dressed in rags and some with really quite upsetting make-up jobs lurching about and trying to grab you. Even though common sense tells you that these aren't zombies but some theatre studies students from Didsbury College, it's still quite unnerving. Your natural reaction is to run, even though you're not sure what they'd do if they caught you, and probably neither are they.

But here's the thing. If this happened at your fairground (you're a fairground manager, did I mention that?), when these zombies start arriving en masse from lord knows where, milling around bloodied and moaning and generally trying to gnaw at customers' throats or disembowel people with axes, well, you'd close the fairground for the night, wouldn't you? You'd give the staff the rest of the shift off and lock up. Come back tomorrow bright and early, maybe, but definitely call it a night.

Not here they haven't. They don't even seem to regard the influx of the baying crazed undead as much more than a minor inconvenience, like a burst pipe or some kid being sick on the waltzer (as I once was in Southport in 1975). They are carrying on with things quite normally over at the penalty shoot-out stall (£2.50 a go, three kicks). Naturally, I pay for a go, having my eye on the Messi Barcelona shirt. The man says it's harder than you think and he's right. I get one in the target hole but miss the rest. But then I did have a clown with a chainsaw trying to eviscerate me.

I'm not being insulting by the way. It was an actual clown, and he certainly ruined my chances of the Messi shirt. The fact that one of the re-animated corpses should be dressed as a scary clown and have access to a chainsaw is puzzling too. It's almost as if he knew he was going to get roped into an assault on a Manchester fairground. (Incidentally, if you really do want to see a cracking oddball zombie horror set in Manchester and the Lake District, seek out Jorge Grao's wonderfully barmy Spanish Italian 1974 cult classic movie *The Living Dead at the Manchester Morgue*.)

As you've surmised, there doesn't seem to be a coherent narrative. Essentially it boils down to a shedload of zombies running amok and terrorising random civilians and screaming nurses. From what I can see, the few who do get cornered by one, perhaps by the hook-a-duck stall, or the one where chucking balls at a target could win you a large pink orang-utan, get taken away to a sort of M.A.S.H. type triage centre and made up as zombie recruits. I don't want this to happen to me, because I have my eye on the iPad mini top prize at said hook-a-duck stall, where one of the lesser prizes is four isotonic drinks. I don't win – it seems impossible – but I do have a nice chat to the smiley lady stall holder and a bit of a play with her small feisty Jack Russell, neither of whom seem put out by the full-scale zombie apocalypse happening all around them.

The rummest element of a fairly rum set up is that in the midst of all this fantasy military versus bloodthirsty zombies stuff, the actual army are here recruiting. The reservists of the Queen's Own Yeomanry no less. Well, I guess we'll need to call up the TAs in the event of a zombie apocalypse so it's as well to be prepared. They ask us if we want a go in their armoured car, which strikes me as a brilliant way of getting you to join up. Sadly it's probably more effective letting you fire off a few imaginary rounds at a stampeding mob of mutants than showing you a film about building a new well for a village in Burkina Faso. The guy from the Yeomanry, a chubby little fellow with glasses and a cap with a feather on, says that they can't use the actual rear mounted machine gun 'for reasons of space'. I would have thought it was for reasons of 'not killing a load of people in a mass carnage' but I let this pass.

In theory, you could have four hours of this, but I think – fun though it was – an hour was about enough, especially since it was raining so you couldn't go on the outdoor rides. This was a real shame as I quite fancied going on the giant teacups with a bloke with one eye dangling out on his optic nerve and a gangrenous face. As we leave, my friend Helen nonchalantly steps over a drooling halfwit zombie lying on the ground who swipes at her ankle with a bloodied stump. She carries on chatting unperturbed. 'Wow,' I say, 'didn't you see that?'

'Oh yes,' she replies, 'but I'm from Clitheroe. All the fairs are like this up there …'

Clitheroe is certainly 'up there'. It overlooks the Ribble Valley, the town on the rocky hill, as its Anglo–Saxon name 'Clyderhow' tells us; a name that survived even when their reign didn't. Invading Norman Roger De Lacy made the town his fiefdom and built the smallest

Norman keep in England there, which on a winter night feels colder than the Urals and just as steeped in dark and bloody history. From the Pendle Witches to the haunted pubs of the Trough of Bowland, this is spooky, darkest Lancashire, a county which, according to historian Rachel Hasted, was once 'fabled for its theft, violence and sexual laxity, where the church was honoured without much understanding of its doctrines by the common people'

Clitheroe and Pendle's dark past has been Lancashire lore and legend for centuries, but turning it into a marketable leisure proposition is another of our local innovations. Clitheroe tourist literature positively revels in this saturnine side of its character. It tells you as proudly of the haunted stepping stones over the Ribble, which every seven years drown an unsuspecting traveller, as it does of the award winning Byrne's wine store and, my favourite, Cowmans Famous Sausage Shop with its 75 different varieties of succulent banger.

This kind of thing – the ghosts, not the sausages – lured the team behind the wonderfully silly *Most Haunted* TV show to Clitheroe, and, in its wake, great swathes of nutjobs – sorry dedicated paranormal researchers – have beat an uphill path to the town. My browsing eye was caught instantly by 'Scariest Demon Ever Actually Caught On Tape' in which two lads from Dorset – who seem to have made 58 of these short films previously so you have to admire their commitment – went at night to 'Cliffrow Carstle... home of many hauntins and light anomarlies an that' and, what a stroke of luck, seem to find some blood and evidence of a demon he spots in the keep 'just wandrin around'. (I hate phonetic transcriptions of local accents but here, I think, it adds to an appreciation of the film.)

'If there's a spirit here now, could you just, err, stand in that li'l archway over there. We've come all this wayter speak to you ... and it'd be brilliant if you could just wave or summink ... it'd be really amazing if you could do that ...' Something then jumps out of the dark at them – we don't see this and we only have their word for it – and, with a shriek, the camera goes black. ('I apologise to the viewers but my 'and must have arcidentally touched the arff button.') As a finale, the lads use a shortwave radio to try and pick up what are called in the trade EVP (Electric Voice Phenomena), and in among what are clearly random bursts of BBC Lancashire and Clitheroe Cabs, we are told (via captions) that the ghosts are relaying messages such as 'Kill me', 'I silenced you' and 'Ahmed'. To me, these sounded more like 'car fourteen', 'half past two' and, yes, 'Ahmed', who probably works late shifts at BBC Lancashire or Clitheroe Cabs.

I'm headed up towards that castle now, though, silhouetted a menacing black against the gathering dusk. An unnaturally cold night everyone is saying, and there's rain in the chill wind that comes in from Pendle Hill. A rook caws, perched in a mossy arrow-slit in the ancient crenelated wall, and as I near the keep, I see a figure awaiting me. It is a man dressed in antique funeral dress, a top hat, a cravat, and a frock coat flapping like a bat wing in the wind. It is a strange, unearthly sight, full of foreboding. But I am not afraid, because I rang him up a couple of days ago and asked him to meet me here at seven o'clock on Tuesday.

Simon Entwistle does all this stuff properly, with thoroughly researched and superbly told tales of sinister history and macabre folklore. He is a genial man, at odds with his morbid attire, and he notices me shivering. 'Unnaturally cold, isn't it?' he says, with a twinkle.

In his previous life (though not literally) Simon was a groundsman in the town with a passion for history. Making small talk as we enter the castle grounds, he mentions that he lost out by one vote on becoming mayor but as his wife hated the idea of being mayoress, she was delighted. An American friend said 'you're in the wrong job', and he decided to turn that passion for history into work, at first informally and now very successfully.

His astute wife told him, with his knowledge and flair, he should cash in on the *Most Haunted* team's seven days visit and so he did, doing 15 tours that week for 100 people at a time. He had arranged for a friend to jump out from behind a gravestone at a certain point in his tour, but his mate stayed put, gazing at the sky and claiming, 'I saw a spaceship.' Similarly, erstwhile resident Scouse medium of *Most Haunted* Derek Acorah said that one of the nearby houses was 'full of aliens'. Here, Simon does a really rather good impression of Derek and later I see from his website that he has a sideline in an 'uncanny knack of impersonating accents, and people, and can also create some unbelievably realistic sound effects. Chainsaws, machine guns, horses, dentist drills, strangled dogs, passing trains', etc.

As he cautions me away from the edge of the keep, he tells me that he couldn't do the gravestone stunt now even if his mate was up for it, and the skies were clear of UFOs. Health and safety has put a stop to such malarkey, and Simon's tours now have public liability insurance of a million pounds. We're standing looking down on the pretty little town. There's bunting up, but the streets are deserted. It's charming but perhaps a little spooky, especially if you're on a ghost walk. Simon disabuses me of any sinister notions though. 'Despite all the history and the stuff I talk about, Clitheroe has the lowest crime rate in the north. It's quite a right-wing town though. When some local kid with a joint was arrested, the local paper headline was "Drug Baron Captured!"'

Across the town, over the rooftops, through a lowering mist, you can see the green heathery bulk of Pendle Hill, along with Saddleworth Moor, surely the hill with the darkest history in the north. I can't do justice to the whole strange and horrific tale of the Pendle Witches in a paragraph, but in essence, in 1612, 12 local women were tried as witches, found guilty and executed, victims of a combination of state sexism, the devious patriarchy of men like Justice of the Peace Roger Nowell, local infighting, corrupt officialdom, religious fundamentalism and the mental instability of some of the accused.

In the shadow of the hill lie the little villages where these events took place. In one of them, Roughlee, they've erected a statue to one of the most famous victims, Alice Nutter, and in 2012 hundreds of people, some dressed as witches, marched up the hill to commemorate the women, much to the concern of the bishop of Burnley. Local MP Jack Straw, then Home Secretary, was petitioned to pardon the women, but this was refused. Astonishingly, the convictions stand.

The same year, writer and local girl Jeanette Winterson published a superb, coldly intense novella about the matter called *The Daylight Gate*. I ask Simon if he's read it. 'Oh yes,' he says, with deep and evident admiration. Less nuanced maybe but more regularly visible than Winterson's prose, all the events are commemorated in the black double-decker 'Witch Way' bus which serves the local area and bears the logo of a witch on a broomstick flying across the moon.

Looking out from the keep at Pendle stands the statue of a First World War soldier, and Simon tells me the story of a young Great War infantryman who 'had no gripe with the Germans', and his widowed bride, that is more ordinary people's history than a ghost story and very moving.

In the wall of the keep itself, there's a large ugly hole. Though the local kids say that the devil himself threw a stone at it, the truth is that it was a cannonball fired from across the fields during the English Civil War, something that reminds me of the richness of the stories in this little island. That hole, that wound that looks so raw and livid in the castle wall, was fired by a breaching cannon across those damp fields 500 years ago; the wall itself built by the de Lacy's, warlike invading Frenchmen who live on in the names of local pubs. Down in the town stands a fine house called The Almonds. It is named after a family who were one of the 26 burgesses of the de Lacy's, locals given good jobs to keep them onside. Then, half a millennium later, it was bought by local comedian Jimmy Clitheroe, a fifties star who renamed himself after the town and would drive through it regally in his Rolls-Royce.

Simon and I turn and look the other way and into what would have been, until 1974, Yorkshire. A vale called Bashall Eaves is gorgeous but solemn in this failing light. Lonely now, it would have been even lonelier when, in 1934, a bachelor farmer called John Dawson was walking home one winter's night from Edisford Bridge Hotel. He heard a click behind him and felt a tap on his back. Thinking not much of it he went home, had his supper and went to bed where he slept soundly.

Next morning, his sheets were soaked in blood from a gaping wound in his back. Taken to hospital, a surgeon removed a small filed rod of hardened steel embedded four inches deep in his back. Three days later, Dawson was dead, and his murder remains unsolved, but was believed to be some bitter local feud, possibly over a girl.

The community clammed up. 'It was like talking to a brick wall,' said the London detective in charge of the investigation. The subject is still taboo locally, and I wouldn't say too much about it in the bar at the Edisford Bridge Hotel, which still exists. Indeed, a weird home-made gun, which may have been the murder weapon, was found in a barn next to the pub only a few years ago. Some of this new information came to light after the publication of a good book about the subject called *Wall of Silence* by Jennifer Lee Cobban, a local author. It's out of print now but you can pick one up on eBay for 15 quid or so.

We walk up Clitheroe High Street and past the Swan and Royal pub, which has entertained some famous residents in its day. Gandhi spent a night here while touring the Lancashire cotton mills, and Winston Churchill stayed when he came to see the world's first jet engine built and designed in Clitheroe by Sir Frank Whittle.

They had an undisturbed night's sleep as far as we know. They were lucky. For years, the landlords of the inn received complaints about bedroom number five. Guests complained that the walls were too thin and regularly asked to be moved because they were constantly being woken by a baby crying until in 1957 renovation work took place in the hotel's attic. Builders uncovered a parcel made up of a bundle of Victorian newspapers. A thick crust of dust covered the package and when it was unwrapped, the last sheet contained a baby's skeleton. The newspaper was dated March 1879.

I'm not going to relate all Simon's stories because they're good ones, he tells them brilliantly, and you should go on the walk for yourself. He peppers them with nice little *coup de théâtre* moments and I liked how detailed they are, without the kind of 'many years ago' vagueness that characterises the obviously false.

It took a pint and a whisky chaser in the Swan with Two Necks in Pendleton to get me warm again. Mulling the ghost walk and waiting for my pie and chips, I thought about those two strains in our character, and how you could argue that they are there in how we work and live and how we play. It's a very northern mix I think, the chilly and the cheery, nights spent in laughter on streets full of ghosts. Every night when the *Lancashire Evening Post and Chronicle* arrived at my nana's house (best headline, 'Paper Knife Stolen'; best apocryphal headline, 'Sir Vivian Fuchs Off To Antarctica'), she would turn to the 'deaths' bit of the 'births, deaths and marriages', just as some people might to the gossip columns or the sports pages, and read it with a grim smile of satisfaction, immersed in life's miseries and the passing of her friends.

As Morrissey sang on 'Sweet and Tender Hooligan', 'In the midst of life, we are in death … etcetera … etcetera etcetera etcetera'. We know just what he means with that stony northern mix of the maudlin and the matter of fact. Stan Laurel, the comic genius of Ulverston, said to his doctor on his deathbed that he wished he were skiing. 'I didn't know you liked skiing, Stan,' the nurse said. 'I don't,' replied Laurel 'but I'd rather be doing that than this.'

Peter Tinniswood's fabulous creation Uncle Mort put it like this, 'I've got faith in the old tried and trusted values of the north of England. We'll never give in. Come 2084, the north will be alive and kicking … with rampant gloom and despondency.'

Uncle Mort's gallows wit is a very northern trope, much more characteristic of us in its ruminative gloom than that of more infamous and stereotyped north country gagsters like Bernard Manning or Roy Chubby Brown. In truth, northern working-class humour is much stranger, much deeper than Manning's arid hate or Brown's coarseness.

Their tone, for me, is much more that of London 'funnymen', more cocksure and belligerent, more Mike Reid than Al Read.

Al Read, Sid Field, Frank Randle and Rob Wilton are now famous for their lack of fame, for the fact that while bolder and brasher voices like Max Miller, The Crazy Gang, Charlie Chester, Arthur Askey (who along with wisecracking smart alecs like Tarby and Stan Boardman prove that Scousers are different) and goofy but heroic Lancastrian George Formby were national treasures, Randle and Field's comedy never made it south of Crewe station. Their style set a template for a kind of rueful if not entirely black humour rooted in the same world view that you can see in Lowry, Peter Tinniswood, Alan Bennett, Victoria Wood and more; the notion that life is a baffling, humiliating and unpredictable farce, bookended by silence, more usually scarred by work and family ties than improved by them, and made tolerable only by sex, beer, skiving and by the adopting of an absurdist whimsy in the face of it all that Camus would have approved of.

A hangdog deadpan melancholy has always made us laugh up north. We find failure and thwarted ambition touching and very funny, be it Victoria Wood's desperate singleton Kelly Marie Tunstall, Alan Bennett's Mum and her social gaucheness, or Eric Morecambe leaving quietly downstage for the number 72, rain-coated and crestfallen, a Larkin of the Last Bus.

I can remember the silences that would descend on my living room of a seventies Saturday evening whenever a cockney comic would appear on the big variety shows of the day. 'Flash Harry type' would be the disapproving conclusion, in the same withering and dismissive tone of voice reserved for flamboyant Chelsea wingers or celebrity hairdressers.

Max Miller, Jim Davidson, Mike Reid, Sid James, with their crass sexual boasting and desire to get one over on the other guy, rang utterly false to us. They are show-offs, braggarts, the kind of bloke we avoid in the pub.

Peter Kay, the most successful and quintessentially northern comedian of his generation, may be the last word in ebullience. But his humour is that of limited horizons and the trials of the everyday, and based on painfully accurate domestic detail, such as getting the mismatched 'emergency chairs' out when the relatives come round at Christmas, the dexterity with the remote control needed to book cheap holidays off Ceefax, or your dad's early eighties pride in his green leatherette cases for his video cassettes. Kay's sometime colleague Dave Spikey has a joke I love: 'I once got a puncture in a place called Hindley Green, on the outskirts of Wigan. I pulled into the garage and said, "Have you got an Airline?" He said, "Piss off, we've not even got a bus station."' This is funny wherever you come from. But if you've ever been to Hindley Green, it's hilarious and a little tragic.

Kay may be a classic northern circuit comic but his rise to fame came through the comedy clubs, which is a modern innovation just like zombie apocalypses, ghost walks or, for that matter, laser quest, quiz nights, locked room HintHunt games, or even Grindr and the varyingly dubious social media hook-up sites.

Stand-up comedy has been with us since the aforementioned greats of the late music hall and variety, but the comedy club is a modern development. A 'comic' would appear on the halls or in the clubs as part of a package of varied entertainment; a song here, a dance there, a ventriloquist, a magician, perhaps even someone who would 'fill the stage with flags' or spin plates. That's why so many northern comics like Morecambe and Wise also had soft shoe or tap or some other variant of song and dance – comedy acts sometimes arose out of the 'patter' between numbers. Dedicated comedy clubs were an eighties phenomenon, taking hold in bigger cities, usually with big youth and student populations who became the new and core audience for live comedy.

I'd been tipped off to the XS Malarkey comedy club in the heart of Manchester's student quarter by a fine comic and actor of my acquaintance Justin Moorhouse, who I first met in a Farnworth Labour Club on the set of the *Phoenix Nights* sitcom. The club has been going every Tuesday night since 1998 and described by the

Guardian as 'a great example of how a club should be run'. It has played host to all the stars, cult or otherwise, of its comedic era; multi-award winning, much loved and not for profit.

You can tell you're in a student pub when they don't sell whisky of any description but do sell 'Jägerbombs', 'shots' or any number of small scarlet bottles of flavoured sugared water with glucose and a dash of vodka called TurboDoom or Vermillion SkullCrush or Satan's Eggnog – all alcohol by volume roughly 2%. This has the dual effect of making me feel a) hugely sophisticated and b) enormously old. (I'm reminded of the time I asked for Scotch and Dry Ginger in a Salford boozer and the barman said, 'What do you think this is, *Life on Mars?*)

The reason I didn't know XS Malarkey maybe is because I've lost any appetite I ever had for stand-up comedy. I suppose I must have had one once as I can still remember every gag of *The Comedians* album of the seventies' ITV comedy show my Irish grannie had (George Roper, Dougie Brown and Ken Goodwin were my favourites I seem to recall, I didn't like Manning much even then). British stand-up now often seems to consist of overgrown male students telling me in a plonking sneer that people who believe in god are 'idiots', or that celebrities, television shows or cartoons are 'a bit rubbish' or that former Tory chairman Eric Pickles is 'fat'. Moreover they seem to get an awful lot of chances to tell me this, on pretty much every TV programme aired after nine o'clock at night, a tsunami of strident man-baby entitledness, with no jokes.

So it was nice to see that the first comic up at XS Malarkey on the Tuesday I was there was a young Canadian woman. Were it not for the occasional gag about blow jobs and periods, there was a rather sweet, slightly over-eager and nervy enthusiasm about her that you might even have described as 'jolly hockey sticks'. She was engaging enough and in my notes I have written down that I 'liked joke about student loan or baby'. Clearly I thought that I would remember the actual joke when I re-read it. This, of course, as John Cleese's irate customer said in Python's Cheese Shop sketch, is 'an act of the purest optimism'.

Maybe someone who was there could remind me. It definitely made me laugh into my pint of gassy lager.

Stand-up comedy, a staple of working-class leisure through music hall, holiday camps and working men's clubs, declined somewhat in fashion during the sixties and seventies. Then in 1979, Britain's first 'hip' US-style stand-up club, The Comedy Store, opened in London, and a network quickly spread across the UK, with the dominant style on offer being observational or satirical, rather than randy milkmen and mothers-in-law. Though some think the live comedy circuit is declining because of TV, that medium – with its raging insatiable appetite for comics on its many panel shows – can prove a massive career boost. John Bishop went from selling just nine tickets for the basement club of the Leicester Square Theatre to selling out Wembley Arena a year later, with the same act, thanks to one appearance on *Michael McIntyre's Comedy Roadshow*.

The Zoo pub where Malarkey is held is considerably smaller than Wembley, and there are considerably less than 12,550 in tonight, but they are lively, receptive and young. We are deep in the heart of Manchester's densely populated student stretch, the Oxford Road corridor, with the fabulous new library at one end and the clubs and kebab shops of Rusholme at the other, a metaphorical and literal journey from bookish to bibulous. In the Victorian era, this area was notorious for its squalor and destitution; the area around Oxford Road train station, 'Little Ireland', was what shocked Engels into writing his *The Condition of the Working Classes in England*. Nowadays, though the BBC has decamped to MediaCity, Salford, the area is still vibrant and, according to the council's blurb, 'now a focus for knowledge-driven, innovation-orientated economic growth'. Most of Manchester's 60,000 students will pass along here every day and a couple of hundred of them are here tonight.

Compère Toby shuffles on stage and is withering about the audience in a very funny, affectedly decrepit and sour way. They love it. He makes a very rude remark about his ex-wife – in the audience –

and then laughingly but genuinely apologises over a storm of appalled giggles. To do this thing properly, I realise, you have to have no filter really, to abandon any fear or shame or need to be liked. It reminds me of something I once heard novelist John Niven say, 'You have to write as if both your parents are dead.'

Next on the bill is Michael Legge, a comic I know and who comes to join Justin and me for a pint. He seems more relaxed than I would be in the circumstances, given what he's about to do (Will Ferrell called stand-up 'hard, lonely and vicious'). But then, he does know what he's doing and the audience seem sweet and generous. I always thought stand-up comedy clubs were bear pits. 'A lot of them are,' says Michael. 'You should come down to the Frog and Bucket (another Manchester club) on a Friday night when the stag dos and the lads are in. I once was getting so much hassle and aggro from some pissed guy in the audience that I actually said, "I'm not sure why you're here, mate, you're not enjoying it. Why don't you do something else?" And he got up, and he was a huge bloke, and said, "I've just got out of prison after 13 years. I can do what I want." And I had to agree really.'

Michael drains his pint and walks straight on stage. He bounds into a very funny twist on the old music-hall song 'A, You're Adorable', which I'll let you go and see for yourself rather than mirthlessly describe in print. Interestingly, the audience get this, but a later reference to eighties musical *Starlight Express* seems to go straight over their collective head. Michael goes down well, though, and seems pleased as he comes off stage and I hand him another pint.

He's got a gig in London tomorrow so he's getting the Megabus back tonight after midnight rather than a hotel in Manchester. Michael's very good at this comedy lark. He's always working, he's highly rated by his peers and audiences love him. But as I think of him in the dank, pissy chill of an empty city-centre bus station in the small hours, I realise that, of the thousand or so working comics in Britain, most are neither playing to nine people in a basement or 12,000 in an arena, but somewhere vaguely and for them tantalisingly in between.

Michael drains his pint and leaves to claim a spot at the bus station. I still fancy that whisky that I never got, and so I draw up a mental checklist of the pubs nearby, 'boozers' if you are plain speaking, 'hostelries' if you are that kind of 'hail fellow, well met' drinker. Somewhere I could get a night cap or two.

It was almost time to call it a night, and call time on a year of enjoying the leisure of the working north. But there was time for one for the road, and I knew just the place.

EPILOGUE

DRINKING UP

The Briton's Protection. Don't be put off by the name. Yes, it sounds like the kind of place where snarling, bull-necked men drink gassy lager in front of the Chelsea game, or perhaps where a chap in a Barbour jacket asks mine genial host, Geoff, for his tankard. It isn't like that at all. But come to think of it, yes, do be put off by the name. It means I'll get served quicker.

The Briton's Protection is a famous Manchester pub. Legendary may not be too strong a word. It stands on the corner of a busy road junction, just by an unprepossessing road bridge off Deansgate and next door to the Bridgewater Hall, which is why about 9.30 you'll often find the second violins and the bassoons dashing in for a pint. It's stood here since 1795, when it was called The Ancient Briton. But by the time it featured in the *Pigot & Dean's New Directory of Manchester & Salford* for 1821, it had been renamed The Briton's Protection, a reference it's thought to the pub being a regular recruiting venue during the Napoleonic Wars, when drunk patrons were often shanghaied into the military.

Should anyone want to pressgang me into service, it's not unusual to find me in one of the pub's six characterful rooms. Maybe by the open fires in the bar parlour on a winter's night, or on a stool in the front bar under the gleaming russet ceramic tiles, with their distinctly old school municipal flavour, or in the corridor by the large mural of the Peterloo Massacre that lines the walls. Maybe on a summer's night in the tidy white-washed beer patio, Manchester weather permitting. It is always busy, with the odd popstar, film director or writer mixed in among the clientele of office workers, tourists, shoppers and old hands who have been supping here for decades. It keeps good real ales, there are home-made venison, hare and turkey pies on offer, as well as 300 malt whiskies.

Like the Buffet Bar at Stalybridge station, this makes it sound akin to Orwell's Moon Under Water, i.e too good to be true. But The Briton's Protection is very real. It's one of my and many another's favourite Mancunian watering holes, and there are plenty of great ones to choose from. There's The Eagle by Elbow's Salford studios, a pub with a music venue in the partly converted terraced house next door. The Port Street Beer House is what craft beer enthusiasts call a 'catwalk bar', designed to show off mouth-watering ales at sometimes eye-watering prices. The Molly House in the gay village does great tapas, cooked behind the bar by a genial Ecuadorian, and I have hatched radio series in The Kings Arms in Salford, owned by Housemartins and Beautiful South singer Paul Heaton, and featuring his quirky collection of 'Do Not Disturb' signs on the walls.

But it was right that, if we were to finish our voyage into the northern night with a pint and a chaser somewhere, it should be here. In 2008, I threw a little 'do' in the upstairs function room to launch a book called *Pies and Prejudice*, so it seems fitting now that it's become a second home, and that that book has led to this one, to raise a glass here.

Britain invented the pub as we know it, although it evolved from what you might call a fashionable Italian wine bar. As every proverbial schoolboy knows, the Romans brought us roads, and with them came *tabernae*, roadside inns for the traveller's refreshment. When the Romans left Britain, the Anglo-Saxons, Jutes and Vikings worked a variant on these 'taverns' that formed the basis of our pub system today. Alehouses developed out of ordinary domestic dwellings. An 'alewife', the precursor of today's landlady, would hoist a green bush up on a pole to signify she had ale brewed and ready to drink. These 'public houses' became community hubs as well as places to booze and grew so popular that King Edgar limited their spread to one per village. He also introduced a drinking measure whereby a peg was placed on the side of a barrel as a means of controlling the amount of alcohol an individual could consume. This gave rise to the expression 'to take someone down a peg'. Two famous early British pubs were the Tabard Inn in Southwark, immortalised by Geoffrey Chaucer in his *Canterbury Tales*, and Ye Olde Trip to Jerusalem in Nottingham where Richard the Lionheart recruited for his crusade to the Holy Land.

In 1577 there were around 17,000 alehouses, 2,000 inns and 400 taverns throughout England and Wales. Their rampant popularity was not just due to a populace desperate to get hammered, however. Remember that beer, fermented and brewed, was a much safer drinking option than water in the early modern world. 'Small beer' was the term for the very weak ale given to women and children, and persists as a term for a trifling matter. The hard stuff arrived in the eighteenth century, when cheap brandy from France and gin from Holland ushered in the social crisis and moral panics found in Hogarth's etching 'Gin Lane' and other moralising accounts of the times.

During the nineteenth century, pubs and inns developed a mild system of segregation similar to the railways. Pubs would typically be split into several rooms and bars in order to cater for the preferences of the differing type and class of customer. You can the find the vestiges of those days of 'internal zoning' in the labyrinthine layout of pubs like The Briton's Protection, or the Stalyvegas Buffet Bar, or the Liverpool 'Phil' on Hope Street. It was the case in my teens in the long-gone Market Tavern in Wigan; its warren of back rooms, still with the old but sadly non-functioning bells for waitress service, were perfect for underage drinkers, trysts, political conspiracies and gossip.

I like a big pub with nooks and crannies, and I like it even more if it's in a city or town centre. Town centre pubs are usually busy which is best. Finding some places empty and deserted is a delight – a swimming pool or a railway carriage, a golf course, I imagine. But an empty pub, like an empty restaurant, makes your heart sink. I like a brisk feel and a healthily mixed clientele. None of that Slaughtered Lamb insular weirdness, that 'you're not from round here, are you boy' silence when you walk in.

Even Christopher Snowden of right-wing think tank the Institute of Economic Affairs spotted the difference when he wrote, 'When politicians and metropolitan pundits disingenuously pay homage to the "great British pub", these are not the kind of establishments they have in mind at all. Their vision of a pub is essentially a mid-priced restaurant with horse brassings on the wall; somewhere to take their children on a Sunday afternoon. Somewhere to read *The Sunday Times* for four hours while nursing a solitary pint.'

A different kind of pub is the one in the worker's blood. The official history books will tell you that Karl Marx wrote *Das Kapital* in the reading room of the British Museum, but the landlord of the Museum Tavern across the road tells visitors to his establishment that he 'researched' it in the corner of the bar, nursing a stout and a brandy. The boozer has been both spark and dampener of our radical fires, as heard in that famous old war cry of the left, 'As soon as this pub closes, the revolution starts', immortalised in Alex Glasgow's funny and sweet song of the same name.

The pub as a metaphor for the ordinary man at his leisure has a rich pedigree in literature. In T S Eliot's 'The Waste Land', a Queen Vic-like East End watering hole becomes a symbol for the emptiness of modern culture. A young woman tells the odd tale of losing all her teeth while a cockney voice tolls 'HURRY UP PLEASE IT'S TIME'.

More sympathetically, in Graham Swift's *Last Orders*, the regulars at the Coach turn out to have rich and complex lives and histories that he celebrates. And the opening section of Alan Sillitoe's *Saturday Night and Sunday Morning* finds Arthur Seaton drunk in the fervid, sloshing wildness of a Nottingham pub at the weekend.

The rowdy gang of singers who sat at the scattered tables saw Arthur walk unsteadily to the head of the stairs, and though they must all have know he was dead drunk, and must have seen the danger he would soon be in, no one attempted to talk to him or lead him back to his seat. With eleven pints of beer and seven small gins playing hide-and-seek inside his stomach, he fell from the topmost stair to the bottom …

Floors shook and widows rattled and leaves of aspidistras wilted in the fumes of beer and smoke. Notts County had beaten the visiting team, and the members of the White Horse supporters club were quartered upstairs …

For it was Saturday night, the best and bingeist glad-time of the week, one of the fifty-two holidays in the slow-turning Big Wheel of the year, a violent preamble to a prostrate Sabbath.

You can feel the heat and sweat and alcohol tang coming off the page, and feel it pulsing off the screen in the famous film version. It speaks of excess and indulgence but that is only part of the story. In the absence of what Priestley identified as well-lit and book-lined rooms to take their ease in at home, the pub was also a place of solace for the tired worker, somewhere to slake their thirst in quiet conversation, perhaps, foot on the rail, to the slow, contemplative music of the snooker ball's gentle clack.

Do not underestimate the need for manual workers to slake that thirst. Middle-class wits may mock the workman's tea with its slosh of milk and four sugars but, as a letter writer to the *New Statesman* pointed out, you need sugar for energy and liquid for rehydration if you are in hard physical work, less so if you spend your day gazing at a flickering computer screen. Christopher Snowden was perhaps exaggerating the attitude of some to working-class pub culture, but maybe not much, when he wrote:

> The aim of the chattering classes is not unlike that of the early Anti-Saloon League ... to rid the country of what they see as the scourge of drink-led, politically incorrect, smoke-filled, privately run, child unfriendly, sports-watching boozers that are frequented mainly by working class men – pubs that have customers who are indifferent to food because they don't go there to eat. Proper pubs, in other words; havens from sterile, prod-nosed Britain. A place for grown ups.

A constant, melancholic refrain of modern life is that pubs are in decline and under threat. Hilaire Belloc was bemoaning this nearly a century ago: 'When you have lost your inns, drown your empty selves, for you will have lost the last of England.' Cheap supermarket booze is blamed, and young people 'pre-loading' at home or in the park on bargain vodkapops before staggering to the club. Or perhaps, as Stephen Williams, former Lib Dem minister in the Department for Communities and Local Government, put it, because traditionally white working-class areas have become home to teetotal Muslim immigrants. Blackburn has lost more pubs than any other British town.

But, at the risk of harsh judgement, it may be that it's just bad pubs that are dying out. At either end of my mum and dad's street two pubs have been steel-shuttered and security-taped for months. But then they were perhaps the two worst pubs I have ever been in; desolate and nasty, serving indifferent food and tasteless beer. By contrast, none of my favourite pubs seems in any imminent decline, town or country. There's always a queue for the bar in the Port Street Beer House and The Briton's, and on a Bank Holiday Monday you'll need to book a table at the Boot & Shoe in Greystoke near Ullswater, a village pub with the buzzy feel of a town centre one, and not a tankard in sight.

You can get quietly or noisily leathered in these places (providing you behave), but a good pub provides much more than that and, traditionalists take note, this wasn't always the case. The pubs of my childhood were cheerless places, from what I could glimpse through the little hatch of the off-sales window. Places where a dartboard or a one-armed bandit represented state of the art recreation. The Briton's offers the occasional storytelling session, quiz nights and folk clubs. The Boot & Shoe hosts a local MP's surgery from time to time. The Port Street Beer House has ethnic street food cooked out back on summer nights, sizzling chilli dogs and samosas and barbecue. They have 'meet the brewer' evenings too, where visiting micro-brewers from Milwaukee and Bruges are treated like rock stars.

An English pub is very different from an American bar or a German bierkeller or a French wine bar. That difference, though, can be as nebulous and unfathomable to foreign guests as our plurals and past tenses. It is an invention of the British people that reflects our national character. Learning the etiquette of pubs is a great social leveller. We all must learn that the note held unshowily but prominently in the hand will alert the hawk-eyed bar staff member as to your place in the serving order. Waving it about, however, will indicate that you are an over-entitled arse. Some of us learn quickly that the occasional 'one for yourself' will get you remembered favourably for a future visit for the modest outlay of about 50p. We learn the complicated protocols of 'splitting a round' and 'doubling up', and when and where it is OK to slip into that gap at the bar during a last orders scrum.

'Sometimes you want to go where everybody knows your name' went the theme tune to long-running comedy *Cheers*. I've been in the bar that inspired it, the Bull & Finch in Boston, and no one knew my name, but I liked it no less for that. Sometimes the very fact that people don't know you from Adam is the reason you go the pub. It could be to escape, to start again or maybe just to sit undisturbed with your book or paper. But of course, having a 'local' is something that at heart every Englishman and woman feels contented with, even if it's just a place that you know and feel comfortable with, rather than expect a slapped back and a 'the usual?'.

Finishing a Cumbrian walk once, some friends and I arrived at the Boot & Shoe at about half-three to find, not unreasonably, the chef gone home and the kitchen shut. Apologetically, Jan the landlady went away and returned to place on our table a huge, teetering cairn of assorted crisps, a jar of chutney and a pile of buttered white bread, for us to make crisp sandwiches while we warmed up and sipped our ale and whisky. A Michelin star would not have made that late afternoon lunch any more delightful.

We have exported the notion of the pub to the world, and the world has embraced it. Their take is different naturally, speaking of charm, exoticism and quirkiness, of boho intimacy and even cool, in a way that might make habitués of the traditional English boozer choke into their chestnut mild. It began with the American crush on the faux-Irish pub, later to blarney its way round the globe. When Woody Allen should have been picking up an Oscar for *Annie Hall*, he was playing the clarinet in Michael's Pub in New York as he did every Monday night. Maybe they kept a really good stout. But in this act, Allen was really saying, 'Hey, I'm just a regular guy who has no truck with the weird shallowness of Tinseltown' (and back in the days when we might have believed him). Soon the world had developed 'a craic habit' with a couple of thousand cod-'Oirish watering holes in some 50 countries.

But recognisably urban English pubs have insinuated themselves into other shores too. China has a blossoming pub culture, a fact that was brought home to me when a friend texted to say that he was playing darts and dominoes and drinking bitter in a 'pub' in Guangzhou province. The government of the People's Republic have tacitly encouraged this, launching campaigns to encourage the consumption of grape wine and beer rather than traditional stronger grain-based spirits and rice wines. A recent feature in the *Financial Times* supplement, nestling between Lucia Van der Post's luxury jewellery reviews and an ad for a yacht charter, was a guide to the pubs of Bangalore, India's Silicon Valley, where the subcontinent's new young software millionaires and super geeks sip pale ale at Formica tables à la the Rovers Return.

I pitched up one night at sunset in Van Buren, Indiana, a quaint and sleepy one-horse town in the middle of the real America, the grain belt of the Midwest. Hungry and thirsty, I found in the middle of town not a bar, but a dark, woody pub that would not have seemed out of place in Bolton or Keighley. It served mild and about a 150 different baked potato fillings. It was run by a guy called Jack Sparks who asked me where I was from, and when I said 'Wigan' pinned a drawing pin in a map of the world in that bit of central Lancashire and told me with pride that he wanted this to be 'the kind of public house you get back in your part of the world'. It was called the Other Place and it got its name, Jack told me, from being across the street from a much more conventional American bar where everyone walked in and asked, 'Is this the place that serves those potatoes?'

When Jack says 'in my part of the world' is he thinking of England or the north? Is there something uniquely northern about a northern pub? I would say not in terms of fixtures or fittings, snacks or décor but maybe in terms of culture. I've never seen anyone order a lager top in a northern pub and I don't think I've seen anyone drinking Mild south of Milton Keynes. The notion of the after work drink and the happy hour I tend to associate with London. The more grimy, manual nature of northern industry dictated that workers would go home and get cleaned up before venturing out again. I was amazed when I first saw how London pubs, especially in the Square Mile, would often clear out by nine o clock and wouldn't open at all at weekends which seemed some vague crime against nature to me.

Oddly, given the north's enthusiasm for pubs (or maybe because of it), the temperance movement began here in Preston in 1832. The Chartists worked a radical riff on this, trying to move it away from its catholic basis into what they called 'temperance Chartism' and seeing the quest for working-class sobriety going hand in hand with the demand for workers' voting rights. Temperance bars were once widespread across the north with one on most high streets. Now only one remains, Fitzpatrick's of Rawtenstall, serving sarsaparilla and dandelion & burdock, blackbeer and raisin, ginger cordial, cream soda, lemon & ginger and blood tonic.

One of the most popular soft drinks in the world was invented as a direct response to the burgeoning temperance movement. In 1908, in Granby Row in downtown Manchester, John Nichols created a new health cordial called Vim Tonic and it soon became a hit in the region's temperance bars. The name soon became shortened to Vimto, and it is still with us and thriving. In fact, I went to its hundredth birthday party in a fashionable Manchester bar and met the current Nichols family, who still run the company.

Mr Nichols told me that the drink is hugely popular in the Arab world, especially at Ramadan, when it is regarded as a smart and gluggable after-sunset tipple. In deference to the brand's popularity with kids and its roots in the temperance movement, the Nichols' have decided that there will never be an 'alcopops' version of Vimto (though of course something very like that can be made by combining it with port and blue WKD; the infamous 'Cheeky Vimto'). But the company had no problem with and indeed encouraged Vimto's use as a mixer. At the centenary party I went to, a mixologist bartender was serving up delicious Vimto cocktails. It was the tail end of a blazingly hot working day in the city and my friend John and I plumped for a long cool drink with lots of ice cold vodka, a dash of Aperol, Vimto, mint and crushed ice. I can still taste it. After the first sip, John turned to me at the bar and said, 'Hmm, it's OK, but I don't think I could have more than seven or eight.'

The pub no longer has the virtual monopoly on working-class leisure that it once did, but as that boozy gang the Institute of Economic Affairs said in a report of December 2014, 'Pessimism about the British pub trade has a long history'. Mass Observation, that earnest, leftist chronicler of British life, was mourning its decline in the 1930s.

Orwell, in a 1943 review of *The Pub and the People*, thought that the passive pleasures of cinema and radio were luring people away from the communality and 'animated conversations' of the pub. Equally gloomy, Christopher Hutt wrote a book called *The Death of the English Pub* in 1973. Around the same time, a TV ad sponsored by the pub trade featured England captain Bobby Moore and his missus popping in to a pub and encouraging us to 'look in at the local', in an attempt to lose the pub's image as a bastion of brutish sullen masculinity.

But temperance be damned. Up here we like a drink. Not for us the January detox and the feeble infantilised refusal to booze on a school night. In the north-east, during the early eighties, a health campaign was launched to curb binge drinking with the slogan 'two or three pints, two or three times a week'. Among Geordie drinking wits, this was soon turned into the mantra 'two or three pints, two or three times a night'. This is simply outrageous, of course, and in our defence all I can say is that we don't like being told what to do, which is why sales of Turkey Twizzlers increased in the north in the weeks after Jamie Oliver's tearful TV tirade against them.

When the BBC opened MediaCity, the brand new purpose built multi-million pound state-of-the-art home of the BBC in the north of England, we all agreed that, rather like the amorous sailors in *South Pacific* bemoaning the lack of Dames, we had pizza restaurants and cinemas, we had libraries and trams, we had museums and galleries and five-a-side and theatres, but what didn't we have: we didn't have a pub. Then, a year or so ago, one opened just next to my radio studio. On hot summer afternoons, as I slave at a microphone, I watch as laughing punters sip ice-cold craft beer or read books over a glass of something fruity and full-bodied. It's hell but I don't blame them.

MediaCity has risen, neon-lit and glamorous, from the old Salford docks. Built by the Manchester Ship Canal Company, the docks were opened in 1894 by Queen Victoria, and at their peak they were the third busiest port in the land. Containerisation did for it though, that and restrictions on the craft that could navigate the ship canal. All through the seventies, the docks dwindled and declined, rusted and silted. It closed in 1982 with the loss of 3,000 jobs, coincidentally about the same number that were created when the BBC moved in here in the noughties.

That move prompted much consternation in the London press. A series of blustering op ed pieces boiled down to dopey screeds of barely-concealed contempt and suspicion, with straplines like 'Auntie's Folly' and 'Bill Turnbull Fears For His Life Every Time He Parks Car Say Friends'. Fleet Street sniggered at the north's evident unsuitability for anything cultural and, on a more personal level, bemoaned the fact that they had to come all the way on a comfortable train to Manchester to appear on *BBC Breakfast* plugging their new book. Here's an example from Giles Coren:

> All sorts of shows that needed no messing about with – *BBC Breakfast*, Richard Bacon's Radio 5 Live show, *Match of the Day* – have been randomly booted up there ... at a cost of what I'm told was around a billion pounds.
>
> When you get here, it is very like High Noon: wide, empty streets, vacated lots, haunted-looking gunslingers, tumbleweed. A few weeks ago a mate of mine got home to London two hours late because someone was shot dead literally outside the door of his studio.
>
> And so I am torn between love and duty, as I was last week when, in order to talk about my book on *BBC Breakfast*, I had to go up the night before, and miss the company of my wife and daughter for 24 hours, because there are no trains early enough from London to travel there on the day ...
>
> So I was forging a path into the Wild (North) West. Opening a trail. One man against the wilderness. Well, one man and his publicist ... from Hodder, whose job it is to shanghai me into these trips.

In my first high fever of rage at these bleatings, I wrote a piece for the *New Statesman* in which I fulminated that it was hard to pinpoint what was so dreadful about this. Was it the tired clichés and untruths about trains and shootings? Was it the laziness of the prose, just the general unctuous metropolitan bellyaching? Whatever, I concluded that surely any reasonable person would think that every penny of the whole billion pound MediaCity site was a bargain, even if its sole purpose was to screw up Giles's day.

I've calmed down a little now. Salford is definitely no St John's Wood. That's why we like it. But maybe I have got that St John's Wood cabal wrong. Maybe their shtick is an affectation, a turn done to please their readers, a bit of easy posturing. Lord knows, we can all be guilty of that. Maybe I have done them a disservice in casting them as over-privileged babies surfing waves of conceit and entitlement. Perhaps, in the same way they have me cast as a chippy left-wing northerner with a grudge, a 2:1 and a romanticised view of council estates, chip shops and class struggle. They may be right and I may be wrong about them, so away with such acrimony. Let's play nice and let's 'accentuate the positive', as the self-help books would have it. I work at MediaCity practically every day and I love it. I love the light and the water, the facilities, the campus-like feel of the place. I love the fact that at night it feels like *Blade Runner*, like Tokyo. It excites the child in me just like those fairground lights and floodlight did and still do.

And in the day, from my desk, I can see over Eccles and suburban Worsley, along the M61, over Atherton and Tyldesley, 'Bent' and 'Bongs' as their weird local names have them. I can see the shapely whaleback Winter Hill. Sometimes anyway. Some days it's buried in clag and wreathed in rain, but some days it wobbles through a summer haze or sparkles in early winter light, and it calls me. I can't see lonely Anglezarke Moor and its flashes of water. But that calls me too. It's waiting, and it knows I'll be back.

*

When I was thinking about how to end this book, I was de
not to descend into soft soap and blather. The north and its
deserve better than gloopy sentiment, even though we are a hope
sentimental lot. I'd written one love letter to the north and I could
simply write another now, the same roads taken but at a somewha
more arthritic pace. But two things happened.

Firstly a general election hoved into view, and as the talk revolved
around sops for big business, and inheritance giveaways for millionaires,
and benefit cuts, and library closures, and the paring away at every
turn of what makes us fair and civilised, I realised that some things
can bear endless repeating. The view from Blackpool Tower and
the Humber Bridge, the moors of Anglezarke and Rookhope, from
Catbells and Werneth Low, the terraces at Rochdale FC and even
the glamorous balconies of MediaCity, Salford, are different from the
view from Primrose or Harrow hills. You can't see us at all from there
it seems. So we shall have to remind them that we are here.

It was once taken for granted that any creative type – writer,
musician, actor, comedian etc – would, however proudly northern
they were, have to at some point decamp to London. Braine, Barstow,
Storey, Delaney and all the burgeoning giants of the Kitchen Sink
school, made the trip eventually and the northern writer eating tripe
in St John's Wood (metaphorically and literally) became a comic trope
like Monty Python's Four Yorkshiremen. They may have celebrated
the north's passion, quick wittedness, humour, virility and such but
they also railed against its small mindedness and lack of sophistication.
Success lay in getting away and it lay southward.

That is no longer the case. Writers of my acquaintance who quit
the towns and cities of their northern birth out of necessity for careers
in London now watch ruefully as their university-aged kids apply
hopefully for places in Leeds, Liverpool, Newcastle and Manchester
lured by affordable and convenient lives in cool, vibrant communities.

In 2014, the radio station BBC 6 Music held a festival in Newcastle
and Gateshead; we decamped en masse, presenters and producers

...agement, to the banks of the Tyne for the weekend. I think
...stle is the best-looking city in Britain; in fact, just one of the
...generally, full of character and beauty and wonderful people. I
...ver miss a chance to go there, so I was off like a shot, through
...he wild and empty country where Hadrian's legions once stomped,
and eventually into Newcastle; the finest train arrival of any city in
England, except maybe Durham, just down the road.

I strolled one evening at sunset with my colleagues, after a great
day of events in the arty quarter around Ouseburn, along the banks
of the river back to the beautiful Sage centre, a curvaceous, chrome
poem high on the Gateshead side of the water. We walked past luxury
hotels, penthouse flats and little market stalls, looking down that
broad and beautiful waterway at the famous bridges, each lovely in its
own way – the Millennium Bridge sleek and modern; the Tyne Bridge
mighty and dark, like something from Gotham; the Swing, bright and
quirky and fun.

And as the crimson winter sun dropped behind my favourite,
Stephenson's High Level Bridge, a lonely elevated promenade, I could
see what the London staff were thinking as they gazed at the city
coming alive for the night. You could see the cogs turning behind their
widening eyes. You could almost hear their thoughts: Why would I not
want to live here, and see these sights every day, breathe this air, walk
these streets? Perhaps my house won't triple in value overnight, but
I won't live in a financial clearing house, at the whim of an absentee
landlord, in a city whose heart is shrivelling. When Geordie R&B act
the Animals sang 'We Gotta Get Out Of This Place', the 'better life'
they were in search of lay many miles south of the Tyne, presumably in
London. Now the reverse would seem to be true.

I remembered my night at the opera in Leeds and how I raced to
the station down crowded streets, awash with tipsy midweek revellers
in miniskirts and daft hats. They were loud and lairy, a little too much
for comfort maybe. But we are brothers and sisters under the skin,
they and I, and they are good people at heart. My people. I have a

bit of the peasant in me, a clever one I like to think, but I have come to realise that as much as they annoyed me at the time, I'd rather be running with them down a street in Leeds than watching a baking programme at the end of the Northern Line. That's the problem. I'm hopelessly biased. The Northern Line just doesn't go far enough north for me.

When I was a kid my dad would moan that I 'didn't come awake till bedtime'. 'Night Owl' was always one of my favourite northern soul tunes. When I hear a grown person use the phrase 'school night', I shudder a little inside. The days are long gone when I want to stay up every night till dawn. But I still am proud of the fact that the north will follow sport, eat out, learn French, go to art galleries, walk up hills with head-torches, stay up late and have fun. Between the stern compulsion of work and the free creativity of play, in the friction and clash of the two, we find ourselves.

Let us go then and wake up the night, that sleeping patient that Prufrock found etherised upon the table. Let us arm ourselves and be guided by what an old friend of mine from Hindley used to say, 'If I die with 50 pence in my pocket, that's bad budgeting' or, my particular watchword, 'All things in moderation, including moderation'. We're going out, on a school night, if only because that's what the boss doesn't want us to do. The hooter has gone, school's out and, as Richard Hawley of Sheffield put it:

'Tonight the streets are ours.'

Let's go, eh?

ACKNOWLEDGEMENTS

The following people offered invaluable help in many different ways during the writing of this book. Some pointed me to places or books. Some got me into things. Moreover whilst many of the trips and journeys I undertake on my books are solitary adventures (which explains why you might have seen me making furtive notes in a chip shop, museum or nuclear reactor near you) over the course of this book, I was often accompanied by some of the following people. In any event, here they are listed part alphabetically, part chronologically, slightly randomly and mildly nervously as I fear I may have left someone out. If it's you, forgive me.

Clare Hudson
Dee Wallace
East of Eden WI
Elizabeth Alker
Lizzie Hoskin
Lorna Skingley
Helen Hobday
Henrie Rowlatt
Rebecca Gaskell
Simon Entwistle
John Leonard
Faith Wilson
Peter Young, David Morris and all at Dobcross Silver Band

Luke Bainbridge

Justin Moorhouse

Simon Moran

Tony Howard and all at FC United of Manchester

The Tone Deaf Society

Ian and all at Belle Vue Aces Speedway

Jackie, Ian and all at British Crown Green Bowling Association

Peter Salmon

Paddy McAloon

Johnny Marr

Richard Hawley

Maxine Peake

Pawlo Wintoniuk

Elaine Constantine

Elle Rees

Opera North

Durham Literary Festival